JUST WAR AND CHRISTIAN TRADITIONS

JUST WAR AND CHRISTIAN TRADITIONS

EDITED BY

ERIC PATTERSON

AND

J. DARYL CHARLES

FOREWORD BY JOHN ASHCROFT

University of Notre Dame Press

Notre Dame, Indiana

Library of Congress Control Number: 2022947590

ISBN: 978-0-268-20381-8 (Hardback)
ISBN: 978-0-268-20382-5 (Paperback)
ISBN: 978-0-268-20383-2 (WebPDF)
ISBN: 978-0-268-20380-1 (Epub)

CONTENTS

Foreword   vii
John Ashcroft

ONE
Christian Approaches to Just War, Peace, and Security   1
Eric Patterson and J. Daryl Charles

TWO
Catholic Just War Thinking   29
Joseph E. Capizzi

THREE
The Orthodox Church on Just War   59
Darrell Cole

FOUR
Luther's Political Thought and
Its Contribution to the Just War Tradition   85
H. David Baer

FIVE
John Calvin and the Reformed View of War,
Resistance, and Political Duty   123
Keith J. Pavlischek

SIX

Just War and the Church of England   157
Daniel Strand and Nigel Biggar

SEVEN

Methodism and War   181
Mark Tooley

EIGHT

Praying for Peace but Preparing for War:
Baptists and the Just War Tradition   219
Timothy J. Demy

NINE

Anabaptists and the Sword   253
J. Daryl Charles

Contributors   305

Index   311

FOREWORD

John Ashcroft

Can war be just? Can war be rooted in virtues such as justice and liberty, rather than vices like vengeance? This collection of essays contains insights and analysis about a Christian understanding of just war ethics and its application. The essays concern themselves neither with the history of a specific conflict nor the discrete policies of the United States or any other country. As a former American public servant whose responsibilities included significant elements of national security activity, I can attest to the relevance of virtue in US law and history. Just war principles are the foundation of the law of armed conflict and of our global system of sovereign, independent states. Such states not only have rights under international law but are obligated to shoulder moral obligations and responsibilities as well. We should all be grateful that the intersection of liberty and morality is a recurring topic of discussion and debate when our nation confronts the necessity of using force in defense of our national interests.

There is a distinctive American tradition that flows from our understanding of humanity in terms of values. The Declaration of Independence asserts that "all men are created equal" and "endowed by their Creator with unalienable rights." Americans believe that the right to "life, liberty, and the pursuit of happiness" is universal. It is not to be limited in terms of blood, history, language, or soil. To be sure, the United States has made its own wartime errors. Nevertheless, it is valuable to consider how different the American ethics and outcomes of war have been. They stand in sharp contrast to the ethical perspectives of many other nations, which have drawn sharp distinctions between themselves and their competitors based on matters of primordial culture, race, language, and ethnicity.

Fundamental values and ideals helped shape American citizens as they developed as a nation. The foundations of our republic include, importantly, the Bible and Christian teaching (especially insights associated with the Reformation). Citizens influenced by zealous pastors such as Jonathan Mayhew and Samuel West deliberated whether or not it was just for the colonial legislatures to employ force to protect against London's red-coated Hessian mercenaries.[1] The debates of the time were grounded in a Judeo-Christian worldview, characterized by principles of political equality (i.e., the Golden Rule), the notion of liberty (rooted in the Bible and energized by the Reformation), and the rule of law (notably, the Ten Commandments and Rom. 13). This emphasis on moral reflection and deliberation among an engaged, literate citizenry (another legacy of the Reformation) prompted spirited public debates about the morality of going to war and how war would be fought for centuries to come.

One of the greatest examples of this American creed, rooted in Judeo-Christian values, can be found in the career of Abraham Lincoln. Lincoln was deeply concerned about the morality of warfare. He himself enlisted for a brief time in 1832 in the Illinois militia during the Black Hawk War. Later, as US congressman, Lincoln introduced the "Spot Resolutions" in order to question the precipitating *casus belli* of the Mexican-American War (1846–48).[2] As president, Lincoln wrestled with questions of law, justice, and morality, from how to treat the rebellious South to the proper punishment in the individual case of a teenage sentry who fell asleep at his post (the traditional penalty was execution). Lincoln's words, in his two inaugural speeches and the Gettysburg Address, present a compelling vision of justice and liberty, rather than vengeance and destruction, despite the cruelties and hardship of war.

A nation's values are explicit in how that nation honors those who have fought. Historically, the majority of American battle dead have lost their lives on foreign soil in wars of liberation. The American Battle Monuments Commission maintains US cemeteries in ten foreign countries and reports another sixteen monuments in foreign countries memorializing those missing in action.[3] Those cemeteries — in Italy, France, Belgium, Luxembourg, and elsewhere — remind us of American soldiers who liberated others, from Cubans in concentration camps in 1899 to Bosnians and Kosovars at the end of the twentieth century.

American virtue is best seen in its restraint and generosity at war's end. Consider the noble goals Woodrow Wilson envisaged in 1918: self-determination, collective security, and freedom of the seas. The fact that the United States, unlike its allies, did not take any German or Ottoman colonies testifies to America's restraint and devotion to human dignity and self-governance as universal values. At the end of the Second World War the United States not only helped rebuild former adversaries but also worked patiently to expand freedom against old colonialisms abroad and racism at home. Whether fighting terrorists or rogue regimes or strategic competitors, the US objective has typically been to preserve and extend the international order and human liberty.

A commitment to just war thinking focuses attention on the Creator's endowment of human dignity, not merely American prerogatives. The just war principles of legitimate political authority, battlefield restraint, the rule of law, and the goal of a better peace are all rooted in Judeo-Christian conceptions of the purpose of government. These include, as Augustine noted, love of neighbor and the critical evaluation of both behavior and motives.[4]

Consequently, it is imperative that we reflect on the lessons, both positive and negative, of US history and the ways that the American people have generally sought to embrace and extend liberty, often at great cost to themselves. Whether applied to the United States or beyond, the collective analysis and thoughtful evaluation presented in the following pages provides an essential resource for understanding the distinctly Judeo-Christian roots and denominational frameworks undergirding the moral structure for statesmanship and policy referred to as just war thinking.

NOTES

1. A typical example of this is Samuel West's claim that "the same principles which oblige us to submit to government do equally oblige us to resist tyranny." Some of the writing referred to at the time included the work of Peter Martyr Vermigli (who advocated resistance), John Ponet (whose *A Short Treatise on Political Power* supported tyrannicide), John Knox, and others who argued that resistance was justified—even morally required in some cases—if the national political authority became corrupt and tyrannical. The appropriate body to take such action, it was generally argued, was intermediate political authorities (for example, chartered colonial governments) acting within the rule of law to preserve the security, rights, and freedom of the citizens. The most famous

American making such claims was Jonathan Mayhew, notably in his 1750 "A Discourse concerning the Unlimited Submission and Non-Resistance to the High Powers." This sermon was printed and reprinted numerous times in the colonies and in London; John Adams famously said that everyone had read it in the colonies. For more on this line of thinking, see Mayhew's sermon at Founding.com, Claremont Institute, https://founding.com/founders-library/ preachers-pen/a-discourse-concerning-the-unlimited-submission-and-non -resistance-to-the-high-powers-1750-jonathan-mayhew/, as well as Steven M. Dworetz's *The Unvarnished Doctrine: Locke, Liberalism and the American Revolution* (Durham, NC: Duke University Press, 1990).

    2. See Abraham Lincoln, "Resolutions in the U.S. House of Representatives, December 22, 1847," in *Abraham Lincoln: His Speeches and Writings*, ed. Roy P. Basler (Boston: Da Capo Press, 2001), 199–202.

    3. See, e.g., Ben Rappaport, "How Many American Troops Are Buried in Foreign Lands," NBC News Digital, May 30, 2016, https://www.nbcnews.com /news/us-news/how-many-american-troops-are-buried-foreign-lands-n580951.

    4. Augustine, *Letter to Boniface* (also known as *Letter 189*), written in AD 418; see *St. Augustine Letters, 165–203*, vol. 4, trans. Wilfrid Parsons, The Fathers of the Church (Washington, DC: Catholic University of America Press, 1981), 266–71.

ONE

Christian Approaches to
Just War, Peace, and Security

Eric Patterson and J. Daryl Charles

In AD 418, a senior Roman military officer wrote one of a series of letters to Augustine, the bishop of Hippo. That individual, Boniface, asked whether or not he — as a Christian — could kill in his vocation as a soldier.[1] The two had such an intimate friendship, and Boniface was so insistent, that the messenger waited on the spot while Augustine quickly penned a response that today is known as *Letter 189*.[2] Augustine exhorted Boniface to fulfill his calling and fight against temporal enemies who seek to destroy the peace, while distinguishing this calling from the clergy's vocation of spiritual warfare. Augustine cited the need for political order found in Romans 13 and pointed to venerable warriors from the Scriptures, including David in the Old Testament and Cornelius in the New Testament. In a fatherly tone, Augustine urged Boniface to act out of love for neighbor (*caritas*) as well as a love for justice, which would cause him to have a firm but restrained hand when engaging his foes. In this letter, as elsewhere in his writings, Augustine reminds the reader that the intentions of the heart matter most: one can be motivated by righteous indignation and love of neighbor, or one can act on greed, hatred, lust, and the desire to dominate.

1

Augustine did not create a novel way of thinking. His use of just war principles was rooted in the Holy Scriptures, classical natural law thinking, and practical discussions in the early church about public service in an empire characterized by idolatry. The principles on which Augustine elaborated in his correspondence to Boniface and in other writings have been handed down through the centuries in all of the major Christian traditions: Catholic, Orthodox, Anglican, Lutheran, Reformed, Baptist, Wesleyan, and their many evangelical progeny of the past century. Moreover, the principles of just war thinking, such as reserving the use of force to legitimate political authorities acting on behalf of a just cause as well as limits to distinguish combatants from noncombatants and private property, have become formalized in the laws of armed conflict today.

The idea of Christian just war thinking is not a historical footnote; rather, it is part of a much larger corpus of Christian writing connected to issues of statecraft, good governance, leadership, responsibility, political accountability, restraint, stewardship, political order, justice, and peace in a fallen world.[3] Just war teaching is found in the catechisms of Catholic and Orthodox churches and in the writings of Luther, Calvin, and others. The vast majority of twenty-first-century Christians are part of denominations or traditions that affirm just war thinking—whether they realize it or not.

Today, however, it appears that just war thinking is falling by the wayside among Christians. For instance, a trend among many Catholics and mainline Protestant denominations in recent decades is to adumbrate a new "presumption against force," rather than seeing the roles of law enforcement and the military as necessary and virtuous vocations in the pursuit of justice and peace. Protestant evangelicals, unfortunately, are typically unaware of the historic teachings on just war thinking and thus poorly equipped as Christian citizens to engage thoughtfully on issues of war and peace, despite the fact that from Kosovo to Kandahar the United States and its allies have been perpetually at war for the last two decades. In some cases, evangelicals avoid national security issues altogether; in other cases, national security is framed only in hyperpatriotic colors. When one looks at major evangelical publications such as *Christianity Today*, *Charisma*, *World*, and the like, one finds fewer than a dozen total articles dealing substantively with Christian just war thinking since 9/11. A review of Christian—and specifically, Protestant-oriented—publishing houses yields similar results; one finds few volumes devoted to Christian approaches to security.

Hence, the need for this volume. Our purpose is to introduce readers—laypersons and clergy alike—to classical Christian thinking across denominational lines on the tradition of just war thinking. Representing a two-millennia-old conversation in our wider cultural tradition, just war thinking (often going by the misnomer "just war theory") is rooted in (a) biblical texts (for example, Rom. 13; Luke 3:14; Acts 10; 1 Pet. 2:13–17); (b) historic Christian thinkers such as Ambrose, Augustine, Aquinas, Luther, Vitoria, Suárez, and Grotius; (c) ethical principles such as the "Golden Rule" and neighbor-love; and (d) natural law principles embedded in Greco-Roman and Judeo-Christian thought. As such, it is a shared tradition that unites the vast majority of the world's Christians across denominational and theological divides.

In a very real sense, this is a "genealogical" project, in that it demonstrates a general continuity in teaching on issues of war, peace, and security over the past two millennia. Like any genealogy, the project will identify the different branches of the "family tree" that have emerged over time due to circumstance and controversy. In addition to the development of the just war idea within Roman Catholic and Orthodox traditions, its evolution and refinement within the varied Protestant branches of the family—for example, Lutheran, Reformed, Anglican, Wesleyan, Baptist, even Anabaptist where applicable—are noteworthy and marked by both convergence and divergence.

This volume will hopefully inform Christians as to their role as active citizens in the public sphere, how they might better understand the role that the church and other institutions (e.g., government) have to play in maintaining "civil society," and how to properly understand vocation, rightly construed (for example, serving as law enforcement agents, business owners, social scientists, politicians and policy analysts, medical professionals, educators, etc., as distinct from the clergy). Even those Christians who are a part of Catholic or mainline Protestant denominations, wherein a commitment to issues of "justice" is front and center, may be wholly unfamiliar with confessional statements, documents, or sources that undergird their particular tradition's teaching. This volume is designed to record a history of ecclesial thinking about war and peace across denominational lines and provide a resource relevant for today's world as Christians think about war and peace, especially given the "postdenominational" character of the present era and the tendency among contemporary Christians to eschew tradition.

One of the distinctives of the present volume is to demonstrate important parallels and distinctions *within and among* various Christian traditions that develop over time. For instance, as Keith Pavlischek's chapter demonstrates, John Calvin argued that the state could use "the sword" to enforce Christian morality and church discipline. Later Presbyterians would generally disavow this basic position, although they have historically affirmed the just war idea. Luther, even when he had a high view of political authority and was not shy about enlisting that authority in the service of the Reformation, would have rejected Calvin's position. Conversely, as David Baer's chapter will show, while Luther emphasized obedience to the state, other Reformers developed a doctrine of the lesser magistrate as an intermediate authority between the tyrant and the citizenry. In this regard, it is significant that the Calvinist view was preached in colonial pulpits prior to the US War for Independence.

Nuances such as these are developed throughout the volume in a denominational context. Whereas each of the subsequent chapters focuses on a specific Christian tradition, such as Joseph Capizzi's on Roman Catholicism or Darrell Cole's on Eastern Orthodox Christianity, this introductory chapter devotes its attention to the historical development of Christian just war thinking. It illuminates contrasts between just war thinking and the alternatives of pacifism and holy war, observing nuanced differences among Christian thinkers on issues such as the role of the state and "lesser evil" politics and stressing shared Christian theological commitments with public policy ramifications (for example, the priority of peace).

THE THEOLOGICAL ROOTS OF
CHRISTIAN JUST WAR THINKING

What is just war thinking? It is an approach to issues of statecraft and peace that focuses attention on three questions: (1) "When is it moral to go to war (*jus ad bellum*)?"; (2) "How can war be fought morally (*jus in bello*)?"; and (3) "How can war be ended in a moral fashion that reinforces peace (*jus post bellum*)?" Figure 1.1 provides the common framework for the application of these just war principles.

Figure 1.1. Just War Criteria

Jus ad Bellum
- *Legitimate authority*: Supreme political authorities are morally responsible for the security of their constituents and therefore are obligated to make decisions about war and peace.
- *Just cause*: Self-defense of citizens' lives, livelihoods, and way of life are typically *just* in their nature; more generally speaking, the cause is likely *just* if it rights a past wrong, punishes wrongdoers, or prevents further wrong.[1]
- *Right intent*: Political motivations are subject to ethical scrutiny; violence intended for the purpose of order, justice, and ultimate conciliation is just, whereas violence for the sake of hatred, revenge, and destruction is not just. For this reason, in normal discourse we speak not of "military violence" but "military force."[2]
- *Likelihood of success*: Political leaders should consider whether or not their action will make a difference in real-world outcomes. This principle is subject to context and judgment, because it may be appropriate to act despite a low likelihood of success (for example, against local genocide). Conversely, it may be inappropriate to act due to low efficacy despite the compelling nature of the case.
- *Proportionality of ends*: Does the preferred outcome justify, in terms of the cost in lives and material resources, this course of action?
- *Last resort*: Have traditional diplomatic and other efforts been reasonably employed in order to avoid outright bloodshed?

Jus in Bello
- *Discrimination*: Has care been taken to reasonably protect the lives and property of legitimate noncombatants?
- *Proportionality*: Are the battlefield tools and tactics employed proportionate to battlefield objectives?

Jus post Bellum[3]
- *Order*: Beginning with existential security, a sovereign government extends its roots through the maturation of government capacity in the military (traditional security), governance (domestic politics), and international security dimensions.
- *Justice*: The matter of "just deserts" includes consideration of individual punishment for those who violated the law of armed conflict and restitution policies for victims when appropriate.
- *Conciliation*: This element involves coming to terms with the past so that parties can imagine and move forward toward a shared future.

1. This formulation derives directly from Augustine, as recorded in Thomas Aquinas's *Summa Theologica* II-II.40 (New York: Christian Classics, 1981).
2. On the distinction between "violence" and "force" in normal discourse, see the discussion below.
3. These criteria are not enshrined in historic just war thinking but are distilled from various sources elaborated on by Patterson initially in 2004. See also Eric Patterson, *Ethics beyond War's End* (Washington, DC: Georgetown University Press, 2012); Patterson, *Ending Wars Well: Order, Justice, and Conciliation in Post-Conflict* (New Haven: Yale University Press, 2012).

Within our own wider cultural heritage, the just war tradition may be viewed as the chief moral grammar by which moral judgments concerning force have been shaped. While elements of the just war idea can be found outside of the Christian tradition, such as in Cicero, it has been largely developed and refined within the Christian moral tradition for the past two millennia. In the words of one political ethicist, "Just war is a way of thinking [about international affairs] that refuses to separate politics from ethics."[4] As described by another ethicist, it is a particular "understanding of political responsibility that is rooted in neighbor-regarding love."[5]

The criteria in figure 1.1 rest on sturdy theological foundations. Often these presuppositions are not clearly spelled out in arguments about the "justness" of such and such a war or conflict. The following are among the moral arguments, rooted in Scripture and natural-law reasoning, and shared by the formal doctrinal statements of most denominational traditions and/or the statements of key Christians in history, that inform just war thinking:

- Both good and evil are a part of human nature—a reality that informs responsible policy considerations.
- Certain universal moral constants in human nature, regardless of culture, are based on the *imago Dei*; hence the importance of the natural moral law since all people and cultures have moral codes that are normative and restrict the taking of human life.
- Justice without force is a myth, since there will always be evil people, and evil must be hindered so that the very goods of human flourishing can be protected.
- A necessary distinction exists between a presumption against war or coercive force and a presumption against injustice and evil.
- A moral distinction exists between criminal behavior and victimhood, between relative guilt and relative innocence.
- Based on neighbor-love and inherent (human) dignity, we are morally obligated to protect people from unjust evils; hence the morality of humanitarian intervention.
- "War" and "peace" are not two discontinuous and incommensurable worlds or universes of discourse, each with its own set of rules, whereby "peace" is the equivalent of morality and "war" is the equivalent of evil. "Peace," therefore, can be *unjust* in character and thus illicit; hence, "peace" must be justly ordered.

- A qualitative moral difference exists between "violence" and "force"—"force" being that measure of power necessary and sufficient to *uphold* law and politics, and "violence" being that use of power which *exceeds* that measure, *destroying* the order of both law and politics.[6] As an instrument, force is morally neutral in and of itself; it can be used for good or ill.
- Both conventional and nonconventional military intervention are necessary in the affairs of nations.
- Many are called to a vocation of public service, including some to protect their fellow citizens as judges, warriors, statesmen, and law-enforcement officers.
- Just war thinking assumes that leaders are stewards: they must soberly consider the *likelihood of success*, count the costs of engaging in war or conflict, and limit destruction of lives and private property.
- The principles of justice that govern entering international conflict do not exist in some universe removed from daily living; rather, they embody justice everywhere and at all times—in civilian and domestic life as well as international affairs. After all, if justice is not universal, then it is not "justice." And if discerning and implementing justice in the context of coercive force is not possible, then we will need to admit that neither is criminal justice attainable at the level of domestic policy, nor are just norms plausible in *any* human context. All that is left is sheer power or personal preference, but not *justice*; one person's mugging, then, is simply another person's good time.
- Just war thinking further assumes that a moral symmetry exists between military ends and means (not just *what* we do but *how* we do it must be just).
- Even when moral judgment can be clouded—or violated—in war and international conflict, this potential itself does not render war or coercive force per se unjustifiable.
- Prudential wisdom is needed, for even when and where full justification for entering conflict or going to war is present, wisdom might caution us *not* to proceed.

And what about peace? The just war tradition is properly understood as peace-seeking not simply in terms of aspiration but also in terms of praxis. Thomas Aquinas wrote that the resort to force, or threat of force, should focus attention on three objectives: *order, justice,* and *peace.*[7] *Order* is providing enduring security and stability for all parties (which undergirds the Pauline argument found in Rom. 13). *Justice* begins with the principle of getting what one deserves ("just deserts") and thus should be a humbling and restraining factor because "all have sinned and fall short of the glory of God" (Rom. 3:23).[8] *Justice* should motivate government action to right past wrongs, prevent future wrongdoing, punish wrongdoers (including those among our own troops), and provide, if possible, some restitution to victims. The end—or the fruit—of justice is *peace. Order* and *justice,* therefore, are the foundations for an enduring peace among citizens and among nations. After all, as the Mafia, terrorists, and pirates well demonstrate, "peace" can be illicit; hence it must be justly ordered. Such a political peace can provide the basis for deepening bonds of conciliatory relationships and the pursuit of common goods, such as diplomatic and economic relations, over time.

ALTERNATIVES: PACIFISM AND HOLY WAR

Pacifism

As voices as diverse as John Helgeland, James Turner Johnson, and J. Daryl Charles observe, history provides no evidence that the early church took a unified pacifist position, even when many second- and third-century Christians were apparently pacifists.[9] There is some debate about why these Christians were pacifists, because Christ offered no explicit teaching on war; however, it is nevertheless clear that one compelling motive was a rejection of sinful Rome.[10] Indeed, the book of Acts recounts how, when confronted with gentiles coming to the Christian faith, James and the leadership in Jerusalem did not force them to Judaize (for example, take on circumcision and Old Testament dietary laws) but did restrict them in the context of two of the religio-political practices common on Roman feast days and at Roman shrines: sexual immorality and consuming food that was first offered to idols (Acts 21:25).[11] This was a commonsense moral limit. Christians, like Jews, repugned the idolatry and emperor cult of Rome and were persecuted by taxation, imprisonment, crucifixion, and performances in the arena (the Roman Circus). In this milieu Christian pacifism — or more accurately, a reluctance to serve in Roman government — was a rejection of the idolatrous claims of the state on the individual.[12] Over time, Christian scholars such as Augustine and Aquinas differentiated between the citizen's duty to the state, including military service, and the pacific duties of the churchman. The latter was to be devoted entirely to spiritual service and therefore could not take up the sword.[13]

More broadly, *pacifism* is a commitment against violence and an allegiance to peace, defined as "nonviolence." In practice, Christian pacifists have been motivated by Christ's commission to love one's neighbor while secular pacifists often parallel this injunction with their own: "Do no harm." Moreover, Christian pacifists have looked back on Christ's example of self-abnegation and resignation to his fate as the archetype for their position. The pacifist faces war with two questions: (1) "How could I, an agent of peace, be so presumptuous as to take someone else's life?" and (2) "How could I be so vain as to employ violence in self-defense rather than resign my fate to God?" In short, the pacifist asserts personal responsibility for his or her own actions, and nothing more.[14]

In the fourth century, Augustine responded to theoretical Christian *pacifism* in a way that laid the foundation for just war thinking. Whereas pacifists focused on employing the transcendent values of Christ's millennial kingdom, Augustine attempted to balance the realities of a fallen world (*civitas terrena*) with the values of the *civitas Dei* (city of God).[15] Interestingly, Augustine's notion of just war also relied heavily on the Jesus's teaching on the second-greatest commandment, to "love your neighbor as yourself" (Matt. 22:39). In domestic society as well as international affairs, how does one go about loving one's neighbor? Augustine argued that within a society, adherence to the rule of law, including punishment of lawbreakers, was one way of loving one's neighbors. When one loves his neighbor (*caritas*), he refrains from harming him and supports the authorities in their efforts to provide security to the citizenry. Moreover, Augustine noted that *caritas* means protecting one's neighbor when the neighbor is attacked, even if one is forced to employ force to protect that individual. For Augustine, the law of love includes punishment (consequences for immoral behavior) and justice (restoration of what was taken, righting past wrongs).[16]

A second critique of pacifism from within the Christian tradition comes from Christian realist Reinhold Niebuhr. Niebuhr was an ardent pacifist until the march of militarism and fascism in Europe and Asia made him abandon this position in the 1930s. Niebuhr respected the "witness" of absolute pacifists who refused to support a war effort in any way, including service in the medical corps or through their taxes, but he denounced those he called "political pacifists." For Niebuhr, political pacifists are those who refuse to make moral distinctions about political categories and to make what Niebuhr called "lesser evil" choices when confronted with political evils. For instance, Niebuhr attacked his contemporaries who argued that going to war in 1939–40 was immoral because both sides, the British Empire and the Third Reich, were equally evil. Niebuhr castigated this "neutrality" as conceited, irresponsible, and naïve because there really *was* a qualitative moral difference between Hitler's Nazism and British rule in India.[17]

The pacifist position has found renewed vigor since the Reformation among various strains of Anabaptists such as Mennonites, Church of the Brethren, and Brethren in Christ, among Quakers, as well as among some mainline Protestants. Since the 1980s Catholic pacifism may be at its strongest point since the early church, and varieties of pacifism are flourishing in mainstream Western society, especially in Western European societies and among American intelligentsia due to the legacy of the Vietnam War, the development of nuclear weapons, US actions in Iraq, and current developments in both eastern Europe and the Pacific region. Typically, contemporary pacifism is generally less rooted in a deep theological tradition than it is indebted to the nonviolent example of a non-Christian, Mahatma Gandhi. In contrast, the Anabaptist chapter in this book, written by J. Daryl Charles, will look carefully at the classical Christian pacifist position, rooted in a robust theological posture and elaborated in the Schleitheim Confession of 1527.

Holy War

The crusade or *holy war* mindset assumes the polar opposite position of pacifism. The crusader believes that violence can be employed in defense of—or to further—eternal values. In practice, holy wars are often reactions to threats that seem to undermine the basic ideals and existence of one's civilization. Thus, the medieval Crusades and the *Reconquista* of the Iberian Peninsula were perceived at the time as "holy" in repulsing the onslaught of Islam in its religious and political forms. Similarly, some contemporary proclamations to take up violent jihad in the Middle East are a response to perceived Western cultural and political domination.

What inspires the individual holy warrior? Of course, as skeptics like to note, it is entirely possible that material gain might stimulate participation, as it did for many during Islam's early wars of conquest, the creation of Spain's empire in the New World, or among some al-Qaeda and more recent Islamist recruits. Nevertheless, many holy warriors are motivated by other concerns. For one, holy warriors may be provoked to action by righteous indignation. Their most personal convictions have not only been questioned but affronted and defiled. The holy warrior feels compelled to action in defense of those ideals held most dear—faith in God and community. The holy warrior may also seek an eternal reward. This does not necessarily indicate a "death wish," only that the individual is convinced that his or her actions are in pursuit of transcendent ends and that such behavior will please the deity he or she worships. Many holy warriors speak of purifying their souls through the struggle; they may also seek to purify the land through total, purging war that cleanses the land of sinners and defilement. Other holy warriors seek glory in both the here and hereafter in the tradition of early martyrs of their faith.

While much could be said about crusaders and jihadis, the basic principle needing acknowledgment is that holy war can be based on zealous love for one's faith and that this justifies employing violence by the holy warrior. What is deeply problematic about holy war is that if the end is absolute—namely, the defense of God's name—then it is difficult to provide any ethical rationale for limiting the means employed. Holy warriors are not content with a "settlement" for the simple reason that they are attempting to inaugurate God's kingdom on earth or preserve a sacred community. Hence, the "excesses" of holy war: the extermination of entire cities during the rapid expansion of early Islam and the reactionary Christian crusades, the Inquisition, the wars of the Counter-Reformation, the quasi-religious philosophy of the *kamikaze*, and the ethno-religious cleansing at the hands of Hindu and Buddhist "nationalists" in India and Burma. More recently, we have seen how even nonreligious societies—for example, the former Yugoslavia—can descend to a level of frenzy by "holy war" justifications after a church or mosque is attacked or one's coreligionists are killed. For the holy warrior, the end justifies any means.

In the sixteenth century, a Catholic friar and professor at the University of Salamanca, Francisco de Vitoria, responded to Europe's two frontal wars: defense against the Turks in the East as well as Spain's activities in the New World. Vitoria argued, following Augustine and Aquinas, that wars can be just only if fought by legitimate authorities with right intent on behalf of a just cause. However, Vitoria asserted numerous limits on the prosecution of war, *even when* those prosecuting it are defending the faith. For instance, he argued that it is wrong to kill noncombatants such as women, children, "harmless agricultural folk," "clerics and members of religious orders," and even enemy prisoners who are no longer a threat. Vitoria writes, "The reason for this restriction is clear: for these persons are innocent, neither is it needful to the attainment of victory that they should be slain. It would be heretical to say that it is licit to kill them. . . . Accordingly, the innocent may not be slain by (primary) intent, when it is possible to distinguish them from the guilty."[18] Vitoria's use of just war thinking suggests limits on the resort to and the prosecution of war, even in defense of the faith against infidels.

But what does Christianity have to say about two historical instances of holy war—that commanded by God in the Old Testament book of Joshua and the other commanded by a pope two millennia later? Most Christians, it needs stating, have long distinguished between these two. When it comes to the Old Testament case, we have significant teaching that Catholics, Orthodox, and Protestants have agreed upon—by the likes of Augustine, Calvin, Luther, and others. This teaching sees the period recorded in the books of Joshua and Judges thus: an omnipotent and loving God commanded all peoples to honor him, and in case after case humanity refused to do so. God, in his sovereignty, commanded that justice be rendered upon various Canaanite peoples for their idolatry and immorality and divinely appointed the Israelites to employ that justice. It was a *holy war* in the sense that it was directly and divinely commanded by God, even when it was bounded to a specific time and place. It is noteworthy that it was limited: Israel was not to employ force outside of geographical borders nor was Israel to use it as a means of global conversion by force (there was a robust vehicle for voluntary conversion in Hebraic law). Israel was not rendering a verdict: God had done so directly, and his commandment was that Israel conquer the land and mete out God's judgment in a way that also returned Israel to its homeland. Christians believe that an omnipotent God is just in making such determinations but that this is a unique case in history, limited solely to theocratic Israel, and does not go beyond explicit divine commands toward peoples such as the Amalekites.

From the Davidic kingship onward, and continuing throughout the New Testament era into the present, there exist no such commands given by God to his people. Consequently, most Christians look skeptically on the papal claims that drove the Crusades to liberate Palestine. If a religious figure operates outside of Scripture and/or God's explicit divine command to enjoin a war of conquest on behalf of religious ends, such action simply does not comport with classical Christian views, whether condoned by a pope in the eleventh century or a Serbian priest in the twentieth century. It is noteworthy that such calls to holy war are rooted first in the individual's clerical authority and second in the claim that holy war will both purify the warrior (through struggle and sacrifice) and purify the land (by cleansing it of unbelievers). Consequently, the Crusades may have technically been a "holy war" (or, better said, a "religious war") because an ecclesiastical official justified them, but that does not make them "holy," "righteous," or "just." Christians do not believe that God has commanded total war on religious grounds in the New Testament era. It is only through the atoning work of Christ that humanity can be purified, not through individual works.

That being said, it is worth at least noting from a historical standpoint what those wars that we designate the "Crusades" and "*Reconquista*" (reconquest) in fact were: they were political, rather than spiritual, reactions to invasion. Within twenty years of the Muslim leader Muhammad's death in 632, Muslim armies blazed across Mesopotamia and conquered most of North Africa and Cyprus. In 732, the Muslim advance across Iberia and into Europe was finally checked at the Battle of Tours (France) by Charles Martel; in the East, Muslim armies fanned out to conquer the Persian Empire and moved on toward Byzantium and India. In the decades prior to the call for the first Crusade by Urban II in November 1095, Muslim Turkish armies conquered Baghdad and much of the Byzantine (Christian) territory that makes up modern Turkey. Pope Urban II was responding, in large part, to the direct appeal for aid by embattled Byzantine Emperor Alexios I Komnenos. Hence, it is accurate to describe the Crusades as a political response by the West that had strategic and economic impulses that were packaged in religious justifications authorized

by ecclesiastical authority. It took centuries for the Christian monarchs of
Spain and Portugal to win back the Iberian Peninsula; the wars for Pales-
tine were never a long-term success and at times actually pitted Byzantine
Christians (what became the Eastern Orthodox Church) and other Near
Eastern Christians against Western (Roman Catholic) Christians.

Our point is this: geo-politics is not "holy war." Christians should be
able to distinguish the unique situation that Moses and early Israelite
leaders faced in responding to direct, divine command, while in a one-of-
a-kind covenantal relationship with God, from the claims in the New
Testament era made by religious figures who would justify, on their own
clerical authority, some form of total warfare.

DEBATES WITHIN THE CHRISTIAN
JUST WAR TRADITION

Nearly all Christians today worship in religious traditions or denominations that have at some point in their history affirmed classic just war
thinking, even when it is true that many nondenominational congregations are unaware of their theological genealogy. In the chapters that follow, the reader will sense general agreement on major principles yet observe important nuances that are debated among Christians who think
seriously about war, peace, and security. Differences in perspective will
typically revolve around fine, but important, distinctions, such as that between "force" and "violence," that between the moral obligations of the
private citizen and those of a public official, or that which guides nonconventional over conventional warfare.

"Dirty Hands" and "Lesser Evil" Arguments

Is the profession of arms virtuous, or is it a "lesser evil" practice? Do police
and soldiers necessarily have "dirty hands" when using force? These are
overlapping debates that elucidate important distinctions and for which
classical just war thinking has a response.

One view, held by some Christians and associated with theologian
Reinhold Niebuhr's "Christian realism," is that we are all sinners living in
a fallen world. Our world is rife with sin, violence, and injustice, and thus,
to quote Niebuhr, "The sad duty of politics is to establish justice in a sinful

world."[19] What is "sad" is not simply that justice must be established and defended but that doing so implicates public officials and security personnel in violence. For Niebuhr, the policeman who shoots the murderer just before a second murder takes place has blood on his hands; his duty is tragic and perhaps even sinful because he has shed blood.

For Niebuhr and others like him, Christians have a duty to employ force (a lesser evil) to stop a greater evil, such as Hitler's victory. This is a consequentialist argument insofar as the end somewhat justifies the means. Niebuhr wrote, "There are historic situations in which refusal to defend the inheritance of a civilization, however imperfect, against tyranny and aggression may result in consequences even worse than war." We agree! Unfortunately, however, the root of Niebuhr's argument is a "lesser evil" calculus: our self-defense of civilization — for example, against the threat of Nazism in the context of the Second World War — causes us to sin by employing violence, and thus it is a lesser evil than allowing the Nazis to triumph. But at the end of the day, we are implicated in evil actions. Hereby both the soldier and the statesman sin.

In contrast to these views held by some Christians, the classical Christian understanding is that God calls some to wield the sword under right authority (Rom. 13) and that doing so is praiseworthy.[20] It is *good* to promote security, punish wrongdoers, right past wrongs, defend the weak, and prevent additional wrong. Mark Tooley's chapter on John Wesley and early Methodism emphasizes this very point: Wesley thought "law and order" to be so important that he was willing to raise up a regiment of Methodist volunteers during a time of national crisis. The enforcement of law and the establishment of security is an ontological good, meaning that the advancement of the common good ("commonweal") is virtuous and right: it is not just a comparative good (i.e., a "lesser evil"). To be clear, the police officer is a hero and not a criminal; that is to say, the loss of life is the responsibility of *the murderer himself* for acting wrongly and putting himself into that position. The police officer self-sacrificially puts himself in harm's way on behalf of his fellow citizens. The same is true for the prosecuting attorney and judge ruling in capital cases as well as for soldiers acting in self-defense of their homeland. This, of course, is not to give *carte blanche* to any action by the president, police officers, or military personnel, but it is to argue that people fulfilling their vocation in a fallen world should be praised rather than scapegoated.[21] The true villains are murderous criminals and terrorists.

Force and the Presumption against Force

Throughout history, it was the view of most people in the West—whether Christian or not—that the use of force was an inherent part of justice, politics, and security. Carl von Clausewitz famously wrote that the use of the military instrument was "politics by other means," and certainly the routine work of law enforcement and penal systems was designed with the common good in mind.

In contrast, in recent years a different view has arisen. James Turner Johnson has unflatteringly identified this view as an "innovation" in just war thinking.[22] Commonly associated with an article published by James Childress in 1978, this argument proceeds on the assumption that the just war tradition severely limits war and that, at its core, there is actually an inherent presumption against war.[23] Perhaps the best place to see this logic played out is in *The Challenge of Peace*, a pastoral letter published by the National Conference of Catholic Bishops in 1983. The basic argument, written in early 1980s language suggestive of a nuclear apocalypse, is that Christianity's emphasis on love of neighbor and comparative justice have always made war, at best, a "sad necessity." But in the climate of 1980s and early-1990s contemporary Catholic discourse, war came to be viewed quite simply as immoral and insane because it would invariably devolve into a nuclear holocaust.[24]

What is "innovative"—or more accurately, revisionist—about this view is that it argues that the normative state of affairs is an existential peace and that justice is not related to coercion, force, self-defense, and punishment. The "presumption against" position is not only impractical but, importantly, out of alignment with the presuppositions of the classic just war position and moral reality.

At the heart of this debate is the distinction between *force* and *violence*. *Force* is lawful, restrained, and motivated toward the end of peace. *Violence*, in contrast, is unlawful, unrestrained, often perpetrated by those without authority, and motivated by something other than love. The Bible and the Christian tradition teach that legitimate political authorities have a moral duty to vigilantly employ restrained force to counter lawlessness in domestic and international society. The key, therefore, lies in motivation and how force is employed. We can recognize firm but loving parental discipline: it is quite different from anger-induced, unrestrained child-beating. So, too, we can discern the difference between law enforcement killing a murderous kidnapper to save a child and unlawful police brutality. In short, violence is different from force: it is illegitimate, unrestrained, beyond the law, motivated by an anger verging on hatred, and dehumanizing. The same differentiation holds true with the application of military force, in which there is a difference between lawful, restrained, morally guided fighting on the battlefield and immoral, unrestrained violence. The distinction between *force* and *violence*, therefore, demonstrates the problem of the trope "presumption against force." Instead, classic teaching on the responsibilities faced by legitimate authority focuses attention on a "presumption for order and justice" and a "presumption against unlawful violence."

The Levels-of-Analysis Error

The question is often asked, "Didn't Jesus teach us to turn the other cheek?" What is typically meant by this question is something to this effect: "Don't I, as an individual, have a Christian responsibility to be longsuffering when my neighbor criticizes or attacks me? Wasn't this the example of Jesus Christ himself?" The answer to this question is a narrow, qualified affirmative, in the recognition that there are many other questions left unasked and unanswered. C. S. Lewis rightly commented, in a paraphrase of Martin Luther, "Does anyone suppose that our Lord's hearers understood him to mean that if a homicidal maniac, attempting to murder a third party, tried to knock me out of the way, I must step aside and let him get his victim?" Lewis concluded that Jesus's hearers knew Jesus was speaking about the "frictions of daily life among villagers."[25]

The essential misunderstanding regarding Jesus's directive to "turn the other cheek" can be illustrated by what international-relations scholars label *levels of analysis*.[26] Social and political life, including law enforcement and national security, occur at three different levels of analysis: the individual, domestic politics, and international arenas. In other words, I have a face-to-face relationship with individuals around me, such as my next-door neighbor and my work colleagues. At the same time, I am a member of groups (church, Rotary International, soccer team) and a citizen within the Commonwealth of Virginia and the United States of America. Separately, our government in Washington, DC, is composed of people who represent over three hundred million citizens and who are in relations with other governments as well as nonstate actors such as terrorists, criminal cartels, the United Nations, foreign business enterprises, and so on.

Christ consistently criticized the legalistic, personalized vendettas rooted in the Near Eastern honor culture of his Jewish listeners as suggested by "an eye for an eye."[27] Instead, he called for individuals to be patient, kind, and generous to their neighbors. Nevertheless, neither he nor John the Baptist nor the apostles told soldiers, tax collectors, or other government officials to quit their jobs because the job itself was sinful or "tainted."[28] Rather, the consistent tenor of Jesus's and apostolic teaching is to act justly when one is in a position of authority.

Romans 12 and 13 give us a picture of how the levels of analysis work in society. In these chapters, individual Christians are called to be humble and to use their gifts for the greater good. Additionally, the individual Christian is also called to be loving and forbearing and to "overcome evil with good" (Rom. 12:21). However, the very next sentence calls for accountability to governing authorities and adjures the reader that "there is no authority except from God, and those authorities that exist have been instituted by God" (13:1). The apostle goes on to say that government, what today we often call "the state," has the responsibility for order and justice ("the sword," 13:4) and that Christians, based on conscience, are to be actively supportive, even to the extent of paying taxes (13:7).

Government provides for social order and justice. It consists of individual people serving, but its job is assuredly *not* to turn the other cheek. It has a different role to play than I do as an individual engaging the people who live on my street or who work at my job. And "it" is not just a faceless institution; government is made up of flesh-and-blood humans from accountants to computer programmers to judges to soldiers. In this sense government is a "body with many members" just as civil society and the church are bodies "with many members" all working for the common good.

Imagine for a moment that a US Navy admiral is home on leave mowing his lawn. Perhaps his neighbor vulgarly criticizes him for crossing a property boundary or cutting back the bushes too far or crushing a sprinkler. For the admiral as an individual and a Christian, this would be the time to "turn the other cheek." This same admiral, when in command of a carrier strike fleet dedicated to protecting America and its allies from enemies, may employ lawful force. He represents the government (a third level of analysis), whereas at home he was in the role of individual (a first level of analysis). Each level has different ways of expressing the responsibility to love one's neighbor and one's fellow citizens.

The Role of the State

Yet another issue that Christians debate is the role of the state, or more precisely, the role of government. While it obviously goes beyond the confines of this introductory chapter to adequately summarize two millennia of Christian views on politics and government, there are some points of departure from mainstream thinking that are worth noting. Considering these variances reveals important differences at the level of assumptions about the role of church, government, and the individual that are to be found in various Christian traditions.

One view that is historically marginal, but theologically significant, is that Christians should be salt and light in society but not participate in the administration of society. We will call this the Anabaptist view. As J. Daryl Charles will show in his chapter, this view comes to expression in the earliest Anabaptist confessions of faith and specifically in the Schleitheim Confession of 1527, an assessment of which is outlined in this volume's treatment of Anabaptism. At its heart, the Anabaptist view of government understands governing bodies to be a necessary evil in a fallen world. It believes that those who participate in government tragically must engage in the sins of coercion, violence, and death; hence, it is no place of service for the Christian who is committed to peace. What is important here, for our purposes, is the view that temporal government is *not* a divinely ordered institution in this world in the way that the family and church are. This view suggests that public service occupations, such as in the administration of justice or law enforcement, are not Holy Spirit–empowered vocations but rather a "necessary evil" reserved for sinners to administer. Consequently, this outlook has a strictly separationist view of not only the institutions of church and state but of the ideational space between politics and lived Christianity.

A second, quite different view is some sort of fusion of church and state, both institutionally and socially. By way of illustration, Thomas Bruneau labels Latin America's historic church-state relationship as the "Christendom model."[29] Because every part of life relates to one's salvation, the church therefore relates to every sector of society and every part of the individual's life. Thus, there is no sacred-versus-secular distinction, and the church plays a role in every part of social and community life. Clearly, such was the Roman Catholic Church's view in Europe for the better part of a millennium, and it is analogous in some ways to the state-centric role that many autocephalous Orthodox churches had in the past. The "Christendom model" suggests a fusion of the institutions of church and state, with the institutional church directly influencing policy, law, and social mores to an extent far beyond today's democratic norms. In the chapter on the Orthodox Church, Darrell Cole describes the unique approach that Eastern Orthodoxy has taken on these issues over the past millennium, with the church in a formal but supporting role to the state. When it comes to contemporary Catholicism, one of the points emphasized by contributor Joseph Capizzi is that the "Christendom model" has obviously fallen out of favor throughout almost all of the Christian world, including all Catholic-majority countries (with the exception of the Vatican as an ecclesiastical state with its own protective services).

The third stream of thinking about the state is associated with the Protestant Reformation and various interpretive commentaries and statements from Luther, Calvin, the Anglican tradition, some Baptists (particularly in North America), and their theological descendants. We will simply designate this the "Protestant model." On the one hand, Protestants agree with Anabaptists that Christians have a unique role to play as salt and light in society. Protestants also are cautious about creating with the state an idolatrous allegiance that trumps one's identity in Christ. On the other hand, Protestants agree with some assumptions of the "Christendom model," based on broader Christian teaching and drawing on examples from both the Old and New Testaments such as the service of Nehemiah, Daniel, Cornelius, and others. Together these suggest that Christian ideas and Christian believers have a role to play in government and society.

Nonetheless, the Protestant tradition has continually drawn a set of distinctions between the institutions of church and state; and Catholics, at least since Vatican II, have largely agreed. We will see this particularly evident in the chapters on Lutheranism and Calvinism by David Baer and Keith Pavlischek, respectively. These chapters note important distinctions between different public service "vocations" or "offices" as well as distinctions as to where to draw boundaries between the temporal and spiritual jurisdictions of church and state. What unites almost all Protestants is the notion that Christian values should be articulated in the public sphere and shape policy, including policies having to do with war and peace. But, as later chapters by Mark Tooley (Methodism) and Timothy J. Demy (Baptists) attest, there are many nuances and points of departure among Protestant traditions on these issues.

The chapters that follow outline, from faithful denominational perspectives, the positions of major church traditions on issues of war, peace, and security. The authors are experts in their field and as scholars are rooted in the Christian heritage. But, as we conclude this introduction, it is worth asking: "How does a Christian work for peace today?"

One answer is to begin by dispelling a false dichotomy that arises from a presumption that peace and peacemaking are entirely distinct from entering war or conflict. This way of thinking is simply mistaken. Desperately needed is a holistic approach to Christian thinking and to understanding Christian public servants who engage at every phase of human interaction, including government service, politics, diplomacy, humanitarian aid, and security in our fallen world.

The US military as well as humanitarian agencies provide a helpful framework here. Experts in these arenas understand that there is a long prewar phase before bullets fly in any conventional sort of conflict. That is when formal diplomacy, led by ambassadors and representatives from the US Department of State or the British Foreign and Commonwealth Office—to use but two examples—are at work. At the same time, members of civil society engage in innumerable activities designed to advance peace and the common good, including—for example—Track 2 diplomacy, which refers to nongovernmental actors who advance peace and dispel misunderstanding by engaging one another and/or government agencies outside of traditional government-to-government channels.

Clearly, when it comes to the prewar phases of international relations, there is much space in which Christians might be engaged. For instance, Christians (and other faith-based groups) are often the ones who attempt to ameliorate the conditions of poverty and instability that might make some believe that war is necessary in the first place. Often there are Christians, based on their clerical authority as bishops or priests or due to their leadership of faith-based NGOs (for example, the president of World Vision or Catholic Relief Services), who have private channels of communication that can be utilized for the purposes of communication and safe meetings. This Track 2 diplomacy can also bring belligerents into a safe space for dialogue to end war. The Catholic Church provided such relationships and space for the end of Mozambique's civil war in 1992; similarly, in 2019, the pope and the archbishop of Canterbury worked to bring South Sudan's warring factions to the Vatican for a "retreat" to advance peace. As Eric Patterson has documented, such individuals and organizations can play a similar role in providing a sanctuary for negotiations to end a conflict.[30]

When political instability goes beyond tension to outright conflict, Christians are also needed on the battlefield, from the highest leadership posts down to army privates in the trenches. We want such individuals to be motivated by neighbor-love and a commitment to justice, which will translate into not only love of one's family at home but love of one's comrades, love of one's country, and desire to build the common good, with a commitment to restrained force in pursuit of a better security. At war's end, we need Christians to be serving in law enforcement and in the justice system to punish wrongdoing, restrain future wrong, and help establish a just and enduring order. We also want Christians in the medical and mental health services to provide succor and treatment.

When war ends, it is noteworthy that the first to leave are the UN peacekeepers or the invading forces, leaving many local people behind in situations of injury, destitution, and loss. Often Christians and other faith-based actors commit to demonstrate true charity by caring for the needs of average citizens affected by war in places such as Africa, Central Asia, Latin America, and the Far East.

Yet it is rare to hear pastors and priests laud the work of such professionals and equally rare for congregations to join in prayer for warriors, politicians, diplomats, and aid workers who are responding—at their own peril—to the geopolitical hazards of fallen humanity. We live in a fallen and insecure world. Some Christians are called to work in situations of violence and instability to help their fellow man. The chapters that follow seek to provide classic Christian teaching from denominational perspectives on how Christians should think, theologically and prudentially, and pray about issues of war, peace, and security.

NOTES

1. Augustine wrote letters to a Roman military leader named Boniface as well as to an ecclesiastical figure named Boniface. The two should not be confused.

2. St. Augustine, *Letter to Boniface* (*Letter 189*), written in AD 418; see *St. Augustine Letters, 165–203*, vol. 4, trans. Wilfrid Parsons, The Fathers of the Church (Washington, DC: Catholic University of America Press, 1981), 266–71; also *Letter 189*, in *The Confessions and Letters of St. Augustine, with a Sketch of His Life and Work*, Christian Classics Ethereal Library, https://ccel.org/ccel/schaff/npnf101/npnf101.vii.1.CLXXXIX.html.

3. This argument is made by Joseph E. Capizzi, *Politics, Justice, and War: Christian Governance and the Ethics of Warfare* (Oxford: Oxford University Press, 2015); see also Eric Patterson, *Just War Thinking: Morality and Pragmatism in the Struggle against Contemporary Threats* (Lanham, MD: Lexington Books, 2007).

4. Jean Bethke Elshtain, "Just War and Humanitarian Intervention," *Proceedings of the Annual Meeting of the American Society of International Law* 95 (2001): 1–12.

5. Paul Ramsey, *The Just War: Force and Political Responsibility* (Lanham, MD: Rowman & Littlefield, 2002; first published 1968), 151.

6. Thus John Courtney Murray, *We Hold These Truths: Catholic Reflections on the American Proposition* (New York: Sheed and Ward, 1960), 288.

7. Thomas Aquinas, *Summa Theologica* II-II.40, art. 1, obj. 4 [and answer].

8. Unless otherwise noted, all quotations from the Bible are taken from the New Revised Standard Version.

9. John Helgeland, "Christians and the Roman Army from Marcus Aurelius to Constantine," in *Aufstieg und Niedergang der römischen Welt: Geschichte und Kultur Roms im Spiegel der neueren Forschung*, part 2, *Principat*, ed. Hildegard Temporini and Wolfgang Haase (Berlin: de Gruyter, 1979), 23.1.724–834; James Turner Johnson, *The Quest for Peace: Three Moral Traditions in Western Cultural History* (Princeton: Princeton University Press, 1987), 3–66; J. Daryl Charles, "Pacifists, Patriots, or Both? Second Thoughts on Pre-Constantinian Early-Christian Attitudes toward Soldiering and War," *Logos: A Journal of Catholic Thought and Culture* 13, no. 2 (Spring 2010): 17–55. Helgeland's analysis is an exhaustive historical examination of early Christian attitudes toward war and soldiering. Johnson's examination of the early patristic era highlights sociological realities that played a role in early Christian views of war and soldiering. And Charles focuses on the historical context and position of early church fathers such as Tertullian and Origen—both of whom are typically cited as representatives of the church's supposed pacifistic thinking and both of whom acknowledged

that Christians were serving in the Roman military. Charles also points out that even the influential church historian Roland Bainton, a Quaker pacifist, suggests that the occupation of soldiering was likely not completely off-limits to early Christians; see in this regard Roland Bainton, *Christian Attitudes toward War and Peace* (New York: Abingdon, 1960): 66, 81. Reaching conclusions similar to those of Helgeland, Johnson, and Charles regarding the early Christian centuries are Louis J. Swift, *The Early Fathers on War and Military Service*, Message of the Fathers of the Church 19 (Wilmington, DE: Michael Glazier, 1983), and John Helgeland, Robert J. Daly, and J. Patout Burns, *Christians and the Military: The Early Experience* (Minneapolis: Fortress, 1985).

10. Frederick H. Russell discusses how the limited teaching of Christ on violence ultimately resulted in early church leaders, such as Origen and later Ambrose and Augustine, having to define a Christian position on military service, allegiance to the state, and war in general. See his *The Just War in the Middle Ages* (Cambridge: Cambridge University Press, 1975), chap. 2.

11. Significantly, the first gentile convert reported to have been baptized was none other than a Roman centurion (Acts 10 and 11). It is telling that in a context of repentance and conversion, the centurion was not called out of military service. This incident parallels another significant context of repentance reported in the Gospels: John the Baptist instructing soldiers on their moral obligations. Two specific obligations are identified: being content with their wages and treating people justly (Luke 3:14).

12. A somewhat one-sided view of the historic Christian pacifist position is Geoffrey Nuttall, *Christian Pacifism in History* (Berkeley: World Without War Council, 1971). For a more thoughtful look at historical and contemporary Christian pacifism from perhaps its most famous contemporary defender, see John Howard Yoder, *The Original Revolution: Essays on Christian Pacifism*, Christian Peace Shelf Series (Scottdale, PA: Herald Press, 2003). A history of the application of pacifism in American politics is also provided by Theron F. Schlabach et al., *Proclaim Peace: Christian Pacifism from Unexpected Quarters* (Urbana: University of Illinois Press, 1997).

13. For a brief introduction to this entire controversy, see James Turner Johnson, "Just War, as It Was and Is," *First Things* 149 (January 2005): 19.

14. John Langan takes a slightly different approach to varieties of pacifism. He distinguishes those who withdraw from the controversy surrounding a given war from those who take an activist and ideological or politicized pacifist stance. See his "Just War Theory after the Gulf War," *Theological Studies* 53, no. 1 (1992): 99–100.

15. Augustine's *The City of God* is his famous treatise contrasting the *civitas Dei* and the *civitas terrena*. However, we gather much of his just war thinking

from his voluminous correspondence, such as "To Publicola" and "To Marcellinus." Many of these letters are available in classic compilations from the Catholic University of America Press as well as in a new series by New City Press.

16. In the context of "criminal justice," charity, as Augustine viewed it, is being expressed in three directions: (1) it is directed toward the offender, who is being prevented from doing evil; (2) it is directed toward society at large, which is watching; and (3) it is directed toward future or potential offenders, who might be considering the possibility of evil behavior.

17. See Reinhold Niebuhr, "An Open Letter to Richard Roberts," *Christianity and Society* 5 (Summer 1940): 30–33. This argument is updated in thoughtful chapters by Paul Ramsey, William V. O'Brien, and Jean Bethke Elshtain published in Elshtain's edited volume *Just War Theory* (New York: New York University Press, 1992).

18. Francisco de Vitoria, quoted in Richard Shelly Hartigan, "Francisco de Vitoria and Civilian Immunity," in *Political Theory* 1, no. 1 (1973): 83. The Latin text from which this citation is drawn can be found in Vitoria's work *De Indis et de iure belli reflectiones*, ed. Ernest Nys, trans. J. P. Bate (Washington, DC: Carnegie Institution of Washington, 1917), 449.

19. Reinhold Niebuhr, "The Christian Faith and the World Crisis," *Christianity and Crisis* 1 (1941): 5–6.

20. This argument is forcefully made by Keith J. Pavlischek in "Reinhold Niebuhr, Christian Realism, and Just War Theory: A Critique," in *Christianity and Power Politics Today: Christian Realism and Contemporary Political Dilemmas*, ed. Eric Patterson (New York: Palgrave Macmillan, 2008), 53–71.

21. This point needs emphasis especially in our own day. As we write (summer of 2021), the United States — and we write from a North American perspective — has experienced over a year of social-political, cultural, and racial unrest. A dominant theme, advanced not only by social activists but by virtually all in the electronic and print media and by most of the academy, is that police and law enforcement agents have heaped guilt upon guilt on themselves through their "unjust" treatment of parts of the wider population and that both law enforcement and the criminal justice system are *inherently* flawed. As one who has spent part of his professional career doing public-policy work in the arena of criminal justice, I (Daryl) can attest that this narrative is a false one (even while acknowledging that few people might agree with me, given the chaotic cultural moment). The argument that we as editors are advancing here is *not* that there are not cases of error or abuse in the wider system; it is, rather, that those who serve in police work and law enforcement truly *are* to be honored by virtue of the largely self-sacrificial nature of their work — namely, the mandate to protect the common good. The truth is this: life would be hell on earth without police, law

enforcement, and public authorities committed to *preventing and punishing* criminal offenders. No one would wish such an existence, and one does not need to be a religious believer to acknowledge this fundamental truth. To pursue this theme, however, brings us too far afield from the topic at hand.

22. Johnson, "Just War, as It Was and Is," 19.

23. James F. Childress's essay "Just-War Theories: The Bases, Interrelations, Priorities, and Functions of Their Criteria," originally published in *Theological Studies Journal* 39 (September 1978): 427–45, was reprinted under the title "Just War Criteria" in *War or Peace? The Search for New Answers* (Maryknoll, NY: Orbis Books, 1980), 40–58.

24. See *The Challenge of Peace: God's Promise and Our Response* (Washington, DC: National Conference of Catholic Bishops, 1983), https://www.usccb.org/upload/challenge-peace-gods-promise-our-response-1983.pdf, and its successor, *The Harvest of Justice Is Sown in Peace* (Washington, DC: National Conference of Catholic Bishops, 1993), https://www.usccb.org/resources/harvest-justice-sown-peace. For a response, see Johnson, "Just War, as It Was and Is," 19.

25. C. S. Lewis, "Why I Am Not a Pacifist," in *The Weight of Glory, and Other Addresses* (New York: HarperCollins, 1980; first published 1949), 87.

26. Kenneth J. Waltz first elaborated this idea as the "three images" of international politics in his book *Man, the State, and War* (New York: Columbia University Press, 1959).

27. Frequent confusion attends interpretation of Jesus's instruction as recorded in Matt. 5:38–42. The "You have heard it said . . . but I tell you . . ." is intended to correct rabbinic distortions and contemporary application of the *lex talion*, not to abolish it as a standard of justice (i.e., proportionality). In Jesus's day, the *lex* was not infrequently employed to justify unethical and retaliatory actions by individuals, especially in financial matters. This distortion is illustrated by the fourfold illustration employed by Jesus: turning the other cheek, giving one's cloak, going the extra mile, and giving to anyone who asks. All of these refer to *personal* interactions and not matters of statecraft or public policy.

28. Again, recall that the first baptized gentile convert was a Roman centurion (Acts 10).

29. Thomas Bruneau, *The Political Transformation of the Brazilian Catholic Church* (Cambridge: Cambridge University Press, 1974).

30. See Eric Patterson, "Religion, War, and Peace: Leavening the Levels of Analysis," in *The Routledge Handbook of Religion and Security*, ed. Chris Seiple, Dennis R. Hoover, and Pauletta Otis (London: Routledge, 2012), 115–24; Patterson, *Politics in a Religious World: Building a Religiously Informed US Foreign Policy* (New York: Continuum, 2011).

WORKS CITED

Augustine of Hippo. *Letter 189.* In *The Confessions and Letters of St. Augustine, with a Sketch of His Life and Work.* Christian Classics Ethereal Library. https://ccel.org/ccel/schaff/npnf101/npnf101.vii.1.CLXXXIX.html.

Bainton, Roland. *Christian Attitudes toward War and Peace.* New York: Abingdon, 1960.

Bruneau, Thomas. *The Political Transformation of the Brazilian Catholic Church.* Cambridge: Cambridge University Press, 1974.

Capizzi, Joseph E. *Politics, Justice, and War: Christian Governance and the Ethics of Warfare.* Oxford: Oxford University Press, 2015.

The Challenge of Peace: God's Promise and Our Response. Washington, DC: National Conference of Catholic Bishops, 1983. https://www.usccb.org/upload/challenge-peace-gods-promise-our-response-1983.pdf.

Charles, J. Daryl. "Pacifists, Patriots, or Both? Second Thoughts on Pre-Constantinian Early-Christian Attitudes toward Soldiering and War." *Logos: A Journal of Catholic Thought and Culture* 13, no. 2 (Spring 2010): 17–55.

Childress, James F. "Just-War Theories: The Bases, Interrelations, Priorities, and Functions of Their Criteria." *Theological Studies Journal* 39 (September 1978): 427–45. Reprinted as "Just War Criteria." In *War or Peace? The Search for New Answers,* 40–58. Maryknoll, NY: Orbis Books, 1980.

Elshtain, Jean Bethke. "Just War and Humanitarian Intervention." *Proceedings of the Annual Meeting of the American Society of International Law* 95 (2001): 1–12.

———, ed. *Just War Theory.* New York: New York University Press, 1992.

Hartigan, Richard Shelly. "Francisco de Vitoria and Civilian Immunity." *Political Theory* 1, no. 1 (1973): 79–91.

The Harvest of Justice Is Sown in Peace. Washington, DC: National Conference of Catholic Bishops, 1993. https://www.usccb.org/resources/harvest-justice-sown-peace.

Helgeland, John. "Christians and the Roman Army from Marcus Aurelius to Constantine." In *Aufstieg und Niedergang der römischen Welt: Geschichte und Kultur Roms im Spiegel der neueren Forschung,* part 2, *Principat,* edited by Hildegard Temporini and Wolfgang Haase, 23.1.724–834. Berlin: de Gruyter, 1979.

Helgeland, John, Robert J. Daly, and J. Patout Burns. *Christians and the Military: The Early Experience.* Minneapolis: Fortress, 1985.

Johnson, James Turner. "Just War, as It Was and Is." *First Things* 149 (January 2005): 14–24.

————. *The Quest for Peace: Three Moral Traditions in Western Cultural History*. Princeton: Princeton University Press, 1987.

Langan, John. "Just War Theory after the Gulf War." *Theological Studies* 53, no. 1 (1992): 99–100.

Lewis, C. S. "Why I Am Not a Pacifist." In *The Weight of Glory, and Other Addresses*, 64–90. New York: HarperCollins, 1980. First published 1949.

Murray, John Courtney. *We Hold These Truths: Catholic Reflections on the American Proposition*. New York: Sheed and Ward, 1960.

Niebuhr, Reinhold. "The Christian Faith and the World Crisis." *Christianity and Crisis* 1 (1941): 4–6.

————. "An Open Letter to Richard Roberts." *Christianity and Society* 5 (Summer 1940): 30–33.

Nuttall, Geoffrey. *Christian Pacifism in History*. Berkeley, CA: World Without War Council, 1971.

Patterson, Eric D. *Just War Thinking: Morality and Pragmatism in the Struggle against Contemporary Threats*. Lanham, MD: Lexington Books, 2007.

————. *Politics in a Religious World: Building a Religiously Informed US Foreign Policy*. New York: Continuum, 2011.

————. "Religion, War, and Peace: Leavening the Levels of Analysis." In *The Routledge Handbook of Religion and Security*, edited by Chris Seiple, Dennis R. Hoover, and Pauletta Otis, 115–24. London: Routledge, 2012.

Pavlischek, Keith J. "Reinhold Niebuhr, Christian Realism, and Just War Theory: A Critique." In *Christianity and Power Politics Today: Christian Realism and Contemporary Political Dilemmas*, edited by Eric Patterson, 53–71. New York: Palgrave Macmillan, 2008.

Ramsey, Paul. *The Just War: Force and Political Responsibility*. Lanham, MD: Rowman & Littlefield, 2002. First published 1968.

Russell, Frederick H. *The Just War in the Middle Ages*. Cambridge: Cambridge University Press, 1975.

Schlabach, Theron F., et al. *Proclaim Peace: Christian Pacifism from Unexpected Quarters*. Urbana: University of Illinois Press, 1997.

Swift, Louis J. *The Early Fathers on War and Military Service*. Message of the Fathers of the Church 19. Wilmington, DE: Michael Glazier, 1983.

Thomas Aquinas. *Summa Theologica*. New York: Christian Classics, 1981.

Vitoria, Francisco de. *De Indis et de iure belli reflectiones*. Edited by Ernest Nys. Translated by J. P. Bate. Washington, DC: Carnegie Institution of Washington, 1917.

Waltz, Kenneth J. *Man, the State, and War*. New York: Columbia University Press, 1959.

Yoder, John Howard. *The Original Revolution: Essays on Christian Pacifism*. Christian Peace Shelf Series. Scottdale, PA: Herald Press, 2003.

TWO

Catholic Just War Thinking

Joseph E. Capizzi

The Catechism of the Catholic Church, published in 1992 during the pontificate of John Paul II and updated in its official Latin edition in 1997, discusses "just war" in its third part, "Life in Christ," section two, "The Ten Commandments," chapter two, "You Shall Love Your Neighbor as Yourself," article 5, "The Fifth Commandment." There, and in several other sections of the Catechism discussed below, war and legitimate defense are discussed in the context of the requirements of love and the duties associated with legitimate defense that fall to those in authority, and derivatively, to citizens subordinate to that authority. The Catechism makes plain two things: that war is sometimes permissible and that war— even "just war"—is always accompanied by "evils and injustices."[1] These elements—the placement of war in the context of both love and politics and the acknowledgment of war's permissibility and accompaniment by evils and injustices—are constant features of the tradition's view of war and will frame the analysis that follows. Together these elements allow us to claim the Catholic position on war as a recognition of its permissibility as an expression of care for the neighbor—a position consistent with the requirements of charity when ordered to the goods of community and peace served by governing authority.

For some time, a pacifist sentiment inside and beyond the church has argued that the just war position involves an apostasy from the original commitments of the earliest Christians. According to this view, the early Christian communities prevented each other from military service, embracing instead an ethic of political "radicality" that made space for nonviolent resistance or even nonresistant witness.[2] Among the reasons given for this Christian renunciation of violence are the direct words of Jesus that are thought to counsel nonresistance, the idolatrous oath associated with service in the Roman military, and different eschatological assumptions held by early and subsequent Christians. According to Mennonite theologian John Howard Yoder, the early Christian confident faith in the imminence of Christ's victory and inauguration of his kingdom led Christians to embrace "absolute nonresistance in discipleship and to abandonment of all loyalties which counter that obedience, including the desire to be effective immediately or to make oneself responsible for civil justice."[3] Yoder therefore rejected Reinhold Niebuhr's argument against Christian pacifism as irrelevant and irresponsible.[4] Faithfulness and obedience, not apostasy and "effect," were that to which Christ called his disciples.

Yoder's argument in *The Politics of Jesus* and elsewhere proved enormously successful in convincing many Christians toward this view.[5] Most well known is the effect that Yoder's argument had on Methodist theologian Stanley Hauerwas's "conversion" to pacifist witness and his embrace and development of many Yoderian themes.[6] Less well known, however, is the impact that Yoder made on English-speaking Catholic thinkers on just war, especially in the United States. In fact, any writing on contemporary just war and Christian conceptions of politics must note the "ecumenical" characteristic of recent discussion and the effects of intercommunal dialogue. Catholics, Methodists, Lutherans, Anglicans, and others often write in direct contact with each other. The Catholic view of just war today reflects these influences, including their responses to the enormous influence of Yoder and his protégé Hauerwas. Drew Christiansen, S.J., one of the more prominent just war writers who collaborated with the US Conference of Catholic Bishops on its statements on war and peace, writes of Yoder's significant "influence on how Catholic theologians and exegetes undertook social interpretation of the scripture."[7] Yoder's influence on even Catholic thinking about war cannot be underestimated, especially in his claim of a post-"Constantinian" apostasy in the church from ineffective and nonresistant discipleship toward "taking control of the world" in the name of justice.[8]

There is no legitimate basis for arguing about the ostensible "pacifism" of the early Christian community. Myriads of articles and essays representing different perspectives cannot alter the sound judgment on display in Phillip Wynn's recent volume *Augustine on War and Military Service*. According to Wynn, there was no united Christian view on war and peace before Constantine. No one has been able to "discover a clear and internally consistent view of war as a general phenomenon in the writings of early Christians. Anyone seeking to impose such a singular view on others was reduced to cobbling together a pastiche of authorities whose contradictions had to be smoothed out or obliterated."[9] Wynn's point, of course, counters facile historical reconstructions meant to serve either the pacifist or just war cases. Early Christian opposition to service in war abounded, yet this coexisted with at least some Christian participation in and service to the Roman military.

Some Catholic responses to the emergence of Yoderian thought on war accepted Yoder's history and theological claims about eschatology. These embraced his argument that the "Constantinian" moment was most significant for Christian—and Catholic—reflection on the need for social relevance. These authors thereby accepted both the historical claims of a "fall" from a peaceable ethic characterizing the early church until Constantine and the subsequent conversion of the empire, in addition to the adoption of the use of lethal force as exceptional behavior by Christians now in positions of governing power. From this point of view, Christian participation in war finds justification as an exception to Christ's commands to love even one's enemy in the name of being responsible or effective. Neither governors nor soldiers, then, are peacemakers, but exist alongside a parallel tradition of those committed to peace.[10] Governors and soldiers set aside Christian moral principles of witness in favor of remaining socially relevant. Their service at best is a concession to a fallen world, but it is not part of Christian discipleship or witness to the kingdom.

The just war accounts built on this basis use it as a tool of exception-making to the practices of peacemaking. The tools of the account are used to indicate to Christians the appropriate times to set aside their faith in favor of social responsibility. Just war becomes "akin to pacifism," then, in sharing a presumption against the use of violence and viewing war as a "boundary situation."[11] This account generally accepts the history of an early pacifist Christian community—one for which "killing was unanimously and clearly forbidden"—that experienced a fall subsequent to the conversion of Emperor Constantine.[12] Among the most telling instances of this embrace is the claim found in the National Conference of Catholic Bishops' 1983 pastoral letter, which fails to regard as peacemaking the use of force in accordance with just war principles.[13] Instead, often peace and even just war are opposed to each other. Among the difficulties faced by those who reply to Yoder's concerns is that they fail by Yoder's own analysis. As Yoder himself argued, accounts that view just war as exercises in exception-making generally "slide the scale" downward. Each exception carves a bigger space for the next one, until before long just war analysis "loses its teeth."[14]

But the historic Catholic position on just war did not view service in war as an exception to peacemaking or to Christ's commands to love even the enemy, as we shall see. In addition, the lived experiences of many Christians in the military indicates their assumption that military and Christian service coincide. And not only can we reconstruct a just war approach consonant with scriptural injunctions to be peacemakers; we can question the underlying assumption of pacifism as peacemaking. As Methodist theologian Theodore R. Weber writes,

> There is no reason to assume that non-pacifists cannot be peacemakers, or that pacifists, as such, are effective in peacemaking. As long as human beings are driven by original sin, worldly peace will always be a particular organization of power—some variable combination of force and consent. The art of peacemaking is to move hostile relations toward some denser combination of common consent. . . . Christian peacemaking, in practical terms, requires attention to the reordering and limitation of force in the reorganization of power.[15]

THE CATECHISM ON THE USE OF FORCE

The use of force as an instrument of peace has long been the position of Catholic thought on just war. We will proceed by looking at the current state of the question as expressed in recent official Catholic statements, including *Gaudium et spes* (1965) and the Catechism, supplemented by a few other papal statements. We will dip back into a few points in the tradition to help ourselves understand the claims made in these recent statements, looking at Augustine, Francisco de Vitoria, and then a lesser-known individual, Robert Bellarmine, for insight.[16] Obviously, the choice of these figures has a certain "randomness" to it and should not be taken as more than illustrative of a more complex theological and philosophical tradition worthy of greater precision. Nevertheless, the first individual, Augustine, is a key figure in the tradition of all the magisterial Christian communities; the second, Vitoria, represents an influential Thomistic voice from the beginning of the modern era; and the third, Bellarmine, is chosen in part because of his obscurity on the issue of war. Bellarmine was a late sixteenth-/early seventeenth-century Jesuit theologian, born just four years before Martin Luther's death in 1546. His theological and political positions consistently got him into trouble with popes and his theological and political contemporaries. His view on *indirecta potestas* (roughly, papal "indirect power" in temporal affairs) disturbed popes and monarchs alike. Though he wrote only a few decades after Luther and Vitoria, the world he faced had changed significantly. In some respects, his thought reflects the heavy influence of Vitoria (who also died in 1546), but it departs from him in others. Bellarmine is chosen, in other words, to support the claim of a relatively unified view of war that finds wide expression from varied theological and historical perspectives.

The Catechism begins its discussion of killing (within which the discussion on war arises) by pointing to the fifth commandment's prohibition of killing. Exodus 20:13 states, "You shall not kill." That prohibition, as the Catechism points out, finds specification later in Scripture — at Exodus 23:7, for instance, on which the Catechism comments: "The deliberate murder of an innocent person is gravely contrary to the dignity of the human being, to the golden rule, and to the holiness of the Creator. The law forbidding it is universally valid: it obliges each and everyone, always and everywhere" (CCC, no. 2261). Innocence and guilt, therefore, become critical components of the commandment's interpretation, and as the Catechism suggests in this passage, deliberate killing of the innocent is understood as *malum in se* in the tradition. Nothing can justify the deliberate (or intentional) taking of innocent human life. Scripture prohibits the intentional killing of innocent human beings.[17]

But legitimate defense can be permitted, the Catechism asserts, immediately after stating and explaining the prohibition on intentional killing. Respect for human life enjoined by the commandment is thus far only negative: *never* take innocent human life; *do not* attack the innocent. But legitimate defense begins to fill out the requirements of the commandment beyond the prohibition. Not only must we avoid directly taking innocent human life; we must live in a way respectful of human life, including our own. At this point, the Catechism connects the prohibition to love; on its own, after all, an act of abiding by a prohibition may or may not be moved by love. But the commandment is "brought to perfection," according to Pope John Paul II, when it "culminates in the positive commandment which obliges us to be responsible for our neighbor as for ourselves: 'You shall love your neighbor as yourself' (Lev. 19:18)."[18] The prohibition on killing innocent life then carries with it the injunction to care for those threatened by others. Love requires more than that we not murder; it requires love of self and neighbor to the point of responsibility for their well-being. This might amount to trying to make history "come out right," as Yoder would say of the just war approach, or using violence as part of a "self-deceptive story that we are in control," as Hauerwas argued.[19] But contrarily, it is in fact obedience to the command to love the neighbor, whatever outcome might result.

Therefore, contrary to some of the views influenced by contemporary pacifist thinking, the killing that occurs in legitimate defense "of persons and societies is *not an exception* to the prohibition against the murder of the innocent that constitutes intentional killing" (CCC, no. 2263; emphasis added). The killing that occurs in legitimate defense is another kind of action altogether. For instance, in self-defense, in the killing of the aggressor the intention of the act is ordered toward defense of self and not to the killing of the aggressor. Killing in self-defense therefore requires no special authorization of those responsible for the community, nor need it entail an inordinate self-love. Instead, killing in self-defense, the Catechism continues, can express the appropriate regard of self to which we are called by Christ. Drawing on St. Thomas Aquinas at *Summa Theologica* II-II, question 64, article 7, the Catechism states, "Love toward oneself remains a fundamental principle of morality. Therefore, it is legitimate to insist on respect for one's own right to life. Someone who defends his life is not guilty of murder even if he is forced to deal his aggressor a lethal blow"

(CCC, no. 2264). The Catechism thus expresses self-defense as consonant with the commandment to love and therefore not exceptional to the prohibition against murder. The distinction between guilt and innocence grounds the premise separating this killing from murderous killing; absent that distinction, the act-analysis collapses.

Question 64, article 7 of the *Secunda Secundae*, to which the Catechism refers, is the locus of Aquinas's view on what has since been called the "double effect." There Aquinas explains that any act can have more than one effect and that acts are defined (i.e., they acquire their species, in his terms) largely by the agent's intention. In the case of self-defense, the intention is to save one's self from the act of aggression, and the killing effect is "beside," or alongside, the intention (*praeter intentionem*). That desire of self-preservation is natural, according to him, and therefore not unlawful for the individual, even absent authorization by a recognized authority. Nonetheless, he continues, an act with a licit intention (like the intention to preserve oneself against aggression) and proper circumstances (an individual being attacked by an unjust aggressor) can become illicit if it is out of proportion to its end (*si non sit proportionatus fini*).

The language employed by Aquinas at this point will resonate with anyone familiar with just war thinking. Here he explains the judicious use of force necessary in a situation of duress to preserve a genuine good: the good of existence and derivative good of bodily integrity. However, that good can only be preserved in a manner proportionate to the end. Built into his explanation, in other words, are the criteria of just cause, right intention, and proportionality. Implicit therein lurk the criteria of discrimination and legitimate authority, inasmuch as the exercise of any self-defense presupposes an unjust attacker. Some wrong is being done to which the defender is responding appropriately, both in the sense of properly loving him or herself and of properly loving the attacker by not intending to kill or using disproportionate means. The individual in this case does not determine the justice of his own defensive response against someone attacking him. Such judgments can only be made by those in governing authority responsible for the care of the common good. The victim, therefore, cannot directly intend the death of the assailant; she can only intend to defend herself, even in a manner she foresees will bring about the assailant's death, so long as that remains proportionate to the end of self-defense. The entire act employs the framework of judicious use of force now called "just war."

The consistent teaching of the church on self-defense recognizes this as a "right" deriving from a good love, the love of self that is ordered to the justice we owe God. Because we are to love ourselves as parts of God's creation, we may not inappropriately value our lives. The justice we owe God as created beings of a certain kind sets limits upon that love. Indeed, as individuals, we can recognize goods higher than our self-preservation, including goods of other human beings and the good of religion. We may, therefore, allow our lives to be sacrificed for those goods. The justice we owe to God may in some cases demand as much. So, while there is a right to legitimate defense of self, we can recognize superior obligations limiting our recourse to that right.

Of course, the language of rights is newer than the tradition to which it refers. In the past, Catholic theologians and philosophers would have referred to the "permissibility" or "licitness" of self-defensive action, emphasizing its sound standing in canonical law. (Thus, Aquinas's discussion, in the *Secunda Secundae* [question 40, article 1], begins by asking "whether war is always sinful?") But they would have also thereby signaled the absence of any duty or obligation to preserve one's life in this manner. While there is a natural instinct for self-preservation, the tradition would recognize that an individual might have good reasons, including witness to the faith, to allow the assailant to complete his business.

That is not true, however, for those in governing authority. As the Catechism says in the very next paragraph, "Legitimate defense can be not only a right but a grave duty for one who is responsible for the lives of others. The defense of the common good requires that an unjust aggressor be rendered unable to cause harm. For this reason, those who legitimately hold authority also have the right to use arms to repel aggressors against the civil community entrusted to their responsibility" (CCC, no. 2265). For those in governing authority, the use of force is more than a right. Governing authority is responsible for the care of the community it serves, and that responsibility produces the duty to exercise loving concern even to the point of using force on its behalf. In other words, the framework of judicious use of force present in situations of self-defense remains present in situations of communal defense against aggression.

In this passage and subsequent ones, we can see the close connection of the justification for the force used in war to the justification for the use of force in domestic affairs. Governing authority is responsible for the care of the civil community. Care usually requires internal maintenance: the policing and judging associated with the uses of force in domestic (or, worse but more common for us, "state") governance. That care, however, built upon the principles associated with judgment and punishing, extends outward when the community faces aggressors against the civil community as such. So, the very next paragraph of the Catechism says, "The efforts of the state to curb the spread of behavior harmful to people's rights and to the basic rules of civil society correspond to the requirement of safeguarding the common good. Legitimate public authority has the right and duty to inflict punishment proportionate to the gravity of the offense" (CCC, no. 2266). Thus, the logic in which the Catechism's discussion of war arises is the logic of legitimate defense of the community by those in authority; in other words, the logic of punishment continues a tradition of thinking tracing back at least as far as Alexander of Hales and drawing on concepts nascent in Augustine.[20]

The logic of punishment has long been a Catholic approach to the use of force in war. In the next section, we will support the Catechism's placement of war in the context of punishment by looking at the way this mirrors earlier placement by theologians like Vitoria and Robert Bellarmine, the latter in particular. The first step is to acknowledge, as the Catechism does, that the sine qua non of war is the absence of a superior juridical authority to whom one could turn for the judgment of a situation. The distinction between the use of force in a community understood as "policing" or "punishment" and the use of force to defend a community against another community is that superior authority's absence. The Catechism quotes the pastoral constitution *Gaudium et spes*, which states, "As long as the danger of war remains and there is no competent and sufficiently powerful authority at the international level, governments cannot be denied the right to legitimate defense once every means of peaceful settlement has been exhausted."[21]

BELLARMINE AND THE CATHOLIC TRADITION ON WAR AS PUNISHMENT

The close connection of punishment and war historically has been a common theme in Catholic theology. Bellarmine follows this tradition in his *Disputationes de controversiis Christianae fidei* (often abbreviated as

Controversiae), in which he first claims the power of the pope to intervene indirectly in temporal matters that touch on spiritual ones (*potestas papalis indirecta*). The section in which his analysis of temporal power and war occurs is part of the *Controversia de ecclesia militante* (On the militant church), in particular chapter 14 ("Licere Christianis aliquando bella gerere" [If it is sometimes permissible for Christians to fight wars]) and chapter 15 ("Quot sint et quo justi belli conditiones" [What and how many are the conditions of fighting in war?]). Before he gets there, however, he traces the argumentative conceit of many of his predecessors in first discussing the relationship of temporal and spiritual power more generally. Thus, chapter 12 concerns Christian participation in public trials, which he claims is permissible. It is appropriate, he says, for the prince to exercise judgment. Judgment between guilt and innocence is the basic foundation of law. The next chapter, 13, establishes that the Christian magistrate may use the sword (*gladio*) on those who disturb public peace (*perturbatore publicae quietis*). The defense of capital punishment by Christian theologians of Bellarmine's era and earlier was standard. Bellarmine draws on scripture and theological precedent in its defense. In addition, he points out that this killing is not contrary or exceptional to the commandment not to kill. Instead, punishment by death is a different kind of act. Quoting St. Jerome in his commentary on Jeremiah 22, Bellarmine writes, "To punish murderers and impious men is not shedding blood, but applying laws." He confirms this by appeal to Augustine, again to the point that punishing criminals does not violate the precept "Thou shalt not kill."

Rather, extending the logic of killing as a form of punishment, Bellarmine argues that scripture and tradition prohibit retaliation. "When Christ said 'Do not resist evil,' He did not prohibit just defense, but retaliation" (*Cum dicitur, non resistere malo, no prohiberi justam defensionem, sed repercussionem*). While vengeance is prohibited, a just defense, either in punishment or in war, is not. Thus, when he turns in the next chapter (14) to the proposition that war is permissible for Christians, Bellarmine is prepared to do so only on the condition that war continues to serve the judgment characteristic of governance. War cannot pursue vengeance or retaliation. "War," he writes with remarkable contemporary relevance, "does not pertain to private revenge but to public justice, and just as loving one's enemy, which everyone must, does not prevent the judge and the executioner from doing their duty, so it does not prevent the soldiers and emperors from doing theirs."[22] Another way of putting this is that vengeance is incompatible with charity and that war—while not motivated necessarily by the supernatural virtue of charity—cannot entail incompatible "movements of the will, such as hatred."[23] Bellarmine extends the Catholic view that war is not incompatible with the charity demanded of Christ's followers, even though the activity involves bringing force, including lethal force, against aggressors.

Soldiers, emperors (who here represent governing authorities), judges, and executioners (standing in for all those involved in domestic execution of justice) all could lapse into hating their enemies. And for this reason Bellarmine warns against such while making an important distinction. Appealing to Augustine's remarks on Psalm 37 and jarring contemporary consciences, he states, "Wishing death on one's enemy and even accomplishing it is not evil according to the order of justice, if it is done not because of hatred toward man, but because of love of justice and the common good."[24] In these comments Bellarmine is largely following the tradition. He cites Augustine, Hilary, Jerome, and scripture, among other sources that he calls "fathers." For him and for them, the governing authority has responsibility for a real community of human beings. That responsibility entails enforcement of laws themselves that require judging between guilt and innocence. It is possible for public offices to serve the principle of charity to which Christians are called; they are not incompatible with peacemaking. And with striking relevance to contemporary concerns about the "necessary" opposition of war and peace, he observes: "They say war is opposed to peace, and that peace is a good and effect of charity, therefore war is evil. I reply that war is the opposite of peace in such a way that it is also a means toward peace, and this is the difference between a just and an unjust war. . . . A just war is the opposite of an evil peace and leads to a good peace."[25]

The distinction between punishment and war concerns political context. From the Catholic perspective, and indeed from the perspective of international law, the presupposition of war is the absence of a common tribunal or political authority that can adjudicate disputes among nations or states. Were that authority in place, it could make a judgment concerning the wrong committed that is necessary to war (the *justa causa*) and then levy the appropriate punishment. The absence of an authority capable of making that judgment is a necessary condition of war. In the past, as

Bellarmine explains, there were many authorities not subject to others in temporal matters that could therefore authorize war. Here he lists "all kings, the Republic of Venice, and similar entities, and also certain dukes and counts who are not subject to anybody."[26] A plurality of political types existed that are not present today or that, if present, are rendered invisible by international law, which reserves to itself and to states the sole authority to wage war. No monopoly on the use of force existed; even dukes and counts could authorize war, and in the case of defensive war, anyone could proceed, since "self-defense is lawful for anybody, not only a prince."[27]

Legitimate authority and just cause are to be understood as closely connected. Given the propriety of responding in order to defend a genuine good, the cause of self-defense permits ignoring, or setting aside, concerns about authorization. But other "just causes," such as wrongs done against a political *community*, immediately entail those in positions of governance responsible for that community. Generally speaking, governing authorities can only punish those in their communities. War, however, which presupposes a context lacking recognized governing authority to adjudicate the wrong, requires something different: "A prince," Bellarmine writes, "is only a judge of his own subjects and therefore cannot punish all the crimes committed by others, but only those crimes that are detrimental to his subjects; for even if he is not an ordinary judge of other people, he is nevertheless a defender of his own, and by reason of this necessity he behaves in a certain sense as the judge of those who wronged his people, so that he can punish them with the sword."[28] Responsive to the threat to his community by another, the prince extends his authority of judgment into the offending community and places them within his scope of judgment. This act is perilous and must be done with great care. War, Bellarmine writes, is a genuine means to peace, but "a very serious and dangerous one." The just cause, therefore, must be of a grave sort. And as soon as the offending party offers satisfaction, it must be accepted. War "is a very grave punishment," Bellarmine continues, "by which not only he who sinned is punished, but many innocent people are also involved accidentally."[29]

The responsibility of authority connected to judgment of a particular people sets limits on authority: authority of judgment is always connected to a political community. In that capacity, authority can expand to protect that same community when it is "wronged" by another community or another political authority. In those cases, political authority "behaves" like a judge of that second community.[30] Only a *justa causa* can extend the authority of political community in this way, and only for the purpose of addressing that wrong. Therein the prince acts effectively as a judge of two communities: the one he has primary responsibility for and the second whose wrong act has stretched his authority over it.

Bellarmine is not alone in describing this double position occupied by the prince during war. Earlier, Vitoria had done the same. In his famous *relectio*, or lecture, "On the Indians, or On the Law of War" (1539), Vitoria described how only a prior wrong action could produce a just cause necessary for war. In response, "just cause" creates the temporary, emergency situation wherein a prince in a just war acts as a judge over his community and the offending community. The emergency situation allows the prince to act as though he is the authority even of the offending community — when he is obviously not — even to the point of allowing him to correct the wrong and punish afterward, should he be victorious. The victor, notes Vitoria, "must think of himself as a judge sitting in judgment between two commonwealths — one the injured party and the other the offender; he must not pass sentence as a prosecutor, but as a judge."[31]

The temporary dual position occupied by governing authority during war guides us toward another background supposition of the Catholic view of war, particularly apparent in understanding war through the punishment model. The supposition is that the world itself is a commonwealth, unified under the rule of Christ, though fractured and divided by sin. The punishment framework exposes the fundamental distinction operating in just war analysis — a distinction not between peoples or states but between guilt and innocence. The unity of the world community sets limits on conduct in war. Inasmuch as war seeks to pursue peace — the "right intention" of war — it presupposes a goal of reconfiguring politics toward a more inclusive order of those who ought to be unified by virtue of their membership in the human community. Only those who threaten that order are licitly attacked; anyone who poses no threat must be treated as a potential member of that peace to which all are called.

Bellarmine's remarkable discussion here prescinds from so-called *jus in bello* categories and speaks of the "modus" of fighting, which entails that "no innocents should be harmed" (*nulli innocenti noceatur*) and draws on John the Baptist in Luke 3: "Do violence to no man, neither accuse falsely; and be content with your wages." Drawing on this text and a tradition of thinking about its implications, Bellarmine says that John "prohibits the injuries soldiers usually inflict upon innocent people by force or by treachery, either against their person or their property."[32] Soldiers, therefore, may not, for instance, pillage or steal or even take from these innocents if the soldiers have not been paid by their king (*rex*) or commander (*dux*).

Bellarmine then divides the category of those whom soldiers must not injure (*quibus milites damnum inferre non possunt*) into three. First are all those who do not belong to the commonwealth of the enemies, which presupposes the "pre-nation-state situation" of soldiers marauding across a diverse and confused map of peoples, some of whom are "enemies" and some not. Soldiers must not punish or harm these citizens, nor take it out on them if the soldiers have not been paid. Second are those classes of people (those in "roles") not marked out for fighting, including "priests, monks, those who live in convents, pilgrims, merchants, peasants . . . , and the beasts by which they plow or bring the seeds."[33] Bellarmine's focus on social function indicates a role demarcation of contemporary relevance around machines, factories, and so on that serve functions of daily living. International humanitarian laws protecting these segments of society thus follow a long tradition of thinking about the different roles that citizens perform and their different levels of vulnerability to attack. Third are people not suited to or fit for war (*hominum ineptorum ad bellum*), including children, the elderly, and women who might even be part of the enemy city, for though it is permissible to capture or rob them, they must not be killed unless by chance and by accident (*nisi forte casu et per accidens occidantur*). Bellarmine's comments suggest a total prohibition on inflicting death on those not in the city. They must not be killed, perhaps, even if by chance or accident.

He then discusses killing "unintentionally," as when a soldier shoots into a battalion and kills a woman or child or even a priest; here he does not sin (*miles jaculatur in cuneum hostium* [enemy company/battalion] *et forte occidit puerum, aut mulierem, aut etiam sacerdotem, non peccat*). But, if he can avoid killing them and yet kills them intentionally, he does sin (*sed tunc peccat, cum ex intentione occidit, et potest, si velit, non occidere*). In support of these claims, Bellarmine appeals to both reason (*ratio naturalis hoc docet*) and the word of God. Bellarmine's nuanced discussion about innocence and guilt suggests the importance of these considerations as they apply to the use of force in a manner compatible with Christian precepts.

War, though itself a symptom of the disruption caused by human sinfulness, nonetheless can remain an instrument of peace (*est medium quoddam ad pacem*, in Bellarmine's words), so long as it abides by principles derivative of the fundamental unity of humankind. Acknowledging the reality of a community larger than the political community presided over by a prince (what we typically call a "state" or "nation-state") does not presuppose a "universalist," "imperial," or "cosmopolitan" ethic, as is often criticized in our day. Instead, the acknowledgment provides the coherence necessary to think of a morality binding even the practice of war. States draw on an order beyond themselves that their own sovereignty presupposes and requires. Sovereign regarding *what*? Regarding the existence of other states vying for and expressing their own sovereignty in a coherent, if conflictual, order of states marked out by an implicit and explicit international law. The German lawyer Heinrich A. Rommen expresses it this way: "To be a responsible member of the international community presupposes independence and self-sufficiency in the internal order. The duty of the state in international cooperation for the realization of the international common good is the complement of its undisturbed right of existence as an independent, sovereign national order."[34] Sovereignty of individual political communities presupposes the order of which they are a part, just as the sovereignty of the individual presupposes the community of which she is a part. Sovereignty always raises a "with regard to what or to whom?" question, solved in the case of war by reference to the wider community that becomes the context within which peace is pursued.

War, therefore, can never be justified merely by reference to state goods. Were that possible, discovering a law binding all states as parties to war would be difficult, if not impossible. War as an instrument of peace requires an order of "coexistence and cooperation . . . which realizes the common good of the community of nations," in the apt words of Rommen.[35] "Any commonwealth is part of the world as a whole," wrote Vitoria; hence, "I should regard any war which is useful to one commonwealth or kingdom but of proven harm to the world . . . as, by that very token, unjust."[36] The prince ascending to that odd, temporal condition of a judge of two communities can only do so because the measure of his justice already exceeds his own community. He judges his community by a measure that judges his neighbors and, of course, judges him as well. He stands there not as accuser but as himself potentially accused for his defense of his people and his treatment of all those innocents harmed by their defense. To be an instrument of peace, war must be disciplined by its service to a good inclusive of all, victim and aggressor. When war escapes the disciplining logic of politics and punishment, it threatens to consume anything and anyone perceived as an enemy.

The characterization of war as punishment chafes against intelligible contemporary concerns about the comprehensiveness of modern wars and about punishment itself. The contemporary era rightly worries that war—at least state-versus-state war—cannot be controlled and devastates competing states and their populations. All modern wars are Pyrrhic ones. Once begun, they seem to expand morally and geographically, consuming populations and neighboring states. In addition, a lost confidence in the exercise of contemporary punishment within states creates doubts about any exercise of punishment outside of domestic state contexts.[37] The exercise of punishment in contemporary societies seems contaminated by racial and economic bias, damaged by arbitrariness, and poisoned by corruption. With confidence in domestic punishment diminished, there are little grounds for appealing to it as the international framework of war-waging.

Reflecting these concerns, international law codified in international humanitarian law (IHL) and in the articles of the United Nations has narrowed the justification to which individual states can appeal when considering forceful defense against armed attack.[38] That narrowing down to defense against ongoing aggression appears also in Catholic circles. In the Catholic case, at least, the pressure on the narrowing appears to stem mostly from judgments about proportionality, as opposed to juridical concerns about the capacity of governing authorities to judge cause or intention. For instance, Pope Pius XII's 1944 Christmas address seems to recognize the contemporary irrelevance of war—"The theory of war as an apt and proportionate means of solving international conflicts is now out of date"—a position that gets repeated by subsequent popes in their addresses on war.[39] In similar terms, popes since Pius XII have claimed the obsolescence of war, again usually by appealing to the totalizing characteristics of modern wars. The best summary of this view comes from Pope John XXIII in *Pacem in terris* (1963). Explicitly connecting the character of modern war to his judgment, he writes:

Men nowadays are becoming more and more convinced that any disputes which may arise between nations must be resolved by negotiation and agreement, and not by recourse to arms. We acknowledge that this conviction owes its origin chiefly to the terrifying destructive force of modern weapons. It arises from fear of the ghastly and catastrophic consequences of their use. Thus, in this age which boasts of its atomic power, it no longer makes sense to maintain that war is a fit instrument with which to repair the violation of justice.[40]

But the pope's claims about the inaptness of modern war are not based solely on proportion. The context in which, for instance, Pope Pius XII makes the claim follows up on a juridical point about "the formation of an organ for the maintenance of peace, an organ invested by common consent with supreme power."[41] Likewise, Pope John XXIII's claim about the growing conviction against recourse to arms leads into a series of paragraphs under the heading "relationship of men and of political communities with the world community." There Pope John describes the conditions necessary for the formation of a world political authority that can attend to the common good of the world community and thereby reduce if not eliminate recourse to arms. The international order presupposed by war begs for a political apparatus at its service. War is the bluntest of instruments; one reaches for it only in the absence of anything offering greater precision. War tears where it should cut; it leaves hideous and enduring scars where better instruments would not; it devastates what finer surgery would preserve. War's own endurance speaks not only to its utility but to the absence of something that could do its job better.

Claims about war made by popes and by bishops' councils, then, typically refer to the nature of modern war and to the political context making possible the state-versus-state wars of recent history. In other words, acknowledging implicitly and occasionally explicitly that the use of force is an instrument serving the ends of government, popes and others have judged that modern circumstances evacuate force's effectiveness in pursuit of those ends. The irony from the perspective of just war analysis is that the analysis serves to tether or subordinate force to those ends; consequently, many recent statements announce the irrelevance of just war analysis because that analysis suggests the disproportion of force. They claim the obsolescence of the very analysis upon which their own analysis depends. Yet such claims about proportionality of force to the ends it serves are always susceptible to prudential scrutiny. Many of the claims about the disproportionality of "modern" war since World War I have proven accurate, but many have not. None of these claims foresaw the emergence of asymmetrical warfare; none of them anticipated that aerial war—so indiscriminate in the mid-to-late twentieth century—would usher in aerial technologies of remarkable precision and discrimination.[42] Therefore, it is appropriate to connect the claims about modern war beyond questions of proportionality to political context.

WAR AND POLITICAL AUTHORITY

Modern Catholic judgments on war, therefore, typically accompany claims for more robust political authority at the global level. *Pacem in terris*, Pope John XXIII's 1963 encyclical, thus emphasized the need for a "general authority equipped with world-wide power and adequate means for achieving the universal common good."[43] A world political authority alone can respond to the good of the global human family. Its necessity is not occasioned only by the ongoing presence of war, but also by other challenges that human society faces at a global level. In *Caritas in veritate* (2009), Pope Benedict XVI repeated Pope John XXIII's call for a world political authority to respond to the financial and economic crises. "Such an authority would need to be regulated by law, to observe consistently the principles of subsidiarity and solidarity, to seek to establish the common good."[44] The language—echoed in the pastoral constitution of the Second Vatican Council, *Gaudium et spes* (1965)—frightens realists and nationalists in positing both a "universal common good" and an authority with the power to serve it. A world political authority sounds almost dystopian in its apparent opposition to state sovereignty and in the power one supposes it must possess.

Yet the idea beneath the Catholic claim usually operates implicitly in realist analyses and in much Christian theology. On the one hand, the notion of a universal common good derives from Christian theological claims about the unity of the family created by God, fallen by its own activity, and redeemed by Christ. Human fallenness finds expression in the discord and conflict characteristic of life in community. Sometimes that rises to the level of violence. But just as persons are capable of living in communities at the familial, tribal, and national levels, so can we speak of their membership in a global community based on their common creatureliness. The aspiration of a political community responsive to that community expresses nothing more than the reality of that global community. And, instead of being opposed to state sovereignty, as we saw above, the Catholic claim rests state sovereignty in the existence of a good beyond the state.[45] Each state—that is, each political community—has a discrete temporal common good. Though independent and genuinely self-sufficient in many respects, the fact of personhood always stretches beyond local constraints. There is therefore no settled political reality, a fact borne out in history by the constant transformation of political communities and the differing forms (tribes, cities, regional polities, empires, nation-states) that have existed to serve human goods. To think otherwise—for example, to think that the nation-state arrangement expresses some final political settlement—runs contrary to Christian claims about human flourishing in the world.

In addition, much Christian—including Catholic—theological analysis presupposes the existence of an objective order judging any existing political authority. That order binds all political authority and endeavors to subject it to the rule of Christ. Wittingly or unwittingly, all political authorities take their seats at Christ's foot. Whatever authority they exercise is exercised at his pleasure and for his purposes. Such sovereignty as they experience is always and in every way contingent upon the fullness of sovereignty of the King of Kings. Medievals understood this better than moderns, as politics prior to the nation-state system had a clearer sense of the limitations of sovereignty. The emergence of states and the claims associated with sovereign equality (*par in parem non habet imperium*—equals have no dominion over equals) emboldened political authority to view itself as utterly independent of other sources of authority.[46] Sovereign equality shreds the hierarchical conception at the basis of war as punishment. This not only unleashes a conception of unlimited sovereignty possessed by each state; it eviscerates the capacity of any state to stand in judgment of another. The behavior of a prince acting in the mode of judge for his own community and of the aggressing community, so prevalent in prior conceptions of war, recedes and is replaced by states as equals, making equally powerful claims having no possibility of adjudication beyond war. "On the basis of such reasoning," Rommen writes, "war is [merely] a technical means of national policy; devoid of morality . . ."[47]

Wars persist so long as that world political authority remains only aspirational. But the aspiration toward political authority is not hopeless because we have no world political authority. World political authority is nonexistent because of the resilience and power of human sinfulness. But there is no theological reason to think the nation-state a privileged form of political community. Indeed, there are good philosophical reasons for preferring smaller political communities, like cities on the Greek model. Serious questions remain unresolved about modern nation-states' capacity to attend to genuine human goods. The Catholic view requires no political form; it suggests instead the existence of multiple levels of human community, each necessitating adequate political expression. When Catholic teaching points to the need for a political response to the global common good, it does so cognizant of the theoretical and practical obstacles to the realization of that response. Pope Benedict wrote that "such an authority would need to be regulated by law, to observe consistently the principles of subsidiarity and solidarity, to seek to establish the common good."[48] Until the aspiration becomes reality, as Paul Ramsey observed, "it will remain among the duties of statesmanship (though, of course, not its only responsibility) sometimes to resort to war on behalf of a juster order and a relatively more secure peace."[49]

The foregoing points to the tenacity of certain convictions in Catholic thinking about war. First, that war presupposes a political act of judgment to which even the state is subordinate. War presupposes a judgment between guilt and innocence drawing on a conception of morality broader than the morality of any political community. From that basis alone could something like "humanitarian intervention" or even revolution ever be justified. We have seen how the practice of the art of judgment internally serves as the model for judgment at the international level, even to the point of the tradition positing the political authority temporarily assuming the role of judge over both the community it serves and the one it confronts. That would not be possible, absent the conviction that its judgment was drawing upon a measure of guilt and innocence to which *all parties* were subordinate, as well as a hierarchical conception of authority with Christ at its head and all political authority derivative thereof.

Second, the political act of judgment points backward to the cause (the thing judged by political authority) and political context that brought a particular conflict into being and that together with a forward-looking perspective of judgment, punishment, and repair or restoration sets the parameters of just political action. By this wide, longitudinal perspective, war remains a political act responsive to the conditions of peacemaking. Absent that longitudinal quality and, for example, focusing on the insularity of communal self-defense, war would cease to be peacemaking; in that case it would become susceptible to the critiques of Yoder and Hauer- was noted earlier. War as peacemaking always keeps in view "the grounds of possible reconciliation between victim and perpetrator, both of whom express the image of God."[50]

Third, war in the Catholic tradition therefore resists locating it in the context of self-defense, but keeps it in the triadic context of punishment, as seen in the Catechism. Though sections 2307–9 speak explicitly of the "right of lawful self-defense," the animating logic of the Catechism's discussion makes clear that it is speaking of the defense of the common good for which political authority has responsibility. The language of legitimate self-defense draws directly upon the sections (2264–66) that describe legitimate self-defense as a category of punishment. This tradition drew on and continues to draw on "a moral analogy between ordinary acts of judgment internal to government and a praxis of judgment that used the means of armed conflict to reach beyond the self-contained and self-complacent sphere of autonomous political society to deal with crimes committed by nations against each other."[51] The imagery upon which this Christian tradition draws is not of antagonistic struggle between two opposing forces, but of a third party that inserts itself between those parties in their service. Oliver O'Donovan expresses this well when he notes the Christian rejection of war as antagonistic praxis. In rejecting war so conceived, "[Christians] had a message to proclaim about the end of history: the episodic collapse and recovery of sociality was something God had done away with once and for all in the cross and exaltation of Christ. The unification of all rule in his rule, the subordination of all sovereignty under his sovereignty forbade them to think that sheer unmediated antagonism could . . . be admitted as a possibility."[52]

Fourth, and finally, Catholic teaching on war insists that war is a tragedy and an evil. The tradition contains no glorification of war and much lamenting of its ongoing necessity. War is a failure of governance and consequence of human sin: in a particular conflict, those in judgment have failed to find other means of peace. For a variety of reasons, the international community has failed to put into place the political conditions sufficient to pursue peace without lapsing into war. It has allowed the "episodic collapse and recovery" to persist, in part drawn to the mythology surrounding the glorification of war. But the Christian tradition has always insisted, as recent popes have sought to remind us, that in its devastation—no matter how small or large—war remains an evil. The tradition has followed Augustine's moving words about even a just war:

> For it is the wrongdoing of the opposing party which compels the wise man to wage just wars; and this wrongdoing, even though it gave rise to no war, would still be matter of grief to man because it is man's wrongdoing. Let every one, then, who thinks with pain on all these great evils, so horrible, so ruthless, acknowledge that this is misery and if any one either endures or thinks of them without mental pain, this is a more miserable plight still, for he thinks himself happy because he has lost human feeling.[53]

Pope Francis added his voice to the chorus of popes concerned about the devastation associated especially with modern war. In *Laudato si'* (2015), he connected the encyclical's environmental emphasis to the damages of war. "War always does grave harm to the environment and to the cultural riches of peoples, risks which are magnified when one considers nuclear arms and biological weapons."[54] Even just wars bring evil, the tradition tells us. Augustine wrote of the horrifying moral and material evils associated with war; the tradition followed him in this regard. War might be a necessity as a consequence of human sin and discord; it should never be desired for its own sake, but resorted to only for its instrumental character in pursuit of peace. "The will must want peace, only necessity should bring war," Augustine counseled Boniface, a Roman commander Augustine clearly found wanting in his incapacity to lead while prioritizing his lusts over his command.[55]

From the Catholic perspective, war is a problem of law. The law of the decalogue, the context within which the Catechism discusses war, remains the appropriate context within which to discuss the moral demands on those fashioning themselves peacemakers. All those who seek to serve the peace Christ inaugurated must order all their acts toward peace. The tradition has seen Augustine, Thomas Aquinas, Vitoria, Bellarmine, and many others claim that the aim of war is peace; "it is unlawful to undertake war for any other end."[56] Peace and war are not always opposed; Augustine warned of the false peace posturing as an absence of war, a warning repeated consistently by popes, theologians, and bishops' conferences to this day.

Sometimes, of course, war is chosen to disrupt peace; and sometimes wars become obstacles to peace by their inability to abide by the laws designed to keep them directed toward peace. Nonetheless, in a world disrupted by sin, war—or more accurately, the use of lethal force—retains its instrumentality as the extension of the political act of judgment into the realm of relations among nations. War can be an act of peacemaking, as the tradition we have reviewed continues to assert, and peacemaking is an activity to which all Christians are called. *That reality* can never be set aside.

NOTES

1. All references to the Catechism of the Catholic Church will henceforth refer to it as "CCC" followed by the section number; here, for instance, CCC, no. 2307. The CCC is available via the Vatican website, http://www.vatican.va/archive/ENG0015/_INDEX.HTM.

2. See, for example, John Howard Yoder, *The Politics of Jesus*, 2nd ed. (Grand Rapids, MI: Eerdmans, 1994).

3. John Howard Yoder, "Peace without Eschatology," in *The Royal Priesthood*, ed. Michael G. Cartwright (Grand Rapids, MI: Eerdmans, 1994), 158. The essay originally appeared as a pamphlet in 1961.

4. Reinhold Niebuhr, "Why the Christian Church Is not Pacifist," in *The Essential Reinhold Niebuhr: Selected Essays and Addresses*, ed. Robert McAfee Brown (New Haven: Yale University Press, 1986), 102–19. The essay was first published as a pamphlet in 1940.

5. See also Yoder's *The Priestly Kingdom: Social Ethics as Gospel* (Notre Dame, IN: University of Notre Dame Press, 1985) and *When War Is Unjust: Being Honest in Just War Thinking*, 2nd ed. (Eugene, OR: Wipf & Stock, 1996).

6. See, among others, Stanley Hauerwas, *The Peaceable Kingdom: A Primer* (Notre Dame, IN: University of Notre Dame Press, 1983); Hauerwas, *War and the American Difference: Theological Reflections on Violence and National Identity* (Grand Rapids, MI: Baker Academic, 2011).

7. Drew Christiansen, "The Ethics of Peacemaking: The Genesis of *Called Together to Be Peacemakers*," *Journal of Ecumenical Studies* 45, no. 3 (January 2010): 402.

8. See, for example, John Howard Yoder, "Christ, the Hope of the World," in *The Original Revolution: Essays in Christian Pacifism* (Scottdale, PA: Herald Press, 1971), 148–82, repr. in Michael G. Cartwright, ed., *The Royal Priesthood* (Grand Rapids, MI: Eerdmans, 1994), 192–218.

9. Phillip Wynn, *Augustine on War and Military Service* (Minneapolis: Fortress, 2013), 70, 35. See also J. Daryl Charles, "Pacifists, Patriots, or Both? Second Thoughts on Pre-Constantinian Early-Christian Attitudes toward Soldering and War," *Logos: A Journal of Catholic Thought and Culture* 13, no. 2 (Spring 2010): 17–55.

10. See *The Challenge of Peace: God's Promise and Our Response* (Washington, DC: National Conference of Catholic Bishops, 1983), https://www.usccb.org/upload/challenge-peace-gods-promise-our-response-1983.pdf, no. 74, which refers to "complementary" ways of defending the common good.

11. Lisa Sowle Cahill, *Love Your Enemies: Discipleship, Pacifism, and Just War Theory* (Minneapolis: Augsburg, 1994), 13.

12. So, for example, Lisa Sowle Cahill, *Blessed Are the Peacemakers: Pacifism, Just War, and Peacebuilding* (Minneapolis: Fortress, 2019), 72. But see Louis J. Swift, *The Early Fathers on War and Military Service* (Wilmington, DE: Michael Glazier, 1983), who writes against the idea of apostasy. The move from the early period to post-Constantine, he states, "represents a major shift rather than a reversal in Christian thinking, a shift that was made possible by earlier ambiguities and disagreements concerning the use of coercion and made necessary by the altered political circumstances in which Christians now found themselves" (29).

13. *Challenge of Peace*; see also *The Harvest of Justice Is Sown in Peace* (Washington, DC: National Conference of Catholic Bishops, 1994), which amplifies the role of "peacemaking."

14. Yoder, *When War Is Unjust*, esp. chap. 5.

15. Theodore R. Weber, *Politics in the Order of Salvation: Transforming Wesleyan Political Ethics* (Nashville: Abingdon, 2001), 376.

16. Appeals to "tradition" are always tricky and can be done as ways of closing conversation. I will use this term as a shorthand only, to refer to a view of war that can be constructed especially at its apogee, in the sixteenth and seventeenth centuries, and that itself gets diminished by alternative views of war ascending with the rise of nation-states. Nonetheless, this view persists, as I shall show, in Catholic teaching to this day, even if it contends with the influence of other views internal and external to Catholic teaching.

17. See also Pope John Paul II, *Evangelium vitae* (1995), no. 57 (available via the Vatican website, http://w2.vatican.va/content/john-paul-ii/en/encyclicals/documents/hf_jp-ii_enc_25031995_evangelium-vitae.html): "Therefore, by the authority which Christ conferred upon Peter and his Successors, and in

communion with the Bishops of the Catholic Church, I confirm that *the direct and voluntary killing of an innocent human being is always gravely immoral.* This doctrine, based upon that unwritten law which man, in the light of reason, finds in his own heart (cf. Rom 2:14–15), is reaffirmed by Sacred Scripture, transmitted by the Tradition of the Church and taught by the ordinary and universal Magisterium" (emphasis added). Pope John Paul II arguably invokes the language of papal infallibility.

18. John Paul II, *Evangelium vitae*, no. 40.

19. See Hauerwas, *Peaceable Kingdom*, 94, 87.

20. Compare here Alexander of Hales, *Summa Theologica* III, n. 466 ("Whether war can be licit"). For a good translation and helpful commentary, see Gregory M. Reichberg, Henrik Syse, and Endre Begby, eds., *The Ethics of War: Classic and Contemporary Readings* (Oxford: Blackwell, 2006), 156–59.

21. *Gaudium et spes* (1965), Pastoral Constitution of the Second Vatican Council, no. 79, available via the Vatican website, http://www.vatican.va/archive /hist_councils/ii_vatican_council/documents/vat-ii_const_19651207_gaudium -et-spes_en.html.

22. Bellarmine's works are available in Latin online. For the sections of *Controversiae* used here, see http://cdigital.dgb.uanl.mx/la/1080015572_C /1080015574_T3/1080015574_03.pdf. See Robert Bellarmine, *On Temporal and Spiritual Authority*, ed. and trans. Stefania Tutino (Indianapolis: Liberty Fund, 2012).

23. Gregory M. Reichberg, "The Moral Typology of Peace and War," *Review of Metaphysics* 64, no. 3 (March 2011): 472.

24. Bellarmine, *On Temporal and Spiritual Authority*, 67.

25. Ibid.

26. Ibid., 68.

27. Ibid.

28. Ibid., 69.

29. Ibid., 70–71.

30. Bellarmine's phrase is *etiam quodammodo judex eorum*: the prince acts "somehow" as their judge.

31. Francisco de Vitoria, *On the Law of War*, generally, but see especially 3.9.60, in *Vitoria: Political Writings*, ed. Anthony Pagden and Jeremy Lawrance, Cambridge Texts in the History of Political Thought (Cambridge: Cambridge University Press, 1991), 327.

32. Bellarmine, *On Temporal and Spiritual Authority*, 72–73.

33. Ibid., 73. Bellarmine here quotes the tradition; Tutino, the editor, writes that Bellarmine is quoting "from the first book of Gregory IX's *Decretales*, title 34, chap. 2, and it was issued by Alexander III in 1179."

34. Heinrich A. Rommen, *The State in Catholic Thought: A Treatise on Political Philosophy* (New York: Cluny Media, 2016), 617. The volume was originally published in German in 1935.

35. Ibid., 616.

36. Francisco de Vitoria, *On Civil Power*, q. 1, art. 10, in Pagden and Lawrance, *Vitoria: Political Writings*, 21, quoted in Joseph E. Capizzi, *Politics, Justice, and War: Christian Governance and the Ethics of Warfare* (Oxford: Oxford University Press, 2015), 65.

37. On the other hand, there is a surprising and sometimes uncritical confidence in regional or global institutions of punishment, like the United Nations or the International Criminal Court.

38. See Charter of the United Nations (United Nations), chap. 7, arts. 39–51, https://www.un.org/en/sections/un-charter/chapter-vii/index.html.

39. Pope Pius XII, *Christmas Message 1944* (New York: Paulist Press, 1945), no. 63.

40. Pope John XXIII, *Pacem in terris* (1963), nos. 126–27, available via the Vatican website, http://w2.vatican.va/content/john-xxiii/en/encyclicals/documents/hf_j-xxiii_enc_11041963_pacem.html.

41. Pius XII, *Christmas Message 1944*, no. 62.

42. This is not meant to deny other significant moral considerations raised by either asymmetrical war or modern technologies like unmanned aerial vehicles (UAVs).

43. Pope John XXIII, *Pacem in terris*, no. 138.

44. Pope Benedict XVI, *Caritas in veritate* (2009), no. 68, available via the Vatican website, http://w2.vatican.va/content/benedict-xvi/en/encyclicals/documents/hf_ben-xvi_enc_20090629_caritas-in-veritate.html.

45. Much more could be said about "sovereignty." Hereon see Capizzi, *Politics, Justice, and War*, 45–47; Oliver O'Donovan, *The Ways of Judgment* (Grand Rapids, MI: Eerdmans, 2005), 3–12, 186–210.

46. See David Luban, "War as Punishment," *Philosophy and Public Affairs* 39, no. 4 (2012): 299–330; Hadassa A. Noorda, "The Principle of Sovereign Equality with Respect to Wars with Non-State Actors," *Philosophia* 41 (2013): 337–47.

47. Rommen, *State in Catholic Thought*, 619.

48. Benedict XVI, *Caritas in veritate* (2009), no. 67, available via the Vatican website, http://w2.vatican.va/content/benedict-xvi/en/encyclicals/documents/hf_ben-xvi_enc_20090629_caritas-in-veritate.html.

49. Paul Ramsey, "The Vatican Council on Modern War," in *The Just War: Force and Political Responsibility* (Lanham, MD: Rowman and Littlefield, 1968; repr., 2002), 381.

50. Capizzi, *Politics, Justice, and War*, 122.

51. Oliver O'Donovan, *The Just War Revisited*, Current Issues in Theology (Cambridge: Cambridge University Press, 2003), 18.

52. Ibid., 5.

53. Augustine, *The City of God*, trans. Marcus Dods (New York: Modern Library, 1950), 683.

54. Pope Francis, *Laudato si'* (2015), no. 57, available via the Vatican website, http://w2.vatican.va/content/francesco/en/encyclicals/documents/papa -francesco_20150524_enciclica-laudato-si.html.

55. Augustine, *Letter 189*, para. 6 (*Pacem habere debet voluntas, bellum necessitas*). This letter is quoted by many, including Bellarmine, *On Temporal and Spiritual Authority*, 71.

56. Bellarmine, *On Temporal and Spiritual Authority*, 70.

WORKS CITED

Alexander of Hales. *Summa Theologica*. In Reichberg, Syse, and Begby, *Ethics of War*, 156–59. Oxford: Blackwell, 2006.

Augustine. *The City of God*. translated by Marcus Dods. New York: Modern Library, 1950.

Bellarmine, Robert. *On Temporal and Spiritual Authority*. Edited and translated by Stefania Tutino. Indianapolis: Liberty Fund, 2012.

Benedict XVI. *Caritas in veritate* (2009). Available via the Vatican website, http://w2.vatican.va/content/benedict-xvi/en/encyclicals/documents/hf _ben-xvi_enc_20090629_caritas-in-veritate.html.

Cahill, Lisa Sowle. *Blessed Are the Peacemakers: Pacifism, Just War, and Peacebuilding*. Minneapolis: Fortress, 2019.

———. *Love Your Enemies: Discipleship, Pacifism, and Just War Theory*. Minneapolis: Augsburg, 1994.

Capizzi, Joseph E. *Politics, Justice, and War: Christian Governance and the Ethics of Warfare*. Oxford: Oxford University Press, 2015.

Catechism of the Catholic Church. Available via the Vatican website, http:// www.vatican.va/archive/ENG0015/_INDEX.HTM" http://www.vatican .va/archive/ENG0015/_INDEX.HTM.

The Challenge of Peace: God's Promise and Our Response. Washington, DC: National Conference of Catholic Bishops, 1983. https://www.usccb.org/upload /challenge-peace-gods-promise-our-response-1983.pdf.

Charles, J. Daryl. "Pacifists, Patriots, or Both? Second Thoughts on Pre-Constantinian Early-Christian Attitudes toward Soldering and War." *Logos: A Journal of Catholic Thought and Culture* 13, no. 2 (Spring 2010): 17–55.

Charter of the United Nations. The United Nations. https://www.un.org/en
    /about-us/un-charter/full-text.

Christiansen, Drew. "The Ethics of Peacemaking: The Genesis of *Called Together
    to Be Peacemakers.*" *Journal of Ecumenical Studies* 45, no. 3 (January 2010):
    385–416.

Francis. *Laudato si'* (2015). Available via the Vatican website, http://w2.vatican.
    va/content/francesco/en/encyclicals/documents/papa-francesco_20150524
    _enciclica-laudato-si.html.

Gaudium et spes (1965). Pastoral Constitution of the Second Vatican Council.
    Available via the Vatican website, http://www.vatican.va/archive/hist
    _councils/ii_vatican_council/documents/vat-ii_const_19651207_gaudium
    -et-spes_en.html.

The Harvest of Justice Is Sown in Peace. Washington, DC: National Conference of
    Catholic Bishops, 1994. https://www.usccb.org/resources/harvest-justice
    -sown-peace.

Hauerwas, Stanley. *The Peaceable Kingdom: A Primer.* Notre Dame, IN: Univer-
    sity of Notre Dame Press, 1983.

———. *War and the American Difference: Theological Reflections on Violence and
    National Identity.* Grand Rapids, MI: Baker Academic, 2011.

John XXIII. *Pacem in terris* (1963). Available via the Vatican website, http://w2
    .vatican.va/content/john-xxiii/en/encyclicals/documents/hf_j-xxiii_enc
    _11041963_pacem.html.

John Paul II. *Evangelium vitae* (1995). Available via the Vatican website, http://
    w2.vatican.va/content/john-paul-ii/en/encyclicals/documents/hf_jp-ii
    _enc_25031995_evangelium-vitae.html.

Luban, David. "War as Punishment." *Philosophy and Public Affairs* 39, no. 4
    (2012): 299–330.

Niebuhr, Reinhold. "Why the Christian Church Is Not Pacifist." In *The Essential
    Reinhold Niebuhr: Selected Essays and Addresses*, edited by Robert McAfee
    Brown, 102–19. New Haven: Yale University Press, 1986. First published
    1940.

Noorda, Hadassa A. "The Principle of Sovereign Equality with Respect to Wars
    with Non-State Actors." *Philosophia* 41 (2013): 337–47.

O'Donovan, Oliver. *The Just War Revisited.* Current Issues in Theology. Cam-
    bridge: Cambridge University Press, 2003.

———. *The Ways of Judgment.* Grand Rapids, MI: Eerdmans, 2005.

Pius XII. *Christmas Message 1944.* New York: Paulist Press, 1945.

Ramsey, Paul. "The Vatican Council on Modern War." In *The Just War: Force and
    Political Responsibility*, 369–90. Lanham, MD: Rowman and Littlefield,
    1968. Reprinted 2002.

Reichberg, Gregory M. "The Moral Typology of Peace and War." *Review of Metaphysics* 64, no. 3 (March 2011): 467–87.

Reichberg, Gregory M., Henrik Syse, and Endre Begby, eds. *The Ethics of War: Classic and Contemporary Readings*. Oxford: Blackwell, 2006.

Rommen, Heinrich A. *The State in Catholic Thought: A Treatise on Political Philosophy*. New York: Cluny Media, 2016.

Swift, Louis J. *The Early Fathers on War and Military Service*. Wilmington, DE: Michael Glazier, 1983.

Vitoria, Francisco de. *On Civil Power*. In *Vitoria: Political Writings*, edited by Anthony Pagden and Jeremy Lawrance, 1–44. Cambridge Texts in the History of Political Thought. Cambridge: Cambridge University Press, 1991.

———. *On the Law of War*. In *Vitoria: Political Writings*, edited by Anthony Pagden and Jeremy Lawrance, 295–98. Cambridge Texts in the History of Political Thought. Cambridge: Cambridge University Press, 1991.

Weber, Theodore R. *Politics in the Order of Salvation: Transforming Wesleyan Political Ethics*. Nashville: Abingdon, 2001.

Wynn, Phillip. *Augustine on War and Military Service*. Minneapolis: Fortress, 2013.

Yoder, John Howard. "Christ, the Hope of the World." In *The Original Revolution: Essays in Christian Pacifism*, 148–82. Scottdale, PA: Herald Press, 1971. Reprinted in *The Royal Priesthood*, edited by Michael G. Cartwright, 192–218. Grand Rapids, MI: Eerdmans, 1994.

———. "Peace without Eschatology." In *The Royal Priesthood*, edited by Michael G. Cartwright, 143–67. Grand Rapids, MI: Eerdmans, 1994. First published 1961.

———. *The Politics of Jesus*. 2nd ed. Grand Rapids, MI: Eerdmans, 1994.

———. *The Priestly Kingdom: Social Ethics as Gospel*. Notre Dame, IN: University of Notre Dame Press, 1985.

———. *When War Is Unjust: Being Honest in Just War Thinking*. 2nd ed. Eugene, OR: Wipf & Stock, 1996.

THREE

The Orthodox Church on Just War

Darrell Cole

THE ORTHODOX CHURCH

The Orthodox Church comprises all Christians in communion with the Ecumenical Patriarch of Constantinople and in communion with one another who accept the faith stated in the seven ecumenical councils. The Orthodox Church, with its religious and cultural center in the Byzantine Empire (which began with the transfer of the capital of the Roman Empire to Constantinople in 324 and lasted until the fall of the city in 1453), separated from the Western Church under the bishop of Rome in 1054. There are fifteen autocephalous (self-governing) churches within the Orthodox faith along with diaspora churches throughout the world, such as the Orthodox Church in America,[1] that are autonomous but not self-governing. They come under the jurisdiction of one of the autocephalous churches. Churches that are Orthodox (literally, "right worship" or "right belief") are in full agreement about Christian teaching that was "once delivered to the saints" (Jude 3) and claim to have maintained unbroken continuity with the church founded by Jesus. Moreover, according to that claim they continue to offer to the world the right way to faithfully worship

59

God and to provide access to a life of grace. Indeed, the Orthodox describe their distinctive character as a church in terms of its changeless nature and its sense of maintaining continuity with the traditions handed down by the apostles and the early fathers.[2]

This chapter outlines the just war tradition as it is found within the Orthodox church, beginning with the early fathers who dealt with the moral problems of the relationship between church and state and what this means for the just use of force. In these sources we find clearly formulated principles of a just use of force: right authority, just cause in self-or-other-defense, intention to establish or protect peace and good order, and a commitment to fight with moderation. I then turn to the written lives of the Orthodox saints, Orthodox liturgies, and devotional texts, for they reinforce and build upon the moral principles found in the early fathers and offer some distinctions from Western Christian, particularly Protestant, approaches to statecraft. This is followed by a discussion of the development of Russian thinking on the Orthodox idea of just war in the twentieth century, given its influence on the Orthodox Church (for example, in Eastern Europe). The chapter concludes with some observations about how notable contemporary Orthodox ethicists in the West ground the just war tradition in natural law thinking, even when they differ on whether or not the moral character of the just war should be portrayed as a lesser evil or as a lesser good.

THE PATRISTIC FOUNDATION OF CHURCH, STATE, AND WAR

We cannot overestimate the weight given to the early fathers in shaping for the church what counts as "right belief." The fundamental theological principles of Orthodoxy are worked out in the early, undivided church.[3] Scripture is, of course, the basic fundamental source of theology, but Orthodoxy has always held that biblical exegesis belongs to the church, particularly to the fathers. This early tradition is the "gateway to the theology of revelation" and represents how the Holy Spirit is "experienced within the Church of Christ as the charism of truth."[4] None of this is to agree with Paul Valliere's complaint that most pre-nineteenth-century Orthodox theology is merely a set of "footnotes" to the patristic tradition,[5] but it is to say that any answer to questions about what Orthodoxy teaches must focus first upon what the fathers taught. Indeed, the theological politics that reaches full flower in the Byzantine Empire and is still normative for the Orthodox today is built upon patristic moral theology. The moral theory evident in the early fathers gives shape to the basic Byzantine beliefs about the relationship between church and state and, thus, set the context for how the Orthodox think about the just use of force. As contemporary Orthodox scholar Alexander Webster puts it, all the strands of the patristic age were woven together in the Byzantine Empire, wherein everyone was encouraged to realize the ideal of a "virtuous community and voluntary philanthropy."[6] The just use of force is part of this ideal.

The Byzantine harmony of church and state is built upon the idea that there are two ways of living in the church: a purely spiritual way concerned only with heavenly matters and a secular way that takes direct responsibility for secular matters. The spiritual elite leave behind all earthly jobs, including those of civil authority. They may provide spiritual help to the state—which suggests continuity with the apostolic teaching of Peter and Paul (1 Pet. 2:13–17; Rom. 13:1–7) that the state itself is not conceived of as an inherently evil institution—but they may never take up the duties of political or military office. We note here the importance of the monastic tradition in shaping Orthodox theology. Paul Robinson is right to suggest that the relative absence of systematic thinking on war in the Orthodox Church can be explained, at least in part, by the mystical nature of Orthodox theology, which can lead to a neglect of physical world problems.[7] For the Orthodox, there should always be a healthy tension between the spiritual ideal as lived out in a monastic community and the earthly practical concern for our neighbors who live in the world. The tension reminds the faithful of the ideal that can be lost if we become too focused on earthly matters. However, the ascetic and mystical characteristic of Orthodox theology does not prevent the church from carrying out its "national services."[8] The tension nevertheless did tend to prove a hindrance in constructing a just war tradition as fully articulated as what we find in the West. Moral principles concerning the use of force are to be found in Orthodoxy, but the impetus was never there to formulate formal categories such as *jus ad bellum* and *jus in bello*. There is no systematic presentation of the principles of just war in Orthodoxy. Nevertheless, we begin to see in Clement of Alexandria, and in later key sources, moral concerns and responses so similar to what was later formulated more explicitly and fully in the West that we do not go wrong in positing a basic harmony between Eastern and Western fathers on the tradition of just war.

Clement of Alexandria

Clement of Alexandria (ca. 150–215) is the first important figure to shape Orthodox thinking on the use of force. Clement's formative contribution to the morality of war must be understood within his larger moral scheme of the Christian moral life as a two-level system, with ordinary Christians having secular vocations and occupying the lower level and with extraordinary Christians—Gnostics—having spiritual vocations and occupying the upper level.[9] Throughout his major work, *The Instructor*, Clement makes it clear that Christians with an earthly vocation are certainly true Christians even if they lack the time to devote themselves to the spiritual disciplines that are thought necessary to advance far in the Christian life.

Clement argues that wherever Christians may find themselves in their spiritual development, they are to value peace. Christ will bring perfect peace at the end of the present age, but here and now, peace is a good that the church should nurture as much as possible. The peace of a well-ordered society is primary for Clement and underpins the very purpose of a just use of force. Christians should be trained and made into an army of peace.[10] Nevertheless, we learn through the mouth of John the Baptist that Jesus does not command soldiers to give up their job but to soldier justly as a vocation of peace.[11] In fact, Clement teaches that Christians may be able to develop a fuller understanding of God as revealed in Scripture as soldiers:

> For man has been otherwise constituted by nature, so as to have fellowship with God. We . . . set each animal to that for which it is by nature fitted; so, placing our finger on what is man's peculiar and distinguishing characteristic above other creatures, we invite him . . . as a heavenly plant to the knowledge of God, counseling him to furnish himself with what is sufficient provision for eternity, namely piety. Practice husbandry . . . if you are a husbandman but know God. . . . Sail the sea you who are devoted to navigation, yet call on the winds of the heavenly Pilot. Has knowledge taken hold of you while engaged in military service? Listen to the commander who orders what is right.[12]

The key to moral progress for the soldier is to obey just commands, which bring about an ordered peace. Clement leans upon the natural moral law as a guide for earthly pursuits, but justice as part of the natural law is, under the guidance of the church, to seek a peace in which the spiritual good may be sought by all. The moral limitations of the use of force are built into the very theological justification of force, which is a peace-seeking justice. To seek such peace and order by fighting is a moral good even if it is not the moral best. Clement's idea of earthly vocations as lesser (if real) goods is the lens through which Orthodox approaches to the use of force must be understood.

Origen

Soldiering is an earthly vocation fulfilled within the structure of the state. The state is worth supporting for the sake of an ordered peace. The monastic character of Orthodoxy did not lead to wholesale rejection of the state as a real good. Even that otherwise champion of pacifism (at least in the sense that Christians should never use force), Origen (ca. 185–254), taught that the state serves a necessary function for an ordered and peaceful life. Origen is often considered the greatest pre-Constantinian theologian, vastly influential and revered by the Orthodox Church despite his heretical idea about the eventual salvation of all creatures. In his *Contra Celsum*, Origen attempts to defend Christianity against spiritual, moral, social, and political crimes. Origen follows Clement in holding that there are two ways of Christian living: an earthly way with earthly occupations and a more excellent way for superior attainments in wisdom and truth.[13] But Origen does not completely dismiss concern for secular life. For our present purposes, a key passage in his writing needs identifying in which Origen answers the charge that Christians are not patriotic. The charge does not rest with mere pacifism but with the refusal to participate in any way in public and civil life.[14] Origen's first reply is that if everyone were Christian, then everyone would be truly just and there would be no need for war, since Christians know what true justice looks like and would keep the peace. But he then makes an extraordinary move by arguing that Christians should be given the same civil status as pagan priests—namely, the status of those who are required to offer not physical service to the military but instead prayers on behalf of the emperor and soldiers. This, he insists, is so that the emperor and soldiers may be successful in battle. Christians "should be fighting as priests and worshippers of God, keeping their right hands pure and by their prayers to God striving for those who fight in a righteous cause and for the emperor who reigns righteously, in order that everything which is opposed to and hostile to those who act rightly may be destroyed."[15] The just cause is the peace and good order that makes any kind of civil and spiritual life possible. Thus, Origen argues for the moral goodness of a right use of force even while forbidding Christian physical participation in that goodness. The earthly state is a good, and for this reason Christians ought to be patriotic. But they should show that patriotism by praying for the success of the military operations that keep everyone safe. Thus, Origen's pacifism is not of a strict nature; that is to say, he does not hold that the use of force is inherently evil. God himself uses force, and Origen, although a master at allegorizing Scripture, is never tempted to allegorize away divine use of force in Scripture in a way that would deny the historical facts. The use of force is simply forbidden to Christians.

Eusebius of Caesarea

Origen could not conceive of Christian physical participation in war any more than he could conceive of Christian participation in any secular field. However, one important admirer of Origen had no qualms about Christian physical participation in just wars, and that was Eusebius of Caesarea (ca. 266–339). Eusebius accepts Clement's two-level moral system of Christianity and argues that each level has its own kind of moral hero and its own kind of moral progression. In Eusebius's hands, Origen is the consummate Hellenistic holy man and the model for those who aspire to the upper level of spirituality. But—and this would have significant ramifications for how the Orthodox Church thought about the military—the emperor Constantine, a political leader and a warrior, is the consummate Christian soldier and a model for the lower level of Christianity.

Eusebius argued that the Old Testament prophecies concerning universal peace and harmony are partially fulfilled in the Christianization of the empire.[16] Church and state are now wedded together, a "symphony" of the earthly and the spiritual that is the foundational model for what political order should look like. Christians who fight for the state are actually fulfilling sacred history. Eusebius agreed with Origen's argument that the spiritual elite must limit their support for the emperor to a spiritual realm;

prayer and the spiritual help are found in the church. This prompts Eusebius to be the first church father to propose the office of chaplain. He ad-
vises that Christian bishops should be invited to provide Constantine's
army with the means of divine worship.[17] Orthodox churches have provided chaplains to the military on this very basis.

Eusebius went further. He was adamant that both the spiritual and
secular lifestyles be recognized within the church, arguing as follows:

> Two lifestyles have been established in the Christian Church. The first,
> which goes beyond nature and the usual manner of life, is not involved
> at all with [earthly matters]. Out of an extraordinary love for things
> heavenly it departs from the common and customary pattern and is
> devoted wholly to the worship of God. . . . The other is subordinate and
> more concerned with human affairs. . . . It lays down the practical rules
> for those fighting in a just war. . . . For such individuals there is a sec-
> ondary state of perfection which is suitable in its own way for their kind
> of life. Thus no one is excluded from sharing the Savior's coming.[18]

Ordinary Christians should and must fight for the emperor—that is, for
the establishment of a good political order. Christians do no evil by fighting for the empire, and, in fact, do moral good, achieving a secondary kind
of moral progression while remaining in the earthly job of soldiering.
Christians in the military progress morally by practicing the virtue of justice; it is the fighting of just wars—that is, wars for the peace and order of
the state—that enables the soldier to progress. Because just wars are
fought for the sake of peace and order, those political leaders who would
disrupt good order for selfish gain and establish tyranny—for example,
Maxentius and Maximin (and, later, Licinius)—should not be followed.[19]
Eusebius's position is reflected in canon 12 of the Council of Nicaea,
which condemns Christians who serve in the army of Licinius. Thus, we
find in Eusebius the establishment of two just war principles: right authority (the state) and just cause (protection of the state).

Byzantine Symphony and Natural Law

Eusebius's model of church and state, and how the military ought to be
viewed within that model, became normative for the Orthodox Church.
Orthodoxy has never recognized the rigid line of separation of church and

state that is so crucial to the development of Western politics (and theological politics) in the post-Reformation era. Ideally, church and state should function as a single organism. John Meyendorff is right to argue that the Orthodox ideal cannot be reduced to a crude sort of Caesaropapism in which the emperor tells the church what to believe and how to care for souls.[20] Nor, as Bishop Kallistos Ware points out, does the Orthodox ideal reduce the church to a department of state that has no say in the moral direction of the state.[21] The Orthodox ideal first formulated by Eusebius does mean that there should be two distinct elements in society—the priesthood and imperial power—that work independently yet in harmony together for the full human flourishing of all. This arrangement has often been characterized as a "symphony" of authority whereby political authorities cannot dictate doctrine and spiritual authorities cannot dictate political policy. Nevertheless, Orthodoxy recognizes that Christ has redeemed all of creation, including the political authorities. At its divinely appointed best, the state should be a "living image of God's government in heaven."[22]

The justice that the church demands of the political authorities is that which is found in the natural law and is part of the moral thinking of all human beings. Natural law thinking is God-thinking. Orthodoxy has always taught that the purpose of all human beings is to achieve God-likeness—what is called *theosis*. Despite the presence of indwelling sin, everyone has some knowledge of God and the good. This natural moral law is the basis of ethical standards and is specified most clearly in the Decalogue. The more we follow the natural moral law, the more we become what God intends us to be. It is true that the natural moral law does not lead to full *theosis*; however, as we see in Clement and Eusebius, Christian political leaders and soldiers who follow it do make some progress in *theosis*. To follow it is to exhibit the moral standards set by God in a way that makes human society possible even in a fallen world. The church has a duty to witness not only to the possibility of *theosis* for all people but to the necessity of following the natural moral law. As Eusebius makes clear, earthly vocations exist inside the church. And insofar as the church makes room for earthly vocations, it is attempting the realization of the symphony theory of church-state relations. The ideal should always be attempted for the common good. The church should want the state to realize that it can achieve justice only insofar as it follows the rules of morality as spelled out in the Decalogue. Earthly human existence is improved upon when we seek the rules of justice given to us in the natural moral law. The church, then, has a dual role because it possesses both a negative view of the state — the state is run by and for people who are indwelt by sin and deceived by their own selfish desires — as well as a positive theology of the state — as a sphere in which people can live in peace and security and wherein they are also free to seek the more important spiritual good of *theosis*. Thus, the church since the time of Eusebius has held that it should prompt the state "to establish just relations within society and among political communities."[23] The church witnesses to the fact that human beings cannot be what they are meant to be unless they follow justice. When the state uses force for the purpose of enacting justice, then it is following the natural law witnessed to by the church.

St. Basil the Great

Eusebius's way of thinking about a just use of force left a lasting influence on Orthodoxy and is supported even in the Cappadocian Father Basil the Great (ca. 329–79), who, while distinguishing between war and murder, would penalize Christian soldiers for inevitable immoderation in battle.[24] Basil is doing no more than recognizing the moral hazards of battle, particularly extended types of war in which the just end up doing unjust things. War can be corrupting to the most just of commanders and soldiers, and the longer the fighting lasts, the greater the chances of moral lapses (we need only think of Allied behavior in World War II for a cautionary note). As John Anthony McGuckin has argued, Basil is clearly indicating that "even for the best of motives" the shedding of blood requires penance. At the same time, just warriors are noble to the extent that they have maintained a proper spiritual attitude in conquering "the very chaos and wickedness they have been forced to be a part of all around them."[25] In fact, Basil agrees with Eusebius that Christians in the military can achieve a kind of perfection: "I have become acquainted with a man who demonstrates that it is possible even in the military profession to maintain perfect love for God and that a Christian ought to be characterized not by the clothes that he wears but by the disposition of his soul."[26]

The disposition of the soul — the very character of the person — is what is at stake. The virtues of love and justice can be formed even in members of the military. But this would mean that soldiers cannot fight unjust wars. Simply being brave in battle does not count. You must have justice on your side. What is more, soldiers must always use force with moderation. Although Basil does not specify what counts as moderation, the way is clearly paved for concerns about minimal use of force and discrimination.

St. John Chrysostom

The next church father to shape Orthodox thinking on the state and war is John Chrysostom (ca. 349–407), archbishop of Constantinople, who is held by the Orthodox as one of the Three Holy Hierarchs (along with Basil the Great and St. Gregory Nazianzus). Chrysostom taught that the governing authorities have their power from God for the benefit of everyone, even if they misuse that power.[27] The protection of the state is necessary because the state is the very structure provided by God to make the attainment of virtue possible by providing peace and order through punishment of the wicked and honoring of the good. The state provides "peace to thee and the blessings of civil institutions," in addition to other "countless blessings."[28] Chrysostom has no illusions about a possible pacifist earthly political order. To remove the state would be to remove those who bear arms to protect us and would lead to a condition of life whereby "all things would go to ruin and neither city nor country nor private nor public buildings nor anything else stand, but all the world will be turned upside down, while the more powerful devour the weaker."[29]

Nevertheless, Chrysostom teaches that we ought not to take up "unnecessary and unprofitable wars."[30] Here Chrysostom is making a clear distinction between necessary and unnecessary wars. Necessary wars are those fought for the protection of the commonwealth. Thus, Chrysostom adds his support for the moral principle of self-defense as a just cause for the use of force. Citizens can do their business only when the military does theirs by "keeping guard, beating off enemies."[31] Chrysostom then makes a connection between the virtues of love and justice. Because the military is necessary for peace and order, Chrysostom follows Paul in urging everyone to pay taxes in order to support the state and military. He argues that it is a duty of love for the sake of justice. The honor shown to the civil authorities by obedience and the paying of taxes for the sake of those who maintain peace and order is a form of love owed to all. Love, for Chrysostom, is the "beginning and end of virtue."[32] All law is fulfilled in love. All justice is fulfilled in love. Love is, hence, the motivating force behind Christian support of the state.[33]

St. Ambrose of Milan

Orthodoxy does not claim its theological patrimony to be merely "Eastern." The consensus of the early undivided church has always been held as the norm for the Orthodox everywhere. One important Western early Father, Ambrose of Milan (ca. 339–97), contributes to the Orthodox understanding of how the relationship between church and state is worked out with respect to the state's use of force. Ambrose, who served in a high government office before he became a bishop, holds that earthly government is a divine institution created to ensure peaceful and well-ordered life. Ambrose insists that imperial rule and the use of the military are under the church, which gives moral guidance concerning the use of force—not in the sense of suggesting tactics but in drawing clear boundaries about what can count as a just use of force. The emperor is not simply answerable to God for how he uses force; he is answerable to the church.[34] All citizens ought to give aid to the state so that it might maintain its function of providing peace and order.[35] This does not mean that everyone should use force. Ambrose follows his Eastern theological forebears in insisting that no private person and no clergyman should engage in acts of force.[36]

The use of force is a different matter for those who are responsible for the just ordering performed by the state. The emperor and those who serve him have a divine duty to preserve good order for the sake of everyone, especially the church. Working along the same theological lines as Chrysostom, Ambrose provides a link between the virtues of love and justice to show why the use of force can be praiseworthy in the hands of the military. When Ambrose discusses justice in *On Duties*, he argues that "in accordance with the will of God and the union of nature, we ought to be of mutual help one to the other, and to vie with each other in doing duties, to lay all our advantages as it were before all, and (to use the words of Scripture) to bring help one to the other from a feeling of devotion or of duty."[37] He follows this by saying that the glory of justice lies in its authority to "bring help to others" and "even undergoes dangers for others."[38]

Ambrose is responding to the concern voiced by Basil about moderation in soldiering. Similar to Chrysostom, Ambrose makes charity the very essence of justice, or, as one notable Ambrose scholar puts it, justice is "integrated with charity."[39] Charity makes justice more likely by working against the motives of self-interest. What this means for how the soldier should use force can be seen first in Ambrose's *Discourses on Luke*. Commenting therein upon John the Baptist putting moral limits on soldiers without telling them to give up their occupation, Ambrose urges soldiers to practice compassion in their earthly vocation: "For compassion is the fullness of the virtues, and, therefore, the form of the virtue is placed before all."[40] Then, in Ambrose's letter to the emperor Theodosius concerning a massacre by the military garrison at Thessalonica,[41] we get a clear example of how this works itself out in practical terms. The people of Thessalonica had rioted against a Roman garrison and killed its commander. As a reprisal, Theodosius slaughtered seven thousand citizens who were attending an exhibition in the Circus. Ambrose follows the path laid down by Eusebius and subjects the emperor to ecclesiastical control through ecclesiastical penalty. The reprisal was disproportionate and the innocent were targeted along with the guilty. Ambrose will not stand for such an unjust act; he holds up King David as an exemplar to the emperor and urges him to repent of his sin. Only in this way could Theodosius overcome his natural impetuosity (the very temptation of the soldier that worried Basil).

Ultimately, Theodosius gave in to Ambrose and did penance, and in so doing acknowledged his accountability to the church for the imposition of his unjust use of force. Thus, Eusebius, and then Ambrose, establish very firmly the principle that the state's use of force does not fall entirely outside the church's sphere of authority. This principle is maintained in Orthodox theological politics to our own day. Those who wish to remain within the church must use force responsibly, which means using a minimum amount of force in a way that does not recklessly endanger innocent lives. The goal of being a merciful user of force suggests that the notions of a minimum use of force and discrimination are built into the very theological foundation for how Christians should think about the just use of force.

Just wars for Ambrose are always either defensive in nature[42] or waged for the punishment of wrongdoing,[43] and as such fought with the controlling idea that the whole purpose of a just war is to reestablish peace when war is over.[44] In this context, King David is singled out as the paradigm of the just warrior. David never waged war unless driven to it and was "brave in battle, patient in adversity, peaceful in Jerusalem, merciful in victory."[45] Thus, we see that for any war to be considered just, it must be a last resort, defensive in nature—in defense of country or church—or a punishment of wrong, and it must be waged mercifully and in such a way that a well-ordered peace can be established.

LIVES OF ORTHODOX SAINTS, LITURGIES, AND DEVOTIONAL TEXTS

The normative themes on justice and war evident in the early fathers are reinforced in the popular medieval literature on the lives of the saints, in which we see in action the common virtues of wisdom, justice, courage, and self-control informed by the all-encompassing virtue of charity.[46] Christian soldier-saints in the pre-Constantinian Roman army often underwent martyrdom for their faith because of their refusal to engage in the required pagan ceremonies. The striking thing about these early written accounts is that the military profession itself was not seen as something at odds with faith in Christ. Soldiering per se was seen as a morally acceptable profession. Only the pagan practices were considered immoral. The post-Constantinian lives of soldier-saints, pictured in numerous icons as slaying their unjust enemies, present models of the just use of force. Their acts of force are always for the protection of the innocent, the defenseless, or the church. In Russian religious literature in particular, G. P. Fedotov has argued that the lives of the soldier-saints give us a model of "the idea of a just war," whereby those in political authority are to fight in defense of their rights and heritage and for the people of their land.[47] Alexander Nevsky is, as Alexander Webster has argued, "the ideal of the regal warrior saint."[48] Nevsky, who died in 1263, fought against the Teutonic Knights and the Lithuanians who invaded Russia. He also came to terms with the Mongol Genghis Khan when there was no hope of success to achieve peace through war,[49] thereby suggesting a just war principle not explicitly stated by a church father—namely, reasonable hope for success.

Orthodox liturgies and devotional texts as well reveal a clear support of the idea of just war. In the Divine Liturgy of St. Basil, for example, prayers are made for "this country and all civil authorities" in their just use of force.[50] In *The Great Book of Needs*, we find prayers for the defeat of enemies and success for the military.[51] There even exist in Orthodoxy liturgical rites for the blessing of weapons traced back to the Byzantine era.[52] The practice recently became notable again in the Russian Orthodox

Church with Vladimir Putin's return to power in 2012, as part of an effort by Putin and the church to get the church more visibly active in public life. We note that this particular church blessing of the weapons of Russia is controversial not because of the practice itself, but because the weapons are thought by many to be used for unjust purposes in the Ukraine and Crimea. No one in the Ukrainian Church protested the rite itself, which reflects the church's commitment to a just use of force.[53]

In this regard it also needs pointing out that the nature of autocephalous churches within Orthodoxy does not preclude disharmony among the faithful who are otherwise in communion together. There can be sharp disagreements among Orthodox churches that exist among nation-states in conflict (as, indeed, has too often been the case for Western churches as well). In Ukrainian Orthodox eyes, the Russian Orthodox Church is supporting an unjust use of force by the Russian military in Crimea and Ukraine. In Russian Orthodox eyes, the Russian military is protecting Russian people living in those areas. Neither side doubts the possibility of a just use of force. They disagree about the justice of this particular use of force.

We end this section by noting the absence of the holy-war idea in Orthodoxy. Eusebius and Ambrose certainly shared the idea that the state ought to come to the defense of the church, but there is no effort by the early fathers to spread Christianity by means of the sword. Nor do we find any notion of a holy war in the lives of the saints or in the liturgies and devotional texts. The acts of force employed by soldier-saints are characterized as holy acts when they defend their country and church, but these are always acts of defense, never of offense. Thus, Orthodoxy has always taught that the church ought to be protected by the state, and it is always a just use of force when the state does so, but such uses of force for the church are necessary only when the church is being attacked. There should be no offensive wars to spread the church.

TWENTIETH-CENTURY RUSSIAN DEVELOPMENT AND INFLUENCE

Russian thinkers (novelists, philosophers, clerics, theologians) led the way in contributing to the Orthodox approach to moral questions surrounding war in the twentieth century. This should come as no surprise since Russia was—and still is—a powerful nation-state in which Orthodoxy remains the dominant form of religion and wherein the problems of the just use of force are most evident and in need of theological reflection. Paul Robinson helpfully covers many of the sources of moral thought, pointing out the pervasive influence of Dostoevsky's theological idea—traced throughout *The Brothers Karamazov*—that all human beings are partly guilty for all evil.[54] When applied to war, Dostoevsky's line of reasoning leads to the conclusion that, even in a self-defensive just war, we are still partly responsible for having to fight such a war. This does not mean that there are no just wars or that we should never fight a just war. However, it does mean that Dostoevsky wants Christians to be aware that something has gone wrong to bring us to the circumstances that make it necessary for us to go to war and that those engaged in defensive war share as well in the guilt of the cause of the war, even if not to the same degree. This line of reasoning shares with Basil a concern for the inevitable evil that follows war-fighting, so that, as we fight a just war, we must be constantly aware of our own moral condition, which can lead to the kind of excessive violence that undermines the very moral foundation for the just use of force formulated by the early fathers. From the time of Dostoevsky, Russian Orthodoxy has tended to think of just war as a "lesser evil," and this tendency would be far-reaching in the Orthodox world. Thus, for example, we find Russian Metropolitan Antonin of Galicia and Kiev commenting on World War I that it was an "evil," albeit a "lesser evil" than being overrun by Germany.[55] Similarly, Serbian Orthodox bishop St. Nikolas Velimirovic writes in 1929 that war is always "a poison, which kills, but which at the same time cures and heals."[56]

A just war as an acceptable lesser evil is not as robust a defense of just war as we typically find in the Western expression of the just war tradition, but we must remember that it was Augustine, the veritable father of the Western tradition, who lamented that wars were ever necessary and that they were always an occasion for tears.[57] Yet the Orthodox, particularly in Basil and in its Russian strain, appear to be getting at something deeper than regret. Russian philosopher Ivan Il'in goes so far as to argue that even necessary wars are an "unsinful perpetration of injustice" and a "spiritual compromise."[58] Il'in is not attempting to dissuade the faithful from fighting just wars, but like Dostoevsky he is eager to get them to come to terms with their own guilt in the midst of the necessity and, like Basil, to warn them to be careful to avoid the worst moral violations.

Every political order, including manifestly corrupt ones, does well in protecting its citizens from unjust aggression. Rome was ruled by a pagan emperor (likely the infamous Nero) when Paul advised his Roman readers to support the state (Rom. 13:1–7). Russian novelist Alexander Solzhenitsyn, who served in the Soviet army in World War II and later was thrown into a gulag for alleged unfavorable comments about Stalin in personal letters, argued for the justice of wars even for otherwise corrupt regimes like the Soviet Union. Writing in exile after his release, Solzhenitsyn recognized the evil of the Soviet Union and criticized its unjust use of the military; at the same time he maintained that the defense of country against an unjust aggressor is a moral good.[59] The fate of Russians under Nazi domination, for example, would have been worse than what was faced under the Soviets. His point, firmly grounded in Chrysostom's exposition of Paul in the Epistle to the Romans, is that political regimes govern states, and even if they govern them abusively in many ways, they are not called upon to be completely self-sacrificial. War may be a necessary evil, but states must protect their own citizens from outside aggression. Archimandrite Tikhon (who happens to be Vladimir Putin's confessor) follows this way of thinking when he declares that resistance for the sake of neighbors and the whole of society is a must for the governing authorities; therefore, we should "do everything to confront this evil."[60]

The Russian Orthodox Church reaffirmed its commitment to the just war tradition when it used the occasion of the fall of the Soviet Union in 1990 to reaffirm its moral and theological principles of the relationship of church and state with the release of the document *The Basis of the Social Concept*. This document teaches that the "social concept"—that is, the basic relationship between church and state—is built on the partly eschatological peace promised as a gift from God.[61] This final and perfect peace from God—a peace that Eusebius thought could be achieved to a great degree under Constantine—is not fully realizable in this age, and yet it is still a work that God gives to human beings to achieve as fully as possible in this life. Therefore, peacemaking is one of the primary tasks of the church. War always involves a violation of peace, and for this reason it is always evil. In other words, for the Russian Church, war names an activity in which someone is doing evil and being an unjust aggressor, but it is not evil to use just force to respond to the unjust aggressor who is responsible for violating the peace.

Following the early fathers, the bishops declare that the moral law from God is the basis of the relative (i.e., less than perfect) peace, order, and justice that earthly political authorities are supposed to seek. God commands us to love our enemies and pray for them. He also commands that we lay down our lives for our neighbors, which may lead us to use force against our enemies. These are not contradictory ideas. There is no inconsistency between loving and praying for someone and preventing them from doing evil to their neighbors. The bishops make the same connection between love and justice that we first saw formulated by the early fathers. Justice in international relations should always be based upon the principles of love of neighbor and understanding the needs of others—never using immoral means to protect neighbors or country. Somewhat remarkable to Western eyes is the fact that the bishops appeal to Augustine for what counts as justice in war and what counts as immoral means to protect others. The criteria they list are found in the fathers' thinking surveyed in this chapter: desire for the restoration of justice, legitimate authority (whereby no force can be used by people not under that authority), peaceful means having been tried to restore justice (last resort), reasonable hope for success, and the absence of direct hostilities against civilians.

CONTEMPORARY DEBATES AND CONTRIBUTIONS

The moral tension in Orthodox thinking on war, particularly in the wake of Russian influence and development, can bewilder those of a post-Augustinian Western mindset. In Orthodox thinking, there exists a desire to affirm that the state has a duty to use force to protect its people, yet at the same time we find an effort to craft moral language that refuses to admit that the just use of force can be anything more than a lesser good—and sometimes not even that, a fact that evidences not mere tension but outright confusion. So, for example, George Dragas, dean of Holy Cross Theological School in Massachusetts, states flatly that "there is no just war."[62] And Vassilios Giultsis, professor of Christian ethics at the University of Thessalonika in Greece, denies that war can ever be even a necessary evil.[63] In a worldwide gathering in Minsk of forty Orthodox theologians in 1989, sponsored by the World Council of Churches, participants published a statement condemning all war as evil but maintaining that it was sometimes necessary in order to protect the innocent.[64] On the official website of the Orthodox Church in America, in answer to questions about war and nonviolence, the reader is told that the use of violence is always an evil, though a possible acceptable evil, in order to prevent even greater evil.[65] This tension might be healthy if and where it reminds us that something has gone terribly wrong when we must resort to force, that we should be doing all we can to prevent such circumstances from occurring, and that we should be very watchful of our own fallen fears and desires when contemplating fighting and how we fight. At the same time, the just war tradition should provide the Orthodox with the markers that help guide us in such decisions—moral markers that exclude the designation of "evil" in our response.

The moral tension in Russian Orthodox thinking on just war has been the source of an important moral disagreement about how to characterize the nature of just war. *Is it a lesser evil or a lesser good?* The disagreement is evident in the writings of two notable contemporary Orthodox ethicists— Stanley Harakas and Alexander Webster—who have dealt with the subject of war and peace. Harakas once argued that Orthodoxy shares with the West a similar just war doctrine,[66] but later he repudiated this view in favor of a more measured approach in the vein of Basil and twentieth-century Russian thinking.[67] Harakas grounds Orthodox thinking on war in the overall concern for peace and the right of self-or-other-defense that is anchored in the natural law tradition. He follows Chrysostom in holding that the state exercises authority for the sake of the governed.[68] The state is governed by rules of justice that provide for safe and peaceful conditions. Appealing to the church fathers, Harakas argues that while a high value must be placed upon peace, we should not consider it an absolute value "for which everything else must be sacrificed."[69] The use of force is an "inevitable" part of this provision, even though the state should always be looking for peaceful ways to maintain both peace from within and protection from without.[70] Because each nation should promote peace and try all practical means to adjudicate differences by peaceful means, the resort of military means must be a last resort. The church has always emphasized, when possible, the reformation of the offender rather than destruction.[71] Similar to Ambrose, Harakas is touching upon both the means we use to subdue unjust aggressors and how we deal with them once we have defeated them. In this regard Harakas is certainly in line with the mainstream just war position that we should avoid as much as possible using means that are likely to increase ill will and long-lasting bitterness. In addition, a defeated enemy should be treated with dignity and respect. Such action makes for a more lasting peace.

Harakas is nevertheless reluctant to declare any war a good thing, because it always occurs when one nation refuses to recognize the rights of other nations or its own citizens. Thus, war always represents an "ethical failure."[72] In 2001 Harakas turned to the same moral theme on war following the terrorist attacks on the United States. He argued that the United States must defend itself "without seeking to harm the other beyond what is necessary to stop the attack,"[73] but that such self-defense still requires repentance insofar as it is a falling away of our goal of peace. Just wars are necessary evils that are undertaken to protect our neighbors. They are examples of involuntary sin or involuntary evil (similar to Il'in's "unsinful injustice") to the extent that to refusal to respond with force in such cases brings about even greater evil.

Webster takes issue with this moral confusion, and his robust defense of just war as a positive (albeit lesser) good brings us back to the moral position held by the majority of the early fathers and reflected in the "written lives" of the saints, liturgies, and devotional texts. Like Harakas, Webster locates the grounding of Orthodox thinking on just war in the natural law tradition as expounded by the fathers and others within Orthodox theology and practice. He is helpful in showing how the "lesser evil" approach favored by Harakas and espoused by others in the church can lead to moral muddleheadedness and a weakening of our ability to seek the justice that is possible in this life. Justice, it needs reiterating, is one of the virtues championed by the Orthodox Church; such is part of its patristic heritage.[74] For this reason we do not normally think of just acts as *evil* acts. Action in the defense of the innocent is just, is a moral good. On this view, we should no more call a just act in a just war "evil" than we would a police officer's just act against a criminal.

Yes, we should weep over a world that requires a police force and a military, but our weeping is over human sinfulness and humans' propensity for evil, not human efforts to *contain or counter* that evil. We should be grateful that God has blessed us with such means to achieve peace and order and hold authorities accountable to the rules of justice. The criteria of the just war tradition elucidate those moral principles that pertain to

the state's obligation to protect its citizens, as well as to help protect those of other nations who are suffering egregiously. That protection, alas, is not some "necessary evil"; it is, rather, a necessary "good."

On the Orthodox view, war is always to be entered into with regret, not with the purpose of causing shame on those who must make such decisions and fight to carry them out, but rather with the reminder that there will be cause for tears for those with a shred of the *imago Dei* left in them. Indeed, there will be pain, suffering, destruction, and death in the most just of wars. Thankfully, the church possesses a moral tradition that offers wisdom to guide us in such lamentable circumstances.

NOTES

1. The Orthodox Church in America assumed autocephalous status in 1970 but is still in the process of gaining recognition and has not been accepted by the Patriarchate of Constantinople. See John Anthony McGuckin, *The Orthodox Church: An Introduction to Its History, Doctrine, and Spiritual Culture* (Oxford: Wiley-Blackwell, 2008), 30.

2. Kallistos Ware, *The Orthodox Church* (New York: Penguin Books, 1993), 196.

3. Panagiotis E. Bratsiotis, "The Fundamental Principles and Main Characteristics of the Orthodox Church," in *The Orthodox Ethos*, ed. A. J. Philippou (Oxford: Holywell Press, 1964), 124. This essay was first published in *The Ecumenical Review* 12, no. 2 (1960): 155–63.

4. McGuckin, *Orthodox Church*, 90–91.

5. Paul Valliere, *Modern Russian Theology: Bukharev, Soloviev, Bulgakov—Orthodox Theology in a New Key* (Edinburgh: T&T Clark; Grand Rapids, MI: Eerdmans, 2000), 22.

6. Alexander F. C. Webster and Darrell Cole, *The Virtue of War: Reclaiming the Classical Tradition East and West* (Salisbury, MA: Regina Orthodox Press, 2004), 26.

7. Paul Robinson, "The Justification of War in Russian History and Philosophy," in *Just War in Comparative Perspective*, ed. Paul Robinson (London: Routledge, 2003), 62.

8. Bratsiotis, "Fundamental Principles," 228.

9. Although Salvatore Lilla argues for a series of stages of development, there is clearly an upper and lower level based upon how much time one can devote to a monastic lifestyle. The term "Gnostic" here should be understood in its literal sense of "a knower," as one who truly understands Scripture, and not as

someone involved in a heretical sect. Hereon see Salvatore R. C. Lilla, *Clement of Alexandria: A Study of Christian Platonism and Gnosticism* (London: Oxford University Press 1971), 60–111.

10. Clement of Alexandria, *The Instructor* 1.12.98; Clement of Alexandria, *Miscellanies* 4.8.61; Clement of Alexandria, *Exhortation to the Heathen* 11.116–71.

11. Clement of Alexandria, *Instructor* 3.12.91.

12. Clement of Alexandria, *Exhortation to the Heathen*, in *The Ante-Nicene Christian Library*, ed. Alexander Roberts and James Donaldson (Edinburgh: T&T Clark, 1867), 4:92.

13. Origen, *Contra Celsum*, trans. Henry Chadwick (Cambridge: Cambridge University Press, 1953), 5.33.

14. Ibid., 8.68.

15. Ibid., 8.73, 509.

16. Eusebius, *In Praise of Constantine* 16.3–7.

17. Eusebius, *Life of Constantine* 4.65.2–3.

18. Eusebius, *Demonstration of the Gospel* 1.8, an English translation of which appears in Louis J. Swift, *The Early Fathers on War and Military Service* (Wilmington, DE: Michael Glazier, 1983), 88–89.

19. Eusebius, *Ecclesiastical History* 9.9.2; 10.8.2–3.

20. John Meyendorff, *The Byzantine Legacy in the Orthodox Church* (Crestwood, NY: St. Vladimir's Seminary Press, 1992), 50–52.

21. Ware, *Orthodox Church*, 42.

22. Ibid.

23. Vigen Guroian, *Incarnate Love* (Notre Dame, IN: University of Notre Dame Press, 1987), 135.

24. Basil, *Letter 188*, 13.

25. McGuckin, *Orthodox Church*, 407. McGuckin is surely right that Basil's comments on war represent a theological tradition that "stubbornly clings to a less congratulatory theory of the morality of war" (483), but he overprivileges Basil's part in the tradition—Basil's thoughts are hardly the last or most influential word on the subject in Orthodoxy—and his comments, *pace* McGuckin, do not constitute a "No Entry" sign to any potential just war tradition within Orthodox theology (405).

26. Basil, *Letter 106* ["To a soldier"], translated in *The Early Fathers on War and Military Service*, by Louis J. Swift (Wilmington, DE: Michael Glazier, 1983), 94.

27. John Chrysostom, *Homily XXIII (Rom. XIII.1)*, in *The Nicene and Post-Nicene Fathers of the Christian Church*, series 1, vol. 11, ed. Philip Schaff (Grand Rapids, MI: Eerdmans, 1956), 512.

28. Ibid., 513.
29. Ibid.
30. Ibid., 511.
31. Ibid., 512.
32. Ibid., 515.
33. In his *Homilies on Acts*, Chrysostom singles out Cornelius, the first gentile convert recorded in the book of Acts, as a model of the virtuous Christian military figure. Cornelius combines the virtues of love and justice that Paul commends in his letter to the Romans. He takes care of the soldiers underneath him, he has faith and piety, his "doctrine and manner of life" are acceptable to God, and "in all points" he is "virtuous and irreproachable." See Chrysostom, *Homily XXII (Acts X.1–4)*, in *Homilies on Acts*, in *The Nicene and Post Nicene Fathers of the Christian Church*, series 1, vol. 11, edited by Philip Schaff (Grand Rapids, MI: Eerdmans, 1956), 134–40; Chrysostom, *Homily XXIII (Acts X.23–24)*, in *Homilies on Acts*, in *The Nicene and Post Nicene Fathers of the Christian Church*, series 1, vol. 11, edited by Philip Schaff (Grand Rapids, MI: Eerdmans, 1956) 141–48.
34. Neil B. McLynn provides a helpful discussion of Ambrose's dealings with emperors on this point in his *Ambrose of Milan: Church and Court in a Christian Capital* (Berkeley: University of California Press, 1994).
35. Ambrose of Milan, *On Duties* 1.134–35, in *Nicene and Post-Nicene Fathers*, series 2 (hereafter *NPNF*[2]), vol. 10, p. 23.
36. Ibid., 3.27 (*NPNF*[2], 10:71–72); 1.175 (*NPNF*[2], 10:30).
37. Ibid., 1.135 (*NPNF*[2], 10:23).
38. Ibid., 1.136 (*NPNF*[2], 10:23).
39. Angelo Paredi, *Saint Ambrose: His Life and Times* (Notre Dame, IN: University of Notre Dame Press, 1964), 318.
40. Ambrose of Milan, *Exposition of the Holy Gospel according to Saint Luke*, trans. Theodosia Tomkinson (Etna, CA: Center for Traditionalist Orthodox Studies, 2003), 2.76–77.
41. Ambrose, *Letter 51*.
42. Ambrose, *On Duties* 1.176–77.30; 1.129.22.
43. Ibid., 3.19.110.
44. Ambrose, *Discourse on Psalm 118*, 21.17.
45. Ambrose, *On Duties* 1.114 (*NPNF*[2], 10:20).
46. Webster provides an excellent extended discussion of these materials in Webster and Cole, *Virtue of War*, 78–91.
47. G. P. Fedotov, *The Middle Ages — The Thirteenth to the Fifteenth Centuries*, ed. John Meyendorff, vol. 2 of *The Russian Religious Mind*, Collected Works Series (Cambridge, MA: Harvard University Press, 1966), 175.

48. Webster and Cole, *Virtue of War*, 83.

49. Serge A. Zenkovsky, *Medieval Russia's Epics, Chronicles, and Tales*, 2nd ed. (New York: E. P. Dutton & Co., 1974), 233.

50. *Service Book of the Orthodox Church* (South Canaan, PA: St. Tikhon's Seminary Press, 1984), 2:58.

51. *Services of Supplication* in *The Great Book of Needs* (South Canaan: St. Tikhon's Seminary Press, 1999). 4:130–50.

52. Alexander P. Kazhdan, ed., *Oxford Dictionary of Byzantium* (London: Oxford University Press, 1991), 2:1373.

53. "Ukrainian Orthodox Priests Establish Independent Church," BBC, December 15, 2018, https://www.bbc.com/news/world-europe-46575548. Ukrainian President Petro Paroshenko announced an independent Ukrainian Church separate from Russia on December 15, 2018. He stated that national sovereignty depended upon "spiritual independence" from Russia. The Ukraine Church is seeking autocephalous status from the Ecumenical Patriarch of Constantinople. The drive for independence was fueled by Russia's annexing of Crimea and seizure of Ukrainian territory. The Moscow branch of the Ukrainian Church was thought by Ukrainians to be a tool of the Kremlin. The KGB is widely assumed to have infiltrated the Russian Church during the USSR regime, and many believe the KGB's successor, the Federal Security Services (FSS), to have close links to top Russian clerics.

54. Robinson, "Justification of War."

55. Alexander F. C. Webster, *The Pacifist Option: The Moral Argument against War in Eastern Orthodox Theology* (Washington, DC: International Scholars Publications, 1998), 84.

56. Hildo Boss and Jim Forest, eds., *For the Peace from Above: An Orthodox Resource Book on War, Peace and Nationalism*, rev. ed. (Rollinsford, NH: Orthodox Research Institute, 2011), 224.

57. Augustine, *City of God* 19.7.

58. Robinson, "The Justification of War," 72.

59. Alexander Solzhenitsyn, "Repentance and Self-Limitation in the Life of Nations," in *From under the Rubble*, ed. Alexander Solzhenitsyn, trans. A. M. Brock et al. (Boston: Little, Brown, 1975), 142.

60. Robinson, "Justification of War," 70.

61. *The Basis of the Social Concept* (Russian Orthodox Church, 1990), http://orthodoxrights.org/documents/the-basis-of-the-social-concept. See section 8, "War and Peace."

62. Georges Dragas, "Justice and Peace in the Orthodox Tradition," in *Justice, Peace, and Integrity of Creation: Insights from Orthodoxy*, Gennadios Limouris (Geneva: WCC Publications, 1990), 42.

63. Vassilios Giultsis, "An Ethical Approach to Justice and Peace," in Limouris, *Justice, Peace, and tegrity*, 38.

64. Limouris, *Justice, Peace, and Integrity*, 17–18.

65. "War and Non-violence," Orthodox Church in America, https://oca .org/questions/society/war-and-non-violence.

66. Stanley Harakas, "Is There an Orthodox Just War Position?," *Orthodox America* 1, no. 2 (1992).

67. Stanley Harakas, *The Living Faith: The Praxis of Eastern Orthodox Ethics* (Minneapolis: Light and Life Publishing, 1993).

68. Ibid., 266.

69. Ibid., 212.

70. Ibid., 262, 274.

71. Ibid., 287.

72. Ibid., 289.

73. Stanley Harakas, "Thinking about Peace and War as Orthodox Christians," *Praxis* 3, no.1 (January 2002): 28.

74. Webster and Cole, *Virtue of War*, 109. Webster's contribution to *Virtue of War* is an expansion of an earlier essay, "Justifiable War in Eastern Orthodox Christianity," in *Just War in Comparative Perspective*, ed. Paul Robinson (London: Routledge, 2003), 40–61. Webster also deals helpfully with the issues of war and peace in *The Price of Prophecy: Orthodox Churches on Peace, Freedom and Security*, rev. ed. (Washington, DC: Ethics & Public Policy Center, 1995).

WORKS CITED

Ambrose of Milan. *Exposition of the Holy Gospel according to Saint Luke*. Translated by Theodosia Tomkinson. Etna, CA: Center For Traditionalist Orthodox Studies, 2003.

———. *On Duties*. In *The Nicene and Post-Nicene Fathers of the Christian Church*, series 2, vol. 10, *St. Ambrose*, edited by Philip Schaff and Henry Wace, 1–90. Grand Rapids, MI: Eerdmans, 1983.

Basil. *Letter 106* ["To a soldier"]. In *The Nicene and Post-Nicene Fathers of the Christian Church*, series 2, vol. 8, *St. Basil*, edited by Philip Schaff and Henry Wace, 186. Grand Rapids, MI: Eerdmans, 1983.

The Basis of the Social Concept. Russian Orthodox Church, 1990. https://www .bbc.com/news/world-europe-46575548.

Boss, Hildo, and Jim Forest, eds. *For the Peace from Above: An Orthodox Resource Book on War, Peace and Nationalism*. Rev. ed. Rollinsford, NH: Orthodox Research Institute, 2011.

Bratsiotis, Panagiotis E. "The Fundamental Principles and Main Characteristics of the Orthodox Church." in *The Orthodox Ethos*, edited by A. J. Philippou,

23–31. Oxford: Holywell Press, 1964. First published in *The Ecumenical Review* 12, no. 2 (1960): 155–63.

Clement of Alexandria. *Exhortation to the Heathen.* In *The Ante-Nicene Christian Library*, edited by Alexander Roberts and James Donaldson, 4:171–206. Edinburgh: T&T Clark, 1867.

———. *The Price of Prophecy: Orthodox Churches on Peace, Freedom and Security.* Rev. ed. Washington, DC: Ethics & Public Policy Center, 1995.

Dragas, Georges. "Justice and Peace in the Orthodox Tradition." In *Justice, Peace, and Integrity of Creation: Insights from Orthodoxy*, edited by Gennadios Limouris, 40–44. Geneva: WCC Publications, 1990.

Die griechischen christlichen Schriftsteller der ersten drei Jahrhunderte. Band 6, *Eusebius.* Leipzig: J. C. Hinrich, 1913.

Eusebius. *Demonstration of the Gospel.* In *The Early Fathers on War and Military Service*, by Louis J. Swift, 88–89. Wilmington, DE: Michael Glazier, 1983.

Fedotov, G. P. *The Middle Ages: The Thirteenth to the Fifteenth Centuries.* Edited by John Meyendorff. Vol. 2 of *The Russian Religious Mind.* Collected Works Series. Cambridge, MA: Harvard University Press, 1966.

Guroian, Vigen. *Incarnate Love.* Notre Dame, IN: University of Notre Dame Press, 1987.

Harakas, Stanley. "Is There an Orthodox Just War Position?" *Orthodox America* 1, no. 2 (1992).

———. *The Living Faith: The Praxis of Eastern Orthodox Ethics.* Minneapolis: Light and Life Publishing, 1993.

———. "Thinking about Peace and War as Orthodox Christians." *Praxis* 3, no.1 (January 2002): 28–29.

John Chrysostom. *Homily XXII (Acts X.1–4).* In *Homilies on Acts*, in *The Nicene and Post Nicene Fathers of the Christian Church*, series 1, vol. 11, edited by Philip Schaff, 134–40. Grand Rapids, MI: Eerdmans, 1956.

———. *Homily XXIII (Acts X.23–24).* In *Homilies on Acts*, in *The Nicene and Post Nicene Fathers of the Christian Church*, series 1, vol. 11, edited by Philip Schaff, 141–48. Grand Rapids, MI: Eerdmans, 1956.

———. *Homily XXIII (Rom. XIII.1).* In *The Nicene and Post-Nicene Fathers of the Christian Church*, series 1, vol. 11, edited by Philip Schaff, 511–16. Grand Rapids, MI: Eerdmans, 1956.

Kazhdan, Alexander P., ed. *Oxford Dictionary of Byzantium.* London: Oxford University Press, 1991.

Lilla, Salvatore R. C. *Clement of Alexandria: A Study of Christian Platonism and Gnosticism.* London: Oxford University Press 1971.

McGuckin, John Anthony. *The Orthodox Church: An Introduction to Its History, Doctrine, and Spiritual Culture.* Oxford: Wiley-Blackwell, 2008.

4

McLynn, Neil B. *Ambrose of Milan: Church and Court in a Christian Capital.* Berkeley: University of California Press, 1994.

Meyendorff, John. *The Byzantine Legacy in the Orthodox Church.* Crestwood, NY: St. Vladimir's Seminary Press, 1992.

Origen. *Contra Celsum.* Translated by Henry Chadwick. Cambridge: Cambridge University Press, 1953.

Paredi, Angelo. *Saint Ambrose: His Life and Times.* Notre Dame, IN: University of Notre Dame Press, 1964.

Robinson, Paul. "The Justification of War in Russian History and Philosophy." In *Just War in Comparative Perspective*, edited by Paul Robinson, 62–75. London: Routledge, 2003.

Service Book of the Orthodox Church. South Canaan, PA: St. Tikhon's Seminary Press, 1984.

"Services of Supplication." In *The Great Book of Needs*, NN–NN. South Canaan, PA: St. Tikhon's Seminary Press, 1999.

Solzhenitsyn, Alexander. "Repentance and Self-Limitation in the Life of Nations." In *From under the Rubble*, edited by Alexander Solzhenitsyn. Translated by A. M. Brock et al., 105–43. Washington, DC: Regnery Gateway, 1981.

Swift, Louis J. *The Early Fathers on War and Military Service.* Wilmington, DE: Michael Glazier, 1983.

"Ukrainian Orthodox Priests Establish Independent Church." BBC, December 15, 2018. https://www.bbc.com/news/world-europe-46575548.

Valliere, Paul. *Modern Russian Theology: Bukharev, Soloviev, Bulgakov—Orthodox Theology in a New Key.* Edinburgh: T&T Clark; Grand Rapids, MI: Eerdmans, 2000.

"War and Non-violence." Orthodox Church in America. https://oca.org/questions/society/war-and-non-violence.

Ware, Kallistos. *The Orthodox Church.* New York: Penguin Books, 1993.

Webster, Alexander F. C. "Justifiable War in Eastern Orthodox Christianity." In *Just War in Comparative Perspective*, edited by Paul Robinson, 40–61. London: Routledge, 2003.

———. *The Pacifist Option: The Moral Argument against War in Eastern Orthodox Theology.* Washington, DC: International Scholars Publications, 1998.

Webster, Alexander F. C., and Darrell Cole. *The Virtue of War: Reclaiming the Classical Tradition East and West.* Salisbury, MA: Regina Orthodox Press, 2004.

Zenkovsky, Serge A. *Medieval Russia's Epics, Chronicles, and Tales.* 2nd ed. New York: E. P. Dutton & Co., 1974.

———. *The Instructor.* In *The Ante-Nicene Christian Library*, edited by Alexander Roberts and James Donaldson, 4:209–96. Edinburgh: T&T Clark, 1867.

FOUR

Luther's Political Thought and Its Contribution to the Just War Tradition

H. David Baer

Martin Luther's place in the history of Christian political thought and his contribution to the just war tradition are significant, but underappreciated and often mischaracterized. According to a widely held stereotype, Luther articulated an early form of absolutism, supposedly teaching that rulers, having received their authority straight from God, were morally unconstrained in the use of power and were owed unthinking obedience from their subjects.[1] In order to preserve this stereotype, those holding this stereotype pass over Luther's innovations to the just war tradition — his rejection of the crusade, his restriction of just cause to defense, and his assertion of a moral right of conscientious objection. The temptation to neglect the full corpus of Luther's work is compounded by the fact that his reflections on politics and the use of force are not only found in a few well-known treatises but also sprinkled across biblical commentaries, sermons, and letters that have remained hidden and untranslated in well over one hundred volumes of the so-called Weimarer Ausgabe (WA).[2] The fact that in the last fifteen years of his life Luther developed arguments for resisting political authority that went beyond standard medieval justifications of tyrannicide is almost completely unknown outside of a small, specialized group of historians. Thus, a detailed and careful overview of Luther's political thought in relation to the problem of war, rebellion, and the use of force can fill a large lacuna in contemporary just war scholarship.

The present chapter begins with an examination of Luther against the backdrop of his own world. That rehearsal is followed by a clarification of those theological convictions that underpinned his view of political authority, the church, and Christian obligation in society—convictions that have had an enormous influence on the subsequent centuries of Western Protestant thought. This in turn leads to an assessment of Luther's contributions to the just war tradition and of the development of Luther's thinking about political obedience. The chapter concludes with a look at some of the most recent statements made by Lutheran denominations on war, peace, and security.

MARTIN LUTHER, LUTHERANISM, AND THE DEBATES OF HIS TIME

In addition to the challenges associated with researching Luther in a serious way, the predisposition to misrepresent him originates, also, from his historical significance. Luther is an inherently polarizing figure. The historical events he set in motion were, to put it mildly, enormously consequential, a fact apparent already to his contemporaries. Ever since the Reformation, Luther has been the object of both unbridled polemic and unrestrained hagiography. More than a few characterizations of him have been overly determined by the preoccupations of his interpreters, by their attitude toward things like the Enlightenment, the Reformation, nationalism, modernity, and so on. To get at the real Luther one must set aside modern reference points and work to see him in his own time and place, which was quite removed from ours.

Luther's reformation took place in the Holy Roman Empire, a historical contingency indispensable to its success. Had Luther lived elsewhere, he might have been burnt at the stake and forgotten. That instead he transformed Europe had a lot to do with the political possibilities provided by the empire—a complex, geographically expansive entity that cannot be grasped in terms of a nation-state. To think of the Holy Roman

Empire as premodern Germany would be a mistake. The borders of the empire, never precisely defined, included not merely what today is Germany but also modern Austria, the Czech Republic, Switzerland, and Luxembourg as well as parts of Poland, Denmark, Belgium, the Netherlands, France, and Italy.[3] The Kingdom of Hungary, while not part of the empire, was closely associated with it, as was for important periods the Kingdom of Spain. Within these vast borders were independent kingdoms, principalities, free cities, and ecclesiastical estates. Unlike the centralized monarchies that developed in England and France, political authority within the empire was textured, distributed, and mixed.[4] The Holy Roman emperor, who ruled over the empire as a whole, did not inherit his position but was elected.

For a century preceding Luther the empire had been undergoing a series of imperial reforms, which had the unintended effect of aiding the Reformation.[5] One reform, for example, granted imperial estates a right to vote at meetings of the Imperial Diet. Consequently, when Luther was excommunicated by the pope, princes sympathetic to Luther pushed to have his case heard by the Diet in Worms. Even after Luther was condemned, many princes refused to enforce the ban. Eight years later, when the emperor tried to bring disobedient princes in line at the Diet of Speyer, nineteen imperial estates "protested" that they could not be forced to violate their conscience. The following year the "Protestants" presented a statement of faith at the Diet of Augsburg, the so-called Augsburg Confession, which became the foundational confession of the Lutheran church.[6]

The evangelical (or Protestant) camp also benefited from what might be called the geopolitical environment. Charles V, Holy Roman emperor and king of Spain, fought intermittent wars against France and the papacy. In addition, Charles confronted the Ottomans, who, led by the great sultan Suleiman the Magnificent, were expanding into Europe. In 1526, five years after Luther was condemned at Worms, Suleiman conquered and partitioned the Kingdom of Hungary. Three years later he laid siege to Vienna. To fight the Ottomans, Charles needed support from evangelical princes in the empire, which meant treading softly, at least temporarily, on the religious question.

The Lutheran reformation thus unfolded within an inescapably political context. Although Luther understood himself to be expounding the pure Word of God, the political protection afforded to him and his associates affected the development of his reform, especially its political teaching. Luther was called upon repeatedly to speak to the questions of the day: What sort of obedience do Protestant subjects owe Catholic princes? Under what conditions can Christians wage war with a clear conscience? How should the princes respond to the Peasants' War? What should Christians do about the Ottoman threat? Could Protestant princes defend themselves against an attack from the emperor? In speaking to such questions Luther sought to give principled answers rooted in immutable theological truth, but even so, he was always answering particular questions tied closely to the course of events. This accounts for shifts in his thinking and presents problems of interpretation. In terms of foundations, Luther consistently approached political questions within a theological framework established by his understanding of the two kingdoms and the three estates. However, the answers he gave to specific questions about war and resistance changed. Although some of those changes were quite dramatic, they can be explained by sympathetic interpreters who relate them to an overarching system of thought that remains consistent. Less sympathetic interpreters, of course, explain the shifts in Luther's thought less sympathetically. A definitive account of Luther's political theology does not exist and is probably impossible to deliver. While Luther is a theologian who repays careful study, we should not expect him to answer contemporary questions directly.

THE THEOLOGICAL FOUNDATIONS OF LUTHER'S POLITICAL THOUGHT

Two Kingdoms

The best-known and most systematic presentation of Luther's political thought is his treatise *Temporal Authority: To What Extent It Should Be Obeyed*, which was published in response to the decrees of several rulers within the empire prohibiting the sale of Luther's books and ordering confiscation of his translation of the New Testament.[7] *Temporal Authority* devotes considerable attention to the question of political obedience, counseling civil disobedience but not rebellion in instances where legitimate authorities overstep the limits of their authority. Luther also discusses the origin and purpose of secular government in a way that makes clear he intends to set forth its theological foundations.

A crucial part of that foundation is a distinction between the kingdom of God and the kingdom of earth. This is often referred to, somewhat misleadingly, as Luther's "two kingdoms doctrine."[8] Luther does not articulate a doctrine so much as set forth a distinction between two basic communities, one aligned with Christ and the other with sin. This distinction is reminiscent of Augustine's two cities, yet despite the Augustinian resonances, Luther's two kingdoms doctrine is formulated with the social structures of the Holy Roman Empire clearly in view.[9]

For Luther, the most important political implication of the distinction between two kingdoms is a strict demarcation between spiritual and secular government. Each kingdom has its own government. The kingdom of God consists of all true Christians, who live directly under the spiritual reign of Christ. The kingdom of earth consists of all persons subject to sin who need worldly, or secular, government. The kingdom of God has no need for worldly law or government, because true Christians do everything the law requires on their own. The kingdom of earth, however, needs secular government to maintain law and order, because sinners left to their own devices would devour each other in chaos. The kingdom of God has a spiritual government, which is nothing less than Christ's direct rule over the soul. The kingdom of earth has a worldly government that rules over external things and maintains an external peace. Secular government preserves peace, punishes the wicked, and protects the innocent with the sword — that is, through the use of force.[10]

Although the two kingdoms are distinct, Christians nonetheless participate in both. This is because the division described by the two kingdoms runs through the heart of each believer. Insofar as they are perfect, Christians belong to the kingdom of God, but insofar as they are still ruled by sin, Christians belong to the kingdom of earth.[11] Moreover, even perfect Christians can exercise the office of the sword in the kingdom of earth. This is because, as Paul makes clear in Romans 13, government is God's work and creation. "If it is God's work and creation, then it is good," Luther says, "so good that everyone can use it in a Christian and salutary way."[12] To fill the office of government is a work of love, because government protects the innocent, promotes justice, and maintains peace. As

Luther writes famously, "If you see that there is a lack of hangmen, constables, judges, lords, or princes, and you find that you are qualified, you should offer your services and seek the position, that the essential governmental authority may not be despised and become enfeebled or perish."[13] Although Christians do not wield the sword to protect themselves, love for the neighbor constrains them to exercise the sword on behalf of others.

Luther was quite proud of *Temporal Authority*, boasting, "Not since the time of the apostles have the temporal sword and temporal government been so clearly described or so highly praised as by me."[14] This self-congratulation notwithstanding, the treatise is difficult to interpret. The two governments and the two kingdoms are distinct conceptual pairs, but they overlap in ways that can be confusing. The spiritual government aligns closely with the kingdom of God, but secular government does not appear to align with the kingdom of earth. The two governments should not be confused with church and state. The church of the Holy Roman Empire was an elaborate web of social and political institutions sometimes referred to as the *ecclesiastical estate*. The spiritual government Luther describes is the invisible reign of Christ over the communion of saints. In fact, the distinction between Christ's spiritual government and the ecclesiastical estate played a central role in Luther's polemic against the medieval church. Further, what Luther calls *secular authority* should not be confused with the modern state. The Holy Roman Empire was a decentralized mixed monarchy with different sorts of political powers (including princes, bishops, and free cities) exercising legitimate political authority underneath the distant authority of the Holy Roman emperor. Luther did not have a concept of the state, if by "state" we mean a centralized, impersonal administrative structure. He understood political authority largely in terms of the personal governance exercised by princes.[15]

There is also an asymmetry in the definition of the two governments. The spiritual government is the *invisible*, spiritual governance of Christ, but secular government is the *visible*, physical rule of princes. The two governments do not parallel each other, but operate on different planes. This asymmetry suggests that the argument of *Temporal Authority* is incomplete in certain respects. To understand Luther's political theology fully one must relate the two kingdoms described in *Temporal Authority* to Luther's understanding of the three estates.

The Three Estates

In many places in his writings Luther refers to three "estates" or "orders." When writing in Latin he labels these consistently as *ecclesia* (the church), *oeconomica* (household), and *politia* (government). Although these were traditional concepts not new with Luther, Luther reinterpreted them significantly in light of his two kingdoms doctrine.[16] That said, the complete nature of his reinterpretation is open to interpretation. Luther never discussed the matter systematically in a treatise similar to *Temporal Authority*, and I can only offer what I take to be a reasonable interpretation of his views.

Clearly the two kingdoms have an eschatological dimension that the three estates do not. The two kingdoms arise from a conflict between God and the devil that will come to an end on the Last Day. The kingdom of earth is therefore temporary. The three estates, by contrast, are orders of creation. Although they have been damaged by the fall and corrupted by sin, insofar as they express God's original intention for humankind, they will presumably continue in some form even in eternity.[17] The estates appear to have an ontological character that runs deeper, and is more fundamental, than the distinction between the two kingdoms.[18]

As divine institutions expressing God's will for creation, the estates are unified by "the common order of Christian love, in which one serves not only the three orders, but also serves every needy person in general with all kinds of benevolent deeds."[19] At one point Luther says an angelic hierarchy stands above the three estates, protecting them and assisting in their rule. The estates themselves are constantly assaulted by the devil, in such a way that grace cannot be proclaimed in the church without error, the household cannot be managed without the rod, and government cannot preserve peace without the sword.[20] The two kingdoms thus run through the three estates; or, using a different image, one might say the three estates straddle the two kingdoms.[21] The devil's kingdom has made inroads into the estates, but even so, these divine orders continue to serve the kingdom of God. The task of Christians, working in the estates through their offices, is to advance the kingdom of God and serve the neighbor through obedience to the order of love. To paraphrase the scholar Franz Lau, the two kingdoms are connected to each other through the activity of individual Christians. The Christian lives spiritually under the lordship of Christ through worldly service in the orders.[22]

By reconceptualizing the estates in light of the two kingdoms, Luther laid the foundation for his critique of the ecclesiastical estate. To appreciate the radical nature of that critique one must understand the central social and political role played by the imperial church within the Holy Roman Empire. Bishops and archbishops possessed significant holdings of land and commanded their resources, making them politically active aristocratic lords.[23] Thus when Luther distinguished between the *ecclesiastical* estate and the spiritual kingdom of Christ, he was establishing the predicate for a sweeping criticism of the medieval church. The pope, prince-bishops, and other ecclesiastical lords, by exercising temporal authority over secular affairs were confusing the two kingdoms, according to Luther. To confuse the kingdoms was to undermine the three estates and to assault God's will for creation.

The second estate, *oeconomica*, encompassed a large swath of society, including the family, economic activity, and education. That Luther grouped these activities together reflects the influence of an Aristotelian tradition that understood economics to be rooted in the household.[24] Luther believed *oeconomica* originated in the marriage of Adam and Eve before the fall. Hence, he often referred to this estate as household government (*hausregiment*). Household government is also, in Luther's view, the source of secular government. In the Large Catechism Luther discusses civil government under the fourth commandment, stating: "All other authority is derived and developed out of the authority of parents."[25] Similarly, in a sermon from 1539, Luther says, "Parents are the source and fount from which secular government arises."[26]

This raises a question: Did Luther consider secular government to be a pre- or postlapsarian institution? The answer is not completely clear. In *Temporal Authority* Luther states explicitly that "the law of this temporal sword has existed from the beginning of the world"—although the only task he assigns to the sword is punishment of sin.[27] In his *Commentary on Genesis*, however, Luther says, "Government did not exist before sin, for there was nothing for it to do . . . for the one and principle activity of government is to constrain sin."[28] But in the Large Catechism Luther describes the tasks of government more broadly, saying that civil rulers, like parents, provide "food, house and home, protection and security."[29] This lack of clarity about the origin and purpose of secular government has generated a fair bit of discussion among scholars.[30] Instead of resolving the debate, we might content ourselves with the observation that Luther's position is ambiguous. One interpretation that seems faithful to Luther's spirit might hold that government in a broad sense existed from creation, but that government's use of the sword began only after the fall.[31]

Regardless of when Luther thought secular government first appeared, he was clear about its divine institution. That divine institution secured government's independence from the ecclesiastical estate. Luther rejected the kind of two swords theory associated with the papal bull *Unam sanctam*.[32] According to Pope Boniface VIII, Christ entrusted both the spiritual and temporal sword to the church, placing the temporal under the spiritual: "If the earthly power errs, it shall be judged by the spiritual power."[33] This view was untenable in light of Luther's understanding of the two kingdoms. He rejected it explicitly, writing in his address *To the Christian Nobility*, "Since the temporal power is ordained of God to punish the wicked and protect the good, it should be left free to perform its office in the whole body of Christendom without restriction and without respect to persons, whether it affects pope, bishops, priests, monks, nuns, or anyone else."[34]

That secular government had authority over clerics in temporal affairs did not mean its authority was unlimited. Not only the pope but also temporal authorities could confound the two kingdoms: "Where [government] is given too wide a scope, intolerable and terrible injury follow."[35] When emphasizing the limits of government, Luther often invoked the "tribute passage" ("Render unto Caesar"—Matt. 22:21). In Luther's words, "The soul is not under the authority of Caesar; he can neither teach it nor guide it, neither kill it nor give it life, neither bind it nor loose it."[36] Secular government's authority extends only over external, worldly matters, and never over spiritual things. When government attempts to command the soul, it mixes the two kingdoms and starts to overturn the estates. Luther even went so far, at least in *Temporal Authority*, as to state that secular power should not repress heresy for the sake of public order—a notable departure from the prevailing medieval view.[37]

Luther, therefore, thoroughly reconceived government in light of his two kingdoms doctrine and his theory of the three estates. That reconceptualization informed his reflections on war and inspired significant innovations to the just war tradition.

LUTHER'S CONTRIBUTIONS TO
THE JUST WAR TRADITION

Innovations in Defining Just Cause

Luther understands the right to wage war as grounded in government's divine ordination. War, when just, is merely an extension of government's right to use force to protect and preserve peace: "The very fact that the sword has been instituted by God to punish the evil, protect the good, and preserve peace is powerful and sufficient proof that war and killing along with all the things that accompany wartime and martial law have been instituted by God."[38] In just war terms, this is to assert the criterion of *legitimate political authority*. Only legitimate political authorities may wage war because only they have been entrusted by God with the right to use force and to kill. On this point, Luther's view is consonant with the just war tradition and appears unremarkable.

In a paradoxical way, however, Luther's conception of civil government is steeped in the Middle Ages even while his definition of *just cause* is strikingly modern. Luther discusses the question of war at length in *Whether Soldiers, Too, Can Be Saved.* The treatise was dedicated to a knight who had participated in suppressing the Peasants' War. Luther writes to allay the soldier's conscience, assuring him that the Christian faith is compatible with "being a soldier, going to war, stabbing and killing."[39] The bulk of the treatise, however, is devoted not to justifying Christian participation in war, but rather to examining the conditions in which war is rightly fought. Those questions happened to be animating the evangelical (Lutheran) princes at the time Luther wrote this treatise in 1526. A group of Catholic princes had formed the Deslau League in 1525 with the purpose of stamping out the Reformation. In response, a group of evangelical princes established the Torgau League, an alliance intended to deter any potential Catholic attack. The legitimacy of this defensive alliance was heavily debated in evangelical circles.[40] *Whether Soldiers* must have been written with those debates in mind, because Luther appears to address them.[41]

In this treatise Luther distinguishes between three kinds of war: wars waged by subjects against their superiors, wars waged by superiors against their subjects, and wars waged between persons of equal standing. Luther rules out wars waged against superiors almost completely. The only exception he entertains is a situation where the ruler has gone insane. Madness and tyranny, however, are different things. A tyrant, no matter how unjust, must be endured. Bad rulers are not to be opposed with rebellion, because secular government has been ordained by God.[42] Luther thus clearly implied that, should the emperor move against the evangelical princes with force, the princes must suffer wrong rather than resist. Although the princes held divinely sanctioned authority over their own subjects, vis-à-vis the emperor they were as private persons with no right to bear the sword.[43]

War between lords of equal standing was a completely different matter. Such wars were permitted provided they were defensive. The only *just cause* Luther recognizes is self-defense. As he states, "War against equals should be waged only when it is forced upon us. . . . Such a war is forced upon us when an enemy or neighbor attacks and starts the war";[44] and also, "Whoever starts a war is in the wrong."[45] This unambiguous position, while narrowly restricting the justified causes of war to one, also communicated clearly that Luther would approve a defensive alliance against Catholic princes. That was a significant position for Luther to adopt.[46] As we shall see, Luther would later come to allow for a defensive alliance against even the emperor, modifying his earlier position.

Whether Soldiers, Too, Can Be Saved also illustrates the extent to which Luther's understanding of secular government was premodern. Moderns identify government with the state and tend to think of the state as that entity which, to borrow a phrase from Max Weber, "claims the monopoly of the legitimate use of physical force within a given territory."[47] Luther, however, advances no such concept, nor does he understand the right to use force as devolving downward from a supreme, encompassing authority. Instead, he conceives the right to use force as attached to specific offices (prince, ruler, judge, etc.), which are exercised as part of the third estate of secular government. Since each estate is divinely ordained, the authority of those who hold office within the estates comes directly from God. "In the end," Luther says, "all authority comes from God, whose alone it is; for he is emperor, prince, count, noble, judge, and all else, and he assigns these offices to his subjects as he wills."[48]

Consequently, Luther did not hold a concept of sovereignty like that described as central to the Christian just war tradition by James Turner Johnson. Johnson has argued that by the High Middle Ages a consensus existed within Latin Christendom that only a sovereign—that is, a temporal authority with no superior—had the right to wage war. Members of what he calls the "knightly class" did possess a private "right of arms," but this was only a right to vindicate personal grievances. According to Johnson, the medieval just war tradition distinguished between *duellum*, a private quarrel between knights, and *bellum*, the public use of force by the sovereign on behalf of the common good. "When [medieval canonists] defined the concept of just war," Johnson writes, "they reserved this specific term for the use of arms by a temporal ruler with no temporal superior to correct and punish an injustice already accomplished with the aim of vindicating justice."[49] Regardless of the consensus among medieval canonists, however, Luther did not distinguish between *duellum* and *bellum* in *Whether Soldiers, Too, Can Be Saved*. Had he done so, he could not have considered the possibility of war between equals, much less approved of a defensive alliance against Catholic princes. Moreover, had the view of sovereignty described by Johnson been shared by Lutheran princes and jurists, they could not have developed, in collaboration with Wittenberg theologians, the argument that lesser magistrates may resist an unjust superior authority—an important development to which we will return.

While Luther's view of political authority was premodern, his view of *just cause* was almost contemporary to the view in current international law. Like international law, Luther limited *just cause* to defense.[50] In the sixteenth century, this was an innovation. Medieval thinkers frequently identified a more expansive list of just causes, including avenging injury, exacting retribution, and defending honor. Luther's highly restrictive account of just cause appears to rule out even avenging past injury. The only cause he recognizes is defense against an attack. In this respect, Luther's interpretation of *just cause* resembles the United Nations (UN) Charter, which stipulates that states may only go to war in response to aggression.[51] The UN Charter, however, derives this limitation from the principles of state sovereignty and nonintervention. For Luther, the limitation on *just cause* is related to his theory of the two kingdoms and three estates.

First, Luther conceived secular government's dominion as fairly limited. God provides for society through three estates, each of which has its own domain and form of governance. Many of the functions assigned to the state today would belong to what Luther thought of as *oeconomica*. The primary task of temporal authority was to preserve peace with the sword. That task was carried out by individual officeholders, who as princes bore a representative relationship to their subjects. According to Luther, "The overlord is appointed as a common person and not for himself alone. He is to have the support of his subjects and bear the sword. . . . Seen in relationship to his subjects, he is as many people as he has people under him and attached to him."[52] Because the prince bears the sword as a representative of his subjects, his right to wage war is limited to the protection of his subjects. Hence, just cause is limited to defense.[53]

Second, Luther probably considered peace a greater political value than justice. Although he believed secular government exercised a judicial function—namely, to punish the wicked and protect the good—that judicial function was ordered directly to the preservation of peace. According to Franz Lau, Luther considered peace the *telos* of all the orders.[54] Secular government differs from the other estates in that its task is to restore peace after it has been broken, but the sword itself is ordained for peace. Luther's preference for peace makes him more patient about earthly injustice than others in the just war tradition. Christians, who belong to the spiritual kingdom of God, should expect injustice in the kingdom of earth. Instead of stepping outside the mandate of the orders, they should wait upon God's providence.

Rejection of Crusade

Another work by Luther with significance for the just war tradition is *On War against the Turk*. Written in 1528, at the height of Ottoman expansion into Europe, this treatise is radical in several respects, not least because it breaks with medieval tradition to reject crusading.[55]

Luther's rejection of the crusade emerges from his two kingdoms doctrine. Those who would wage war against the Turkish empire in Christ's name are confusing the kingdoms. Christ does not govern the kingdom of God with the sword, nor can the gospel be defended with force. Only secular government may wield the sword. One must also distinguish clearly between offices. The office of priest and bishop serves spiritual things, whereas the office of prince and judge serves worldly things. Disorder arises when "a bishop or pastor gives up his office and assumes the office of a prince or judge; or, on the other hand, when a prince takes up the office of a bishop."[56] Similarly, "it is not right for the pope, who wants to be a Christian, and the highest and best Christian preacher at that, to lead a church army, or army of Christians, for the church ought not to strive or fight with the sword."[57] Only one who holds the appropriate secular office may wage war against the Turk.

Even when considering the threat of Ottoman conquest, Luther adhered to the restrictive just war principles he set down in *Whether Soldiers, Too, Can Be Saved*. First, any war against the Turk must be strictly defensive. One cannot fight the Turk for reasons like "winning of great honor, glory, and wealth, the extension of territory, or wrath and revenge."[58] Second, such a war can only be waged by the *legitimate political authority*, who in this case is the Holy Roman emperor alone. The Turks were attacking the empire, which the emperor is appointed to protect by virtue of his office. Princes and kings ruling within the empire have an obligation to obey the emperor in assembling an army against the Turk, but the war itself must be fought "at the emperor's command, under his banner, and in his name."[59] This illustrates again how closely Luther linked the right to wage war to the officeholder's responsibility for a specific community. The sovereign was not responsible for justice in a universal sense, and hence he could not wage war to punish injustice committed outside his domain. He could wage war defensively, in response to unjust attacks against his subjects. Moreover, the emperor's defensive war had nothing to do with defending the faith. It was a purely secular matter of protecting the empire.

Luther's rejection of the crusade and, more generally, his reconceptualization of just cause are among his most significant contributions to the just war tradition. Nevertheless, his theological critique of the "Turk" is also important, because it hints at arguments Luther will later use to justify resistance against the emperor.

Simply put, Luther accuses the Turks of destroying the three estates. First, they destroy the ecclesial estate by attacking Christ's kingdom, the gospel, and the sacraments. Second, they destroy the political estate by using the sword to advance their religion. By using the sword to advance their faith the Turks confound the two kingdoms and destroy secular government; "Their government," Luther says, "is not a godly, regular rulership, like others, for the maintenance of peace, the protection of the good, and the punishment of the wicked."[60] Third, the Turks destroy the estate of marriage by allowing men to take as many wives as they will. "In Turkey," claims Luther, "women are held immeasurably cheap and despised; they are bought and sold like cattle."[61]

To destroy the estates is to overturn God's will for human community and give society over to the devil. Luther viewed the Turks in apocalyptic terms; they were an instrument of the devil engaged in ultimate battle against God as a prelude to the end times.[62] The Turkish attack on the three estates was a comprehensive assault on human society; Luther's reasoning is this: "If you take out of the world *veram religionem, veram politiam, veram oeconomiam,* that is, true spiritual life, true temporal government, and true home life, what is left in the world but flesh, world, and the devil."[63] In Luther's view, the Turk sought to replace God's ordered will for creation with a demonic purpose.

Yet the Turks were not alone in this. The papacy was also assaulting the three estates. It attacked the spiritual estate with false teaching and the political estate by its efforts to enforce false teaching with the sword. Lastly, it attacked the estate of marriage by tolerating priests who entered the forbidden marriage of Sodom.[64] Acknowledging the similarity between the Turk and the pope, Luther asked the obvious question, "Ought we not, then, fight the pope as well as the Turk, or, perhaps, rather than the Turk?" His answer, although brief and undeveloped, would assume significance over the course of the subsequent two decades: "If the pope and his followers were to attack the empire with the sword, as the Turk does, he should receive the same treatment as the Turk."[65] Here, unnoticed, was the seed of a doctrine of resistance that would start to emerge after the Diet of Augsburg and come into bloom during the Smalcald War.

THE QUESTION OF RESISTANCE

No aspect of Luther's political thought has been more misrepresented than his position on political obedience. Luther is commonly, and falsely, accused of teaching abject subjection to the powers that be. The reality is that Luther consistently distinguished between disobedience and rebellion. He counseled Christians to disobey the unjust commands of secular government but rejected rebellion, which he considered an attempt to overthrow one of God's divine estates. Luther never abandoned this distinction, although he did redefine the nature of rebellion in later years in a way that allowed him to endorse armed resistance against the emperor. His position on resistance indisputably changed, but it changed within a theological framework that was largely, if not completely, consistent.

The Early Luther on Resistance

The inflection point in the evolution of Luther's thought on resistance was the Diet of Augsburg in 1530, a date we can use to distinguish between the "early" and "later" Luther. The early Luther clearly rejected the possibility of armed resistance against superior political authority. That rejection followed from two broad premises. The first was the distinction between the two kingdoms, which entailed a proscription against self-defense. Christians belong to the kingdom of God, where Christ's injunction against resisting evil obtains. As members of the kingdom of God, Christians may not exercise self-defense, and to rebel against an unjust government would be an exercise of self-defense.[66] Thus, Christians must endure, rather than resist, tyranny. The second premise of Luther's argument was the divine ordination of government. Because secular government has been instituted by God, to rebel against government is to overthrow a divine estate. In this respect rebellion is no ordinary crime, but an assault on the order of creation: "It is like a great fire, which attacks and devastates a whole land."[67]

These weighty considerations on behalf of government did not, however, lead Luther to advocate abject submission to unjust authority. To the contrary, Luther taught that when government oversteps its legitimate boundaries, Christians should disobey in ways that fall short of rebellion. In *Temporal Authority* Luther tells Christians living in Catholic territories to ignore princes ordering them to turn over prohibited books and copies of the New Testament. If, however, the authorities come and confiscate the books, a Christian must suffer the injustice.[68] In *Whether Soldiers* Luther states that soldiers cannot participate in a war they know to be unjust. If the conscientious objector fears his overlord will punish him, he must, says Luther, "take that risk and, with God's help, let whatever happens, happen."[69] Luther himself refused to comply with the edict against his reformation and spent much of his life as an imperial outlaw.

Perhaps the event most responsible for Luther's reputation as an authoritarian is his response to the German Peasants' War of 1524–25. Peasant uprisings had been rumbling through Europe for a good century, but the German Peasants' War implicated Luther's teaching. Many peasants appealed to the Reformation in articulating their grievances, and their movement attracted religious figures critical of medieval society. The most notorious of these was Thomas Müntzer, an educated theologian who had briefly associated with Luther.[70] In 1525 Müntzer led an army of peasants into battle at Frankenhausen, where they were swiftly and brutally slaughtered. Although Luther had publicly condemned Müntzer and never supported the rebellious peasants, critics tried to pin responsibility for the social upheaval on him. Luther's own criticisms of the papacy and the ecclesiastical estate had been fairly radical; hence, the charge that he was overturning the established social order was more than a little plausible. One senses in Luther's response to the Peasants' War a concern that the revolts were discrediting his own reform movement, which, despite Luther's provocative and incautious style, was always only focused on reforming the church. "This rebellion," Luther insisted, "cannot be coming from me."[71]

Luther first addressed the matter in his *Admonition to Peace*. The *Admonition* was written as a reply to the *Twelve Articles*, a relatively moderate statement of peasant demands couched within a broader appeal to the Christian gospel.[72] Although Luther acknowledged the peasants had some reasonable complaints, he still rejected their program. The matter concerned the two kingdoms. The peasants, by cloaking their secular, political demands in the language of the gospel, were confounding the two kingdoms. In the kingdom of God, Christians are governed by the gospel, which tells them to endure evil rather than resist it.[73] To mix the kingdoms is always to assault God's ordered will for society. Thus, the peasants through their rebellion were acting to overturn the entire estate of secular government. "If your enterprise were right," Luther tells the peasants, then "authority, government, law, and order would disappear from the world."[74]

Luther even argues in *Admonition to Peace* that one cannot resist a government that suppresses the gospel. To suppress the gospel is certainly the greatest of evils; "whoever keeps the gospel from me, closes heaven to me and drives me by force into hell.... On peril of losing my soul, I should not permit this."[75] Yet even when salvation is at stake, says Luther, one should not rebel against government, because no government can succeed in suppressing the gospel. The gospel moves freely under the sky. If the ruler of the land or city where you live suppresses the gospel, you can leave. "It is not necessary, for the gospel's sake, for you to capture or occupy the city or place; on the contrary, let the ruler have his city, you follow the gospel."[76]

Shortly after writing the *Admonition*, Luther learned more about the peasants' revolt and, horrified by its scale and violence, quickly penned his

short and infamous tract *Against the Robbing and Murdering Hordes of Peasants*. Now that the revolt was underway, Luther urged the princes to stamp
it out, saying things like "Anyone who is killed fighting on the side of the
rulers may be a true martyr in the eyes of God," and "let everyone who can,
smite, slay, and stab, secretly or openly, remembering that nothing can be
more poisonous, hurtful, or devilish than a rebel."[77] The harshness of the
tract damaged Luther's reputation in reformation circles, especially given
that—as if on Luther's recommendation—the peasants were brutally
slaughtered. At the urging of his friends, Luther eventually wrote *An Open
Letter on the Harsh Book against the Peasants*, in which he explained, but essentially reaffirmed, the position he had taken in *Against the Peasants*.[78]

The Peasants' War put Luther on public record as opposing not only
rebellion but any sort of resistance against a superior authority. Given Luther's enormous prestige, this had obvious and unsettling implications for
the evangelical princes, who feared the emperor might move against them.
Not everyone in the Lutheran camp shared Luther's view, however. As
early as 1523 the Elector of Saxony had asked theologians in Wittenberg
to author "opinions" (*Gutachten*) about whether it was permissible to resist
the emperor in cases of religious persecution. Although Luther answered
this question negatively, the other theologians, including important figures
such as Philipp Melanchthon and Nikolaus von Amsdorf, offered more
qualified answers that seemed to allow for the possibility of resisting the
emperor in certain circumstances.[79] Over time, these members of the Wittenberg circle appeared to have brought Luther over to their point of view.

The Later Luther on Resistance

The Diet of Augsburg marks the turning point in Luther's thinking about
resistance. The Edict of Worms, which condemned Luther and his teaching, had never been successfully enforced. At the 1526 Diet of Speyer the
imperial estates agreed to allow individual princes to decide about religious
practices in their own territories. The evangelicals were thus free to imple-
ment changes to worship in their territories, which contributed to the
spread of the Reformation.[80] However, as the political challenges posed by
the French and the Ottomans receded, Emperor Charles V redirected his
attention to the affairs of the empire and moved to end its religious divisions. In 1530 he convened the Diet of Augsburg. The Lutherans drafted

the Augsburg Confession, which they read in front of the Diet. After they had finished, Charles ordered the Catholic theologians to refute it, which they did six weeks later, producing the so-called *Confutation*. Before he would permit the Lutherans to examine the *Confutation*, however, Charles ordered them to acknowledge they had been refuted. When attempts at negotiation failed, the Diet concluded with the Augsburg Recess, which gave the Protestants six months to submit to the Diet or face military action by the emperor.[81]

The Lutheran princes assembled in Torgau to consider again the question of resistance. The Wittenberg theologians were asked for their opinion, and this time, in the so-called Torgau Declaration, they unambiguously affirmed a right of resistance against the emperor. Although Luther did not author the declaration, he signed it, thereby clearing the path for the formation of the Schmalkaldic League.[82] Luther's change of mind was brought about by a legal argument. Jurists in the Lutheran camp argued that the emperor was constitutionally prohibited from moving against the princes as long as their case had not been decided by the appropriate imperial bodies. If the emperor acted illegally, then the imperial constitution — so argued the jurists — granted the princes a right of defense. In the words of the theologians who wrote the Torgau Declaration, "In previously teaching that resistance to governmental authorities is altogether forbidden, we were unaware that this right has been granted by the government's own laws, which we have diligently taught are to be obeyed at all times."[83] Luther's new position on resistance thus hinged on a contingency within positive law.[84]

At the same time, Luther's willingness to entertain the possibility that the emperor could act unconstitutionally led him to think more thoroughly about the nature of rebellion. In particular, he considered the possibility that a ruler himself could rebel against the estate of government. This idea begins to emerge in Luther's *Warning to His Dear German People*, published soon after the Torgau Declaration. As Luther explained, not every violation of the law is rebellion; rather, rebellion is an attack on government and law itself. Should the emperor and the Catholic camp start a war, they would violate imperial law. They would also be violating divine law, since the point of the war would be to impose religion by force. Because they were attacking human and divine law, "the papists are much closer to the name and the quality which is termed rebellion."[85] To resist the emperor in this circumstance would not be an attack on the estate of government, but an act of defense, and "self-defense against the [papists] cannot be rebellious."[86]

The argument of the *Warning* nevertheless depended heavily on the analysis of the jurists, which one imagines made Luther uncomfortable. To be secure, the right to resistance needed to rest squarely on theological ground. Luther attempted to provide that ground in 1539 in the *Circular Disputation on Matthew 19:21*.[87] This disputation concerns ninety-one theses related to the rich young man told by Christ to give up his wealth, a story Luther somehow used to examine the right of resistance. The progression of the theses is strange in places and difficult to follow, which may help to explain why the *Circular Disputation* has never been translated into English despite its importance.[88]

A crucial argument in the *Circular Disputation* centers on the relationship of the papacy to the three estates. God, Luther says, has established three estates as a bulwark against the devil: *ecclesia, oeconomica*, and *politia*. The pope does not belong to any of these estates. Much to the contrary, he seeks to destroy them. The pope attacks the ecclesial estate by condemning the gospel and trampling on it with canon law; he attacks the estate of government by subjecting civil law to his authority; and he attacks the household estate by prohibiting from marriage those who are free to marry. The pope is thus the monster described by the prophet Daniel, the adversary of God, who seeks to overturn God's will for creation; or to put it succinctly, the pope is the antichrist. The Germans talk of a werewolf, a wolf possessed by a demon, who seeks to destroy everything in his path. When the werewolf comes, one must drive him out.[89]

The prohibition against resistance does not apply to the antichrist. Thus, if the pope starts a war, the princes can resist. The same applies to the emperor if he should start a war on behalf of the pope. In that case, the emperor would become a tool of the pope, placing himself outside the estate of secular government.[90] Luther reiterates this line of argument in a letter from the same period addressed to a certain Johannes Ludicke. Responding to concerns about the legitimacy of resisting the emperor, Luther writes, "The emperor has no cause against the princes as emperor, but the pope would like to make use of a false cause to entangle the emperor in a dangerous war. . . . Therefore, our side has decided that in such a case the emperor would not be the emperor, but a soldier and bandit of the pope."[91]

The scholar Johannes Heckel has argued that Luther held a complex "doctrine of the tyrant" that became clear in the *Circular Disputation*. According to Heckel, Luther distinguished between petty tyrants and world tyrants. The petty tyrant commits acts of injustice but retains the authority of his office. One cannot rebel against a petty tyrant. The world tyrant, however, represents a qualitative difference. He is defined not only by his "unlimited craving for power" but also by "the revolutionary, all-encompassing dimension of his governing principles."[92] The world tyrant assaults the principle of law itself, disregards the two kingdoms, and seeks to overturn God's order of creation. He is an aspiring totalitarian dictator. Against such a world tyrant, one must resist.

Heckel, however, has not won over many with this elegant interpretation.[93] Others, like Hermann Dörries, see the argument in the *Circular Disputation* as restricted narrowly to the sixteenth-century papacy.[94] The truth perhaps lies somewhere in between. Admittedly, Luther's justification of resistance depends on a premise—the pope is the antichrist—which is difficult to generalize for those who do not share his apocalyptic worldview. Nevertheless, the elements of a generalizable doctrine of resistance can be found in Luther's thought and might be formulated as follows: the duty to obey secular authority derives from its mandate as a divine order. When those holding political office turn against that mandate, the obligation to obey no longer applies and one may resist. Not every act of injustice places on officeholder outside the divine mandate, however. The tyrant must attack the orders of creation themselves, seeking to overthrow them, placing his own will against God's will for creation.

Admittedly, Luther never articulated his doctrine of resistance this clearly and succinctly. He did, however, clear the path for other theologians in the Wittenberg circle to develop arguments for a right of resistance immediately after Luther's death.

The Lutheran Doctrine of Resistance

Emperor Charles V finally moved against the Protestants in 1546, shortly after Luther's death, in what is called the Smalcald War. The Protestants were beaten decisively at the Battle of Mühlberg, whereupon Charles V issued the Augsburg Interim, reimposing Catholic worship throughout the empire. Lutherans who refused to accept the Interim fled to the city of

Magdeburg, which was placed under siege by Duke Maurice (Moritz) of
Ducal Saxony. However, the sweeping dictates of the Interim as well as
the emperor's harsh and dubious treatment of two captured Protestant
princes elicited resentment throughout the empire. Even Catholic princes
viewed Charles's actions as unconstitutional and feared for their liberties.
Suddenly, Duke Maurice switched allegiance to the Protestants, abandoned the siege of Magdeburg, and drove the emperor's forces out of Germany. This led to the 1555 Peace of Augsburg, which annulled the Interim
and granted Lutheranism legal status in the empire.

As the Smalcald War unfolded, Lutheran theologians produced two
significant documents developing what is sometimes called the "lesser
magistrates doctrine." The first was a treatise titled *Von der Notwehr* (*On
Defense*), written in 1547 by Justus Menius and Philipp Melanchthon.
The second was the Magdeburg Confession, written in 1550 by Lutherans
under siege in the city of Magdeburg. Both documents reflect the influence
of Luther's *Warning* and the *Circular Disputation*, but they develop their
arguments in a way that is more systematic, coherent, and compelling.

On Defense argues in a way that Luther did not for a natural right of
self-defense, while at the same time following Luther's analysis of secular
government. According to the treatise, government has been ordained by
God to preserve external peace and to punish the wicked, not to command things contrary to divine law. When government commands false
worship, it steps outside its divine mandate and turns against the first table
of the Decalogue. To obey such an authority would be to commit idolatry.
But Christians are to obey God rather than human beings. Confronted
with a superior authority that commands idolatry, each Christian must
resist as he is able, according to his office. Although the church itself has
no defense and must heed the Sermon on the Mount, God has ordained
secular authority for the protection of the church. Thus, if the emperor
moves against the church to impose false religion, the princes should exercise their office to defend the church.[95]

The doctrine of resistance developed in the Magdeburg Confession
builds on Luther's concept of three estates.[96] God has established three
estates, each with a distinct task that should not be mixed with the others.
When secular authority persecutes true piety, it ceases to be an ordinance
of God and becomes an ordinance of the devil. Emperor Charles V seeks
to spread religion with the use of his weapons. This exceeds the boundaries

of his office and encroaches upon the dominion of Christ.[97] To resist such encroachment is not rebellion against God's ordinance. Admittedly, all governments do wrong, and simple injuries do not justify resistance; however, some wrongs surpass even tyranny. When a magistrate turns against what is true and right itself and persecutes God in an attempt to destroy all good works, he becomes the antichrist.[98] In this extreme case, the leader must be curbed by all with whatever power they possess.

This so-called lesser magistrate doctrine is commonly attributed to Calvinism. In point of fact, it was developed before Calvin by Luther and the Wittenberg circle. Some historians have suggested that the Lutheran doctrine of resistance was transmitted to Geneva via the Magdeburg Confession, which influenced Theodore Beza.[99] From Beza the teaching traveled to Scotland, from Scotland to England, and from England to the American colonies. Admittedly, tracing the lines of historical transmission is difficult and sometimes impossible, but even if we do not give Luther credit for the American Declaration of Independence, we can recognize that the doctrine of resistance he developed with the Wittenberg circle constitutes a major contribution to the history of Christian political thought.

THE TRADITION OF LUTHERAN POLITICAL THOUGHT AND LUTHERAN CHURCHES TODAY

As the preceding discussion makes clear, the tradition of Lutheran political thought is rich and substantial. One might suppose it provides an abundance of resources for thinking theologically about war and peace. Yet Lutherans today bear an uncomfortable relationship to their past, largely because of the legacy of Nazi Germany. Ambivalence about their history can make Lutherans reluctant to draw upon their spiritual heritage when thinking about politics. Lutherans, additionally, are hindered in adopting a distinctive stance on political questions for ecclesiological reasons. Unlike the Roman Catholic Church, Lutheran churches do not have a magisterium with the authority to speak definitively on matters of faith and morals. Although Lutheran ecclesiastical leaders exercise oversight within their churches and may (on rare occasions) enforce church discipline, they cannot issue proclamations that bind on conscience the way a pope can. A Lutheran who runs afoul of his or her bishop does not inevitably enter into a dissenting relationship with orthodox Lutheranism. Orthodox Lutheranism is articulated first and foremost in the Augsburg Confession, and to a lesser extent in the writings in the *Book of Concord*. The Augsburg Confession contains an article on civil government that affirms government's right to wage just wars, an affirmation repeated in passing elsewhere in the *Book of Concord*. These affirmations, however, are quite general. Although one might expect Lutherans to be informed by their own tradition when speaking to politics, there are very few affirmations about government and war to which they are confessionally committed.

Even so, Lutheran churches do issue statements on questions of war and peace expressing official positions of some sort, which do not, however, articulate the *official Lutheran Doctrine*. The largely unofficial character of these statements makes them difficult to interpret theologically. They can be understood in at least two ways. One possibility is that the statements are addressed internally to church members. In this case, their purpose might be to educate Lutheran laypeople into their own tradition. Given that Lutheran church leaders do not have the authority to issue doctrinal judgments on questions pertaining to government's use of force, the statements they make would seek to do no more than lay out theological principles to inform the conscience of Lutherans deliberating about matters of public import. Understood this way, church statements are more like study documents than doctrinal pronouncements. They exercise dogmatic restraint, leaving final judgment on the questions they take up to the conscience of individual believers.

A second possibility, however, is that the churches issuing these statements understand themselves to be speaking on behalf of their members to the wider world in the voice of the church. In this case, the statements aim to influence and shape public opinion. To shape public opinion, they also need to address controverted questions with a specificity that goes beyond general principles. Since conscientious people who share the same principles can, and often do, disagree about how best to apply them, statements articulating practical judgments run the risk of expressing the private views of those who have written them, rather than the position of the church understood theologically as the people and body of Christ.[100]

Crafting and issuing church statements is, therefore, a difficult theological task, and we might ask of any Lutheran church statement the following questions: To what extent does the statement draw upon the Lutheran tradition? Does it articulate general principles or seek to make specific policy proposals? If the statement offers specific policy proposals, does it do so with theological authority in the voice of the church? Or does it echo the prevailing view among certain social constituencies? My own tentative observations about Lutheran statements, based on review of a number of them, follow below.

Specifically, I reviewed *For Peace in God's World* (Evangelical Lutheran Church in America), *Vulnerability and Security* (Church of Norway), and *Aus Gottes Frieden leben—für gerechten Frieden sorgen* ("To live from God's peace—to work for just peace," from the EKD, or Lutheran Church in Germany). Each of these statements invokes just war categories, accepts Luther's limitation of just cause to defense, and endorses a moral right of selective conscientious objection. Generally, however, the statements propose modifications or reinterpretations of the just war criteria. *For Peace in God's World* refers to the "just/unjust war tradition," which, according to the statement, begins "with a strong presumption against all war"—a formulation that may echo Luther less than it does a particular interpretation of just war theory originating with James Childress and ethicists trained at the University of Chicago and widely embraced in our day.[101] *Vulnerability and Security* discusses the criteria of just cause, just intention, rightful authority, last resort, and proportionality at some length, adding that the criteria alone are not sufficient to evaluate morally the use of force. Although these statements offer interpretations of just war theory that go beyond Luther, they do so modestly in a plausible effort to bring the Lutheran tradition up to date with the modern world. Far bolder revisions of the just war criteria are proposed in the *Denkschrift* (document) issued by the Lutheran Church in Germany (EKD).

The German statement is written with a level of rigor, precision, and care that at times rivals a papal encyclical. The very thoroughness of the document may have emboldened its authors to move far beyond Luther to embrace a vision of international relations that appears heavily influenced by Immanuel Kant. According to the EKD document, world peace cannot be achieved through an international order composed of independent sovereign states. Neither, however, can it be achieved with a world state. Rather, the path to peace lies in a cooperative international order with mutual rights and duties regulated by international laws and institutions—an argument very much resembling Kant's view in *Perpetual Peace*.[102] According to the church document, modern international law has made the concept of just war obsolete, even if the moral principles that inspired the just war criteria still have use and validity.[103] This strong internationalist vision, although certainly defensible, is also highly controversial (at least outside Germany), a fact that might cause readers to wonder if the document is written more with a German voice than in the voice of the church.

All three of these statements allude in various ways to the two kingdoms distinction, while at the same time downplaying key parts of that teaching. *For Peace in God's World* and *Aus Gottes Frieden leben* locate the question of war within the framework of God's eschatological peace. The emphasis on peace is certainly Lutheran, but Luther himself distinguished more sharply than the statements do between earthly, temporal peace and divine peace. In Luther's thought the fragility of temporal peace arises from the sinful character of the kingdom of earth, and this is the reason that government must use the sword. If Luther believed government's use of force was an inevitable and necessary part of God's work of preservation, contemporary Lutheran statements mostly bypass that part of Luther's thought. Instead, they invoke the two kingdoms distinction to establish that war must have a secular character. According to *Aus Gottes Frieden leben*, the distinction between God's two types of government rules out wars of religion as well as wars waged with ideological objectives.[104] According to *Vulnerability and Security*, Luther's rejection of the crusade excludes wars of religion and also calls into question nationalism.[105] These applications of the two kingdoms doctrine in the latter document are unforced and authentic, even when they skirt around some of the more pessimistic implications of Luther's doctrine—in particular, his view that war and conflict are inevitable so long as the kingdom of earth remains.

None of the three statements mentions Luther's theory of the estates. Perhaps it seems too medieval; or perhaps it has been tainted by historical association with older theological defenses of Hitler. Interestingly enough, however, the American statement evinces traces of the theory, without referring to it explicitly. According to *For Peace in God's World*, "Building earthly peace encompasses all the dimensions of human society."[106] Human society, in turn, can be broken down into three spheres—culture, economics, and politics—which is clearly reminiscent of, if also a little different from, Luther's *ecclesia*, *oeconomica*, and *politia*. After identifying three societal spheres, however, the ELCA statement does not employ the concepts in any meaningful way.

One might say of all the statements that they make use of the Lutheran political tradition in a genuine, but limited and selective, way. The Lutheran tradition, it needs emphasizing, is deeper, richer, and more important than the church documents convey. Luther contributed more directly to the development of modern just war theory than many Christian just war thinkers who have been given more credit. He wrote more on the problem of war and resistance, for example, than either Augustine or Aquinas, two figures touted as fountainheads of the Christian just war tradition. Luther's rejection of the crusade, his restriction of just cause to defense, his endorsement of conscientious objection, and his seminal arguments about the right to resist political authority were major innovations to the just war tradition that also helped change the trajectory of European history. Few theologians can claim more influence.

Luther's political theology, however, is universally—and tragically—underappreciated. This is due in part to a facile Anglo-American scholarly consensus about Luther that developed in the decades after World War II. Just as importantly, however, it is the fault of Lutherans who have failed to know their own tradition and represent it well. As the distortions in Luther scholarship produced by the cataclysmic events of the twentieth century recede into the past, one hopes that the true legacy of the Lutheran political tradition will receive both the attention and recognition it deserves. It remains to be determined whether Lutherans will rediscover the richness of their tradition—a tradition that is rooted in both Augustinian and Thomistic affirmations of a conversation on war and peace that stretches over the last two millennia in the Western cultural heritage.

NOTES

1. The history of this gross mischaracterization is well documented in Uwe Siemon-Netto, *The Fabricated Luther: Refuting Nazi Connections and Other Modern Myths*, 2nd ed. (St. Louis: Concordia, 2007), esp. chap. 2. A typically crude caricature of Luther by a well-respected scholar can be found in Alasdair MacIntyre, *A Short History of Ethics: A History of Moral Philosophy from the Homeric Age to the Twentieth Century* (New York: Macmillan Publishing Company, 1966), 121–45.

2. Martin Luther, *D. Martin Luthers Werke*, Kritische Gesamtausgabe, 120 vols., Weimar ed. (Weimar: Hermann Böhlau, 1883–2009). Hereafter referred to as WA.

3. Peter H. Wilson, *Heart of Europe: A History of the Holy Roman Empire* (Cambridge, MA: Belknap Press of Harvard University Press, 2016), 1.

4. Ibid., 44.

5. Over the last few decades historians have adopted the convention of referring to Protestant *reformations* in the plural, rather than *the* Protestant Reformation. The rationale for this new usage is that the different Protestant groups that emerged around the time of Luther, despite sharing similarities, also shared differences. However, earlier scholars who used to refer to the Protestant *Reformation* with a collective noun were aware of the variegated character of sixteenth-century Protestant groups. The disagreement contemporary historians have with their teachers on this point concerns syntax rather than substance. I prefer the older English usage for reasons of style. For more on collective nouns, see George O. Curme, *A Grammar of the English Language*, vol. 2, *Syntax* (Essex, CT: Verbatim, 1983; first published 1931), 539–40. On imperial reform in the Holy Roman Empire, see Wilson, *Heart of Europe*, 396–420.

6. Straightforward narrative accounts of the course of the Lutheran reformation are hard to come by. See, however, Carter Lindberg, *The European Reformations* (Malden, MA: Blackwell, 1996). A good narrative is also provided in the old classic by Will Durant, *The Story of Civilization*, vol. 6, *The Reformation: A History of European Civilization from Wyclif to Calvin; 1300–1564* (New York: Simon & Schuster, 1957), 438–58. See, as well, Harold J. Grimm, *The Reformation Era: 1500–1650* (New York: Macmillan, 1954; repr., 1965), 143–264.

7. Martin Brecht, *Martin Luther*, vol. 2, *Shaping and Defining the Reformation: 1521–1532*, trans. James L. Schaaf (Minneapolis: Fortress, 1990), 108.

8. The phrase "two kingdoms doctrine" was introduced into Luther scholarship only in the early twentieth century. More recent scholarship has tended to question the notion that Luther had a *doctrine* about the two kingdoms. Luther certainly distinguished between two kingdoms, but what he meant by that distinction and its importance to his overall political thought is a controverted matter. In this essay I use two kingdoms "doctrine" in a loose sense to refer to Luther's basic distinction, offering a reasonable interpretation of the relationship between the two kingdoms and the three estates that I hope is not too controversial. For more on this topic see Per Frostin, *Luther's Two Kingdoms Doctrine: A Critical Study* (Lund: Lund University Press, 1994).

9. For the view that the Augustinian character of the two kingdoms doctrine is overstated, see Ernst Kinder, "Gottesreich und Weltreich bei Augustin und bei Luther," in *Reich Gottes und Welt: Die Lehre Luthers von die Zwei Reichen,*

ed. Heins-Horst Shrey (Darmstadt: Wissenschaftliche Buchgesellscaft, 1969), 42–43; also, Eike Wolgast, *Die Wittenberger Theologie und die Politik der evangelischen Stände* (Gütersloh: Gütersloher Verlagshaus Mohn, 1977), 40–41.

10. *Temporal Authority: To What Extent It Should Be Obeyed*, in *Luther's Works* [hereafter *L.W.*], 45:88–93.

11. Here I interpret Luther's two kingdoms doctrine through the prism of his teaching on justification, and specifically, his concept *simul iustus et peccator* (simultaneously saint and sinner). This is the interpretative view of Eike Wolgast; see his "Luther's Treatment of Political and Societal Life," in *The Oxford Handbook of Martin Luther's Theology*, ed. Robert Kolb et al., (Oxford: Oxford University Press, 2014), 398–99. See, as well, W. D. J. Cargill Thompson, *The Political Thought of Martin Luther*, ed. Philip Broadhead (Sussex, UK: Harvester Press, 1984), 19–25.

12. Luther, *Temporal Authority*, 99.

13. Ibid., 95.

14. Martin Luther, *Whether Soldiers, Too, Can Be Saved*, in *L.W.*, 46:95.

15. Cf. Wolgast, *Die Wittenberger Theologie*, 43–44.

16. Wolgast, "Luther's Treatment of Political and Societal Life," 402.

17. Oswald Bayer, *Martin Luther's Theology: A Contemporary Interpretation*, trans. Thomas H. Trapp (Grand Rapids, MI: Eerdmans, 2008), 325.

18. Cf. ibid., 122–26.

19. Martin Luther, *Confession Concerning Christ's Supper*, in *L.W.*, 37:365.

20. Martin Luther, *Predigt am Michaelstage, 29 September 1539*, in WA, 47:854, lines 2–21.

21. An interpretation somewhat along these lines is suggested by John Witte Jr., *Law and Protestantism: The Legal Teachings of the Lutheran Reformation* (Cambridge: Cambridge University Press, 2002), 89–94.

22. Franz Lau, *Luthers Lehre von den beiden Reichen* (Berlin: Lutherisches Verlagshaus, 1953), 55–57.

23. Wilson, *Heart of Europe*, 87.

24. Bayer, *Martin Luther's Theology*, 142.

25. Martin Luther, Large Catechism, 1.141, in *The Book of Concord: The Confessions of the Evangelical Lutheran Church*, ed. Robert Kolb and Timothy J. Wengert (Minneapolis: Fortress, 2000), 405.

26. Luther, *Predigt am Michaelstage*, in WA, 47:854, lines 7–8.

27. Luther, *Temporal Authority*, 86.

28. Martin Luther, *Genesisvorlesung* [*Commentary on Genesis*], in WA, 42:79, lines 7–8, 12 (my translation). The text reads: *Politia autem ante peccatum nulla fuit, neque enim ea opus fuit.... Hoc enim unum et pracipiuum agit Politia, ut peccatum arceat.* See also *L.W.*, 1:104.

29. Luther, Large Catechism, 1.150 (*Book of Concord*, 407).

30. Franz Lau believes Luther understood government as an "order of creation"; see Lau, *Luthers Lehre*, 35–38. Wolgast, *Die Wittenberger Theologie*, 48, disagrees. Paul Althaus thought Luther's view shifted over time from a narrow view of government as responding to sin to a broader view of government fulfilling additional tasks; see Althaus, *The Ethics of Martin Luther*, trans. Robert C. Schultz (Philadelphia: Fortress, 1972), 51–56.

31. A solution along these lines may be what John T. Pless suggests in his entry "Three Estates" in *Dictionary of Luther and the Lutheran Traditions*, ed. Timothy J. Wengert et al. (Grand Rapids, MI: Baker Academic, 2017), 744–46. Pless notes: "Government, according to Luther, was established in creation out of the household, but the state is established after the fall" (745).

32. Wolgast, *Die Wittenberger Theologie*, 45–47.

33. Boniface VIII, *Unam sanctam*, cited in Brian Tierney, *The Crisis of Church and State, 1050–1300* (Toronto: University of Toronto Press, 1988), 189.

34. Martin Luther, *To the Christian Nobility of the German Nation concerning the Reform of the Christian Estate*, in *L.W.*, 44:130.

35. Ibid., 104.

36. Ibid., 111.

37. Luther, *Temporal Authority*, 114.

38. Luther, *Whether Soldiers*, 95.

39. Ibid.

40. See Brecht, *Martin Luther*, 353–55; Wolgast, *Die Wittenberger Theologie*, 108–14.

41. See the introduction to *Whether Soldiers*, by Robert Schultz, in *L.W.*, 46:90; the introduction is also found in WA, 19:616.

42. Luther, *Whether Soldiers*, 103–8.

43. Ibid., 126.

44. Ibid., 125.

45. Ibid., 118.

46. See Brecht, *Martin Luther*, 352–55; Wolgast, *Die Wittenberger Theologie*, 108–14.

47. Max Weber, "Politics as Vocation," in *From Max Weber: Essays in Sociology*, ed. and trans. H. H. Gerth and C. Wright Mills (New York: Oxford University Press, 1946), 78.

48. Luther, *Whether Soldiers*, 126.

49. James Turner Johnson, *Sovereignty: Moral and Historical Perspectives* (Washington, DC: Georgetown University Press, 2014), 19.

50. Karl Dietrich Erdmann, *Luther über den gerechten und ungerechten Krieg* (Göttingen: Vandenhoeck & Ruprecht, 1984), 13–14.

51. Ibid., 24–25.

52. Luther, *Whether Soldiers*, 126 (WA, 19:652, lines 25–27, 29–31; I have modified the translation in *L.W.*).

53. Luther's understanding of the sovereign's right of war complicates the historical narrative related by James Turner Johnson. Johnson writes: "For Aquinas (and for medieval and early modern just war thought as a whole), the sovereign's obligation to punish evildoing, which is not limited in his discussion to internal disturbances within his own political community but extends to externals as well, might justify the use of the sword against tyrannical rulers over other political communities" (*Sovereignty*, 33). This, however, is not Luther's view.

54. Franz Lau, *"Äußerliche Ordnung" und "weltlich Ding" in Luthers Theologie* (Göttingen: Vandenhoeck & Ruprecht, 1933), 132–33.

55. Wolgast, *Die Wittenberger Theologie*, 57.

56. Martin Luther, *On War against the Turk*, in *L.W.*, 46:166.

57. Ibid., 168.

58. Ibid., 185. See also Wolgast, *Die Wittenberger Theologie*, 57; Erdmann, *Luther über den gerechten und ungerechten Krieg*, 21–23.

59. Luther, *On War against the Turk*, 185.

60. Ibid., 178.

61. Ibid., 181.

62. Brecht, *Martin Luther*, 366.

63. Luther, *On War against the Turk*, 182.

64. Ibid., 197–98.

65. Ibid., 198.

66. Luther, *Temporal Authority*, 101–3.

67. Martin Luther, *Against the Robbing and Murdering Hordes of Peasants* (hereafter *Against the Peasants*), in *L.W.*, 46:50.

68. Luther, *Temporal Authority*, 112.

69. Luther, *Whether Soldiers*, 130.

70. See Brecht, *Martin Luther*, 146–57.

71. Martin Luther, *Admonition to Peace: A Reply to the Twelve Articles of the Peasants in Swabia*, in *L.W.*, 46:20.

72. Brecht, *Martin Luther*, 174.

73. Luther, *Admonition to Peace*, 29.

74. Ibid., 27.

75. Ibid., 36.

76. Ibid.

77. Ibid., 53, 50.

78. Martin Luther, *An Open Letter on the Harsh Book against the Peasants*, in *L.W.*, 46:68–80.

79. See the discussion in Hermann Dörries, *Wort und Stunde* (Göttingen: Vandenhoeck & Ruprecht, 1970), 3:196–203.

80. Lindberg, *European Reformations*, 233–34.

81. Ibid., 240–41; Brecht, *Martin Luther*, 407.

82. See Dörries, *Wort und Stunde*, 3:215–24, as well as the helpful summary found in the editors' preface to Martin Luther, *Dr. Martin Luther's Warning to His Dear German People*, in *L. W.*, 47:5–10.

83. An English translation of the Torgau Declaration is included in the introduction to *Dr. Martin Luther's Warning*, 8. The text is available in more modernized German in *Dr. Martin Luther's Sämmtliche Schriften* (St. Louis: Concordia Publishing House, 1885), 10:562–63.

84. Luther discusses his reasons for signing the Torgau Declaration in a letter to Lazarus Spengler. See Martin Luther to Lazarus Spengler, February 15, 1531, in *L. W.*, 50:9–12 (letter 239).

85. Luther, *Dr. Martin Luther's Warning*, in *L. W.*, 47:20.

86. Ibid.

87. Martin Luther, *Zirkulardisputation über Matth. 19,21* [*Circular Disputation on Matthew 19:21*], in WA, 39.II:34–91.

88. Although the *Circular Disputation* is discussed frequently in the German literature, it is not well known in English. One discussion in English of Luther's evolving stance on resistance is found in Thompson, *Political Thought of Martin Luther*, 91–111.

89. Luther, *Zirkulardisputation über Matth. 19,21*, theses 51–60, in WA, 39.II:42.

90. See Rudolf Hermann, "Luthers Zirkulardisputation über Matth. 19,21," *Luther-Jahrbuch* 23 (1941): 88–89.

91. Martin Luther to Johannes Ludicke, February 18, 1539, in WA, Br 8:367, lines 18–20, 23–24 (letter 3297; my translation). The text reads: *Nihil enim habet Caesar contra principes causae ut Caesar, sed papa vult habere non causas pro causis et ita Caesarem involvere periculoso bello. . . . Ideo nostri iudicarunt Caesarem in hoc casu non Caesarem esse, sed militem et latronem papae.*

92. Johannes Heckel, *Lex Charitatis: A Juristic Disquisition on Law in the Theology of Martin Luther*, ed. and trans. Gottfried G. Krodel (Grand Rapids, MI: Eerdmans, 2010), 113.

93. However, recently Michael P. DeJonge has followed Heckel's analysis fairly closely. See Michael P. DeJonge, *Bonhoeffer's Reception of Luther* (Oxford: Oxford University Press, 2017), 190–95. See also DeJonge's discussion of the *Circular Disputation* in the same volume (250–54).

94. Dörries, *Wort und Stunde*, 3:251–53.

95. Philipp Melanchthon and Justus Menius, *Von der Notwehr*, in *Politischer Widerstand als Protestantische Option*, ed. Hans-Otto Schneider (Leipzig: Evangelische Verlagsanstalt, 2014), 45–85. For more on the history and significance of this treatise, see Luther D. Peterson, "Justus Menius, Philipp Melanchthon,

and the 1547 Treatise, *Von der Notwehr Unterricht,*" *Archiv für Reformationsgeschichte* 81 (1990): 138–57.

96. David M. Whitford does an admirable job demonstrating the elements of continuity between Luther and the Magdeburg Confession; see Whitford, *Tyranny and Resistance: The Magdeburg Confession and the Lutheran Tradition* (St. Louis: Concordia, 2001). Whitford does not, however, discuss the *Circular Disputation,* despite its clear influence on the Magdeburg Confession, and in my view downplays the shifts in Luther's thinking.

97. The Magdeburg Confession, trans. Matthew Colvin (North Charleston, SC: CreateSpace, 2012), 52.

98. Ibid., 59.

99. See Oliver K. Olson, "Theology of Revolution: Magdeburg, 1550–1551," *Sixteenth Century Journal* 3, no. 1 (1972): 56–79; John Witte, *The Reformation of Rights: Law, Religion, and Human Rights in Early Modern Calvinism* (Cambridge: Cambridge University Press, 2007), 106–12.

100. My discussion in the preceding two paragraphs draws heavily on Paul Ramsey, "Speaking on Particulars for the Church to the Church and World," in *Speak Up for Just War or Pacifism: A Critique of the United Methodist Bishops' Pastoral Letter "In Defense of Creation"* (University Park: Pennsylvania State University Press, 1988), 125–47.

101. *For Peace in God's World* (adopted by the Evangelical Lutheran Church in America in 1995), section 4.A (page 11), https://download.elca.org/ELCA%20Resource%20Repository/PeaceSS.pdf. For the "particular interpretation," see James F. Childress, "Just War Theories: The Bases, Interrelations, Priorities, and Functions of Their Criteria," *Theological Studies* 39 (1978): 427–45. For a prominent representative of the "Chicago School," see Lisa Cahill, *Blessed Are the Peacemakers: Pacifism, Just War, and Peacebuilding* (Minneapolis: Fortress, 2019).

102. *Aus Gottes Frieden leben—für gerechten Frieden sorgen: Eine Denkschrift des Rates der Evangelischen Kirche in Deutschland* (Gütersloh: Gütersloher Verlagshaus, 2007), 57–58 (para. 86). See, in this regard, Immanuel Kant, *Perpetual Peace,* ed. and trans. Lewis White Beck, Library of Liberal Arts (Indianapolis: Bobbs-Merrill, 1965).

103. *Aus Gottes Frieden leben,* 68–70 (para. 102).

104. Ibid., 65–66 (para. 98).

105. *Vulnerability and Security: Current Challenges in Security Policy from an Ethical and Theological Perspective* (Commission on International Affairs in Church of Norway Council on Ecumenical and International Relations, n.d. [ca. 2002]), section 3.4, https://kirken.no/globalassets/kirken.no/church-of-norway/dokumenter/kisp_vulnerab_00.pdf.

106. *For Peace in God's World,* section 4.A (page 9).

WORKS CITED

Althaus, Paul. *The Ethics of Martin Luther*. Translated by Robert C. Schultz. Philadelphia: Fortress, 1972.

Aus Gottes Frieden leben—für gerechten Frieden sorgen: Eine Denkschrift des Rates der Evangelischen Kirche in Deutschland. Gütersloh: Gütersloher Verlagshaus, 2007.

Bayer, Oswald. *Martin Luther's Theology: A Contemporary Interpretation*. Translated by Thomas H. Trapp. Grand Rapids, MI: Eerdmans, 2008.

Brecht, Martin. *Martin Luther*. Vol. 2, *Shaping and Defining the Reformation: 1521–1532*. Translated by James L. Schaaf. Minneapolis: Fortress, 1990.

Cahill, Lisa. *Blessed Are the Peacemakers: Pacifism, Just War, and Peacebuilding*. Minneapolis: Fortress, 2019.

Childress, James F. "Just War Theories: The Bases, Interrelations, Priorities, and Functions of Their Criteria." *Theological Studies* 39 (1978): 427–45.

Curme, George O. *A Grammar of the English Language*. Vol. 2, *Syntax*. Essex, CT: Verbatim, 1983. First published 1931.

DeJonge, Michael P. *Bonhoeffer's Reception of Luther*. Oxford: Oxford University Press, 2017.

Demy, Timothy J., Mark J. Larson, and J. Daryl Charles. *The Reformers on War, Peace, and Justice*. Eugene, OR: Pickwick, 2019.

Dörries, Hermann. *Wort und Stunde*. Vol. 3. Göttingen: Vandenhoeck & Ruprecht, 1970.

Durant, Will. *The Story of Civilization*. Vol. 6, *The Reformation: A History of European Civilization from Wyclif to Calvin; 1300–1564*. New York: Simon & Schuster, 1957.

Erdmann, Karl Dietrich. *Luther über den gerechten und ungerechten Krieg*. Göttingen: Vandenhoeck & Ruprecht, 1984.

For Peace in God's World. Adopted by the Evangelical Lutheran Church in America in 1995. https://download.elca.org/ELCA%20Resource%20Repository/PeaceSS.pdf.

Frostin, Per. *Luther's Two Kingdoms Doctrine: A Critical Study*. Lund: Lund University Press, 1994.

Grimm, Harold J. *The Reformation Era: 1500–1650*. New York: Macmillan, 1954. Reprint, 1965.

Heckel, Johannes. *Lex Charitatis: A Juristic Disquisition on Law in the Theology of Martin Luther*. Edited and translated by Gottfried G. Krodel. Grand Rapids, MI: Eerdmans, 2010.

Hermann, Rudolf. "Luthers Zirkulardisputation über Matth. 19,21." *Luther-Jahrbuch* 23 (1941): 35–93.

Johnson, James Turner. *Sovereignty: Moral and Historical Perspectives.* Washington, DC: Georgetown University Press, 2014.

Kant, Immanuel. *Perpetual Peace.* Edited and translated by Lewis White Beck. Library of Liberal Arts. Indianapolis: Bobbs-Merrill, 1965.

Kinder, Ernst. "Gottesreich und Weltreich bei Augustin und bei Luther." In *Reich Gottes und Welt: Die Lehre Luthers von die Zwei Reichen,* edited by Heinz-Horst Shrey, 40–69. Darmstadt: Wissenschaftliche Buchgesellscaft, 1969.

Kolb, Robert, and Timothy J. Wengert, eds. *The Book of Concord: The Confessions of the Evangelical Lutheran Church.* Minneapolis: Fortress, 2000.

Lau, Franz. *"Äußerliche Ordnung" und "weltlich Ding" in Luthers Theologie.* Göttingen: Vandenhoeck & Ruprecht, 1933.

———. *Luthers Lehre von den beiden Reichen.* Berlin: Lutherisches Verlagshaus, 1953.

Lindberg, Carter. *The European Reformations.* Malden, MA: Blackwell, 1996.

Luther, Martin. *Admonition to Peace: A Reply to the Twelve Articles of the Peasants in Swabia.* In *Luther's Works,* vol. 46, edited by Robert C. Schultz, 3–43. Philadelphia: Fortress, 1967.

———. *Against the Robbing and Murdering Hordes of Peasants.* In *Luther's Works,* vol. 46, edited by Robert C. Schultz, 45–55. Philadelphia: Fortress, 1967.

———. *Genesisvorlesung* [*Commentary on Genesis*]. In *Luthers Werke,* vols. 42–44.

———. *Confession Concerning Christ's Supper,* in *Luther's Works,* vol. 37, edited by Robert H. Fischer, 153–372. Philadelphia: Fortress, 1967.

———. *Luthers Werke.* Kritische Gesamtausgabe. Edited by J. F. K. Knaake et al. 120 vols. Weimar: Hermann Böhlau, 1883–2009.

———. *Dr. Martin Luther's Warning to His Dear German People.* In *Luther's Works,* vol. 47, edited by Franklin Sherman, 3–55. Philadelphia: Fortress, 1971.

———. Large Catechism. In *The Book of Concord: The Confessions of the Evangelical Lutheran Church,* edited by Robert Kolb and Timothy J. Wengert, 377–480. Minneapolis: Fortress, 2000.

———. *On War against the Turk.* In *Luther's Works,* vol. 46, edited by Robert C. Schultz, 155–205. Philadelphia: Fortress, 1967.

———. *An Open Letter on the Harsh Book against the Peasants.* In *Luther's Works,* vol. 46, edited by Robert C. Schultz, 68–80. Philadelphia: Fortress, 1967.

———. *Predigt am Michaelstage, 29 September 1539.* In *Luthers Werke,* 47:853–58.

———. *Temporal Authority: To What Extent It Should Be Obeyed.* In *Luther's Works,* vol. 45, edited by Walther I. Brandt, 81–129. Philadelphia: Fortress, 1962.

———. *To the Christian Nobility of the German Nation concerning the Reform of the Christian Estate.* In *Luther's Works,* vol. 44, edited by James Atkinson, 54–216. Philadelphia: Fortress, 1966.

————. *Whether Soldiers, Too, Can Be Saved.* In *Luther's Works*, vol. 46, edited by Robert C. Schultz, 87–138. Philadelphia: Fortress, 1967.

————. *Zirkulardisputation über Matth. 19,21* [*Circular Disputation on Matthew 19:21*]. In *Luthers Werke*, 39.II:34–91.

MacIntyre, Alasdair. *A Short History of Ethics: A History of Moral Philosophy from the Homeric Age to the Twentieth Century.* New York: Macmillan, 1966.

The Magdeburg Confession. Translated by Matthew Colvin. North Charleston, SC: CreateSpace, 2012.

Melanchthon, Philipp, and Justus Menius. *Von der Notwehr.* In *Politischer Widerstand als Protestantische Option*, edited by Hans-Otto Schneider, 45–85. Leipzig: Evangelische Verlagsanstalt, 2014.

Olson, Oliver K. "Theology of Revolution: Magdeburg, 1550–1551." *Sixteenth Century Journal* 3, no. 1 (1972): 56–79.

Peterson, Luther D. "Justus Menius, Philipp Melanchthon, and the 1547 Treatise *Von der Notwehr Unterricht.*" *Archiv für Reformationsgeschichte* 81 (1990): 138–57.

Pless, John T. "Three Estates." In *Dictionary of Luther and the Lutheran Traditions*, edited by Timothy J. Wengert et al., 744–46. Grand Rapids, MI: Baker Academic, 2017.

Ramsey, Paul. "Speaking on Particulars for the Church to the Church and World." In *Speak Up for Just War or Pacifism: A Critique of the United Methodist Bishops' Pastoral Letter "In Defense of Creation,"* 125–47. University Park: Pennsylvania State University Press, 1988.

Siemon-Netto, Uwe. *The Fabricated Luther: Refuting Nazi Connections and Other Modern Myths.* 2nd ed. St. Louis: Concordia, 2007.

Thompson, W. D. J. Cargill. *The Political Thought of Martin Luther.* Edited by Philip Broadhead. Sussex, UK: Harvester Press, 1984.

Tierney, Brian. *The Crisis of Church and State, 1050–1300.* Toronto: University of Toronto Press, 1988.

Torgau Declaration [German]. In *Dr. Martin Luther's Sämmtliche Schriften*, 10:562–63. St. Louis: Concordia Publishing House, 1885.

Vulnerability and Security: Current Challenges in Security Policy from an Ethical and Theological Perspective. Commission on International Affairs in Church of Norway Council on Ecumenical and International Relations, 2001. https://kirken.no/globalassets/kirken.no/church-of-norway/dokumenter/kisp_vulnerab_00.pdf.

Weber, Max. "Politics as Vocation." In *From Max Weber: Essays in Sociology*, edited and translated by H. H. Gerth and C. Wright Mills, 77–128. New York: Oxford University Press, 1946.

Whitford, David M. *Tyranny and Resistance: The Magdeburg Confession and the Lutheran Tradition.* St. Louis: Concordia, 2001.

Wilson, Peter H. *Heart of Europe: A History of the Holy Roman Empire*. Cambridge, MA: Belknap Press of Harvard University Press, 2016.

Witte, John, Jr., *Law and Protestantism: The Legal Teachings of the Lutheran Reformation*. Cambridge: Cambridge University Press, 2002.

———. *The Reformation of Rights: Law, Religion, and Human Rights in Early Modern Calvinism*. Cambridge: Cambridge University Press, 2007.

Wolgast, Eike. *Die Wittenberger Theologie und die Politik der evangelischen Stände*. Gütersloh: Gütersloher Verlagshaus Mohn, 1977.

———. "Luther's Treatment of Political and Societal Life." In *The Oxford Handbook of Martin Luther's Theology*, edited by Robert Kolb et al., 397–413. Oxford: Oxford University Press, 2014.

FIVE

John Calvin and the Reformed View of War, Resistance, and Political Duty

Keith J. Pavlischek

Ethicist Paul Ramsey famously insisted that the just war idea was part and parcel of a Christian theory of statecraft. By "statecraft" Ramsey meant to say that any understanding of the use of military force would be "an outgrowth, entailment, or expression of . . . the relation between force and political responsibility. Whether one moves 'from politics to war' or 'from war to politics,' it is statecraft that is crucial." At a time when just war thinking was thought to be a doctrine unique to Roman Catholicism, Ramsey insisted, to the contrary, that it is the "common possession of all the mainline churches — Lutheran and Calvinistic no less than Roman Catholic."[1] What, then, are the specific features or points of emphasis for the Reformed tradition as it pertains to statecraft, political theology, and just war thinking?

Any attempt to mine the Reformed contribution to the just war tradition must start with John Calvin himself. Calvin's influence on the theology (including the political theology) of not only Reformed and Presbyterian churches but also Protestant thought more generally is impossible to overestimate. The most important and influential figure in the second generation of the Protestant Reformation, Calvin profoundly influenced the thinking of Protestant Christianity during the tumultuous post-Reformation period primarily through his *Institutes of the Christian Religion* as well as through his widely distributed sermons, biblical commentaries, polemical tracts and pamphlets, and other formal writings.[2] Reformed thought on war and political responsibility does not stop with Calvin, but it certainly must start there. Two themes of Calvin's "political theology," or what we might call his "theology of statecraft," are particularly important for understanding Reformed thought on force and political responsibility. The first involves Calvin's views on a classical question of political philosophy, and specifically, his reflections on the nature or "forms" of "regime." Calvin's preference for a mixed regime, or a mixed republic, in contrast to either a monarchical or purely democratic polity, was crucial for his teaching that "magistrates of the people" (*populares magistratus*)[3] had a duty to serve as a check on tyranny, and by armed resistance if necessary. The second theme is Calvin's understanding, both in theory and in practice, of the distinct responsibilities—that is, "callings" or "vocations"—of ecclesiastical and civil authorities. Calvin's approach is neither theocratic—whereby political authorities are subordinate to ecclesiastical authorities—nor Erastian—whereby ecclesiastical authority and discipline are subservient to political authority.[4] Calvin's insistence on the distinction between "the two swords" would form the foundation of his opposition to certain medieval Roman Catholic understandings in which clergy, most notably the pope, would have authority to wage war. Calvin's notion of the "two swords" also distinguishes his own view of just war from the Erastian views of several of his Reformed contemporaries, most notably the Zürich theologian Heinrich Bullinger and a number of later Reformed Puritan thinkers.

CALVIN AND THE FORMS OF REGIME

In his introduction to Calvin's political thought in *John Calvin: On God and Political Duty*, John McNeill writes that Calvin "at times throughout his voluminous writings refuses to choose among the forms of government,"[5] since Calvin believed it to be idle speculation for those who have no part in determining the form of government to dispute about it. Calvin also refused to be dogmatic because, as McNeill observes, the biblical witness with regard to "the piety of some Bible Kings" would tend to exclude "any blanket denunciation" of monarchy as a form of government. "Good government under a king," notes McNeill, "is for him a possibility."[6]

And yet, throughout his writings, Calvin is "habitually severe in his judgment of kings of history and of his own time."[7] As early as the 1543 edition of the *Institutes*, Calvin would confidently assert that "aristocracy, or aristocracy tempered by democracy, far excels all other forms." Calvin retained this phrase in the final 1559 edition, supporting it on the ground that "justice, rectitude, and discernment are rare in kings." He then reinforces his criticism by adding the following: "The vice or inadequacy of men thus renders it safer and more tolerable that many [*plures*] hold the sway [*gubernacula*], so that they may mutually be helpers to each other, teach and admonish one another, and if one asserts himself unfairly, the many may be censors and masters, repressing his willfulness [*libidinem*]."[8] In short, Calvin favored a mixed or plural republic, or as McNeill puts it, "a plural magistracy," in contrast to an absolute monarchy, for the purposes of serving as a check both on the vicious behavior of the masses and on the human frailty or inadequacy of kings. As Calvin biographer William J. Bouwsma observes, Calvin defended a republican form of government despite its unpopularity at the time and despite the problems it might cause for his sympathizers in France who were undergoing harsh persecution at the hands of a Roman Catholic monarchy: "He favored a republic, and he articulated his republicanism with clarity and force in the last chapter of the *Institutes*. That this chapter might have antagonized some readers, notably in France, and that it hardly seems essential to the work as a whole suggests the depth of his republicanism. It may also hint at his awareness of affinities between civic humanism and evangelical Christianity."[9]

Calvin's republicanism, it should be further noted, had an unmistakable democratic element. In his biblical commentary on Micah 5:5, Calvin not only criticizes hereditary monarchy as inhospitable to liberty but finds authorization for the popular election of rulers: "For the condition of the people most to be desired is that in which they create their shepherds by a general vote [*communibus suffragiis*]. For when anyone by force usurps the supreme power, that is tyranny. And where men are born to kingship, this does not seem to be in accordance with liberty."[10] McNeill further observes that when Calvin speaks of an aristocracy as "the rule of principal persons" he is not thinking of a hereditary ruling caste. Because he sees liberty likely to be breached when kings are born to kingship, it is fair to conclude that aristocracy proceeds not by inheritance similar to that of hereditary kingship but rather "through the recognition of [certain principal persons'] qualities by their fellows."[11]

Despite these democratic sympathies, Calvin was anxious to avoid the language of rebellion or revolution, even in the case of a tyrannical monarch. He was decidedly wary of democracy degenerating into anarchy and mob rule. So, for instance, he consistently counseled restraint to the Huguenots despite severe persecution.[12] But the crucial point for Calvin is that even when a hereditary aristocracy has political authority, it ought to be brought to bear for good government and to provide a check on the tyranny of monarchs. McNeill thus suggests that Calvin would be in complete agreement with the Scottish Calvinist John Knox, whose political views on resistance to tyrannical rulers were more radical than Calvin's: "To bridle the fury and rage of princes in free kingdoms and realms . . . it pertains to the nobility, sworn and born to be councilors of the same, and also to the barons and people, whose votes and consent are to be required in all great and weighty matters of the commonwealth."[13] Later in this chapter we will see how Calvin's preference for a republican form of government—that is, a "mixed regime"—plays a foundational role in his, and subsequent, Reformed and Presbyterian theories of armed resistance.

THE TWO SWORDS:
ON THE DISTINCTION BETWEEN
ECCLESIASTICAL AND CIVIL AUTHORITY

Christ wished to bar ministers of his Word from civil rule and earthly authority, observed Calvin. "The office of the pastor is distinct from that of prince," and the two "are so different that they cannot come together in one man."[14] Calvin's insistence on the distinct responsibilities of ecclesiastical and civil authority was no mere speculative theological argument but rather a point of emphasis in Geneva's Ecclesiastical Ordinances, by which the limited jurisdiction of the consistory—the ecclesiastical ruling assembly (similar to a "synod" or a Presbyterian assembly)—was explicitly spelled out: "The ministers have no civil jurisdiction and wield only the spiritual sword of the word of God."[15] But the converse applied as well.

The civil magistrate did not wield the spiritual sword, at least with respect to ecclesiastical discipline and the authority to excommunicate. As Mark Larson writes, "Calvin's commitment to *ecclesiastical* discipline, rather than *magisterial* discipline, was itself a defining characteristic of his version of the Reformed faith." In fact, many of the ministers in Geneva believed he was "usurping power that really belonged to the civil government."[16]

Calvin's insistence on distinct roles for ecclesiastical and civil authorities entailed a decisive break with the tradition of regalian episcopacy, a political practice of the Middle Ages by which, as James Turner Johnson describes it, "the same individual served simultaneously as bishop and as a feudal lord of territories included in his see. Thus spiritual and temporal authority were brought together in the same individual for the territory in question. His role as feudal lord inevitably involved a regalian bishop in military activities, and bishops in such roles claimed and exercised the right to authorize wars and to lead their armies on campaigns. In such circumstances it was difficult in practice to discern where the spiritual office left off and the temporal office began."[17] Martin Luther had earlier denounced this medieval doctrine and practice by insisting that those clergy taking up arms "would be deserting their calling and office to fight with sword against flesh and blood."[18] Calvin, as it turns out, was equally hostile to the practice. In his commentary on Luke 22:38 ("They said, 'Look, Lord, here are two swords.' He replied, 'It is enough.'") Calvin writes, "As to the inference which the Doctors of Canon Law draw from these words—that their mitred bishops have a double jurisdiction—it is not only an offensive allegory, but a detestable mockery, by which they ridicule the word of God."[19]

THE CALLING OR VOCATION OF
THE CIVIL MAGISTRATE:
AGAINST THE ANABAPTISTS

Throughout his life and teaching ministry, Calvin emphasized that all vocations, including those of various tradesmen and craftsmen, were to be done to the glory of God and that a Christian's talents and abilities therein should be upheld and respected. Among the highest "callings" or "vocations" was that of a government official. The "civil magistrate" was a godly office, and in maintaining order and justice it served the kingdom of God.

The importance of Calvin's stress on "vocation" and "calling" was particularly evident in his response to the Anabaptist movement, which would, in turn, provide the foundation for later Reformed criticisms of other sects — such as the Mennonites, Hutterites, and Amish — that traced their beliefs to earlier "Radical Reformation" thinking. These "sectarian" Christian denominations explicitly forbade Christians to serve as soldiers, and to varying degrees that prohibition applied to political office as well.

In 1527 the Anabaptists assembled under the leadership of Michael Sattler and produced a unanimously agreed-upon and representative statement of principles called the Schleitheim Confession. For our purposes, the relevant section of the confession is article 6:

> Sixth. concerning the sword: The sword is ordained of God outside the perfection of Christ. It punishes and puts to death the wicked, and guards and protects the good. In the Law the sword was ordained for the punishment of the wicked and for their death, and the same [sword] is [now] ordained to be used by the worldly magistrates. . . .
>
>   . . . It will be asked concerning the sword, Shall one be a magistrate if one should be chosen as such? The answer is as follows: They wished to make Christ king, but He fled and did not view it as the arrangement of His Father. Thus shall we do as He did, and follow Him, and so shall we not walk in darkness. For He Himself says, He who wishes to come after me, let him deny himself and take up his cross and follow me. Also, He Himself forbids the [employment of] the force of the sword saying, The worldly princes lord it over them, etc., but not so shall it be with you. Further, Paul says, Whom God did foreknow He also did predestinate to be conformed to the image of His Son, etc. Also Peter says, Christ has suffered (not ruled) and left us an example, that ye should follow His steps.
>
>   Finally it will be observed that it is not appropriate for a Christian to serve as a magistrate because of these points: The government magistracy is according to the flesh, but the Christians' is according to the Spirit; their houses and dwelling remain in this world, but the Christians' are in heaven; their citizenship is in this world, but the Christians' citizenship is in heaven; the weapons of their conflict and war are carnal and against the flesh only, but the Christians' weapons

are spiritual, against the fortification of the devil. The worldlings are armed with steel and iron, but the Christians are armed with the armor of God, with truth, righteousness, peace, faith, salvation and the Word of God.[20]

The Anabaptists shared Calvin's emphasis on a strong distinction between the "two swords" held by civil and ecclesiastical authority, but then they went further, arguing that truly biblical Christianity considered not only military service but all politics — and hence all political offices — to be outside the purview of the New Testament. Because Christians share in the "perfection of Christ," the utmost pain and penalty was excommunication from the church, understood as a community of believers radically separated from political authority. In short, "The gospel contained principles for ruling citizens of the kingdom of heaven, but not for the legislation of a secular state in the evil world. Consequently, they held that a Christian may fill no role in the state."[21]

Calvin was eighteen years of age when the Schleitheim Confession was published. Over the subsequent years he responded to the Anabaptists with a plethora of biblical counterarguments. He stressed, for instance, that in ancient Israel, God had raised up numerous kings and even prophets such as Daniel who wielded the sword as part of their civil office, arguing that "we serve the selfsame God as that of the ancient Fathers" and insisting that what "was holy and lawful cannot be reproved among the Christians."[22] Calvin thought it bizarre and incoherent that in both the Old and New Testaments God would "exalt and magnify" the vocation of public office, call those who hold that office a "servant of God" (Rom. 13:4), and yet then insist that a Christian may not hold that office. Moreover, Calvin thought that the Anabaptists, by conceding that the civil authorities had been ordained by God to pursue justice and oppose the wicked, had backed themselves into a theologically incoherent position.

> Here must we note, that this is a moderation which they do make, to correct that which afore time they have said, after they perceived that for the absurdity of their saying, they were rejected of all the world. For this honour did they give unto principalities, and Seniors [*Elders, Senators*] of the world, that they reckoned them among murder and thievery. But perceiving that this could not be born [*sic*], they have

advised themselves gently to retract this Article, using this false co-
lour, that worldly dominion is an ordinance of God, besides [*outside*]
the perfection of Christ. Now by this, they do signify that it is an estate unlawful & forbidden to all Christian men, as they themselves
expound it afterward.[23]

In other words, after being confronted with the anarchistic implications of
declaring as evil not only police and military office but *all* civil authority,
they then reluctantly retreated to a recognition that civil authority was still
"ordained" by God—indeed, conceding that political officeholders were
also "servants of God." However, these "servants" should only be non-
Christians, according to the Anabaptists, because the office itself was pur-
portedly "outside the perfection of Christ." Calvin was not impressed:

> Which is as [if] one would say: I confess that this work is com-
> manded of God; but there is no man that can do it with a good
> conscience, and also whosoever shall do it shall forsake God. I pray
> you, is there any man, that hath but one ounce of brains, that will
> speak after this manner? I would they should answer me, in this one
> thing: Seeing they put no doubt, but that all handicrafts which are
> ordained to serve unto the common utility of mankind, are lawful
> and holy, wherefore do they exclude out of this number, the vocation
> of princes, which doth excel all the others? As for example: They
> deny not but that a Christian man may be a tailor or a shoemaker.
> And yet, these crafts have no express witness in the Scriptures. Where-
> fore then do not they as well permit a Christian man to be a minis-
> ter of Justice, seeing that that estate hath so large approbation &
> praise of the mouth of God? God doth pronounce that Princes and
> all Superiors are his ministers, and that he hath ordained them to be
> defenders of the good and innocent, and to chastise the wicked: and
> that in doing this, they do execute his work, which he hath commit-
> ted into their hands.[24]

In short, Calvin rejected the argument that the vocation of government
service, including that of a soldier or a "magistrate" responsible for bearing
the sword, was out-of-bounds for the individual Christian. He thought it
wildly incoherent to claim that the duties of such officers were good and

acceptable when a non-Christian pagan performed them but somehow wicked when the Christian performed them.

We can see how fully Calvin's followers embraced his rejection of the Anabaptist position on public service when we read the Reformed confessions, all of which explicitly condemn the Schleitheim position. Thus, for example, the Second Helvetic Confession (1566): "We condemn the Anabaptists, who maintain that a Christian should not hold a civil office, that the magistrate has no right to punish any one by death, or to make war, or to demand an oath." The Irish Articles of Religion (1615) state: "It is lawful for Christian men, at the commandment of the magistrate, to bear arms and to serve in just wars." Similarly, chapter 23 of the Westminster Confession of Faith (1646) and chapter 24 of the Savoy Declaration (1658) state: "It is lawful for Christians to accept and execute the office of a magistrate, when called thereunto: in the managing whereof, as they ought especially to maintain piety, justice, and peace, according to the wholesome laws of each commonwealth; so, for that end, they may lawfully, now under the New Testament, wage war, upon just and necessary occasion." Finally, the Thirty-Nine Articles of the Church of England, while not a Reformed Confession though certainly influenced by certain Reformed trends, also insists that "it is lawful for Christian men, at the commandment of the Magistrate, to wear weapons, and serve in the wars."[25]

CALVIN ON POLITICAL AUTHORITY AND THE USE OF FORCE

The key passage summarizing Calvin's theological and biblical understanding of the use of force by political authority is found in the *Institutes*:

> But here a seemingly hard and difficult question arises: if the law of God forbids all Christians to kill [Ex. 20:13; Deut. 5:17; Matt. 5:21] . . . how can magistrates be pious men and shedders of blood at the same time?
>
> Yet if we understand that the magistrate in administering punishments does nothing by himself, but carries out the very judgments of God, we shall not be hampered by this scruple. The law of the Lord forbids killing; but, that murderers may not go unpunished,

the Lawgiver himself puts into the hands of his ministers a sword to be drawn against all murderers. . . .

. . . Now if their [i.e., civil magistrates'] true righteousness is to pursue the guilty and the impious with drawn sword, should they sheathe their sword and keep their hands clean of blood, while abandoned men wickedly range about with slaughter and massacre, they will become guilty of the greatest impiety, far indeed from winning praise for their goodness and righteousness thereby!

. . . But kings and people must sometimes take up arms to execute such a public vengeance. On this basis we may judge wars lawful which are so undertaken. For if power has been given them to preserve the tranquillity of their dominion . . . can they use it more opportunely than to check the fury of one who disturbs both the repose of private individuals and the common tranquillity of all . . . ? . . . Therefore, both natural equity and the nature of the office dictate that princes must be armed not only to restrain the misdeeds of private individuals by judicial punishment, but also to defend by war the dominions entrusted to their safekeeping, if at any time they are under enemy attack.[26]

Several important points directly related to the just war tradition are worth highlighting. First, the Augustinian influence on Calvin's political theology here is unmistakable. Calvin cites Augustine more than any other church father or theologian, and he expressly refers to Augustine twice by name in his discussion of the topic of the magistrate and the sword in book 4, chapter 20 of the *Institutes*.[27] Here, in particular, we find unmistakable echoes of the traditional Augustinian *jus ad bellum* criteria of just cause ("public vengeance") and right intent, which is, in Augustinian terms, "the end of peace" or the *tranquillitas ordinis*. Calvin declares that the reason God has given magistrates the power of the sword (a common biblical and historical metaphor for lethal force) was for the purpose of preserving "the tranquillity of their dominion."[28]

As Augustine before him, Calvin recognized the role of politically authorized force both in the construction of states and in discipling human behavior. At the same time, he "deplored the fact that wars are generally initiated by the greed or ambition of rulers, and conducted by soldiers out of the basest of motives."[29] According to William Bouwsma,

"In a time when aristocratic groups still idealized war, Calvin, like Erasmus, aimed to demythologize it."[30] Bouwsma summarizes Calvin's opposition to "heroic" conceptions that tended to view war in a militaristic[31] fashion in which war becomes an end in itself: "He denounced 'the loftiness of mind that many consider a heroic disposition.' The supposed 'prowess' of men valiant in war reduces them to the level of cats and dogs. 'Nothing is more desirable than peace for the happiest life,' he declared, 'for amidst the tumults of war an abundance of all things is worth noting, for it is corrupted and perishes.'"[32] Calvin deplored the fact that whatever the cause of wars, they "open the gate to robbery, pillage, arson, slaughter, rape, and every violence," insofar as soldiers are so brutalized by combat that they no longer recognize God's image in each other.[33]

Calvin explicitly warns against resorting to war or waging war with base motives. When rulers must resort to arms, "let them not allow themselves to be swayed by any private affection, but be led by concern for the people alone. Otherwise they very wickedly abuse their power, which has been given to them not for their own advantage, but for the benefit and service of others."[34] Calvin is unambiguous. Both the "prince" who resorts to war and the soldiers who fight in war must do so with the right intention and avoid base motives: "Princes must not allow themselves to sport with human blood, nor must soldiers give themselves up to cruelty, from a desire of gain, as if slaughter were their chief business: but must be drawn to it by necessity, and by a regard for public advantage."[35]

Second, Calvin has a sophisticated view of the use of lethal force by political authority or "civil magistrates"—a view that does not contradict the Sixth Commandment's prohibition of killing (Exod. 20:13). Murder, however, suggests something far more profound. The Sixth Commandment, according to Calvin, was not merely a negative precept. "The purpose of this commandment," he writes, is that "the Lord has bound mankind together by a certain unity; hence each man ought to concern himself with the safety of all. To sum up, then, all violence, injury, and any harmful thing at all that may injure our neighbor's body are forbidden to us." And what, for Calvin, follows from this? "We are accordingly commanded, if we find anything of use to us in saving our neighbors' lives, faithfully to employ it if there is anything that makes for their peace, to see to it; if anything harmful, to ward it off; if there are any in danger, to lend a helping hand."[36] That affirmative obligation to aid one's neighbor threatened with harm is central to why Calvin considers it be sinful for the civil magistrate to *refuse* to do his duty—that is, to refuse to employ lethal political force, or, as he puts it, "to keep his sword clean of blood"—when that is required to protect the innocent from violence. Such dereliction of duty by those whose office requires the wielding of the sword would violate the *positive* requirements of the Sixth Commandment.

Third, Calvin argues a fortiori that if it is reasonable and just to expect the civil authorities to punish private individuals who murder and go about committing criminal activity, then how much more reasonable and just when such activity threatens not merely "the repose of private individuals" but the entire commonwealth, the entire society, the common good, or, as Calvin puts it, "the common tranquility of all"? This line of reasoning, of course, is not unique to Calvin. Thomas Aquinas makes a similar argument in *Summa Theologica*: "And just as it is lawful for them to have recourse to the sword in defending that common weal against *internal* disturbances, when they punish evil-doers, according to the words of the Apostle (Rom. 13:4): 'He beareth not the sword in vain: for he is God's minister, an avenger to execute wrath upon him that doth evil'; so too, it is their *business* to have recourse to the sword of war in defending the common weal against *external* enemies."[37]

Fourth, even though Calvin considers war as one of "the general evils that human wickedness has released,"[38] and even though he is unambiguous about the requirement to avoid base motives and will have nothing to do with a militaristic mindset that seeks military fame and glory as an end in itself, Calvin does not consider the resort to lethal force by legitimate political authority to be what Darrell Cole calls a "limited exception to pacifism."[39] What Cole says about the early church fathers (which certainly applies to Augustine, Thomas Aquinas, and scores of medieval Christian theologians) is clearly and unmistakably true for Calvin as well:

> Christian pacifists, of course, think that just war theory developed precisely because early Christians had to figure out a way to harmonize their nonviolent assumptions with the desire to aid their neighbors with acts of force. This is factually wrong. Pacifists cannot point to a single Church Father who helped develop the Christian just war doctrine out of "nonviolent assumptions." On the contrary, just war theory arose out of assumptions of justice and the virtue of charity.

Assumptions of nonviolence had nothing to do with the genesis of Christian just war theory.[40]

Calvin, as we have seen, insists that it would be *impious*—indeed, it would be *disobedient* to the Lord—for the civil magistrate *not* to wield the sword in defense of the innocent and in defense of the commonweal or when, like modern terrorists, "abandoned men wickedly range about with slaughter and massacre."[41] It would be impious or disobedient to God for the civil authorities to sheathe the sword and keep it clean from blood, if the sword is what is required to execute justice on those who engage in such slaughter and massacre.

At this most fundamental level of theological reflection about political responsibility and the use of force (i.e., "statecraft" or "political theology"), Calvin's reflections are far from novel. In fact, he is for the most part articulating the broader Christian theological tradition, as summarized by Augustine and Aquinas. He is not suggesting that the civil magistrate or the soldier is doing evil so that good may come when he—Christian or not—unsheathes his sword. To the contrary, in line with the broader Christian theological tradition, he is teaching that it would be evil if the Christian magistrate, or the Christian soldier, were to keep that sword "clean" if wisdom and prudence dictate that force is necessary to protect the innocent and to defend the commonwealth from human wickedness.

CALVIN, CALVINISTS, AND THE *JUS IN BELLO*: RESTRAINT IN WAR AND THE HOLY WAR IDEA

In *Christian Attitudes toward War and Peace*, Roland Bainton argues, largely on the basis of his study of the Puritan Revolution in England, that the Puritans had adopted the idea of "Holy War" or "the crusading idea," which he famously identified as follows: "The crusading idea requires that the cause shall be holy (and no cause is more holy than religion), that the war shall be fought under God and with his help, that the crusaders shall be godly and their enemies ungodly, that the war shall be prosecuted unsparingly."[42] By "prosecuted unsparingly" Bainton means that this type of warfare is conducted without mercy, with little or no attempt at restraint, and without concern for noncombatants or prisoners of war. James Turner

Johnson has argued at length that this widely cited passage from Bainton is, in fact, "at variance with definitions of Holy War in other contexts." Johnson argues that Bainton "is wrong in his characterization of 'the crusading idea' to define holy war as a conflict which is 'prosecuted unsparingly'"; it does not withstand scrutiny "even for the English Puritans whose practice of warfare he was directly describing."[43]

Since Calvin only hints in the *Institutes* at the ethics of how war is fought (*jus in bello*), and since the Puritans were prominent Calvinists, we must ask where Calvin's own understanding of restraint and humanity in war stands in this broader historical context. More specifically, can Calvin's view be identified with that of the more radical English Puritans, such as William Gouge (1575–1653), whose views on the conduct of war might most plausibly fit Bainton's description of "Holy War" as warfare "prosecuted unsparingly"?

According to Johnson, two related and mutually reinforcing cultural ideas and practices shaped the thinking of noncombatant immunity in medieval Christendom. The first was the Augustinian-rooted insistence that both the prince, in going to war, and the soldier, who is fighting the war, must do so with good intention while avoiding base motives. This was reinforced by medieval canon law, which required that soldiers do penance after battle.[44]

This Augustinian theme—requiring the moral soldier to fight without base passions—developed alongside "the ideals rooted in the customs and attitudes of chivalry, notably prowess, courtesy, and the desire for glory or prestige": "The first of these referred to the goal of the knight to develop skill in arms; the second and third referred to his perception of others. Briefly stated, the knight gained glory by demonstrating his prowess in arms courteously, that is, against worthy opponents and for the protection of the weak and innocent. This is the cultural root of the protection given to women, children, the aged, and the infirm in the fully developed conception of noncombatant immunity achieved in the Western tradition by the fourteenth century."[45] These two themes were reinforced by formal canonical efforts, sparked by the Peace of God movement of the eleventh and twelfth centuries, which sought to specify particular classes of people as immune from attack. Gratian's *Decretum* (1148) specifically identified ecclesiastical classes—inclusive of clergy, monks, and pilgrims—as protected. A century later, in a landmark of canon law, protection was extended to peasants, their property, and their lands in *De Treuga et Pace* ("Of Truces and Peace"): "These two themes—the concept of good moral character in combat as measured by right intention and the chivalric ideals for knightly conduct—tended to reinforce each other and to inculcate a carefulness in the use of armed force. Within the just war tradition this link between the concept of right intention and the development of a concept of noncombatant immunity determined by weakness and inability to protect oneself is clear, and *we know this conception was in place by the fourteenth century.*"[46] Since this broad consensus on restraint in warfare had been well in place before the Protestant Reformation, we can now ask if whether what Calvin and the Reformed had to say about right conduct in war falls within this broader medieval tradition.

On one issue relevant to the *jus in bello*, Calvin did dissent from medieval attempts to limit the damage done by war. The Second Lateran Council (1139) had placed a ban on certain weapons of war, including the crossbow and siege machines, but Calvin, like Luther before him, had little interest in such canonical restrictions. Nor did he object to the use of the newer, more destructive weapons of the sixteenth century, particularly the use of the cannon, the most destructive and powerful weapon of the time.

> Calvin did not have continuity with the mindset manifested at the Second Lateran Council, which forbade crossbows and siege machines. Speaking about the rulers of the time, Calvin declared, "They have thus many footemen, thus many horsemen, thus much artillerie, such and such intelligence, such and such alyances." Here Calvin mentioned the weapon of choice for maximum firepower in the sixteenth century—artillery, the cannon. Did he suggest that such an overwhelming instrument of violence be banned from the field of battle? He did not. He rather affirmed, "True it is that all these things are neceessarie for the warres." In this perspective he stood with Luther, who acknowledged, "It is true that one should have horses and men and weapons and everything that is needed for battle, if they are to be had, so that one does not tempt God."[47]

That Calvin did not embrace medieval ecclesiastical efforts to outlaw certain weapons is a relatively minor issue, since the failure of these attempts had long become obvious before the fifteenth century. "The simple fact," Johnson writes, "is that the ban did not work. The use of bows, crossbows, and siege weapons continued, though the former were often the target of chivalric grumbling."[48] Moreover, since the banned weapons were among the arms used by Muslim armies outside of Christendom, in which the ban did not apply in any case, "the principle of reciprocity meant that they were immediately in use on the Christian side as well."[49]

While Calvin broke with medieval canonical attempts to ban certain weapons as a means to restrain the ravages of war, he clearly did not break with the medieval tradition of humanity and restraint in battle with the treatment of noncombatants.[50] While Calvin hints at the need for humanity in battle in the *Institutes*, his thinking on the laws of war comes into clear focus in his Old Testament commentaries, particularly in his handling of war conducted by Old Testament Israel.

One example of this is how he deals with the treatment of women following battle. In his commentaries, Calvin identifies numerous instances in which political laws for the Israelites had been given to accommodate the hardness of their hearts. The preeminent instance of such a law was divorce, of course, but in many of these he could not, as in the case of divorce, appeal to an authoritative statement by Jesus or the apostles. But with regard to these others, "Calvin judges particular laws as lacking from the standpoint of the reason or the law of nations," one of which is particularly relevant to right conduct in war—specifically, the law that permitted Israelites to enslave and marry women captured in war. Calvin argues that such forced marriages should not have taken place at all, but God allowed it in order "to restrain the lust of victors in war." For this reason, he argues, "God so tempers his indulgence."[51]

At a more fundamental level of biblical interpretation, however, was Calvin's insistence that "Old Testament Israel had a typological function that precluded its simplistic use as an example of Christian polities."[52] Particular civil laws in the Torah no longer remained binding because God had given certain laws to Israel "appropriate for its unique mission as God's sacerdotal kingdom Israel." Calvin explicitly identified the command for Israel to exterminate the Canaanites as such a law.[53] More specifically, in his commentary on Deuteronomy 20:12–13, Calvin directly addresses issues related to noncombatant immunity in the context of siege warfare. This text required all male inhabitants to be killed if a city refused to surrender to the Israelites. But Calvin thought "the permission here given seems to confer too great a license"—a particularly striking comment since he describes such license as being deficient in comparison with the work of "heathen writers," and Cicero in particular.[54] "Since heathen writers command even the conquered to be spared, and enjoin that those should be admitted to mercy who lay down their arms, and cast themselves on the good faith of the General, although the battering-ram may have actually made a breach in the wall, how does God, the father of mercies, give His sanction to indiscriminate bloodshed?"[55] Calvin insisted that the command "to slaughter, which is extended to all the males, is far from perfection" and that, "unquestionably, by the law of charity, even armed men should be spared, if casting away the sword, they crave for mercy."[56] Moreover, Calvin's emphasis on restraint here is even more remarkable in that "Calvin was essentially advocating the law of charity not only in opposition to the biblical text, but also with reference to the standard procedure of siege warfare in the Middle Ages. Once the medieval siege formally began, either with the firing of cannons or siege engines, the commander of the besieging forces had every right, according to the law of arms, to show no mercy to any of the soldiers or any other men in the city."[57] Assuming *arguendo*, that Bainton was right to say that warfare "fought unsparingly" is a necessary characteristic of "Holy War," it should be obvious that Calvin did not endorse either war without restraint or holy war. Calvin's call for restraint in warfare, coupled with his insistence that the God-ordained wars of the Old Testament were unique and related to only that particular event within redemptive history, places his thought firmly within the medieval just war tradition.

However, Calvin's teaching on this point also distinguishes his thought from a minority stream within the Reformed tradition, represented most clearly by Zürich Reformed theologian Heinrich Bullinger,[58] and later by some of the more radical sixteenth-century Puritan revolutionaries, of whom William Gouge is an example.[59] In contrast to Calvin, for instance, Bullinger wrote, "The laws of war are recited in the 20th chapter of Deuteronomy, both profitable and necessary, and therewithal so evident, that they need no words of mine to expound them. Moreover, in every place of scripture these laws of war are still bidden to be kept."[60] Bullinger also envisioned circumstances in which noncombatants, civilians and captured combatants alike, could be killed in time of war against those who are "incurable"—those who had done repeated harm in the past and could be expected to do so in the future—since the civil magistrate is "compelled to make war upon men which are incurable, whom the very judgment of the Lord commandeth and biddeth to kill without mercy."[61]

The most charitable interpretation of Bullinger's comments here might be to suggest that harsh treatment of "incurable rebels" against a legitimate public authority was permissible under customary laws of war at the time. Rebels could be treated much more severely under the laws of war well into the nineteenth century. But Bullinger's comments on one particular passage in the book of Numbers that refers to "the wars as Moses had with the Midianites" suggests that a more charitable interpretation is unwarranted. Larson's comment is apt and to the point: "As Bullinger well knew, Numbers 31 records the execution of noncombatants—captive Midianite women and male infants. Killing 'without pity or mercy' meant violating the limits of war traditionally developed in the doctrine of *jus in bello*. In these statements, Bullinger was drawing away from the medieval Peace of God trajectory, which culminated in later just war teaching. In a real sense, his teaching at this point could have provided a justification for the massacre of Irish combatants and noncombatants alike under Cromwell's Puritan army at Drogheda."[62] Larson and other scholars, including James Turner Johnson,[63] find a key source for the revival of the holy war idea among some Puritans during the English Civil War in the person of Bullinger. The most notable and eminent of these was William Gouge, noted earlier. Gouge, according to Johnson, shared with Bullinger the notion that the Old Testament laws of war and examples of warfare were to be understood as universally valid types. This view was not unique to Calvinists or even to Protestants more generally; it was also held by some Roman Catholic theologians and prelates as well in the post-Reformation period.[64] However, for the English Calvinists, it took a specific form. "Whereas in the case of Israel that command sometimes came directly, it comes to the Puritan Christians through the Bible by faith."[65]

When the Old Testament laws of war are understood to have an abiding legitimacy for a Christian polity, and that view is coupled with an assumption about the righteousness of one's own political community, or with an assumption that one's own political community enjoys a special covenantal relationship with God that is analogous to God's special covenantal relationship with ancient Israel (for example, making claims about being "God's New Israel"), then it is accurate to say that such a notion has veered off the trajectory of the just war tradition in Western thought. At that point the theological and moral logic behind a justification for waging war without restraint is in place. In Gouge's *God's Three Arrowes*, for instance, we find a claim that "Papists profess the Christian Faith, yet are anti-Christians, the directest and deadliest enemies the true Church ever had." However, as Larson notes, this claim by itself does not distinguish Gouge from the just war tradition of restraint in warfare. Such rhetoric, of course, was common in post-Reformation Protestant and Roman Catholic polemics. However, when Gouge adds that "Papists are to Protestants as Amalekites to Israelites," the implication for Protestant armies was surely obvious. The Israelites were commanded in Deuteronomy 25:17–19 to wage holy war against and to exterminate the Amalekites.[66]

Johnson argues that Bullinger and Gouge, along with similar-minded Protestants and Catholics in the post-Reformation period, had all built upon certain medieval Christian justifications of war for the cause of religion, but they did so through a particular method of biblical interpretation — a method very distinct in crucial ways from that of Calvin. For Gouge and some other Puritans during the English Civil Wars, the biblical justification would be coupled with their confidence that their own particular political communities could be understood as analogous to the community of Israel, with its special covenantal relationship with God. This could, in turn, serve as warrant for public authorities to override historical attempts to limit the harm permitted in the conduct of war, particularly to noncombatants and their goods and property.[67] For this reason, Timothy George seems correct in saying that "the movement from just war to holy war in Puritan thought owed much to a biblical hermeneutic which lessoned the distance between old and new covenants and, in fact, gave priority to the former in defining a normative pattern of conduct in civil society."[68]

While Bullinger and Gouge within the Reformed tradition, and others from the Roman Catholic tradition, were reviving some elements of the holy war idea, particularly the notion that war could be waged to promote and advance (true) religion contemporaneously, other authors, notes Johnson, among them Francisco de Vitoria and Hugo Grotius, "were advancing a contrary argument, also based on reasoning inherited from the Middle Ages, that rejected religious reasons as justifying causes for offensive war. The latter position ultimately carried the day and became the basis for the Western moral tradition on war as it developed during the modern period."[69]

It seems clear, especially given the sharp difference between Calvin and both Bullinger and Gouge in how they understood the laws of war and their applicability for Christians, that Calvin himself stood firmly and unmistakably within the latter tradition and has a legitimate claim to be a forerunner to the former. That is to say, Calvin, clearly stood within the developing trajectory of the medieval just war emphasis on restraint in warfare, particularly with regard to noncombatant immunity. In truth, his biblical reflections and commentaries on the issue would find more systematic expression in the natural law theorists who explicitly addressed the requirements of *jus in bello* in the early modern period.

CALVIN ON ARMED RESISTANCE
TO POLITICAL AUTHORITY

Throughout his life Calvin grew consistently more critical of monarchical forms of government, in large measure because of the severe persecution of Reformed Protestants in France. Contemporary events had the effect of reinforcing his classical conviction that monarchies tended to degenerate into tyrannical regimes. Still, the absence of popular consent or approval alone did not warrant active disobedience or active resistance against political authority—not even against a tyrannical monarchy.[70] While Calvin held that Christian citizens should be grateful if they lived under a government that had the consent of the people, he also shared classical reservations about undiluted democracy because it was too easy to fall from popular rule to sedition.

Calvin, of course, did insist that all Christians had a duty to passive disobedience against "the impious and wicked edicts of Kings," pointing to the refusal of Hebrew midwives to obey Pharaoh's order to kill male infants of Hebrew mothers. Those who obey such wicked orders, Calvin insisted, "display by their cowardice an inexcusable contempt for God." But active disobedience to civil authority by private individuals was another matter altogether. Calvin insisted that the apostle Paul's statement that political authorities had been ordained by God meant that to resist them was to resist the ordinance of God (Rom. 13:1–7). If we look to God's Word, Calvin insisted, "We are not only subject to the authority of princes who perform their office toward us uprightly and faithfully as they ought, but also to the authority of all who, by whatever means, have got control of affairs, even though they perform not a whit of the princes' office."[71] Calvin maintained that obedience even to bad kings was required by scripture and that Christians were to consider those "who rule unjustly and incompetently [to] have been raised up by him [God] to punish the wickedness of the people."[72] "Therefore, if we are cruelly tormented by a savage prince, if we are despoiled by one who is avaricious or wanton, if we are neglected by a slothful one, if finally, we are vexed for piety's sake by one who is impious and sacrilegious, let us first be mindful of our own misdeeds, which without a doubt are chastised by such whips of the Lord [cf. Dan. 9:7]. By this, humility will restrain our impatience."[73] And Calvin will further insist that "if the correction of unbridled despotism is the Lord's to avenge, let us not at once think that it is entrusted to us, to whom no command has been given except to obey and to suffer."[74]

However, immediately following his insistence on obedience to even unjust rulers in the *Institutes,* Calvin proclaims, "I am speaking all the while of private individuals," after which follows one of the most famous and ultimately influential passages in the history of Western political thought.

> For if there are now any magistrates of the people, appointed to restrain the willfulness of kings (as in ancient times the ephors were set against Spartan kings, or the tribunes of the people against the Roman consuls, or the demarchs against the senate of the Athenians; and perhaps, as things now are, such power as the three estates exercise in every realm when they hold their chief assemblies), I am so far from forbidding them to withstand . . . the fierce licentiousness of kings, that, if they wink at kings who violently fall upon and assault the lowly folk, I declare that their dissimulation involves nefarious perfidy, because they dishonestly betray the freedom of the people, of which they know that they have been appointed protectors by God's ordinance.[75]

Calvin's firm opposition to private resistance was followed immediately with this thundering demand that magistrates of the people (*populares magistratus*) were obliged to respond to grave injustice against the people. His insistence on obedience by private citizens, as well as his remedy for grave injustice committed by tyrants, serves to highlight Calvin's and the broader Reformed commitment to *order,* the political good secured by the *jus ad bellum* principle of proper political authority. Armed force, even when contemplated for a just cause and right intention, must have a strong claim to legitimate political (or civil) authority. For Calvin, magistrates of the people—parliamentary political bodies—served to meet that requirement, and their specific obligation was to defend the cause of the "lowly folk" they represented.

Calvin's teaching on this subject was supplemented, reinforced, and transmitted by the systematic reflection on the subject by Theodore Beza, Calvin's close confidant and theological successor in Geneva.[76] Beza expounded at length on Calvin's suggestion that the Estates-General in France was an example of *populares magistratus*, which held the authority to depose and even punish a king. Appealing to the Old Testament, the history of France, and political logic, Beza argued that "those who possess the authority to elect a king also have the authority to depose him."[77] The famous Huguenot tract *Vindiciae contra tyrannos* (1579) justifies armed rebellion if those suffering persecution are led by a lesser magistrate. In Scotland, John Knox followed Calvin in refusing to support rebellion by "private persons," but he argued that the nobility could serve as civil magistrates, and in fact had a duty "to defend innocents" in order to "bridle and repress" the tyrant.[78] These justifications for armed resistance to tyranny would influence Reformed Protestants, including French Calvinists (Huguenots) in France, persecuted Dutch Calvinists against the Spanish king Philip II in the Netherlands, Puritans during the English Civil War, and Protestant clergy in the decades leading up to the American Revolution, particularly the Presbyterian and Congregationalist clergy.[79] Reformed pastors and their congregants in the decades leading up to the American Revolution knew quite well that an experiment in self-government had long been well underway and that colonial assemblies could be recognized as "magistrates of the people," as would other representative bodies such as the Continental Congress. Reformed pastors and their congregants and public officials and representatives would seek to steer a middle position between passivity and acquiescence to monarchical tyranny, on the one hand, and support for full blown popular revolutionary movements, on the other.[80]

Finally, this Reformed emphasis on the right and duty of armed resistance of *populares magistratus* was a noteworthy difference between the Reformed and Lutheran Protestant traditions. "No one shall fight or make war against his overlord," argued Luther in *Whether Soldiers, Too, Can Be Saved* on the basis of Romans 13, "for a man owes his overlord obedience, honor, fear." And unlike Calvin, Beza, and subsequent Reformed political thinkers, Luther insisted that what he had been saying with regard to "subjects" (Calvin's "private individuals") "is intended for peasants, citizens of the cities, nobles, counts and princes as well."[81] We find considerably less sympathy here for the idea so prominent in Reformed political theology that parliaments—or Beza's "lesser magistrates"—could depose, let alone punish, a tyrannical monarch.

But if the Reformed differ from Lutheran Protestants on this particular point of political theology, they are very much in line with the broader medieval, and more specifically Thomistic, theological tradition. In *On Kingship*, Aquinas states: "To proceed against the cruelty of tyrants is an action to be undertaken, not through private presumption of the few, but rather by public authority."[82] Aquinas argues, "If to provide itself with a king belongs to the right of a given multitude, it is not unjust that the king be deposed or have his power restricted by the same multitude, if, becoming a tyrant, he abuses the royal power." In fact, Aquinas had even made a carefully circumscribed argument for tyrannicide, basing his position on arguments for just war and capital punishment. In such a case, he observes, "one who liberates his country by killing a tyrant is to be praised and rewarded."[83]

Calvin and Reformed thinkers would essentially mediate and serve as the most important Protestant transmitter and catalyst for at least this part of the Thomistic and medieval idea of resistance to tyranny in the post-Reformation era. This, when conjoined with a clear preference for republican forms of government over monarchies within the context of persecution in the early-modern period, would be perhaps the greatest contribution of Reformed thought to the just war idea in the modern era. Many of the ideas put forward by this strain of Reformation thought find their logical outcomes in support for the Puritan cause in the English Civil War and in the self-defense-against-tyranny argument in the American War for Independence. Furthermore, more specific principles of statecraft and citizenship emanate from this tradition, including the role of the magistrate in maintaining justice through coercive force and the Christian's obligation to participate in the sociopolitical process of maintaining civil society. Today many of these principles are taken for granted in Western culture and society as democratic mores, and part of the reason for this is that too few understand the theological underpinnings and the influence of John Calvin.

NOTES

1. Paul Ramsey, *The Just War: Force and Political Responsibility* (Lanham, MD: Rowman and Littlefield, 1968), xi.

2. W. Stanford Reid, "The Transmission of Calvinism in the Sixteenth Century," in *John Calvin: His Influence in the Western World*, ed. W. Stanford Reid (Grand Rapids, MI: Zondervan, 1982), 33–52.

3. Calvin used the term *populares magistratus*, but Theodore Beza, Calvin's influential Reformed successor in Geneva, also used the term *inferiores magistratus*, or "inferior magistrates." While Calvin's term "magistrates of the people" emphasizes those who constitute a representative body, closely akin to parliamentary bodies, Beza's use of "lesser magistrates" also emphasizes those who ruled at a more local level and who exercised authority over a limited area. See Mark J. Larson, *Calvin's Doctrine of the State: A Reformed Doctrine and Its American Trajectory, The Revolutionary War, and the Founding of the Republic* (Eugene: Wipf & Stock, 2009), 52–59.

4. Matthew J. Tuininga, *Calvin's Political Theology and the Public Engagement of the Church* (Cambridge: Cambridge University Press, 2017). Tuininga's summary of Calvin's understanding of the distinct responsibilities of ecclesiastical and civil authority and how that understanding differed from other political theologies of Calvin's day is worth quoting at length: "In the first half of the sixteenth century, Calvin's two kingdoms theology offered the sharpest distinction between church and commonwealth articulated by a mainstream theologian who did not reject Christian participation in civil government. The papacy claimed that civil government was ultimately subjected to the authority of the pope as the vicar of Christ. Luther and Melanchthon distinguished between the two kingdoms, but relegated matters of discipline and ecclesiastical order to the civil realm. Zwingli, Bullinger and the apologists of royal supremacy in England adopted the caesaropapist position that subjected the church and its discipline to the control of the civil magistracy. And the Anabaptists, when they were not turning toward apocalypticism, separated church and civil government so far apart as to reject Christian participation in civil government. But against his fellow magisterial reformers Calvin insisted on the autonomy of the church from the state with respect to worship, discipline, and poor relief. Against the papacy he rejected claims that the church holds magisterial authority over ecclesiastical or temporal affairs. And against the Anabaptists he insisted on the legitimacy of civil government as an institution in which Christians should participate" (357).

5. John T. McNeill, ed., *John Calvin: On God and Political Duty* (Indianapolis: Bobbs-Merrill Educational Publishing, 1950), xx. For an excellent overview of the broader issue of Calvin and the state, see David H. Hall, "Calvin on

Human Government and the State," in *A Theological Guide to Calvin's Institutes: Essays and Analysis*, ed. David W. Hall and Peter A. Lillback (Phillipsburg, NJ: P&R, 2008), 411–40.

6. McNeill, *John Calvin*, xx.

7. Ibid.

8. John Calvin, *Institutes of the Christian Religion*, 4.20.8 (1559 ed.), cited by McNeill, *John Calvin*, xxii.

9. William J. Bouwsma, *John Calvin: A Sixteenth Century Portrait* (New York: Oxford University Press, 1988), 207.

10. John Calvin, *Joannis Calvini opera quae supersunt omnia*, 59 vols., Corpus Reformatorum (Brunswick, Germany, 1863–1900), 43:374, cited in McNeill, *John Calvin*, xxiii.

11. McNeill, *John Calvin*, xxiii.

12. The increasing persecution of the Huguenots by the French monarchy formed the background for Calvin's lectures on the book of Daniel; here he found an apt analogy to the situation of Daniel and the exiles in Babylon. However, "the primary lesson Calvin drew from the experience of Protestants in France to that of the Israelite exiles in Babylon was not that the faithful should rebel against the government but that they should continue to submit to it, while waiting patiently for God's sure deliverance." Tuininga, *Calvin's Political Theology*, 345.

13. John Knox, "The Regent and the Congregation," in *John Knox: On Rebellion*, ed. Roger A. Mason, Cambridge Texts in the History of Political Thought (Cambridge: Cambridge University Press, 1994), 166.

14. John Calvin, *Institutes of the Christian Religion*, ed. John T. McNeill, trans. Ford Lewis Battles (Philadelphia: Westminster, 1960), 1220 (4.11.8).

15. See the discussion "Ecclesiastical Ordinances," in *The Register of the Company of Pastors of Geneva in the Time of Calvin* (Grand Rapids, MI: Eerdmans, 1966), 49, cited in Larson, *Calvin's Doctrine of the State*, 6. Larson helpfully places Calvin's emphasis here in the broader context of ecclesiastical-civil authority in Geneva: "This specified limitation upon the power of the consistory—this separation between the jurisdiction of the ministers and the jurisdiction of the magistrates—was in sharp contrast to the previous history of Geneva when it was ruled autocratically for centuries by a prince-bishop who possessed both civil and ecclesiastical jurisdiction. Calvin's structure, which distinguished between church government and civil government, was also in marked contrast to the arrangement that had long prevailed in Rome, in which the Pope was both head of the church and the temporal prince of the Papal States. Calvin in no sense was the Pope of Geneva" (7).

16. Larson, *Calvin's Doctrine of the State*, 5n19. Larson further notes that Calvin's beliefs in this area also distinguished him from most of the other Protestant

Reformers, who were convinced that the civil magistrate alone had the power to discipline. This Erastian conception was embraced by Zwingli and Bullinger in Zürich. In Lutheran countries the right to discipline was likewise retained by civil governments.

17. James Turner Johnson, *The Holy War Idea in Western and Islamic Traditions* (University Park: Pennsylvania State University Press, 1997), 84–85.

18. Martin Luther, *On War against the Turk*, in *Luther's Works*, vol. 46, ed. Robert C. Schultz (Philadelphia: Fortress, 1967), 165.

19. John Calvin, *Commentary on a Harmony of the Evangelists*, 224, cited in Larson, *Calvin's Doctrine of the State*, 4.

20. This translation is taken from J. C. Wenger, "The Schleitheim Confession of 1527," *Mennonite Quarterly Review* 19, no. 4 (October 1945): 250–51.

21. Willem Balke, *Calvin and the Anabaptist Radicals*, trans. William J. Heynen (Grand Rapids, MI: Eerdmans, 1981), 260.

22. John Calvin, *The John Calvin Bible Commentaries*, vol. 3, *The Harmony of the Gospels* (Charleston, SC: Createspace), 183; this passage is quoted in Balke, *Calvin and the Anabaptist Radicals*, 261.

23. John Calvin, *A Short Instruction for to Arme All Good Christian People agaynst the Pestiferous Errours of the Common Secte of Anabaptistes* [also known as *Treatise against the Anabaptists*] (1549), available at http://www.truecovenanter.com/calvin/calvin_against_anabaptists.html.

24. Ibid.

25. The Thirty-Nine Articles of the Church of England, art. 37. These related articles can be found at Reformed.org, https://reformed.org/historic-confessions/.

26. Calvin, *Institutes*, 1497–99 (4.20.10–11).

27. Larson, *Calvin's Doctrine of the State*, 26, notes that while Calvin did not explicitly connect his teaching on war with Thomas Aquinas, it is likely that he had read Aquinas's treatment of the subject. Larson finds much stronger evidence that Heinrich Bullinger and Peter Martyr Vermigli, Reformed contemporaries of Calvin in Zürich, had carefully examined Aquinas on the matter of just war, and their views closely mirrored his in both substance and style.

28. Calvin, *Institutes*, 1499 (4.20.11).

29. Bouwsma, *John Calvin*, 57.

30. Bouwsma, *John Calvin*, 57.

31. A. J. Coates, *The Ethics of War* (Manchester: Manchester University Press, 1997). See especially Coates's chapter "Militarism" (40–76), from which this is drawn.

32. Bouwsma, *John Calvin*, 57. Bouwsma quotes Calvin's comments on Gen. 14:1.

33. Bouwsma, *John Calvin*, 57. Bouwsma quotes Calvin's comments on Ezek. 6:11.

34. Ibid.

35. John Calvin, *Commentary on the Harmony of the Evangelists*, 195, cited in Larson, *Calvin's Doctrine of the State*, 74. Calvin here is commenting on the classic text of Luke 3:14, insisting that since the passage approves of the office of the civil magistrate, it necessarily entails an approbation of what civil government entails. "Magistrates require not only an executioner, but other attendants, among whom are the military, without whose assistance and agency it is impossible to maintain peace."

36. Calvin, *Institutes*, 404 (2.8.39).

37. Thomas Aquinas, *Summa Theologica*, trans. Fathers of the English Dominican Province (New York: Christian Classics, 1981), 1274 (II-II.40.7).

38. Bouwsma, *John Calvin*, 57.

39. Darrell Cole, "Listening to Pacifists," *First Things*, August 2002, https:www.firstthings.com/article/2002/08/listening-to-pacifists. This point separates Calvin and the Reformed tradition from contemporary neo-orthodox theologians such as Reinhold Niebuhr and Karl Barth. See Keith Pavlischek. "Reinhold Niebuhr, Christian Realism, and Just War Theory: A Critique," in *Christianity and Power Politics Today: Christian Realism and Contemporary Political Dilemmas*, ed. Eric Patterson (New York: Palgrave Macmillan, 2008), 53–71. While not a pacifist, Barth tends to veer toward viewing the just use of force as a "limited exception to pacifism" in a "Grenzfall" situation; this is clear from John Howard Yoder's *Karl Barth and the Problem of War* (Nashville: Abington, 1970). See especially chap. 4, "Barth's Revision of the Traditional View of War," 37–42.

40. Cole, "Listening to Pacifists."

41. Calvin, *Institutes* (1536 edition), section 44, "Christian Freedom"; here see *Institutes*, trans. Battles, 1498 (4.20.10).

42. Roland Bainton, *Christian Attitudes toward War and Peace* (Nashville: Abingdon, 1960), 148.

43. Johnson, *Holy War Idea*, 45–46. For a more detailed study on the restraints on war within the Western holy war tradition, a study that relates to the just war tradition, see James Turner Johnson, *Ideology, Reason, and the Limitation of War* (Princeton: Princeton University Press, 1975), 134–46.

44. Johnson, *Holy War Idea*, 110: "Through much of the medieval period canon law required that soldiers do penance after battle as a precaution against having sinned by allowing themselves to be overcome by such wrong intentions as listed by Augustine as 'what is to be blamed in war'—the desire for harming, the cruelty of avenging, an unruly and implacable animosity, the rage of rebellion, the lust of domination and the like. Right or wrong intention was understood as

independent of the enemy or the cause; it had to do rather with the moral character of the soldier as an individual."

45. Ibid.

46. Johnson, *Holy War Idea*, 110–11 (emphasis added). See also James Turner Johnson, *Just War Tradition and the Restraint of War* (Princeton: Princeton University Press, 1981), 131–50.

47. Larson, *Calvin's Doctrine of the State*, 38, citing John Calvin, *Sermon 117*, in *Sermons on Deuteronomy*, trans. Arthur Golding (London: Henry Middleton, 1583; repr., Edinburgh: Banner of Truth, 1987), 721, and Luther, *On War against the Turk*, 191.

48. Johnson, *Holy War Idea*, 109.

49. Ibid.

50. Larson helpfully places Calvin's reflections on just conduct in war within the historical context of the Ottoman Empire's advance on Europe in the sixteenth century. Suleyman had attempted but failed to take Vienna in 1529 and then again in 1532, and the threat to Christian Europe was, as we say nowadays, "existential." The "Turks'" reputation for the lack of restraint was sealed with Suleyman's order to take no prisoners following the Battle of Mohac (1526). Suleyman recorded the following in his diary after defeating the Hungarian forces: "The emperor seated on a golden throne, receives the homage of vizers and beys: massacre of 2,000 prisoners: the rain falls in torrents." It is against this historical backdrop that, according to Larson, we should understand "inimical feelings Calvin had about Turkish warfare," when he bemoaned: "Nowadayes the lawe of the Turk reigneth among Christians." *Sermon 119*, in *Sermons on Deuteronomy*, 434, cited in Larson, *Calvin's Doctrine of the State*, 43.

51. Tuininga, *Calvin's Political Theology*, 331, citing Calvin, *Commentary on Deuteronomy* (1563), on Deut. 21:10.

52. Tuininga, Calvin's *Political Theology*, 319.

53. Ibid., 324–25. Other Old Testament laws that fit into this category of laws that are no longer applicable but were unique to Israel included laws about the sharing of manna, the law about breaking down altars and images, laws pertaining to the chief priest, the law of tithes, and laws prohibiting alliances with pagan nations. See ibid., n. 12.

54. Ibid., 332.

55. Calvin, *Commentaries on the Last Four Books of Moses*, 53, cited in Larson, *Calvin's Doctrine of the State*, 45. Calvin is referring to Cicero's *On Duties*: "And while you must have concern for those whom you have conquered by force, you must also take in those who have laid down their arms and seek refuge in the faith of generals, although a battering ram may have crashed against their

wall." See Marcus Tullius Cicero, *On Duties*, Cambridge Texts on the History of Political Thought (Cambridge: Cambridge University Press, 1991), 14.

56. Ibid., 53, cited in Larson, *Calvin's Doctrine of the State*, 47–48.

57. Larson, *Calvin's Doctrine of the State*, 46, citing M. H. Keen, *The Laws of War in the Late Middle Ages* (London: Routledge, 1965), 120.

58. In addition to being the author of the Second Helvetic Confession, the most important Reformed Confession of the sixteenth century, Bullinger also wrote *The Decades* (see Henry Bullinger, *The Decades*, ed. Thomas Harding [Cambridge: Cambridge University Press, 1849]), a collection of sermons on various topics that was mandated reading by English clergy for a time in 1586 and was widely popular among members of the Puritan party otherwise. Among these sermons, sermon 9 of the second decade (*On War*) laid out a mix of political and religious justifications for war. Hereon see Johnson, *Holy War Idea*, 57.

59. See Johnson, *Holy War Idea*, 57–58; Bullinger, sermon 9, in *Decades*, 380, cited in Larson, *Calvin's Doctrine of the State*, 44.

60. Bullinger, sermon 9, in *Decades*, 376, cited in Larson, *Calvin's Doctrine of the State*, 50.

61. Bullinger, sermon 9, in *Decades*, 376, cited in Larson, *Calvin's Doctrine of the State*, 50.

62. Larson, *Calvin's Doctrine of the State*, 50.

63. Johnson, *Holy War Idea*, 58–59. For an extended discussion, see chap. 2 of Johnson, *Ideology, Reason, and the Limitation of War*.

64. Johnson identifies the English Catholic prelate William Cardinal Allen as a Roman Catholic who justified war for religion with a stridency that matched Bullinger. Both insisted that those who profess "true religion" could go to war: against "idolaters," in the case of the Puritan Bullinger, and against "wilde condemned heresies," in the case of the Roman Catholic Allen.

65. Johnson, *Holy War Idea*, 59.

66. William Gouge, *God's Three Arrows* (London: George Miller, 1631), cited in Larson, *Calvin's Doctrine of the State*, 41–42n30.

67. That the move toward holy war in Puritan thought could be traced to the political theology of Bullinger, and not Calvin, is evident not only in Bullinger's understanding that the Old Testament laws of war are still applicable but also in the manner in which Bullinger justified his Erastianism. Tuininga writes, "Bullinger argued that the prophetic office of pastor and the kingly office of magistrate are necessary in the Church, *which he identified as the covenantal community that constitutes the commonwealth, just as they were in Old Testament Israel.... God had given the magistracy as spiritual gift of the church.*" See Tuininga, *Calvin's Political Theology*, 53, citing Bullinger's *Treatise on the Unity of the Old and New Covenants* (emphasis added).

68. Timothy George, "War and Peace in the Puritan Tradition," *Church History* 53, no. 4 (December 1984): 497.

69. Johnson, *Holy War Idea*, 59.

70. Calvin, *Institutes*, 1493–95 (4.20.8).

71. Ibid., 1512 (4.20.25).

72. Ibid.

73. Ibid., 1516 (4.20.29).

74. Ibid., 1518 (4.20.31).

75. Ibid., 1519 (4.20.31).

76. Theodore Beza, *Concerning the Rights on Rulers over Their Subjects and the Duty of Subjects to Their Rulers*, trans. Henri-Louis Gonin (Capetown: H.A.U.M., 1956). Beza wrote his treatise in response to the slaughter of French Huguenots in the Massacre of St. Bartholomew's Day in France.

77. Beza, *Concerning the Rights*, 64, cited in Larson, *Calvin's Doctrine of the State*, 64. Larson's chap. 4 — "Warring by Popular Magistrates" (52–65) — and Tuininga's chap. 9 — "Law Democracy and Resistance to Tyranny" (321–54) — are both essential readings on this subject.

78. Glenn A. Moots and Valerie Ona Morkevicius, "Just Revolution: Protestant Precedents for Resistance and Rebellion," in *Justifying Revolution: Law, Virtue, and Violence in the American War of Independence*, ed. Glenn A. Moots and Phillip Hamilton (Norman: University of Oklahoma Press, 2018), 40. Both Calvin and Bullinger were, however, more cautious than Knox, and the Scottish Reformer was surprised that they were more circumspect after he sought their approval for armed resistance by Protestant nobles against Catholic rulers.

79. Moots and Morkevicius note that older Reformed Protestant literature on resistance reappeared during the American Revolution and that Protestant ministers cited prior "Protestant revolutions" as precedent: "Though historians disagree about the *precise* role of Protestant religion in the Revolution, there is sufficient reason to agree with John Coffey's recent argument that John Pocock's 'British Revolutions' (1641, 1688, and 1776) are better labeled 'Protestant Revolutions.' It is also significant that David Ramsay and Joseph Galloway, two of the earliest historians of the Revolution, identified Protestantism as an important contributor to Patriot justifications for war. Likewise, Patriot leader John Adams, in his three-volume defense of the US Constitution, cited both Bishop Ponet (republished in England in 1642) and the French *Vindiciae Contra Tyrannos* (published in England in 1581, 1648, and 1689) as essential influences on Anglo-American ideas of liberty." "Just Revolution," 48–49.

80. We should be cautious of claiming too much for the Reformed Protestant influence on the American colonists during the decades leading

to the American Revolution, but we can place too little on it as well. Moots and Morkevicius wisely place the Reformed Protestant contributions alongside the work of Grotius, Samuel von Pufendorf, Emmerich de Vattel, and John Locke.

81. Martin Luther, *Whether Soldiers, Too, Can Be Saved*, in *Luther's Works*, vol. 46, ed. Robert C. Schultz (Philadelphia: Fortress), 103, cited in Larson, *Calvin's Doctrine of the State*, 62. Moots and Morkevicius write, "While there were Lutherans in America (and some such as Peter Muhlenberg) who were enthusiastic supporters of the Revolution, many of the English, Scots, Irish, French, Germans and Dutch who came to the New World subscribed to the Reformed Protestant tradition. Sydney Ahlstrom's landmark religious history suggests that by 1776, three quarters of Americans shared a moral and religious background in Reformed Protestantism. This theological movement's theory of resistance and rebellion was even more robust than that of the Lutheran Tradition."

82. Thomas Aquinas, *On Kingship to the King of Cyprus*, ed. I. Thomas Eschmann, trans. Gerald B. Phelan (Toronto: Pontifical Institute of Mediaeval Studies, 1949), 1.6.48, cited in Larson, *Calvin's Doctrine of the State*, 60.

83. Thomas Aquinas, *Commentary on the Sentences of Peter Lombard* 2.44.2, in *From Irenaeus to Grotius: A Sourcebook in Christian Political Thought, 100–1625*, ed. Oliver O'Donovan and Joan Lockwood O'Donovan (Grand Rapids, MI: Eerdmans, 1999), 330. William Saunders nicely summarizes Thomas's argument for tyrannicide: "A tyrant by usurpation has illegitimately seized power and, therefore, is a criminal. When there are no other means available of ridding the community of the tyrant, the community may kill him. According to St. Thomas, the legitimate authority may condemn him to death using the normal course of law. However, if the normal course of law is not available (due to the actions of the tyrant), then the legitimate authority can proceed 'informally' to condemn the tyrant and even grant individuals a mandate to execute the tyrant. A private citizen who takes the life of a tyrant acts with public authority in the same way that a soldier does in war. The key conditions for a justifiable act of tyrannicide in this case include that the killing be necessary to end the usurpation and restore legitimate authority; that there is no higher authority available that is able and willing to depose the usurper; and that there is no probability that the tyrannicide will result in even greater evil than allowing the usurper to remain in power." See William Saunders, "Does the Church Condone Tyrannicide?," Catholic Education Resource Center (first published in *Arlington* [Virginia] *Catholic Herald*, 2003), https://www.catholiceducation.org/en/culture/catholic-contributions/does-the-church-condone-tyrannicide.html.

WORKS CITED

Bainton, Roland. *Christian Attitudes toward War and Peace.* Nashville: Abingdon, 1960.

Balke, Willem. *Calvin and the Anabaptist Radicals.* Translated by William J. Heynen. Grand Rapids, MI: Eerdmans, 1981.

Beza, Theodore. *Concerning the Rights of Rulers over Their Subjects and the Duty of Subjects to Their Rulers.* Translated by Henri-Louis Gonin. Capetown: H.A.U.M., 1956.

Bouwsma, William J. *John Calvin: A Sixteenth Century Portrait.* New York: Oxford University Press, 1988.

Bullinger, Henry [Heinrich]. *The Decades.* Edited by Thomas Harding. Cambridge: Cambridge University Press, 1849.

Calvin, John. *Institutes of the Christian Religion.* 2 vols. Edited by John T. McNeill. Translated by Ford Lewis Battles. Philadelphia: Westminster, 1960.

———. *Sermon 117.* In *Sermons on Deuteronomy,* translated by Arthur Golding, 721–29. London: Henry Middleton, 1583. Reprint, Edinburgh: Banner of Truth, 1987.

———. *A Short Instruction for to Arme All Good Christian People agaynst the Pestiferous Errours of the Common Secte of Anabaptistes* [also known as *Treatise against the Anabaptists*] (1549). True Covenanter, last updated January 29, 2022. http://www.truecovenanter.com/calvin/calvin_against_anabaptists.html.

Cicero, Marcus Tullius. *On Duties.* Edited by M. T. Griffin and E. M. Atkins. Cambridge Texts on the History of Political Thought. Cambridge: Cambridge University Press, 1991.

Coates, A. J. *The Ethics of War.* Manchester: Manchester University Press, 1997.

Cole, Darrell. "Listening to Pacifists." *First Things,* August 2002. https:www.firstthings.com/article/2002/08/listening-to-pacifists.

"Ecclesiastical Ordinances." In *The Register of the Company of Pastors in Geneva in the Time of Calvin,* edited and translated by Philip E. Hughes. Grand Rapids, MI: Eerdmans, 1966.

George, Timothy. "War and Peace in the Puritan Tradition." *Church History* 53, no. 4 (December 1984): 492–503.

Gouge, William. *God's Three Arrowes: Plague, Famine, Sword.* London: George Miller, 1631.

Hall, David H. "Calvin on Human Government and the State." In *A Theological Guide to Calvin's Institutes: Essays and Analysis,* edited by David W. Hall and Peter A. Lillback, 411–40. Phillipsburg, NJ: P&R, 2008.

Irish Articles of Religion (1615). Reformed.org. https://reformed.org/historic-confessions/.

Johnson, James Turner. *The Holy War Idea in Western and Islamic Traditions.* University Park: Pennsylvania State University Press, 1997.

———. *Ideology, Reason, and the Limitation of War.* Princeton: Princeton University Press, 1975.

———. *Just War Tradition and the Restraint of War.* Princeton: Princeton University Press, 1981.

Keen, M. H. *The Laws of War in the Late Middle Ages.* London: Routledge, 1965.

Knox, John. "The Regent and the Congregation." In *John Knox: On Rebellion,* edited by Roger A. Mason, 157–68. Cambridge Texts in the History of Political Thought. Cambridge: Cambridge University Press, 1994.

Larson, Mark J. *Calvin's Doctrine of the State: A Reformed Doctrine and Its American Trajectory, The Revolutionary War, and the Founding of the Republic.* Eugene, OR: Wipf & Stock, 2009.

Luther, Martin. *On War against the Turk.* In *Luther's Works,* vol. 46, edited by Robert C. Schultz, 155–205. Philadelphia: Fortress, 1967.

———. *Whether Soldiers, Too, Can Be Saved.* In *Luther's Works,* vol. 46, edited by Robert C. Schultz, 87–138. Philadelphia: Fortress, 1967.

McNeill, John T., ed. *John Calvin: On God and Political Duty.* Indianapolis: Bobbs-Merrill Educational Publishing, 1950.

Moots, Glenn A., and Valerie Ona Morkevicius. "Just Revolution: Protestant Precedents for Resistance and Rebellion." In *Justifying Revolution: Law, Virtue, and Violence in the American War of Independence,* edited by Glenn A. Moots and Phillip Hamilton, 35–63. Norman: University of Oklahoma Press, 2018.

Pavlischek, Keith. "Reinhold Niebuhr, Christian Realism, and Just War Theory: A Critique." In *Christianity and Power Politics Today: Christian Realism and Contemporary Political Dilemmas,* edited by Eric Patterson, 53–71. New York: Palgrave Macmillan, 2008.

Ramsey, Paul. *The Just War: Force and Political Responsibility.* Lanham, MD: Rowman and Littlefield, 1968.

Reid, W. Stanford. "The Transmission of Calvinism in the Sixteenth Century." In *John Calvin: His Influence in the Western World.* Grand Rapids, MI: Zondervan, 1982.

Saunders, William. "Does the Church Condone Tyrannicide?" Catholic Education Resource Center (first published in *Arlington* [Virginia] *Catholic Herald,* 2003). https://www.catholiceducation.org/en/culture/catholic -contributions/does-the-church-condone-tyrannicide.html.

The Thirty-Nine Articles of the Church of England. Reformed.org. https:// reformed.org/historic-confessions/.

Thomas Aquinas. *Commentary on the Sentences of Peter Lombard.* In *From Irenaeus to Grotius: A Sourcebook in Christian Political Thought, 100–1625*, edited by Oliver O'Donovan and Joan Lockwood O'Donovan, 328–30. Grand Rapids, MI: Eerdmans, 1999.

———. *On Kingship to the King of Cyprus.* Edited by I. Thomas Eschmann. Translated by Gerald B. Phelan. Toronto: Pontifical Institute of Mediaeval Studies, 1949.

———. *Summa Theologica.* Translated by the Fathers of the English Dominican Province. New York: Christian Classics, 1981.

Tuininga, Matthew J. *Calvin's Political Theology and the Public Engagement of the Church.* Cambridge: Cambridge University Press, 2017.

Wenger, J. C. "The Schleitheim Confession of 1527." *Mennonite Quarterly Review* 19, no. 4 (October 1945): 247–53.

Westminster Confession of Faith (1647). Reformed.org. https://reformed.org/historic-confessions/.

Yoder, John Howard. "Barth's Revision of the Traditional View of War." In *Karl Barth and the Problem of War*, 37–42. Nashville: Abingdon, 1970.

SIX

Just War and the Church of England

Daniel Strand and Nigel Biggar

THE CHURCH OF ENGLAND
AND ITS MORAL THEOLOGY

The Church of England came into being in the 1530s during the reign of King Henry VIII by the enacting of a series of laws that removed the English church from papal jurisdiction and placed it under the authority of the English monarch as its "Supreme Governor."[1] This break with Rome was welcomed by churchmen and laity who were sympathetic to the theology of Martin Luther (1483–1546) and other continental Reformers; and under Queen Elizabeth (1533–1603) the church acquired an official, moderately Protestant character. This "Elizabethan Settlement" was not so very settled, however, and in the words of Peter Marshall, who sums up the consensus of contemporary historians, "The Reformation in England was a thorny and protracted process and by no means straightforwardly unidirectional."[2] For much of her reign Elizabeth resisted pressure from "Puritans" to move the church in a markedly Calvinist and anti-Roman Catholic direction, although her moderating resistance was undermined by a combination of military threats from foreign Catholic powers such as

Spain and France and domestic plots by English Catholics to overthrow her. Although the Church of England has remained basically Protestant in its Lutheran soteriology, it has always contained elements of sympathy for the traditions of the undivided, pre-Reformation Church — for example, the "Great Tew Circle" of intellectuals in the 1630s and early 1640s who yearned for the reunion of divided Christendom, as well as the Anglo-Catholic movement from the 1830s, which drew inspiration from the early fathers and the medieval church.

In its ethical thinking, the Church of England (otherwise known as "the Anglican Church") has retained a connection with the pre-Reformation, scholastic tradition. In book 1 of his foundational *Treatise of the Laws of Ecclesiastical Polity*,[3] Richard Hooker (ca. 1554–1600) established Anglican moral theology on foundations owing more to Thomas Aquinas than to Martin Luther. As a consequence, like Roman Catholic moral theology, Anglicanism has sought moral understanding primarily with reference to the natural law and has tended to esteem more highly than its Lutheran, Reformed, or Anabaptist counterparts the power of natural reason to discern what is good and right, albeit aided and corrected by the grace of special revelation. Accordingly, it has also been more ready to accredit sources of moral wisdom other than Scripture — in particular, reason, experience, and empirical science.

In addition, the Anglican Church has inherited from Thomist moral theology a high regard for moral reasoning in the form of "casuistry"— that is, the development of moral norms in the process of their application to concrete cases. This has found expression in an Anglican casuistical tradition, which flourished in the seventeenth century in the hands of divines such as William Perkins (1558–1602), William Ames (1576–1633), Robert Sanderson (1587–1663), Joseph Hall (1574–1656), and Jeremy Taylor (1613–67), and which Kenneth Kirk (1886–1954) sought to revive in the 1920s.[4]

INFLUENCES ON ANGLICAN THOUGHT ABOUT WAR AND PEACE

In its attitude toward the use of force by the state, the Church of England has always officially belonged to the so-called magisterial Reformation, rather than the so-called radical Reformation. That is to say, it has upheld the God-given duty of Christian rulers or magistrates to use force—if need be, violent force—to maintain law and order and suppress crime. The classic biblical authority for this view is, of course, Romans 13:1–7, according to which God ordained public authorities to use "the sword" to curb the wicked.

It is true that this refers to the maintenance of civil, domestic law and order, not international law and order among states. However, it was not until well into the nineteenth century that England invented a civil police force. Until then, there was no distinction between those charged with keeping the lawful peace within English society and those charged with imposing it on the outside. Militia and, later on, the standing army, *were* the police. War, therefore, was viewed merely as an interstate extension and analogue of domestic policing. As Luther himself put it: "For the very fact that the sword has been instituted by God to punish the evil, protect the good, and preserve the peace is powerful and sufficient proof that war and killing along with all the things that accompany wartime and martial law have been instituted by God. What else is war but the punishment of wrong and evil? Why does anyone go to war, except because he desires peace and obedience?"[5]

We have observed how Anglican moral theology did not sever itself from late-medieval scholastic thinking, in general, nor from just war thinking in particular. As we shall see below, the works of early Anglican moral theologians such as William Ames drew explicitly from this tradition in their own arguments about conducting war justly. In his *De conscientia et ejus jure vel casibus libri quinque* (1630), Ames states the basic *jus ad bellum* criteria that can be found in the formulation of Thomas Aquinas (1225–74) in the *Summa Theologica* (1268–71), which were developed by his later disciples Francisco de Vitoria (1483–1546) and Francisco Suárez (1548–1617).[6] While Aquinas himself did not invent the classic "just war" tradition, he organized and summarized the tradition of discussion in a way that would prove influential on subsequent formulations. Gratian's *Decretum*, a comprehensive and systematic corpus of canon law published around 1140, was the single greatest influence on Aquinas. The other major influence was Augustine of Hippo (354–430), who provided Aquinas with the basic theological contours for his discussion of war—namely, as an exercise of *caritas* or charity.

In its Thirty-nine Articles of Religion, the Church of England sought to position itself in relation to Roman Catholics, Reformed or Calvinist Protestants, and, to a lesser extent, Anabaptists. Unlike more comprehensive confessional statements, the Thirty-nine Articles were not intended to cover all aspects of the Christian faith but, rather, to make clear the church's positions on certain important and controversial issues. One of these issues was the role of the civil magistrate relative to war. The Articles went through a number of revisions before their final form was inserted into the Book of Common Prayer in 1571. Archbishop Thomas Cranmer (1489–1556), the Articles' primary author, composed early versions that were decidedly more Reformed than the final form. However, when the final version is compared with the 1553 Forty-Two Articles of Religion, it can be seen that the section on the "Civil Magistrates" had not changed much at all. In both cases, the authority of the civil magistrate to execute capital punishment upon wrongdoers and to bear weapons and engage in warfare is upheld as God ordained. More significantly, these magisterial duties are regarded as incumbent upon Christians — in implicit contradiction of the Anabaptists' view that, while the use of "the sword" is divinely authorized, it is forbidden to the disciples of Christ.

In the Augsburg Confession (1530), which exerted great influence on Cranmer's own formulations in the different drafts of the Thirty-nine Articles, opposition to the Anabaptists is made explicit in the affirmation of the magistrate's duty to wield the sword to punish wrongdoers and engage in just wars. Augsburg also emphasized the goodness of political life as ordained by God and asserted that Christians should participate without reservation in the political order through the offices of judging or soldiering.

The text of the Thirty-nine Articles of Religion states in a brief and concise manner the duties of the civil magistrate before God, emphasizing the God-ordained role of the magistrate to "rule all estates and degrees committed to their charge by God, whether they be Ecclesiastical or Temporal, and restrain with the civil sword the stubborn and evil-doers."[7] Unlike Augsburg, however, the Thirty-nine Articles primarily emphasize the role of monarch as sovereign rather than Christians' duty and freedom to participate in the various offices of civil society.

Cranmer and the Thirty-nine Articles do not invoke Augustine directly, nor does the Augsburg Confession, at least not in the way that Luther did in his own writings on political authority. The realism that Luther draws from Augustine in his blunt view of the magistrate as the hangman who must punish evil is not stated explicitly in either of these confessions. However, we can see the influence of Luther and Augustine's realism in an earlier edition of the Thirty-nine Articles that was only discovered recently. Cranmer composed the earlier Thirteen Articles in 1538 in preparation for discussion with German Lutherans. It is notable that the discussion of the civil magistrate here is quite long and articulate, from which we may infer that the question of the role of the magistrate was more pressing in England than on the continent. Two other things are worth highlighting in Cranmer's exposition. First, he quotes Augustine and demonstrates a Luther-like view of civil government as restraining wickedness and punishing evil—although he comes closer to Calvin in his advocacy of kings and princes as the defenders of true religion. Second, Cranmer asserts that magistrates are "to undertake just war for the defense and safety of themselves and their state,"[8] before continuing at some length to enumerate others' duties.

In this earlier version we see a much richer and more expansive view of the magistrate and civil government than in the final Thirty-nine Articles. We also get a better sense of the influences that shaped Cranmer's view of politics and war. He stands firmly within the stream of Reformation thinking on warfare and civil government—which was Augustinian in its basic orientation—while reading Augustine in a variety of ways.

HISTORICAL CONTRIBUTIONS TO THINKING ABOUT WAR AND PEACE

The Ethical Hinterland: Reason and Casuistry

Anglican contributions to "just war" thinking have been shaped by the style of early Anglican ethical thinking. We have already noted how Richard Hooker established Anglican moral theology on foundations closer to Aquinas than to Luther. We have also noted its comparatively positive appraisal of the ability of natural reason to make moral judgments. In contrast, other streams of the Reformation, having a much less positive view of the rational capacities of fallen humanity, tended to start from special revelation in scripture or to use direct citations from Scripture to back their moral reasoning and conclusions. Accordingly, Anglican ethics has been more inclined than other Protestant traditions to appreciate moral wisdom in nonscriptural sources. This proclivity is evident, for example, in Archbishop of Canterbury William Temple (1881–1944), who took seriously the contributions to ethical debates from the social and natural sciences. We can also see it in the Church of England's custom since the 1950s of forming multidisciplinary working parties to address ethical issues, parties that have included philosophers, natural and social scientists, and practitioners, as well as theologians.

Another element that we have seen Anglican moral theology preserve from its pre-Reformation, scholastic inheritance is its appreciation of casuistry. This style of moral reasoning suffered searing criticism from Luther, as it did later from Karl Barth (1886–1968). Its moral judgments arise from the careful interpretation of general or specific rules in relation to concrete cases, rather than from direct appeal to Scripture or, in the case of Barth, from hearing a concrete command of God. Luther was strongly critical of casuistry because of its use in the late medieval penitential system. As a means for determining the gravity of confessed sins, it tended toward a legalism and moralism that eclipsed, in Luther's thinking, the more important spiritual depth of sin and the religious faith in God's grace required for salvation.

Contrary to Luther, English Puritan divines such as William Perkins and William Ames became convinced of the pastoral need for the provision of precise moral guidance along the lines of scholastic moral theology. However, Perkins and Ames did not merely adopt the Catholic tradition; rather, they adapted it to Protestant theological presuppositions. The innovation, then, of the Anglican reworking of casuistry was, in the words of Nigel Biggar, to set it "loose from the confessional, aiming to reach a judgement, not retrospectively about the gravity of sins confessed, but prospectively about the right course of action to be taken."[9]

Developments in "Just War" Doctrine

In Ames's *De conscientia* there is a straightforward presentation of the *jus ad bellum* criteria that we find in Aquinas. For instance, in answering question 1 in chapter 33 of book 5 Ames enumerates the just conditions for warfare as just cause, proper authority, and right intention. In answering the next question (q. 2), Ames lays out the conditions for *jus in bello*, in accordance with a just mode of acting. Next, he discusses further issues such as whether a Christian prince should call on the aid of an infidel (in answering question 3), to what extent combatants waging war must agree with the justice of its cause (in answering question 4), how much of a sin it is to wage war with a wrong intention (in answering question 5), and whether it is just to use plots and tricks in war (in answering question 8).

Ames's reflections on "just war" were not the Church of England's earliest contribution. Alberico Gentili (1552–1608) was an Italian Protestant who fled to England, where he became Regius Professor of Civil Law at Oxford. Widely recognized as one of the leading jurists of his day, Gentili was a Roman legal scholar and humanist who had been trained in civil law at the University of Perugia, following the tradition of Bartolus of Saxoferrato (1313–57) and Bartolus's disciple Baldus (1327–1406). Best known for his work *De jure belli, libri tres* (1588–89, 1598), Gentili combined a strong historical treatment of the practice of warfare with normative analysis. His discussion of *just cause* was extensive, covering some eighteen chapters. His work would prove to be a significant reference point for Hugo Grotius (1583–1645) in the following century.

Following ancient Roman jurists, Gentili defines *war* as "a just contest of arms"[10]—a formal contest between sovereign equals. Drawing upon the work of legal humanists, he argues that war is akin to the legal process by which litigants enter into proceedings in good faith. Since it may be unclear upon entering the contest of arms who rightly possesses the *just cause*, both sides should observe the same rules of behavior. Theory is different from application, however. Applying the criteria of just war to concrete cases will often yield ambiguous and inconclusive results. The reality of the difficulty of determining the just cause of a war leads Gentili to argue that "war may be waged justly on both sides."[11] Perhaps the most notable—and controversial—feature of his work is his argument in favor of "preventative," as distinct from "preemptive," war. The latter is a defensive action taken at the eleventh hour against an attack that is known to be in the process of being realized and that will be launched at midnight. The former is a "defensive" action taken against a party that might, at some indeterminate time in the future, become an active threat, but is not presently. Gentili hints at this when he writes that "one ought not to delay, or wait to avenge at one's peril an injury which one has received, if one may at once strike at the root of the growing plant and check the attempts of an adversary who is meditating evil."[12] But his meaning becomes more explicit later: "We must therefore oppose [powerful and ambitious chiefs]; and it is better to provide that men should not acquire too great power, than to be obliged to seek a remedy later, when they have already become too powerful. . . . But to conclude: a defence is just which anticipates dangers that are already meditated and prepared, *and also those which are not meditated, but are probable [verisimilia] and possible [possibilia]*."[13]

Gentili's work on the ethics of war was a major influence on Hugo Grotius's seminal work, *De jure belli et pacis* (1625), which was later translated into English by William Whewell (1794–1866). Whewell, who was the Knightbridge Professor of Moral Theology and Casuistical Divinity at the University of Cambridge, also devoted a small portion of his work *Elements of Morality, Including Polity* (1855) to addressing "the rights of war." Following Grotius, he argued that the limitation of warfare by international law is a recognition that it is limited by certain moral constraints. The right to undertake war (*jus ad bellum*) can only be exercised by a state that is authorized to act in defense of its citizens—as distinct from non-state actors—and that therefore has some prima facie claim to be acting in accord with justice. In terms of justice in fighting wars (*jus in bello*), combatants who have surrendered must no longer be treated as active belligerents, since they cannot properly be considered "an object of hostility." War is waged against the "public force" of an opposing state, and when a combatant is captured or surrenders, then he is no longer part of that public force and should therefore be accorded a different status with different protections. In addition, while the killing of prisoners may be understandable in certain circumstances, the legal prohibition of such killing would be a more desirable norm.[14] Use of deception in general is acceptable, as are military ambushes, but the use of assassins and poisoners is a violation of the public nature of warfare. Good faith also requires that mutually recognized modes of communication, such as the truce, be recognized.[15] With regard to noncombatants, an invading army "supersedes the higher functions of the State in the invaded country," and thus possesses the right to tax populations and levy a "contribution." Private property is to be respected, and persons not involved in hostile activities should be free to go about their normal work.[16] If noncombatants engage in guerrilla warfare, they ought to lose their protection as noncombatants, since they violate the fundamental distinction between combatant and noncombatant.[17]

Neutral parties may not aid belligerents by carrying munitions to them or transporting goods to a place that has been declared under blockade.[18]

Two further notable Anglican contributions to just war thinking were made during the Second World War. George Bell (1883–1958), bishop of Chichester, argued that war with Germany, though regrettable and tragic, was just and necessary. The Nazi State had become an absolute tyranny over both the church and people in Germany and, therefore, had to be opposed at all costs: "By making the State an absolute, they subordinate truth, goodness, mercy and justice to the supposed interests of the State as interpreted by the contemporary leader and party. By regarding the individual citizen as existing for the sake of the State, they take all genuine worth away from the individual personality."[19] Bell drew upon the Roman Catholic tradition of "just war" criteria to defend the cause of the war against Germany. In order for a war to be just it must first have been declared by a legitimate authority; second, have just and grave cause, proportionate to evils it brings about; third, only be undertaken after all means of peaceful solution of the conflict have been exhausted without success; fourth, have serious chances of success; and, fifth, be carried out with the right intention.[20] Yet, while Bell was highly critical of the controversial "area" bombing of German cities, his colleague, William Temple, initially held that civilian deaths were permissible, so long as they were not directly intended.[21]

THE JUST DEFENSE OF NATIONAL LIFE

An important element of Anglican political thought in the nineteenth and twentieth centuries that informs the just cause for war is the value of independent national life. Frederick Dennison Maurice (1805–72) affirmed "the sanctity of national life"[22] as a positive value worth defending, arguing that to value a nation's laws, government, and language is something quite different from viewing foreigners with contempt. Further, Maurice presented a view of Christ's kingdom as containing many nations, "a kingdom of all nations," emphasizing the plural nature of the kingdom as opposed to a homogenous "world-empire."[23] War, within Maurice's perspective, is a "struggle for Law against Force; for the life of a people as expressed in their laws, their language, their government, against any effort to impose on them a law, a language, a government which is not theirs."[24] Over and against an aggressive imperialist nationalism, Maurice presents an account of nationalism as a reverence and attachment to one's national life and traditions without being outwardly expansionist or inwardly nativist.

The views of Maurice on the sanctity of national life continued into the twentieth century. William Temple, in his 1928 Henry Scott Holland Memorial Lectures, continued to affirm the value of particular nations against the cosmopolitanism of his time. Presenting a high view of the nation-state, Temple affirmed that "each national community is a trustee for the world-wide community, to which it should bring treasures of its own; and to submit to political annihilation may be to defraud mankind of what it alone could have contributed to the general wealth of human experience."[25] Similarly, in the 1935–36 Gifford Lectures, Hensley Henson (1863–1947), bishop of Durham, drew a sharp distinction between *patriotism* and *nationalism*, which is not unfamiliar today: "Patriotism pictures humanity as a composite of many distinctive national types, enriched with the various achievements of history. Nationalism dreams of a subject world, an empire of its own wherein all men serve its interests and minister to its magnificence."[26]

In recent years two leading Anglican moral theologians, Oliver O'Donovan and Nigel Biggar, the former and current holder of the Regius Chair of Moral and Pastoral Theology at Oxford University, have both continued this tradition of affirming the importance of national life against cosmopolitanism. In his *Desire of the Nations: Rediscovering the Roots of Political Theology*, O'Donovan presents the biblical case for international order of plural nations unified by international law as opposed to universal, imperial government. Unlike empire, "law holds equal and independent subjects together without allowing one to master the other."[27] In a similar vein, Nigel Biggar has developed an ethical account of the value of distinctive national institutionalizations of universal goods and of the virtue of a qualified national loyalty. In so doing he has argued against cosmopolitan interpretations of Christian love.[28]

CONTRIBUTIONS TO WAR AND PEACE AFTER THE SECOND WORLD WAR

The work of the Methodist ethicist Paul Ramsey initiated a general resurgence of just war scholarship in the 1960s that directly influenced Anglican moral theology through Oliver O'Donovan, who studied with Ramsey at Princeton in the 1970s. At about the same time, ethical questions raised by nuclear deterrence drove other Anglicans to rediscover just war thinking. The morality of the nuclear deterrent would be the main focus of the Anglican discussion of war in the 1980s, provoking explicit engagement with the just war tradition by both individuals and church bodies.

In 1982, the Board for Social Responsibility of the General Synod of the Church of England published *The Church and the Bomb: Nuclear Weapons and Christian Conscience.*[29] This was one of the most important reports of the post-1945 multidisciplinary working parties and is one of the most substantial Anglican treatments of war to date. It was published at a time when President Ronald Reagan had assumed a more aggressive posture toward the Soviet Union, thereby creating alarm in both America and Europe about the increased possibility of nuclear warfare. The Board's report expressed deep misgivings about the possibility of nuclear war being waged in a limited and proportionate manner. In particular, it confessed to deep skepticism about the possibility of maintaining a "firebreak" between the different levels of nuclear weapons. Although *The Challenge of Peace*, a pastoral letter published the following year by the National Conference of Catholic Bishops (US),[30] shared that skepticism, *The Church and the Bomb* was more stringent in its evaluation, judging that even the defensive use of nuclear weapons would be immoral, because of the disproportion between its destructive effects and the end of achieving just peace. The report argued that the entire program of deterrence is immoral because it either involves the conditional threat to do an immoral action—"the consent to act immorally, even though the act never be performed, is already sinful"[31]—or a bluff that would still make political and military leaders culpable for requiring military subordinates to adopt a sinful intention to use immoral weapons. Further, the report acknowledged that multilateral disarmament would avoid dangerous instability, while recommending that Britain should disarm unilaterally for the purpose of bolstering the Non-Proliferation Treaty and eliminating the possibility of another center of nuclear decision-making.[32] In responding to the report in 1983, however, the General Synod of the Anglican Church adopted a more conservative motion that affirmed "the duty of H.M. [Her Majesty's] Government and her allies to maintain adequate forces to guard against nuclear blackmail and to deter nuclear and non-nuclear aggressors," while urging the government to take "immediate steps in conjunction with her allies to . . . reduce progressively NATO's dependence on nuclear weapons and to decrease nuclear arsenals through[out] the world."[33]

Oliver O'Donovan's first major foray into the debate around nuclear weapons came six years later in the form of an extended essay, *Peace and Certainty: A Theological Essay on Deterrence*, in which he argued against the use of the strategy of nuclear deterrence on moral grounds. The scope of O'Donovan's argument is broad and historical. Rather than arguing in the strictly ethical terms of just war, he offers a broader, theological criticism of "modernity." In line with the Board for Social Responsibility, he agrees that nuclear deterrence is inherently immoral and indefensible as a national policy. In the pursuit of peace at any cost, nuclear deterrence has bought the peace at the price of disproportion: "Disproportion is not an accident of modern deterrence; it is the principle on which it is thought."[34] The root of the problem is the modern world's impatience with the pursuit of peace and proximate justice, which is motivated by an overriding aspiration "for the seat of divinity and the exercise of omnipotence." What deterrence reveals is the idolatrous desire of the proud to exercise divine control over the events of history.[35] In addition, O'Donovan is unconvinced that nuclear deterrence as a policy has worked. It follows that there is nothing to lose in getting rid of deterrence, though he is aware of the dangers of immediate and unilateral disarmament, preferring first to bolster conventional and battlefield nuclear weapons while attempting bilateral disarmament.[36]

O'Donovan went on to develop a more comprehensive theological account of just war reasoning in his *The Just War Revisited* (2003). Here he covers many topics, including economic sanctions as a tool in warfare, counterinsurgency, and war crimes trials, but as with all of O'Donovan's oeuvre, he does so in terms of a distinctive theological account of what war is and the grounds upon which it may take place. War is an act of political judgment analogous to acts of judgment enacted within the domestic sphere. Yet it is not merely the punishing of wrong but an "evangelical counter-praxis" to the "antagonistic praxis" of the aggressor. Just war, even though it is penal in orientation, asserts "a practical claim, that God's mercy and peace may and must be witnessed to in this interim of salvation-history through a praxis of judgment."[37] The underlying thrust of the book, as is visible in the preface, is to develop a "'spirituality' of just-war theory," for "the reflecting subject conscious of his or her own responsible position before God in relation to other members of society who have their own differently responsible positions."[38]

Two other examples of the Anglican application of just war thinking to the nuclear question in the mid-to-late 1980s deserve mention. Richard Harries, shortly before he was named the bishop of Oxford, published *Christianity and War in the Nuclear Age* (1986).[39] (Four years earlier he had also published a book on guerrilla warfare entitled *Should a Christian Support Guerrillas?*)[40] And then David Fisher, a senior civil servant in the Ministry of Defence and an Anglican layman, offered a moral defense of the policy of deterrence in *Morality and the Bomb* (1985).[41] Twenty-five years later, Fisher published *Morality and War: Can War Be Just in the Twenty-First Century?* (2011) as both a defense of the "just war" tradition and an application of it to contemporary cases and issues such as the 1991 Gulf War, the 2003 invasion of Iraq, terrorism, and genocide.[42]

Working in the same stream of the classic just war tradition as O'Donovan, his successor in the Regius chair at Oxford, Nigel Biggar, has added his own distinctive contributions. By applying moral concepts to concrete cases, Biggar's approach bears similarity to the casuistic method that Ramsey deployed so effectively. In his *In Defence of War* (2013), Biggar sought to address a number of important contemporary questions about the nature and application of just war ethics. Not shy about his own Christian theological framework, Biggar engages a number of contemporary interlocutors with both Christian and nonreligious viewpoints. First, he argues not only that the just war tradition comports with the basic convictions of New Testament Christianity but also that the pacifism made popular by Stanley Hauerwas, John Howard Yoder, and Richard Hays, which dominates current Christian ethics, does not hold the moral high ground. Peace is not simple; our country may enjoy peace, but only because we do not stir ourselves to relieve the innocent suffering of another country at the hands of an unjust aggressor. Writes Biggar, "Since acts of pacifist omission can also have grave effects, pacifists, too, must deliberate as best they can about the evils of peace."[43] Second, Biggar responds to the challenge made by pacifists and other critics of war that war cannot be exercised as an act of love, and he does so by providing an account of how anger and retribution can be exercised, in Augustine's phrasing, as "a sort of kind harshness."[44] Both anger at the wrong being committed and the retribution that is "just war" belong to, and are qualified by, a larger process that seeks to bring about peace. Far from advancing mere abstract theory, Biggar draws upon personal accounts of soldiers to demonstrate that "soldiers are usually motivated primarily by love for their comrades" and that "they can regard their enemies with respect, solidarity, and even compassion—all of which are forms of love."[45] This is important because Biggar seeks to consider the possibility of actually living out the just war ethic in battle, not just as a set of moral principles guiding political decision-makers. Further chapters consider the concept of proportionality in terms of the First World War, the nature and authority of international law in terms of the 1999 Kosovo intervention by NATO, and the complexity of reaching an overall moral judgment about a war in terms of the 2003 invasion of Iraq.

CONTEMPORARY CASES

Before addressing responses from within the Church of England to contemporary cases, we need to attend to two features of the present historical context. First, since America has been the dominant military power in the West and the world since the end of the Second World War, and especially since the collapse of the Soviet Union, the views of Britons and, by extension, members of the Church of England are colored by their views of America, which are often ambivalent—combining admiration, affection, skepticism, and resentment. Though there is still a historically rooted appreciation among the British public for the necessity of fighting wars under certain circumstances, this intuition is complicated and qualified by criticism of American global hegemony, consumerism, and political rhetoric that presents America as a quasi-messianic nation called to shed "Light" on the world's "Darkness." Whatever the motivations, a certain anti-American strain persists in the British public at large, especially on the political left, and so in the Church of England, which affects how the church has viewed contemporary wars.

The other contextual feature to be kept in mind, which more directly influences Anglican views of war, is a certain pacifist tendency. As we have already noted, pacifism has never been the official or the dominant position within the Church of England. Nevertheless, a sort of "practical" pacifism, which does not rule out the possibility of just warfare in theory but in practice raises the standards so high as to be well-nigh impossible to meet, does sometimes prevail. Thus, there is a tendency toward wishful thinking—that there always has to be "a better way" than war. For sure, this "practical pacifism" is more common among continental Europeans, especially among Germans, than among the British—for obvious historical reasons. Nevertheless, it is a force to be reckoned with in today's Church of England.

Three recent wars have provoked discussion and exposed tensions within Anglican thinking about warfare—Kosovo, Afghanistan, and Iraq. The war in Kosovo took place between February 1998 and June 1999 and was eventually brought to an end when NATO gave air support to Kosovar-Albanian forces. The Church of England's response, like the general public's, was mixed. Richard Harries, as bishop of Oxford, issued an official statement in March 1999 that criticized the decision to launch air strikes on the basis of just war criteria. Harries argued that other nonmilitary options should have been exhausted before intervention. Moreover, the action, lacking authorization by United Nations Security Council, was illegal, and the effects of the bombing were ill-considered. Later, however, Harries presented a report from the Board for Social Responsibility to the General Synod under the title *Inside Out—the Balkans Conflict*, which raised the question of whether earlier intervention might have been wiser and asking, "How much responsibility do the Churches bear for failing to face up to evil and support the necessary stern measures?"[46]

In response to the Board for Social Responsibility's equivocal reading of the intervention, Nigel Biggar defended NATO's response as morally justifiable. In both a lengthy article published in the *Church Times* and a later book chapter, Biggar argued that the action had been a last resort that had been undertaken on behalf of nineteen countries, thus throwing into doubt the contention that intervention was merely another exercise in gratuitous American imperialism, as the famous British playwright Harold Pinter had asserted. ("The truth is that neither Clinton nor Blair gives a damn about the Kosovar Albanians. This action has been yet another blatant and brutal assertion of U.S. power using NATO as its missile. It sets out to consolidate one thing—American domination of Europe."[47]) Against the claim that the war had been straightforwardly illegal, Biggar argued that a case can be made for the qualification of the black letter law of the UN Charter by customary law or international human rights law. But even if it were granted that the NATO intervention did not meet the requirements of international law, it still remains possible that it was morally justified because legality does not trump morality.[48] Later, Biggar further elaborated his argument that moral law transcends national legal systems and positive international law: "One thing that [the transcendence of moral law] implies is that military action can sometimes be morally justified in the absence of, and even in spite of, statutory international law. Therefore, the ["just war"] doctrine's proponents cannot join those who believe that the legitimacy of military intervention to prevent or halt grave injustice is decided simply by the presence or absence of authorization by the United Nations Security Council."[49]

In response to the terrorist attacks on New York and Washington, DC, in September 2001, the United States and its allies launched a war in Afghanistan, to stop the Taliban regime from providing a safe haven to the terrorist group responsible, al-Qaeda. The Church of England's reaction to this displayed the same ambivalence as its position on Kosovo. At the gathering of its General Synod in November 2001, the Board for Social Responsibility presented a discussion paper under the title "Al-Qaeda and Afghanistan—a Just War?"[50] The paper argued that, while the 9/11 attacks warranted a "counter-terrorist" response, the forms of that response should have been more diverse, encompassing legal action, diplomacy, intelligence gathering, public education, and policing, and not purely military operations. After debate, the synod contented itself with neither endorsing nor condemning the war in Afghanistan, merely carrying a motion that condemned terrorism, affirmed the general just war rule that terrorism may "be opposed in the last resort by the use of proportionate armed force," expressed reservations about the Afghanistan campaign, and observed that world peace can be achieved with "the commitment of governments to work for a peaceful and equitable world order under the auspices of the United Nations."[51]

In contrast to its ambivalent stances on Kosovo and Afghanistan, the Church of England's response to the invasion of Iraq in 2003 was unequivocally negative. Among other things, discussion did provoke thought about the distinction between "preemptive" and "preventative" war. The Church of England's House of Bishops made a submission to Parliament's House of Commons Foreign Affairs Select Committee's inquiry into the "foreign policy aspects of the war against terrorism," in which it argued that the threat posed by Iraq did not rise to the level of an imminent threat, making the invasion a case of an immoral "preventative" war, rather than a morally permissible "preemptive" war. A later submission by the church's Public Affairs Unit in June 2003 affirmed "preemptive" war as a legitimate possibility, while stressing the need for "clear and transparent rules underpinning its use."[52] One such rule is the existence of "demonstrable and compelling evidence of the hostile intent and capability of a perceived aggressor."[53]

QUESTIONS STILL OUTSTANDING

Among the important issues that the Church of England—along with other churches in Europe and the United States—needs to address is the moral legitimacy of waging war as a tool of statecraft. Is the use of force an extension of politics? Is it one more perfectly legitimate item in the tool bag of governments with regard to international relations that is to be used judiciously and prudently? Or is it never to be used in practice since it can never meet the bar of absolute incontrovertibility and complete assurance of moral purity? The answer given too often is that, in practice, war must be avoided at all costs. Deference to the United Nations or preference for some nonmilitary solution is too often a means of evasion, of avoiding the need to grasp nettles, of averting eyes from the unavoidable risk, moral ambiguity, and tragedy of things. Peace is not simple; our preference for "peace" can mean that innocents suffer destruction. If military intervention entails high risks and costs, so too can nonintervention. As we watch destruction and death continue to engulf Syria, in a war in which early and determined military intervention by Western countries might have stanched the bloodshed and imposed a sufficient peace, the Church of England and Anglicans worldwide should contemplate the fact that peace for the West does not mean peace or justice for the rest of the world.

Another issue that bears further reflection is the status of international law and the role of the United Nations with regard to the just waging of war. Can only military interventions that receive authorization from the UN Security Council be considered legal? Is legality the last word? The Church of England tends toward affirmative answers. But Christians, who believe in God-created, culturally transcendent moral law, cannot regard positive, human law as the final word. In light of the moral failures to intervene in Rwanda and Darfur, the church needs to clarify when the letter of international law may be overridden in the name of the moral obligation to defend the innocent from atrocious and massive aggression.

If recent history is any guide, the default deference shown to the UN should, at a minimum, be reexamined. Competing political interests of the Security Council in the past and present have made it nearly impossible to gather support for even some of the most clear-cut cases for humanitarian intervention. Such stalemates will only increase in number as great-power competition between Russia, China, and the United States continues to mount in the near future. Granted the important roles that international institutions play as well as the value of upholding international norms for the peace and prosperity of the world, it remains true that it is particular nations and alliances—chiefly NATO—that have been both able and willing to use force when required, and not the United Nations. All of this points to the need for a more honest conversation within the Church of England about the role that international institutions can realistically play and about the proper limits of deference to them.

This bears directly on a third issue that deserves further thought: the moral status of humanitarian intervention. The past twenty-five years have seen major humanitarian atrocities go unaddressed by the international community, either at all or until it was too late. Now that the Syrian civil war appears to be entering into its final phase, we will soon have to reckon with another conflict, where Western countries and churches were content to sit and watch, while hundreds of thousands of innocent civilians were killed and millions displaced. In this case, international law sanctioned Russia's support of the murderous Assad regime (because the regime consented to it), while forbidding foreign intervention against the regime (because Russia would have vetoed it in the Security Council). While the UN Security Council has been paralyzed, the Assad regime, with Russian support, rained down indiscriminate barrel-bombs and even chemical weapons on its own people in densely populated urban areas. If the Church of England is serious in its attachment to Christian just war thinking, wherein the paradigm of *just cause* is the rescue of the innocent from grave injustice, then it needs to think further about the political realities, as well as the moral imperatives, of humanitarian intervention. The wisdom of the just war tradition, as early Anglican history attests, is that it is able to speak to geopolitical challenges of any age, and in our age those challenges will likely present themselves in the form of international crises that fall short of conventional warfare yet require application of coercive—even lethal—force in order to protect the innocent.

NOTES

1. Note: the monarch is merely the "Supreme Governor," not the "Head," which is Jesus Christ.

2. Peter Marshall, "(Re)defining the English Reformation," *Journal of British Studies* 48, no. 3 (July 2009): 565.

3. Richard Hooker, *Book I: Concerning Law and Its General Kinds*, in *The Laws of Ecclesiastical Polity in Modern English*, ed. Bradford Littlejohn, Bradley Belschner, and Brian Marr, with Sean Duncan (Landrum, SC: The Davenant Institute, 2019), 47–118.

4. Protestant traditions of casuistry disappeared from sight in the early eighteenth century, until Kirk's attempted revival two hundred years later. For an explanation of what happened, see Nigel Biggar, "A Case for Casuistry in the Church," *Modern Theology* 6, no. 1 (1989): 29–51.

5. Martin Luther, *Whether Soldiers, Too, Can Be Saved*, in *Luther's Works*, vol. 46, ed. Robert C. Schultz (Philadelphia: Fortress, 1967), 95.

6. Aquinas discusses war in his larger section on the virtue of love (*caritas*) in *Summa Theologica* II-II.40.

7. See, e.g., Articles of Religion, article 37, available through Center for Reformation Anglicanism, https://www.anglicanism.info/articles-of-religion.

8. Gerald Bray, *Documents of the English Reformation, 1526–1701* (Cambridge: James Clarke & Co., 1994), 204.

9. Nigel Biggar, "The Church of England on War and Peace," in *How the Churches in Germany and England Contribute to Ethical Decision Making* (Hanover: Evangelische Kirche in Deutschland, 2003), 19–31.

10. Alberico Gentili, *De jure belli, libri tres*, vols. 1–2, trans. John C. Rolfe (London: Humphrey Milford, 1933).

11. Gentili, *De jure belli, libri tres*, 1.6, cited in Gregory M. Reichberg, Henrik Syse, and Endre Begby, eds., *The Ethics of War: Classic and Contemporary Readings* (Oxford: Blackwell, 2006), 372.

12. Gentili, *De jure belli, libri tres*, 1.4, cited in Reichberg, Syse, and Begby, *Ethics of War*, 376.

13. Gentili, *De jure belli, libri tres*, 1.14, cited in Reichberg, Syse, and Begby, *Ethics of War*, 377 (emphasis added).

14. William Whewell, *The Elements of Morality, Including Polity*, 4th ed. (Cambridge: Deighton, Gell & Co., 1864), 1061, 1066.

15. Ibid., 1062–63.

16. Ibid., 1067.

17. Ibid., 1071.

18. Ibid., 1073.

19. G. K. A. Bell, *Christianity and World Order* (Harmondsworth: Penguin, 1940), 68.

20. Ibid., 72–73.

21. For a fuller account, see Stephen Lammers, "William Temple and the Bombing of Germany: An Exploration of the Just War Tradition," *Journal of Religious Ethics* 19, no. 1 (Spring 1991): 71–92.

22. F. D. Maurice, *Social Morality* (London: Macmillan, 1893), 183.

23. Ibid., 180.

24. Ibid., 180–81.

25. William Temple, *Christianity and the State*, Henry Scott Holland Memorial Lectures, 1928 (London: Macmillan, 1928), 172.

26. Hensley Henson, *Christian Morality: Natural, Developing, Final*, Gifford Lectures, 1935–36 (Oxford: Clarendon, 1936), 269.

27. Oliver O'Donovan, *Desire of the Nations: Rediscovering the Roots of Political Theology* (Cambridge: Cambridge University Press, 1996), 71.

28. Nigel Biggar, *Between Kin and Cosmopolis: An Ethic of the Nation* (Eugene, OR: Wipf & Stock, 2014), chaps. 1 and 3.

29. *The Church and the Bomb: Nuclear Weapons and Christian Conscience: The Report of a Working Party under the Chairmanship of the Bishop of Salisbury* (London: Hodder and Stoughton, 1982).

30. See *The Challenge of Peace: God's Promise and Our Response* (Washington, DC: National Conference of Catholic Bishops, 1983), https://www.usccb.org/upload/challenge-peace-gods-promise-our-response-1983.pdf.

31. *Church and the Bomb*, 98.

32. Ibid., 160.

33. The Church of England, General Synod, *The Church and the Bomb: The General Synod Debate, February 1983* (London: CIO Publishing, 1983).

34. Oliver O'Donovan, *Peace and Certainty: A Theological Essay on Deterrence* (Oxford: Clarendon, 1989), 6–7.

35. Ibid., 26, 28, 61, 92, 121.

36. Ibid., 109–12.

37. Oliver O'Donovan, *The Just War Revisited*, Current Issues in Theology (Cambridge: Cambridge University Press, 2003), 1, 9.

38. Ibid., ix.

39. Richard Harries, *Christianity and War in the Nuclear Age* (London: Mowbray, 1986).

40. Richard Harries, *Should a Christian Support Guerrillas?* (Guildford: Lutterworth, 1982).

41. David Fisher, *Morality and the Bomb: An Ethical Assessment of Nuclear Deterrence* (London: Croom Helm, 1985).

42. David Fisher, *Morality and War: Can War Be Just in the Twenty-First Century?* (Oxford: Oxford University Press, 2011).

43. Nigel Biggar, *In Defence of War* (Oxford: Oxford University Press, 2013), 33.

44. Ibid., 61.

45. Ibid., 91.

46. Richard Harries, *Inside Out—the Balkans Conflict*, in *General Synod: Report of Proceedings 1999* (London: Church House Publishing, 1999), 313.

47. Harold Pinter, quoted in Audrey Gillan, "Bombing Shames Britain, Pinter Tells Protesters," *Guardian*, June 6, 1999, https://www.theguardian.com /world/1999/jun/07/audreygillan.

48. Biggar, *In Defence of War*, 216.

49. Ibid., 215.

50. "Al-Qaeda and Afghanistan—a Just War?," Church of England's Board for Social Responsibility, GS Misc 662 (London: General Synod, November 2001).

51. *General Synod: Report of Proceedings 2001*, November Group of Sessions, 32/2 (London: Church House Publishing, 2002), 153.

52. Church of England's Public Affairs Unit, *A Submission to the House of Commons Foreign Affairs Select Committee's Inquiry into the Decision to Go to War in Iraq* (London: Church House Publishing, 2003), 3.

53. Ibid., 4.

WORKS CITED

"Al-Qaeda and Afghanistan—a Just War?" Church of England's Board for Social Responsibility, GS Misc 662. London: General Synod, November 2001.

Ames, William. *De conscientia et ejus jure vel casibus libri quinque*. Amsterdam: Jan Jansson, 1630.

Articles of Religion. Center for Reformation Anglicanism. https://www.anglican ism.info/articles-of-religion.

Bell, G. K. A. *Christianity and World Order*. Harmondsworth: Penguin, 1940.

Biggar, Nigel. *Between Kin and Cosmopolis: An Ethic of the Nation*. Eugene, OR: Wipf & Stock, 2014.

———. "A Case for Casuistry in the Church." *Modern Theology* 6, no. 1 (1989): 29–51.

———. "The Church of England on War and Peace." In *How the Churches in Germany and England Contribute to Ethical Decision Making*, 19–31. Hanover: Evangelische Kirche in Deutschland, 2003.

———. *In Defence of War*. Oxford: Oxford University Press, 2013.

Bray, Gerald. *Documents of the English Reformation, 1526–1701.* Cambridge: James Clarke & Co., 1994.

The Challenge of Peace: God's Promise and Our Response. Washington, DC: National Conference of Catholic Bishops, 1983. http://www.usccb.org/upload /challenge-peace-gods-promise-our-response-1983.pdf.

The Church and the Bomb: Nuclear Weapons and Christian Conscience; The Report of a Working Party under the Chairmanship of the Bishop of Salisbury. London: Hodder and Stoughton, 1982.

The Church of England, General Synod. *The Church and the Bomb: The General Synod Debate, February 1983.* London: CIO Publishing, 1983.

Church of England's Public Affairs Unit. *A Submission to the House of Commons Foreign Affairs Select Committee's Inquiry into the Decision to Go to War in Iraq.* London: Church House Publishing, 2003.

Fisher, David. *Morality and the Bomb: An Ethical Assessment of Nuclear Deterrence.* London: Croom Helm, 1985.

———. *Morality and War: Can War Be Just in the Twenty-First Century?* Oxford: Oxford University Press, 2011.

General Synod: Report of Proceedings 1999. London: Church House Publishing, 1999.

General Synod: Report of Proceedings 2001. London: Church House Publishing, 2002.

Gentili, Alberico. *De jure belli, libri tres.* Vols. 1–2. Translated by John C. Rolfe. London: Humphrey Milford, 1933.

Grotius, Hugo. *De jure belli et pacis* [The law of war and peace]. Translated by Francis W. Kelsey, Arthur E. R. Boak, Henry A. Sanders, Jesse S. Reeves, and Herbert F. Wright. Livonia, MI: Lonang Institute, 2011.

Harries, Richard. *Christianity and War in the Nuclear Age.* London: Mowbray, 1986.

———. *Inside Out—the Balkans Conflict.* In *General Synod: Report of Proceedings 1999.* London: Church House Publishing, 1999.

———. *Should a Christian Support Guerrillas?* Guildford: Lutterworth, 1982.

Henson, Hensley. *Christian Morality: Natural, Developing, Final.* Gifford Lectures, 1935–36. Oxford: Clarendon, 1936.

Hooker, Richard. *Book I: Concerning Law and Its General Kinds.* In *The Laws of Ecclesiastical Polity in Modern English*, edited by Bradford Littlejohn, Bradley Belschner, and Brian Marr, with Sean Duncan, 47–118. Landrum, SC: The Davenant Institute, 2019.

Lammers, Stephen. "William Temple and the Bombing of Germany: An Exploration of the Just War Tradition." *Journal of Religious Ethics* 19, no. 1 (Spring 1991): 71–92.

Luther, Martin. *Whether Soldiers, Too, Can Be Saved.* In *Luther's Works*, vol. 46, edited by Robert C. Schultz, 87–138. Philadelphia: Fortress, 1967.

Marshall, Peter. "(Re)defining the English Reformation." *Journal of British Studies* 48, no. 3 (July 2009): 564–86.

Maurice, F. D. *Social Morality.* London: Macmillan, 1893.

O'Donovan, Oliver. *Desire of the Nations: Rediscovering the Roots of Political Theology.* Cambridge: Cambridge University Press, 1996.

———. *The Just War Revisited.* Current Issues in Theology. Cambridge: Cambridge University Press, 2003.

———. *Peace and Certainty: A Theological Essay on Deterrence.* Oxford: Clarendon, 1989.

Reichberg, Gregory M., Henrik Syse, and Endre Begby, eds. *The Ethics of War: Classic and Contemporary Readings.* Oxford: Blackwell, 2006.

Temple, William. *Christianity and the State.* Henry Scott Holland Memorial Lectures, 1928. London: Macmillan, 1928.

Thomas Aquinas. *Summa Theologiae* [with Latin text, English translation, introduction, notes, appendices, and glossary]. Translated by Thomas Gilby. 60 vols. New York: McGraw-Hill, 1964.

Whewell, William. *The Elements of Morality, Including Polity.* 4th ed. Cambridge: Deighton, Gell & Co., 1864.

SEVEN

Methodism and War

Mark Tooley

Methodism began as an early eighteenth-century renewal movement within the Church of England led by Oxford-educated priest John Wesley. Although Wesley's purpose was not to found a new church, Methodism/ Wesleyanism eventually became the main non-Calvinist Protestant stream within Anglosphere Christianity. Today, the largest Wesleyan denomination is the United Methodist Church, which has about six million members in the United States and another six million worldwide. There are dozens of other Wesley-inspired denominations worldwide, with the vast majority having "Methodist" or "Wesleyan" in their name or being affiliated with the Church of the Nazarene (Nazarenes). Wesleyan theological influences were profound in America's Holiness Movement of the late nineteenth century, when the Nazarenes, the Christian Missionary Alliance, and other groups were founded, and in the subsequent Pentecostal revival of the early twentieth century, which saw the formation of denominations such as the Assemblies of God.

This chapter focuses attention specifically on mainline Methodism, primarily in the United States, beginning with the teachings of John Wesley himself, with a view to consider the development of American-Methodist teachings on war, peace, and security. Although Wesley largely adhered to classical Christian teaching on the need for political order and the authority of government officials to use force, he was not systematic in his work on this subject. As we will see, American Methodism shifted theological course over time. For much of the nineteenth century Methodists were typically supportive of US wars, providing theological rationales from that of order based on Romans 13 to judgment. Many Methodists—though not all by any means—saw the liberation of parts of the old Spanish Empire as not just a political transformation but the opportunity for spiritual enlightenment for those populations as well. However, following World War I, many Methodists followed other Christians in the United States, Europe, and Canada in adopting a pacifistic stance that was less theological and more practical: how could the West survive another catastrophe like the Great War? It was immoral to countenance such destruction ever again. Thus, with the exceptional interlude of World War II, which most Methodists—clergy and laity alike—saw as a just war, the mainline Methodists (today's United Methodists) became increasingly pacifistic in the twentieth century, although again, not simply for theological reasons but also due to a growing political leftism that embraced liberation theology from the Vietnam era forward. In recent years we have seen a tug of war between orthodox Christians who would affirm classic just war teaching and those who affirm a pacifistic and leftist orientation. This chapter will attempt to examine these shifts over time and conclude with the important work of Methodist minister and academic Paul Ramsey (1913–88), who succeeded in awakening a generation of classical Christian just war thinking on issues ranging from nuclear weapons to humanitarian intervention.

JOHN WESLEY AND THE FIRST CENTURY OF METHODISM

John Wesley (1703–91) was an Anglican priest, theologian, author, and evangelist. However, he was not a systematic theologian, and he did not specifically write about the ethics of war and peace or just war tradition per se. His occasional reflections about war and civil disorder across his over sixty-five years of active ministry show that he believed magisterial Protestant teaching about the state's vocation to wield the sword in defense of order and justice. Wesley generally supported the wars conducted by Britain during his lifetime, including the suppression of the American Revolution. Methodist chaplains served in the British army. As American Anglican cleric Briane K. Turley wrote in *Methodist History* in 1991,

> John Wesley had much to say about the moral issues of war. However his polemology, like his theology, may be characterized as lacking systematic development. Wesley apparently never wrote a treatise on war that offers a definitive and detailed treatment of the subject for the modern scholar. Nevertheless, careful analysis and gleaning of all of Wesley's writings yield a significant body of data which, when correlated, reveals that Wesley possessed a generally consistent point of view in his appraisal of war. While it is readily admitted that Wesley was unsystematic in much of his writings, it can be said in his favor that he was a master of practical theology.[1]

And as Stephen Rankin of Southern Methodist University wrote in *Methodist Review* in 2011, Wesley's fairly consistent view of war aligned with just war teaching: "When Wesley wrote in favor of the use of military force, the conditions which he had in mind fit easily within just-war criteria. In each case in which he spoke positively of military engagement, he perceived a threat to the (flawed but essentially just) British nation [which he saw as] a demonstration of original sin."[2]

As his writings evince, Wesley inherited a traditional Christian understanding of the state's ordained power to rule, which included a duty to employ force in some circumstances. Rankin summarizes the reformer's perspective in this way: "Wesley believed that a duly established government, in sincere pursuit of justice and good order, had the authority to use the sword. This seems to be Wesley's basic theoretical assumption. His writings show circumstances in which he felt this principle had come into play and he was willing to do what he could in such times—as a loyal British citizen—to help defend the nation."[3] Theodore Weber of Emory University, in his *Politics in the Order of Salvation: Transforming Wesleyan Political Ethics*, describes Wesley in similar terms: "Although Wesley did not use the terminology, his normative attitude towards war and responsibility can be categorized as a form of the just war ethic. He was a peacemaker, but not a pacifist." Weber continues, "The just war stance alone is

Wesleyan in the historical sense. The larger problem is that his writings on war show no real evidence of theologically grounded moral reasoning in arriving at the position. He seems to have been there from the beginning, and to have taken it for granted—more or less—thereafter."[4]

In his assessment of Wesley, Briane Turley observes that despite the lack of comprehensive reflection about just war teaching by Methodism's founder, "enough evidence can be found in Wesley's writings to establish a place for him in history alongside of individuals who, like St. Augustine, Hugo Grotius and Martin Luther, may be properly described as 'just war theorists.'" Turley admits that the evidence available in support of this claim is "implicit rather than explicit in nature," but the "content of Wesley's political philosophy negates even the remotest possibility that he may be properly interpreted as a Christian pacifist in the modern sense." Turley notes that many eighteenth-century Methodists served in the British army and navy without any recorded disapproval from Wesley.[5]

Wesley's view on war flowed from his reverence for Britain's constitutional order and his belief that political authority is ordained by God. His reflection on Romans 13:1 in his *Explanatory Notes on the New Testament*, which were considered doctrine for Methodist preachers, led him to state: "Let every soul be subject unto the higher powers. For there is no power but of God: the powers that be are ordained of God." He further noted:

> Power, in the singular number, is the supreme authority; powers are they who are invested with it. That is more readily acknowledged to be from God than these. The apostle [Paul] affirms it of both. They are all from God, who constituted all in general, and permits each in particular by his providence. The powers that be are appointed by God— It might be rendered, are subordinate to, or, orderly disposed under, God; implying, that they are God's deputies or vicegerents and consequently, their authority being, in effect, his, demands our conscientious obedience.[6]

Wesley believed that the right to kill belonged not to the "will of the people" but only to God, who confers this power upon government for justice and public order. "There is no supreme power, no power of the sword, of life and death, but what is derived from God, the sovereign of all," Wesley said. Turley summarizes Wesley's view: "Human agency does not possess the right to forfeit life; therefore, it cannot confer that right upon the state. Hence, no government possesses the right to wage war; such authority is bestowed upon the state by God alone."[7] Understanding war as ultimately under divine authority, Wesley, according to Rankin, saw the possibility of war in terms of four categories: as evidence of human sinfulness, as evidence of God's judgment, as a "bad witness" for Christian nations, and as justifiable military action.[8]

Instructive for early Methodist thinking on war was the governing Methodist Conference for Wesley's preachers, which first met in 1744 and where it was asked: "Is it lawful to bear arms?" The journal's recorded answer, presumably from Wesley himself as presiding elder, is this: "We incline to think it is: 1. Because there is no command against it in the New Testament; 2. Because Cornelius, a soldier, is commended there."[9] In his *Notes on the New Testament*, Wesley observed of Matthew 26:52, where Christ pronounces, "Put up again thy sword into its place," that "all they that take the sword—Without God's giving it them: without sufficient authority"—are unauthorized.[10] For Wesley, legitimate political authority, ordained by God, alone could take the sword.

Also, in his *Notes*, Wesley recalled a biblical war for laudable purpose. In Genesis 14, Abram went to war to help Lot, prompting Wesley to observe: "We have here an account of the only military action we ever find Abram engaged in; and this he was not prompted to by avarice or ambition, but purely by a principle of charity."[11] Wesley additionally described in his *Notes* how Israel is a divine instrument for vengeance against the Philistines and how heathen nations are left by God in the promised land to test Israel, with Wesley describing war as God's way of keeping Israel reliant on him. As Rankin notes, Wesley saw war in the Old Testament as a soteriological tool.[12]

Upon the invasion of The Stuart Pretender from France in 1745, Wesley supported British military exertions, but as with Israel and the Philistines, he saw the war as chastisement. In his *A Word in Season: or Advice to an Englishman*, he declined to inveigh against the invading aspirant to the British crown and his supporters. Instead, Wesley reflected on why Britain, as target of divine wrath, was subject to the invasion: "Because of our sins; because we have well-nigh 'filled up the measure of our iniquities.'"[13]

In perhaps his most robust affirmation of just war, in 1756, amid the threat of French invasion during the Seven Years War, Wesley himself offered among the Methodist societies to "raise for His Majesty's service at least two hundred volunteers, to be supported by contributions among themselves; and to be ready in case of an invasion to act for a year (if needed so long) at His Majesty's pleasure." His brother Charles mockingly reflected: "I question whether my brother's soldiers, with all his pains and haste to train them up, will not be too tardy to rescue us."[14]

Wesley was not only concerned about external threats to Britain. In 1768 British troops, in what is known as the St. George's Field Massacre, opened fire and killed protesters rioting against the imprisonment of John Wilkes, a critic of the government. The Wilkites became an ongoing disruptive social force that was distressing to Wesley, who thought that the troops had acted correctly. In 1772, in his *Thoughts upon Liberty*, he lamented that the protesters were "spread[ing] deadly poison" in the land,[15] and he noted of the troops that these "men of war do really at this time preserve the peace of the nation."[16]

Another passing comment that reveals Wesley's presumption of force as central to government's purpose was recorded in his journal in 1778, where he observed: "At St. Peter's Church I saw a pleasing sight, the Independent Companies, raised by private persons associating together without any expense to the government. They exercised every day, and, if they answer no other end, at least keep the Papists in order, who are exceedingly alert ever since the army was removed to America."[17] In addition, Wesley saw the British war in America against the colonists as self-defense against "fanatics of liberty" and lawlessness. Wesley thought the British military response was justified after having exhausted other peaceful means, that it was proportionate to the threat of disorder, and that it had good intention insofar as the British were not seeking conquest or vengeance.[18]

As leader of Methodism in Britain, Wesley did not make his views about war a requirement. John Nelson, a Methodist preacher, defied impressment into military service, telling the court, "I shall not fight; for I cannot bow my knee before the lord to pray for a man, and get up and kill him when I have done." However, prominent Methodist preacher John Fletcher, who was close to Wesley and seen as his successor, wrote *The Bible and the Sword* to defend British suppression of the American rebellion.[19] Wesley's opposition to the American Revolution chagrined Francis Asbury, chief circuit-riding founding bishop of American Methodism. Asbury and early American Methodism supported the new US government while largely avoiding direct comment on contemporary political issues, including the War of 1812.

As a political realist who believed in the doctrine of original sin, Wesley understood the importance of military force in sustaining a balance of power to protect liberty and prevent war. In his journal late in life, he commended *Compassionate Address to the Inhabitants of Ireland* (1778), warning that British war against the Americans would leave Britain militarily vulnerable to France and Spain.[20] In that same address Wesley referred to Irish guerrillas in the countryside as "intestine vipers, who are always ready to tear out their mother's bowels." And he declared: "Blessed be God, there are still within the kingdom some thousands of regular troops ... who are ready to march wherever they shall be wanted." Rankin observes that Wesley here offered a "glimpse of how the conceptual anchor of legitimate government authority" permits state force against internal disorder.[21]

While war was sometimes morally justified, Wesley also saw war as the fruit of human sin and the result of heavenly judgment. As Weber notes, Wesley "insists that war is a work of God,"[22] the "misery of war is divine punishment for sin," a "dramatic and painful call to repentance," and an "event in the economy of God — an instrument of God's justice and redemption."[23] In his *A Word in Season*, published during the 1745 Jacobite Rebellion, Wesley asked why his nation was "on the very brink of destruction," and answers: "Because of our sins, because we have well-nigh 'filled up the measure of our iniquities.'"[24] And in his *A Seasonable Address to the More Serious Part of the Inhabitants of Great Britain* (1776), Wesley warned that Britain's conflict in America was a "divine contention" and the consequence of British iniquities around the world, especially the slave trade, cautioning that monarchies "rose by virtue; but they fell by vice." As Weber describes it, "War is the punishment an entire nation draws for the multiplicity of sins, most of which have nothing to do with war."[25]

Wesley specifically cited Britain's slave trade for incurring divine disfavor through war: "But it is certain that iniquity of every kind, and amongst all ranks and orders of men, has and does abound; and as we are punished with the sword, it is not improbable, but one principle sin of our nation is, the blood that we have shed in Asia, Africa, and America."[26] Yet even though wars were a form of divine wrath, Wesley "supported wars of self-defense, and placed a high premium on what he saw as the biblically grounded duty to obey the governing authorities." Wesley objected when his preachers were sometimes coerced into military service through press gangs, but he did not object to their service per se, especially as Methodist preachers in the military evangelized fellow soldiers.[27]

As seen in his famous 1775 observation in *National Sins and Miseries*, Wesley's view toward war, even as a British patriot, was grudging and unromantic:

> And, as if all this were not misery enough, see likewise the fell monster, war! But who can describe the complicated misery which is contained in this? Hark! The cannons roar! A pitchy cloud covers the face of the sky. Noise, confusion, terror, reign over all! Dying groans are on every side. The bodies of men are pierced, torn, hewed in pieces; their blood is poured on the earth like water! Their souls take their flight into the eternal world; perhaps into everlasting misery. The ministers of grace turn away from the horrid scene; the ministers of vengeance triumph. Such already has been the face of things in that once happy land where peace and plenty, even while banished from great part of Europe, smiled for near a hundred years.[28]

Very aware that soldiers may at any point be taken into the "eternal world," Wesley preached often to them, noting: "And surely the fear and the love of God will prepare them either for death or victory." Sometimes he reminded them of Christ's command to "render to Caesar the things that are Caesar's." At the same time, Methodists serving in the military were expected to uphold Christian morality. The 1782 Methodist Conference decreed expulsion for any Methodists practicing military exercises on Sundays. If not naïve about morals in the military, Wesley still reverenced Britain's armed forces, telling a preacher in 1779: "You did well in lending the preaching-house to the Army. I would show them all the respect that is in my power."[29]

Although he was opinionated about the policies that led to war, Wesley's focus always remained on the divine drama of human redemption, of which war was a part. Wesley's perspective, in the words of Weber, was that "God's interests were religious, not political. The larger context of divine action was the reconstitution of the fallen world . . . chastising sinners and idolators, and calling them to repentance." God was the lord of war but not its author, which was human pride and avarice.[30]

While an enthusiast for Britain, Wesley admitted to British moral failures in statecraft. In his *A Concise History of England: From the Earliest Times to the Death of George II*, published in 1775, Wesley chided King Henry V during the Hundred Years War for waging war with wrong intent, having "attacked [France] without the least provocation," lamenting that the king had "filled it with widows and orphans, lamentation, misery, and every species of distress."[31] And in his own day, Wesley similarly denounced war making on noncombatants, writing: "How guilty so ever an enemy may be, it is the duty of brave soldiers to remember that he is only to fight an opposer and not a supplicant," at the same time ruing British excesses against The Pretender's followers in 1746 and noting that the victory "was in every respective decisive, [but] humanity to the conquered would have rendered it glorious."[32] What's more, he lamented the "cruel" and "unjust" conduct in war of Kings Edberg and Edward I, along with the Duke of Marlborough.[33]

Wesley likewise inveighed against mistreatment of wartime prisoners. "War itself is justifiable only on principles of self-preservation," he insisted. "Therefore, it gives no right over prisoners but to hinder their hurting us by confining them. Much less can it give the right to torture, or kill, or even enslave an enemy when the war is over."[34]

Amid his additional concerns about waging war justly, Wesley denounced pillage and plunder. He also opposed bribing an invading army and saw as an "atrocious act" worthy of the "reproach of all good men" the holding of prisoners for ransom. In his *Some Observations on Liberty* of 1776, Wesley warned that Britain even in a just war, as against America, could not rightly fight to "acquire dominion or empire, or to gratify resentment"; rather, it could fight "solely to gain reparation for injury."[35]

Wesley grieved over wars among Christian nations, which he feared defamed the name of Christ; nothing more horrid than war between Christians: "I mean, between those that bear the name of Christ, and profess to 'walk as he also walked.' Now, who can reconcile war, I will not say to religion, but to any degree of reason or common sense?"[36] With the conflict with America in mind, Wesley in 1776 implored: "Let not those who were designed to save the earth destroy it. Let not Christians engage in the controversy in the spirit and temper of the world, and bite and devour one another."[37] Wesley further admonished British and American Christians not to dishonor their Christian witness before the "heathen," by which he presumably meant America's natives, and perhaps African slaves: "Brother goes to war against brother; and that in the very sight of the Heathen. Surely this is a sore evil amongst us! Christians going to war against fellow Christians is a work of the devil, and Christians ought not to have a part in it. If Christians in this situation do not act in a Christ-like way, with wisdom, compassion and love, then unbelievers will be led away into error. Rather, Christians should be the salt and light that Jesus calls them to be in the Sermon on the Mount."[38]

While admitting the particular tragedy of warring Christians, Wesley made clear that war was universal thanks to original sin:

> From whence comes that complication of all the miseries incident to human nature, war? Is it not from the tempers "which war in the soul?" When nation rises up against nation, and kingdom against kingdom, does it not necessarily imply pride, ambition, coveting what is an other's; or envy, or malice, or revenge, on one side, if not on both? Still, then, sin is the baleful source of affliction; and consequently, the flood of miseries which covers the face of the earth—which over-whelms not only single persons, but whole families, towns, cities, kingdoms—is a demonstrative proof of the overflowing of ungodli-ness in every nation under heaven.[39]

Wesley sketched the tragic absurdity of war in this way:

> Here are forty thousand Men gathered together on this Plain. What are they going to do? See, there are thirty or forty thousand more at a little Distance. And these are going to shoot them through the Head or Body, to stab them, or split their Sculls, and send most of their Souls into ev-erlasting Fire, as fast as possibly they can. Why so? What Harm have they done to them? O none at all. They do not as much as know them. But a Man, who is King of France has a quarrel with another Man, who is King of England, so these Frenchmen are to kill as many of those Englishmen as they can, to prove the King of France is in the right.[40]

Wesley further asked, "What farther Proof do we need of the utter Degen-eracy of all Nations, from the plainest Principles of Reason and Virtue? Of the absolute Want both of common Sense and common Humanity, which runs through the whole Race of Mankind?"[41]

Yet Wesley's appreciation for the power of divine grace persuaded him that peacemaking was a viable option for Christians, even as his belief in original sin precluded pacifism. Thus Weber:

> John Wesley was a peacemaker but not a pacifist. He could understand and advocate the possibilities of reasoning towards a solution of international or intra-empire conflict; he believed that war was a stupid way for rational beings to try to resolve their difficulties. Also, he was convinced of the possibilities of gaining peace by repenting and turning to God—even if done only by one party to the conflict. However, he did not advocate attempting to achieve peace by unilateral renunciation of power. His unwavering belief in the presence and persistence of original sin would have worked against such a proposal, had he chosen to reflect openly on it and especially on original sin as a limiting factor in peacemaking. Providing more immediate resistance was his conviction that governments were authorized by God to maintain order and provide defense. Failure to carry out this mandate would be dereliction of duty before God.[42]

Rankin suggests reasons why Wesley had no developed theoretical view on war:

> He lived and served in view of this larger reality—the Kingdom of God. The kingdom of this world would eventually become the Kingdom of our Lord and of his Christ. The renewal movement over which God had providentially set Wesley, was truly more important for the world than geopolitical conflicts and the interests of nation-states. In this regard, I believe it is only a half-truth to identify Wesley as having a just-war position. Doing so does not reflect the pressure forward—the trajectory—toward a peace-oriented vision. The available categories—pacifism, just war, realism—are essentially ahistorical. Wesley's view of salvation, while being thoroughly theological, was also deeply historical.[43]

Turley offers the following appraisal of Wesley and war:

> Apparently, Wesley harbored at least a tacit sense of respect for those whose Christian convictions would not permit them to participate in

any form of armed conflict. Wesley's own political antecedents would never allow more than this. The primary consideration for Wesley was not whether Christians should or should not participate in war. What was important was that the Christian take positive steps toward the realization of a just and lasting peace. It is the Christian who truly recognizes the source of all power, and it is the Christian, advancing the cause of peace, who can face the future in calm assurance that the Lord of history is active in the universe, transforming the darkness of injustice to the light of perfect love.[44]

BEYOND WESLEY:
AMERICAN METHODISM IN THE 1800S

Wesley's failure to outline theoretical just war teaching extensively was part of his larger avoidance of articulating a specifically Wesleyan political theology. Wesley did propose a holistic image of God that included the natural, political, and moral. However, his failure to develop more fully the divine political image left Methodist political theology underdeveloped on issues like war, even when it was not wholly absent.

Early American Methodism, led by Bishop Francis Asbury, inherited Wesley's legacy, but as a distinctly new church, in a different political context. And without Wesley's academic background, with literate but not very educated clergy, it lacked a firm political theology, much less a defined just war teaching. Asbury had carefully avoided public comment during the American Revolution, as Wesley's opposition to the patriot cause impaired Methodist growth in America. After the war, Asbury continued his political avoidance, including non-engagement with the War of 1812, which divided Methodists, as it did the nation, between New England Federalists on the one hand and Southern and frontier Jeffersonians on the other. In Wesleyan fashion, Asbury declared that "doubtless our sins as a nation had provoked the divine indignation against us, and therefore we must expect to suffer."[45]

Methodist preacher Nathan Bangs recounted of the War of 1812 era that "notwithstanding hostile armies were already measuring swords, the God of Israel was still at work for the salvation of the people."[46] He also reported that "the faithful servants of God, keeping aloof as much as possible from the strife of party and the war of words," steadily pursued their way "in search of 'the lost sheep of the house of Israel,'" while some "ministers of the gospel, biased perhaps too much by some influential members of their congregations, refused even to pray for their rulers and country."[47] According to Bangs' narrative, Bishop Asbury, who had adopted this country as his own, and "most cordially loved" its institutions, "declared most plainly and pointedly, on the floor of an annual conference, that he who refused, at this time especially, to pray for the country, deserved not the name of a Christian or a Christian minister, inasmuch as it was specifically enjoined on all such not only to honor magistrates but to "pray for all that are in authority, that we may lead quiet and peaceable lives, in all godliness and honesty."[48] Bangs noted that New York clergy largely decided not to pray for America's rulers, and most of the clergy in eastern states opposed the "measures of the government" regarding the war.

After the War of 1812, Methodism continued its dramatic growth until reaching nearly 1.5 million adherents in 1850 with 13,000 congregations, accounting for perhaps one-third of American religious believers. Methodist pietism largely began to recede in favor of active support for American democracy and often intense political engagement. Methodism was divided between north and south in 1844, but Methodism nationally was generally supportive of the Mexican-American War in 1846–48. It may have even been the most prowar of American's churches. As Luke Schleif writes in *Methodist History*, Methodists saw the Mexican regime as autocratic and beholden to Catholic superstition. Its defeat would open Mexico to Methodist and Protestant evangelism along with democratic republican principles.[49]

Methodist stances toward the Mexican war mirrored Wesley's view that war was simultaneously the fruit of sinful humanity and providential. An official northern Methodist periodical in 1846 noted that wars "come of man's lust, his inordinate desire of power, distinction, and wealth," but also God could force the "wrath of man to praise him" by making wars "subservient to his great and ultimate purposes of mercy to the family of man." As with the Opium Wars, God could use an "unjust war" to reach souls "heretofore shut up in heathen darkness, and the grossest and most demoralizing superstition." The church journal opined that through war "God [had] designs of mercy toward the people of Mexico and its dependencies," with uplift from "a religious, as well as civil point of view," so that the "blessings of civil and religious liberty may be diffused over the provinces conquered by our armies."[50]

An 1846 northern Methodist sermon admitted that the war was terrible but asserted that it was prosecuted with an "enlightened, humane and liberal policy of our government" and would "bring the great body of the Mexican People under the influence and training of American Institutions." Similarly, an official southern Methodist journal argued in 1847 that God was using the war for "the advancement of Society and the ultimate benefit of the world." Another southern Methodist article in 1848 argued that "the present war of the two republics will end in a toleration of Protestantism throughout the land of the Aztecs."[51]

Thirteen years later, Methodist confidence in American republican democracy would fuel even greater support, along regional lines, for the Civil War. Methodism had become the largest and wealthiest church in its region and understood itself to have societal duties, which included support for war. As *The History of American Methodism* describes it, "When debate gave place to military contest, the sense of responsibility for public righteousness merged with patriotic support of the nation at war."[52] Although southern Methodism insisted it was less "political" than the northern church, it spiritually supported the Southern war cause. As the official Methodist journal of Nashville wrote after the firing on Fort Sumter in 1861, "We exhort our countrymen, as they begin in the right, so to keep in the right. This itself is strength: it is more than armies. Preserve local order. Avoid swearing and drunkenness. Remember the Sabbath day. Patriotism is a duty which the Christian religion enjoins and has illustrated by glorious examples. Let prayer be made at the head of regiments."[53] The most famous Methodist pronouncement during and in support of the war came from the Methodist Episcopal Church General Conference in 1864, which reminded President Lincoln of the church's devotion: "In this present struggle for the nation's life many thousands of her members, and a large number of her ministers, have rushed to arms to maintain the cause of God and humanity. They have sealed their devotion to their country with their blood on every battle-field of this terrible war."[54] To which Lincoln responded: "It is no fault in others, that the Methodist Church sends more soldiers to the field, more nurses to the hospital, and more prayers to Heaven, than any."[55] Northern Methodist enthusiasm for the war included pastors often serving as US Army recruiting officers, and some army companies were nearly exclusively composed of particular Methodist congregations. Perhaps as many as 125,000 Methodists served in the northern army. Methodism's most prominent cleric, Bishop Matthew Simpson, a friend to Lincoln, famously sermonized in 1864: "This nation has the sympathy of the masses all over the earth, and if the world is to be raised to its proper place, I would say it with all reverence, God cannot do without America."[56]

America as God's instrument in peace and war was a Methodist theme that continued through the Spanish-American War. William McKinley was America's most devout Methodist president, and Methodist thinking no doubt influenced his seizure of the Philippines, at least in his explanation to visiting Methodist clergy in 1899. After praying in the White House, he resolved that "there was nothing left for us to do but to take them all, and to educate the Filipinos, and uplift and civilize and Christianize them, and by God's grace do the very best we could by them, as our fellow men for whom Christ also died."[57] After McKinley's assassination, McKinley was hailed at the northern Methodist General Conference for having "commanded armies, declared wars, overthrown kingdoms, crushed tyrants, and lifted up the downtrodden," while it was celebrated that war globally was "becoming unpopular" thanks to spreading "Christian civilization."[58]

Methodist support for America at war culminated with World War I. For three years President Wilson strove to remain neutral between the Allies and the Germanic powers, with Methodist support. Pacifism was increasingly influential in the churches, partly from the import of German theology and partly from the resurgence of idealistic pietism. The 1916 General Conference of northern Methodism endorsed a League of Nations that would "protect weak peoples from outrage and oppression and restrain strong peoples from breaking the peace of the world." Church leaders intoned: "If America should now seek to save her life by withholding her service, she would lose her life, and deserve to lose it. Under the inspiration of leadership of the Christian host within its borders, this nation should stand for the righteousness of the Sermon on the Mount in all national and international affairs."[59]

After President Wilson asked Congress to declare war in 1917, Methodists were overwhelmingly supportive. "We protest against the utterance of any word that would either weaken [President Wilson's] hands or give the slightest encouragement or comfort to our national foes," declared the southern bishops in 1918. They urged fighting until the "bitter end" for total victory. "The Methodist Episcopal Church," it was declared, "is supporting this righteous war in every possible way."[60]

Northern bishops were also enthusiastic. Bishop R. J. Cooke of Montana said: "We are in the war in order that righteousness shall prevail upon God's earth." Minnesota bishop Charles Baird Mitchell announced: "I am a pacifist, but I have suspended my pacifism until we get the Kaiser. I am opposed to war, but I am not opposed to this war."[61] Moreover, Methodism supported Wilson's proposed League of Nations. Georgia bishop Warren A. Candler asserted in 1919 that opposition to it by Christians "would be treason to their Lord." Churches must "lend all their influence to any reasonable plan to make as nearly impossible as may be the repetition of such a hideous chapter in human history."[62]

In sum, for most of the nineteenth century up through World War I, many Methodists supported American involvement in war, not just for political reasons but for those that were clearly theological. Part of that rationale was rooted in classic Christian teaching on political order and governmental authority, human sin and fallenness, and just war thinking. At the same time, there were other motivations as well, such as a desire to prosecute the South in pursuit of ending slavery or an understanding of war that suggested it contained an element of divine judgment. Many American Protestants, including Methodists, saw the corrupt Spanish Empire as barbarous and superstitious and believed that American intervention would save lives and open the doors for social progress, including conversion to Protestantism.

THE TWENTIETH CENTURY:
PACIFISM AND SELF-DEFENSE

Pacifism took root in northern Methodist seminaries starting in the 1890s. Its disciples attained Methodist leadership by the 1920s, politically strengthened by the horrors of World War I. Methodism throughout the 1920s and 1930s touted the League of Nations and arms control to overcome global insecurity. As Nazism, fascism, and Japanese militarism proceeded to conquer, official Methodism became increasingly pacifist. Some older bishops warned about future conflict, but most upcoming Methodist leaders in the 1920s and 1930s were largely uninterested in long-term strategic threats. Instead, they abstractly viewed war itself as the main enemy. In 1920 the northern bishops urged "strong grounds against any more wars and against war itself," with "international troubles" to be "adjusted by counsel and arbitration" while advocating reducing armaments to a "minimum consistent with safety."[63]

Northern Methodism's 1924 General Conference observed that millions had died in "a war to end war" and that "methods of peace" were necessary. Leaders insisted that war is the "supreme enemy"; it is "not inevitable," and its "futility is beyond question." Delegates "determined to outlaw the whole war system," and America "should lead the way," they implored. They demanded arms control and US entrance into the League of Nations.[64] Chicago bishop Edwin Hughes enthused: "Now we go forward to bear our testimony against all offensive war and to proclaim that the Hebrew prophets were not misguided fanatics when they foretold the swordless and spearless day of God. God has given us here the vision of a warless world."[65]

Southern Methodist bishops in 1922 commended America for working on peace and disarmament for relief from the "liability of war." They declared: "A permanent peace based on justice cannot come till the sword is taken out of the heart of mankind." The League of Nations, peace treaties, and disarmament conferences can do much, it was conceded, but only the church can turn men away from the "despotic" and "pagan" and toward the "democratic" and "Christian." Only the "crucified and risen Christ" can save a "race ruined by sin," the bishops declared.[66] The 1922 Southern General Conference concluded, "We must loathe war and hate war, and strip it all of its falseness and glamour and let it stand forth in its unveiled hideousness," while declining to denounce war as "murder."[67]

In 1926 the southern bishops urged the "abolition of aggressive war" and "peaceful" settlement of international disputes, along with adherence to a world court.[68] The 1924 northern General Conference had established a World Peace Commission, which asked the 1928 General Conference to "oppose war as a method of settling disputes among nations and groups, as contrary to the spirit and principles of Jesus Christ, and [to] declare that it will not as a Church sanction war." But delegates stopped short of rejecting all war, instead recognizing the "need of an army and navy sufficient to serve as a police power for the protection of life and property on land and sea." Yet they also renounced "war as an instrument of national policy," insisted that church agencies not serve in "preparation for war," and urged "drastic reduction of armaments."[69]

The northern bishops in 1928 implored that Methodism "stand with unstained hands if war is suffered to reappear." And they directed that "complete disarmament of nations" be "synchronized" so that "no one people shall be left helpless in the presence of armed lawlessness."[70] Southern Methodist bishops in 1930 supported the new international Kellogg-Briand Pact to "abolish war as an instrument of national policy," and they urged Congress's support for "international peace." They observed: "The principle of peace thus becomes lodged in the minds of men as the ultimate goal of humanity"; it is "superior in wisdom to the policy of fear and force."[71]

In 1932, the northern bishops declared: "We have gone beyond the day when war-mindedness is of any value in our program of progress." And they surmised that science, by facilitating "mass destruction of life," had "put an end to war-winning." They urged America to "take the lead in the reduction of war machinery," which was the only way for America to "preserve herself" and "help save the world." The bishops saw "militarism" as humanity's "chief enemy."[72] The 1932 northern General Conference more aggressively denounced war, urging international abolition of "aggressive" weapons such as tanks, airplanes, and aircraft carriers. And it requested conscientious objector status for Methodists as for Quakers and other pacifist churches, while seeking an end to all military training in civilian schools and to all compulsory military service.[73] A 1934 survey of roughly one hundred thousand clergy revealed northern Methodists to be the nation's most pacifist denomination.[74] Two years later, the northern General Conference declared, "The threats of war in the world today are so grave that we feel called upon to restate our convictions," which were that Methodism "does not endorse, support, or purpose to participate in war," hoping for "non-violent methods of overcoming evil."[75] The northern bishops admitted that the League of Nations and the Kellogg-Briand Pact, among other antiwar measures, had "shattered." But they still insisted that "advocates of war" are "on the defensive, as never before." They further asserted that "Idealism dwells with the pacifists" and surmised that any "militarist" who quits Methodism because of its "peace pronouncements" has "none other refuge" within Protestantism. They were greatly troubled by an increase in US military spending, and they warned that another world war would fuel "communistic experiments and bullying dictatorships."[76]

Southern bishops complained in 1938 that "all the leading nations of the world are preparing for a threatened cataclysm," and even the United States is "in the race to possess the most formidable fighting machine that mankind has ever known." The bishops insisted: "This whole hellish business must be done away," and war plans "must stop," although they did not explain how.[77] Methodism's 1939 General Conference reuniting north and south endorsed war neutrality and supported conscientious objectors. It pledged "undivided opposition to the spirit of war now raging through the world" and sought to exert "every possible influence for peaceful settlement of international differences." Delegates asked the president and Congress to avoid "the entanglement of our country in a world-wide conflagration of war which we are convinced would bring our civilization into ruins."[78]

In 1940, Methodism's bishops predicted the war in Europe would bankrupt the "so-called Western civilizations." They faulted the war on the basis of the "intensity and extent of this twentieth-century nationalism," and did so without naming any ideologies like Nazism. The bishops denounced the "war system," which entails "atheism, materialism, barbarism, and diabolism." Correlatively, they observed approvingly that more Christians were becoming conscientious objectors, with support from Methodism for their "exaltation of a Christian value," while posing the question of whether a "world-federation" would ensure future world peace, even if opposed by "jingoistic" and "self-centered patriotism."[79] The General Conference of that year resolved that the United States "should remain out of the present conflicts in Europe and in the Far East" and that Methodism "will not officially endorse, support, or participate in war," since church members were "divided" over "what a Christian should do when his own nation becomes involved in war." Delegates also endorsed a "moral embargo" against "aggressor nations," which was primarily aimed at Japan.[80]

December 7, 1941, of course, changed all of this, at least temporarily. In a dramatic shift, after Pearl Harbor the Methodist bishops assured President Franklin Roosevelt that "in this hour of peril" he had their "profound sympathy and loyalty and above all [their] earnest prayers that in this national crisis [he would] have divine guidance and support."[81] In a "Wartime Message" to the churches, the bishops pledged, "In this crisis, as

in all previous crises in our history, the Methodists of America will support our President and our nation." They also anticipated "coming days of
peace," after "victories in war," when the church would help create "agencies and machinery necessary to establish international justice."[82] Then in
1942 the bishops declared their "appreciation of the nobility of the sacrifice which the youth of our Methodist homes and churches are making in
the military service at the call of our nation." And they hoped for the
"destruction of this brutal and unwarranted aggression and the preservation for all mankind of the sacred liberties of free peoples."[83]

Throughout the Second World War, the Methodist World Peace
Commission was dominated by pacifists and affirmed conscientious objectors. The Methodist Youth Fellowship, attracting a thousand young
people to a 1942 meeting, urged the church "not to actively support or
participate in the war" and affirmed the official Methodist 1940 antiwar
stance. In the same year, the Methodist Women's Division president re-
joiced that her prayers were answered when weather prevented a government agent from touting war bonds at a women's assembly.[84]

Some Methodists, like future bishop Nolan Harmon of Virginia,
were unwilling that the 1944 General Conference should oppose war
when the democracies were struggling against the Axis powers. Harmon
had denounced the 1940 antiwar stance as an "embarrassment to every
Methodist chaplain, and a question mark in every Methodist home which
has sent someone into the service." Repeating this position, he warned,
would be a "tragic disappointment." Nevertheless, a committee majority
report in 1944 strongly recommended a renewed antiwar stand and refused to "pray for a military victory." To this Harmon responded: "We have
spent more time in calling attention to the plight of the 600 Methodist
conscientious objectors than we have to three times that many Methodist
boys, dead and buried under crosses on battlefields in the far-flung corners
of the earth." In the end, Harmon insisted, "the ultimate control of moral
evil in this world must be by force." His minority report framed the matter
in the following way: "In this country we are sending over a million young
men from Methodist homes to participate in the conflict. God himself has
a stake in the struggle, and he will uphold them as they fight forces destructive of the moral life of man. In Christ's name we ask for the blessing
of God upon the men in the armed forces, and we pray for victory. We
repudiate the theory that a state, even though imperfect in itself, must not

fight against intolerable wrongs."[85] The report offered respect to pacifists but insisted "we cannot accept their position as the defining position of the Christian Church." And it concluded: "We are well within the Christian position when we assert the necessity of the use of military forces to resist an aggression which would overthrow every right which is held sacred by civilized men."[86] Harmon's minority report passed the General Conference by a vote of 373 to 300. The clergy had voted for it by only 170 to 169, but the laity by 203 to 131.[87] Delegates also approved a follow-up resolution, declaring, "Christianity cannot be nationalistic"; "the methods of Jesus and the methods of war belong to different worlds." The resolution then concluded: "The church must rise in its might and demand an international organization which will make another war impossible."[88]

Methodism's bishops told the 1944 General Conference: "Multiplied thousands of the bravest young men and women of our Church are on battlefields in the ends of the earth struggling to preserve our liberty and protect our Christian ideals. By their suffering and sacrifice they are maintaining the principles of democracy and preserving the freedom of mankind. They are writing another golden page in the book of patriotism."[89]

World War II compelled official Methodism's return to historic Christian teachings about a just war, even if only temporarily. The laity led with their feet, volunteering for the war effort along their fellow citizens. Like most Americans, Methodists were outraged by Japanese atrocities in the Pacific as well as the unfolding tale of Nazi savagery in Europe. The bishops told the 1948 General Conference: "We have enjoyed the privileges of freedom so long that we are in danger of forgetting that eternal vigilance is the price of liberty." They conceded that "invading armies must be met by defending armies, who subsequently take the initiative and destroy the invader." Moreover, they noted, "Wise men will see that the nation is properly prepared to protect itself from aggressors and to maintain its existence in freedom," while seeking security through a "world order" and cooperation with other nations within the United Nations.[90]

Following the war, the 1952 General Conference urged a stronger United Nations to suppress "aggression and war" while repeating its hopes from 1948 of a "world federation of nations."[91] The bishops celebrated the fact that America had "chosen to defend the Republic of Korea, through the United Nations, from the aggression of a Communist invasion," which had been "a costly and sacrificial price to pay for a safer world." Additionally, the bishops paid "tribute to those who, in mortal combat, have given their all that freedom might not perish from the earth," noting that "this burden" was the "pledge of free men everywhere that the only war we seek is a relentless struggle against despotism, poverty, and human bondage."[92] This support for the Korean War would be official Methodism's last support for any major US military action.

BEYOND KOREA:
DISARMAMENT, PACIFISM, AND LIBERATION

In 1960 the bishops urged "mobilizing Christian opinion within our connection in behalf of mutual disarmament, the prohibition of nuclear testing, and the peaceful use of atomic energy." The General Conference called for the "abolition of the use of war by nations" and "complete disarmament, involving both nuclear and conventional weapons, down to the levels required for internal policing." It asserted that "complete disarmament must be universal to be acceptable to all nations" and "enforced by a competent international agency, preferably a strengthened United Nations," with "international means for the peaceful settlement of disputes and controversies between nations." It granted that, indeed, complete disarmament and delegation of enforcement authority to the United Nations was a "stupendous task." Nevertheless, delegates reiterated opposition to compulsory military service and denounced "militarism" while admitting again that Christians disagree over individual participation in war but asserting that believers must not "gloss over the sinfulness of war."[93]

In 1965, responding to the war in Vietnam, the Methodist Board of Christian Social Concerns urged President Johnson to "seek every possible means of ending [the] conflict through United Nations action . . . in preference to further unilateral military action."[94] A few weeks later, the board's executive committee announced: "The bombing of North Vietnam at an accelerating pace raises serious moral questions as to the appropriateness of the means chosen for the implementation of legitimate policy objectives."[95]

Methodism's bishops condemned the war in 1966: "Nowadays we know that neither victory nor defeat . . . is possible for warring nations"; "the present issue is one of human survival," they declared. "We insist that both sides cease their mutual destruction and seek peace."[96] In 1967 the bishops commended President Johnson for seeking negotiations but opposed any "escalation" of the war and urged talks toward South Vietnam's "self-determination" as well as the "phased withdrawal of all foreign troops," with "asylum for those who may require it."[97]

At the General Conference in 1968, at which time the United Methodist Church was born in a merger between Methodism and the Evangelical United Brethren, delegates expressed a "growing concern over the course and consequences of United States foreign policy, especially in Southeast Asia." They called for "self-determination" for South Vietnam and a negotiated peace, with "asylum" provided to "those who cannot safely remain in the country."[98] In pleading, "Is it possible to murder without becoming a murderer?," the bishops denounced war without specifying Vietnam.[99]

In 1970 the bishops declared, "We deplore the present war in Viet Nam," noting that "what began ten years ago as an effort to assist a friendly nation on a modest scale has become a fiasco which presently is impossible to justify and from which we are striving honorably to extricate ourselves."[100] And in 1971 the bishops asked every United Methodist minister to "lead his people into an ecumenical call to 'Prayers for Peace,'" as part of a larger interfaith "witness concerning the moral issues in the Indochina war," which was to begin with prayers of protest outside the White House.[101] The campaign concluded in 1972 with a call for churches to protect draft avoiders, to withhold some taxes, to publish congressional voting records in church bulletins, to focus on the Vietnam War during the presidential campaign, and to urge Congress to end all war funding.[102]

In 1972, the General Conference similarly denounced the Vietnam War as "immoral" and a "crime against humanity," demanding the end of all support for "military activities in the war in Southeast Asia" and urging "reparations to victims of the war."[103] Language was added to the church's *Social Principles* that stated the following: "We believe war is incompatible with the teachings and example of Christ. We therefore reject war as an instrument of national foreign policy." Just war scholar Paul Ramsey of Princeton University, an ordained United Methodist minister, served on the committee crafting this language. He proposed changing the language to "war is ultimately incompatible" but was voted down by 5 to 4.[104]

From 1972 until 2000 United Methodism officially was pacifist. United Methodist officials opposed the Reagan-era military defense buildup; the General Board of Church and Society expressed "deep distress upon the transfer of billions of dollars from the social needs of people to the production of massive new weapons and strategic defense systems";[105] and the bishops to the 1984 General Conference urged "total disarmament by disbanding armies, navies, and air forces over the face of the earth," while denouncing the "doctrine of the Just War" as a "ridiculous anachronism."[106] In 1986, the bishops released their statement *In Defense of Creation: The Nuclear Crisis and a Just Peace*, which denounced nuclear deterrence but fell short of demanding unilateral disarmament, suggesting "interim possession of such weapons for a strictly limited time" as part of an *"ethic of reciprocity"* during agreed-on stages "to reduce and ultimately to eliminate their nuclear arms."[107]

As Methodism was opposing US arms spending as contrary to peace, the church's Board of Global Ministries was disbursing grants to groups supportive of the Marxist guerrillas in El Salvador and the Marxist Sandinista regime in Nicaragua, under the influence of "liberation theology," which often equated violent Marxist revolution with expanding God's kingdom on behalf of the poor.[108] And in a similar vein, in 1989 General Board of Church and Society (GBCS) chief Thom White Wolf Fassett denounced the US military intervention in Panama to overthrow dictator Manuel Noriega as no "valid act of a civilized nation."[109] US military action against Saddam Hussein in Iraq a year later was also widely denounced, with San Francisco bishop Melvin Talbert imploring United Methodists to "demonstrate and speak out against" US aggression, while warning, "We are on the brink of a nuclear war."[110]

The 1992 General Conference called for "complete strategic disarmament" of all nuclear weapons and opposed any antimissile defense system, since an "effective international nonproliferation regime" would prevent nations from deploying nukes.[111] Regarding terrorism, it urged the US president to "repudiate violence and adhere to the statement that retaliation could be a terrorist act in itself and the killing and victimizing of innocent people."[112]

The 2000 General Conference added just war language to the *Social Principles*: "Most Christians regretfully realize that when peaceful alternatives have failed, the force of arms may be preferable to unchecked aggression, tyranny, and genocide." However, it left the following language intact: "We believe war is incompatible with the teachings and example of Christ. We therefore reject war as an instrument of national foreign policy."[113] After 9/11, however, United Methodist officials ignored the added just war language and selectively stressed the pacifist stance. The bishops responded to 9/11 by declaring that "violence in all of its forms and expressions is contrary to God's purpose for the world."[114] One bishop admitted: "We didn't take the time to struggle with the Wesleyan perspective of war and peace." And over the next several years the bishops and other church officials would denounce US military operations in Afghanistan and Iraq.[115]

CONCLUSION:
CLASSIC JUST WAR THINKING
AND PAUL RAMSEY

As of 2016, the United Methodist official teaching on war and peace declares the following:

> We believe war is incompatible with the teachings and example of Christ. We therefore reject war as an instrument of national foreign policy. We oppose unilateral first/preemptive strike actions and strategies on the part of any government. As disciples of Christ, we are called to love our enemies, seek justice, and serve as reconcilers of conflict. We insist that the first moral duty of all nations is to work together to resolve by peaceful means every dispute that arises between or among them. We advocate the extension and strengthening of international treaties and institutions that provide a framework within the rule of law for responding to aggression, terrorism, and genocide. We believe that human values must outweigh military claims as governments determine their priorities; that the militarization of society must be challenged and stopped; that the manufacture, sale, and deployment of armaments must be reduced and controlled; and that the production, possession, or use of nuclear weapons be condemned. Consequently, we endorse general and complete disarmament under strict and effective international control.[116]

As to the church's teaching on military service, we read:

> We deplore war and urge the peaceful settlement of all disputes among nations. From the beginning, the Christian conscience has struggled with the harsh realities of violence and war, for these evils

clearly frustrate God's loving purposes for humankind. We yearn for the day when there will be no more war and people will live together in peace and justice. Some of us believe that war, and other acts of violence, are never acceptable to Christians. We also acknowledge that many Christians believe that, when peaceful alternatives have failed, the force of arms may regretfully be preferable to unchecked aggression, tyranny and genocide. We honor the witness of pacifists who will not allow us to become complacent about war and violence. We also respect those who support the use of force, but only in extreme situations and only when the need is clear beyond reasonable doubt, and through appropriate international organizations. We urge the establishment of the rule of law in international affairs as a means of elimination of war, violence, and coercion in these affairs.

We reject national policies of enforced military service as incompatible with the gospel. We acknowledge the agonizing tension created by the demand for military service by national governments. We urge all young adults to seek the counsel of the Church as they reach a conscientious decision concerning the nature of their responsibility as citizens. Pastors are called upon to be available for counseling with all young adults who face conscription or who are considering voluntary enlistment in the armed forces, including those who conscientiously refuse to cooperate with a system of conscription.

We support and extend the ministry of the Church to those persons who conscientiously oppose all war, or any particular war, and who therefore refuse to serve in the armed forces or to cooperate with systems of military conscription. We also support and extend the Church's ministry to all persons. This includes those who conscientiously choose to serve in the armed forces or to accept alternative service. When persons choose to serve in the armed forces, we support their right to adequate care for injuries suffered, and advocate for sufficient resources to meet their physical and mental health needs, both during and after their service. We are aware that we can become guilty both by military action and by conscientious objection, and that we all are dependent on God's forgiveness.[117]

Thus, United Methodism, which is the largest Wesleyan church in the world, officially admits that some adherents may adhere to a just war perspective even when the church is still predominantly pacifist. It largely ignores the teachings of its founder, John Wesley, most of its history, and almost certainly the beliefs of most members.

Paul Ramsey, when challenging official Methodist pacifism in 1988, admitted that historic Methodism teaches perfectionism for believers. But does this perfectionism apply to nations? Or should politicians and citizens expect "political holiness" and "perfect love," of which Wesley spoke, to descend? Answering his own question, Ramsey wrote: "It is God's redeemed people, individually and collectively, who are going on to perfection and to a World of Love. That is the 'progressive' element stressed in the Wesleyan heritage; that is the meaning of our legacy joining knowledge with vital piety, and of yearning for holiness." But Ramsey warned his fellow Methodists: "Whenever this is directed (without differentiation between church and world) toward secular problems (however urgent), we swap our birthright for a 'pot of message,' while also sometimes speaking impossible dreams to states and instilling unearthly (i.e., misplaced) hope in laypeople." Modern Methodism, in often seeking to impose pacifism on statecraft, has, as Ramsey described, assumed that there is no "great eschatological discontinuity" en route to God's peaceful kingdom and "no great discontinuity" between creation and fall.[118]

Historic Methodism, at least the variety founded by Wesley, imposed no such discontinuity and assumed just war principles, even if not specifically articulating them. Since he is a Methodist, Ramsey's emergence as the late twentieth century's primary Protestant exponent of just war teaching is paradoxical. His scholarship offers at least some hope that Methodism can and will offer a comprehensive interpretation of the just war tradition.

NOTES

1. Briane K. Turley, "John Wesley and War," *Methodist History* 29, no. 2 (January 1991): 96.

2. Stephen W. Rankin, "John Wesley and War: Guidance for Modern-Day Heirs?," *Methodist Review* 3 (2011): 136.

3. Ibid., 112.

4. Theodore Weber, *Politics in the Order of Salvation: Transforming Wesleyan Political Ethics* (Nashville: Abingdon, 2001), 353.

5. Turley, "John Wesley and War," 98.

6. John Wesley, *Wesley's Notes on the Bible*, on Rom. 13:1, Christian Classics Ethereal Library, www.ccel.org/ccel/wesley/notes.i.vii.xiv.html.

7. Turley, "John Wesley and War," 104.

8. Rankin, "John Wesley and War," 103.

9. *Minutes of the Methodist Conferences: From the First, Held in London by the Late Rev. John Wesley, A.M., in the Year 1744* (London: John Mason of the Wesleyan Methodist Church, 1862), 1:25.

10. John Wesley, "John Wesley's Explanatory Notes – Matthew 26," Sermon Index.net, www.sermonindex.net/modules/articles/index.php?view=article&aid=26197.

11. *Notes on the First Book of Moses Called Genesis*, on Gen. 14:13, Wesley Center Online, Wesley Center for Applied Theology, Northwest Nazarene University, http://wesley.nnu.edu/john-wesley/john-wesleys-notes-on-the-bible/notes-on-the-first-book-of-moses-called-genesis/#Chapter%2BXIV.

12. Rankin, "John Wesley and War," 128.

13. John Wesley, *A Word in Season: Or, Advice to an Englishman*, in *The Works of John Wesley* (Grand Rapids, MI: Zondervan, n.d.; repr. of edition published by the Wesleyan Conference Office, London, 1872), 11:183.

14. John Telford, ed., *The Letters of the Rev. John Wesley*, 8 vols. (London: Epworth Press, 1931), 3:164; Charles Wesley, *The Journal of Charles Wesley*, ed. S. T. Kimbrough Jr. and Kenneth G. C. Newport (Nashville: Kingswood Books, 2007), 2:200.

15. John Wesley, *Free Thoughts on the Present State of Public Affairs*, in *Works of John Wesley* (Zondervan), 11:33.

16. John Wesley, *Thoughts upon Liberty*, in *Works of John Wesley* (Zondervan), 11:44.

17. John Wesley and Thomas Jackson, *The Journal of the Rev. John Wesley, from October 14th, 1735, to October 24th, 1790* (London: Wesleyan Conference Office, 1903), 113.

18. Weber, *Politics in the Order of Salvation*, 382–84.

19. Ibid., 354.

20. John Wesley, *Free Thoughts on the Present State*, 19. See also Wesley, *Compassionate Address to the Inhabitants of Ireland*, in *Works of John Wesley* (Zondervan), 11:149–53.

21. Rankin, "John Wesley and War," 119.

22. Weber, *Politics in the Order of Salvation*, 138.

23. Ibid., 362.

24. Wesley, *Word in Season*, 183.

25. Weber, *Politics in the Order of Salvation*, 364.

26. Rankin, "John Wesley and War," 117.

27. Weber, *Politics in the Order of Salvation*, 365.

28. John Wesley, *National Sins and Miseries*, sermon delivered on November 12, 1775, www.churchages.net/en/sermon/wesley/national-sins-and-miseries.

29. Telford, *Letters of the Rev. John Wesley*, 4:352.

30. Weber, *Politics in the Order of Salvation*, 368–69.

31. John Wesley, *A Concise History of England: From the Earliest Times to the Death of George II* (London: R. Hawes, 1776), 2:25.

32. Ibid., 4:227.

33. Ibid., 1:33; 4:90.

34. John Wesley, *Thoughts on Slavery*, in *The Works of John Wesley* (Kansas City: Beacon Hill Press, 1979), 11:71.

35. John Wesley, *Some Observations on Liberty*, in *Works of John Wesley* (Zondervan), 11:115.

36. John Wesley, *The Doctrine of Original Sin, according to Scripture, Reason, and Experience*, in *Works of John Wesley* (Zondervan), 9:192–93.

37. John Wesley, *A Seasonable Address to the More Serious Part of the Inhabitants of Great Britain, Respecting the Unhappy Contest between Us and Our American Brethren: With an Occasional Word Interspersed to Those of a Different Complexion; By a Lover of Peace*, in *Works of John Wesley* (Zondervan), 11:121.

38. Ibid., 11:122.

39. John Wesley, *Doctrine of Original Sin*, 237–38.

40. John Wesley, *Doctrine of Original Sin*, 221.

41. John Wesley and John Taylor, *The Doctrine of Original Sin: According to Scripture, Reason, and Experience* (Bristol: F. Farley, 1757), 58–59.

42. Weber, *Politics in the Order of Salvation*, 377.

43. Rankin, "John Wesley and War," 138.

44. Turley, "John Wesley and War," 96.

45. Nathan Bangs, *A History of the Methodist Episcopal Church*, vol. 2, *From the Year 1793 to the Year 1816* (New York: Carlton & Phillips, 1853), 352.

46. Ibid., 353.

47. Ibid., 354.

48. Ibid., 355–56. Asbury was quoting 1 Tim. 2:1–2: "I exhort therefore, that . . . prayers . . . be made . . . for all that are in authority; that we may lead a quiet and peaceable life in all godliness and honesty."

49. Luke Schleif, "That Her Religion May Be Uprooted: The Methodists and the Mexican-American War," *Methodist History* 52, no.1 (October 2013): 19–21.

50. "General Intelligence: Domestic," *Christian Advocate and Journal*, November 11, 1846.

51. "Some Remarks on the Twelfth Chapter of Revelation," *Quarterly Review of the Methodist Episcopal Church, South* 2 (July 1848): 474.

52. Emory Stevens Bucke, *The History of American Methodism* (New York: Abingdon, 1964), 207.

53. Ibid., 207–8.

54. Joseph Cummings, "Address of the General Conference to President Lincoln," in *Journal of the General Conference of the Methodist Episcopal Church Held in Philadelphia, Philadelphia, Pa., 1864*, ed. William L. Harris (New York: Carlton & Porter, 1864), 379.

55. Abraham Lincoln, "President Lincoln's Reply to the Address," in Harris, *Journal of the General Conference of the Methodist Episcopal Church*, 80. Ibid., 215.

56. Matthew Simpson, lecture delivered at the Academy of Music, New York, November 3, 1864, published in *The Life of Bishop Matthew Simpson of the Methodist Episcopal Church*, by George R. Crooks (New York: Harper & Brothers, 1890). The quotation appears on p. 380.

57. James Rusling, "Interview with President William McKinley," *Christian Advocate*, January 22, 1903, 17, https://www.digitalhistory.uh.edu/disp_textbook.cfm?smtID=3&psid=1257.

58. *Journal of the Fourteenth General Conference* (Nashville: Publishing House, Methodist Episcopal Church, South, 1902), 272–78.

59. "Methodists Offer Aid to President," *New York Times*, May 28, 1916, 18.

60. *Journal of the Eighteenth General Conference* (Nashville: Publishing House, Methodist Episcopal Church, South, 1918), 341–42.

61. "War Attitude of Methodists," *Miami Herald Record*, October 26, 1917, 7.

62. "Churches Must Endorse League or Be Traitors to the Lord," *Atlantic Constitution*, March 2, 1919, 4.

63. *Journal of the Twenty-Eighth Delegated General Conference of the Methodist Episcopal Church* (New York: Methodist Book Concern, 1920), 3.

64. *Journal of the Twenty-Ninth Delegated General Conference of the Methodist Episcopal Church* (New York: Methodist Book Concern, 1924), 527–73.

65. "Religion: In Springfield," *Time*, June 9, 1925.

66. *Journal of the Nineteenth General Conference* (Nashville: Methodist Publishing House, Methodist Episcopal Church, South, 1922), 338–39.

67. *Journal of the Nineteenth General Conference* (Nashville: Methodist Publishing House, Methodist Episcopal Church, South, 1922), 338–39.

68. *Journal of the Twentieth General Conference* (Nashville: Methodist Publishing House, Methodist Episcopal Church, South, 1926), 300–301.

69. *General Conference Reports and Resolutions of the Methodist Episcopal Church* (New York: Methodist Book Concern, 1928), 599.

70. *Journal of the Thirtieth Delegated General Conference of the Methodist Episcopal Church* (New York: Methodist Book Concern, 1928), 191–92.

71. *Journal of the Twenty-First General Conference* (Nashville: Publishing House, Methodist Episcopal Church, South, 1930), 374.

72. *Journal of the Thirty-First Delegated General Conference of the Methodist Episcopal Church* (New York: Methodist Book Concern, 1932), 188.

73. *General Conference Reports and Resolutions of the Methodist Episcopal Church* (New York: Methodist Book Concern, 1932), 561–63.

74. "Religion: Churchmen on War," *Time*, May 21, 1934, http://content .time.com/time/subscriber/article/0,33009,747448,00.html.

75. *General Conference Reports and Resolutions of the Methodist Episcopal Church* (New York: Methodist Book Concern, 1936), 660–61.

76. *Journal of the Thirty-Second Delegated General Conference of the Methodist Episcopal Church* (New York: Methodist Book Concern, 1936), 140–41.

77. *Journal of the Twenty-Third General Conference* (Nashville: Publishing House, Methodist Episcopal Church, South, 1938), 248–49.

78. *Resolutions of the Methodist Church General Conference* (Nashville: Methodist Publishing House, 1939), 698–99.

79. *Journal of the First General Conference of the Methodist Church* (Nashville: Methodist Publishing House, 1940), 168–71.

80. "Methodists Favor 'Moral Embargo,'" *Baltimore Sun*, May 7, 1940, 15.

81. "Methodists Wire Support to President," *Atlanta Constitution*, December 11, 1941, 12.

82. Robert L. Wilson, *Biases and Blindspots: Methodism and Foreign Policy since World War II* (Wilmore, KY: Good News Books, 1988), 23–25.

83. Herman Will, *The Will for Peace* (Washington, DC: General Board of Church and Society, 1984), 64.

84. Ibid., 65–67.

85. Nolan Harmon, *Ninety Years and Counting: Autobiography of Nolan B. Harmon* (Nashville: Upper Room, 1983), 206–10.

86. *Miscellaneous Resolutions, Methodist Church General Conference, 1944* (Nashville: Methodist Publishing House, 1944), 574–75.

87. "Methodists Vote Support of War, Reversing Position Taken in 1940," *New York Times*, May 5, 1944, 21.

88. Will, *Will for Peace*, 72–73.

89. *Journal of the 1944 General Conference of the Methodist Church* (Nashville: Methodist Publishing House, 1944), 178.

90. *Journal of the 1948 General Conference of the Methodist Church* (Nashville: Methodist Publishing House, 1948), 179–90.

91. *Journal of the 1952 General Conference of the Methodist Church* (Nashville: Methodist Publishing House, 1952), 643–49.

92. Ibid., 154–97.

93. *Journal of the 1960 General Conference of the Methodist Church* (Nashville: Methodist Publishing House, 1960), 699–705.

94. "Methodist Officials Ask End of Viet Nam Conflict," *Concern*, March 1, 1965, 15.

95. "Statement of Vietnam," *Concern*, April 15, 1965, 5.

96. "Resolution on Vietnam," *Concern*, December 1, 1966, 9.

97. "Bishops' Statement on Vietnam," *Concern*, December 1, 1967, 8.

98. *The Book of Resolutions of The United Methodist Church 1968* (Nashville: United Methodist Publishing House, 1968), 10–12.

99. *Journal of the 1968 General Conference of the United Methodist Church* (Nashville: United Methodist Publishing House, 1968), 251–54.

100. *Journal of the 1970 General Conference of the United Methodist Church* (Nashville: United Methodist Publishing House, 1970), 194.

101. "Religious 'Witness' Formed on War Issues," *Christian Advocate*, December 23, 1971.

102. "Anti-War Witness Plan Grows," *Christian Advocate*, February 3, 1972, 23.

103. *The Book of Resolutions of The United Methodist Church 1972* (Nashville: United Methodist Publishing House, 1972), 9–21.

104. Paul Ramsey, *Speak Up for Just War or Pacifism: A Critique of the United Methodist Bishops' Pastoral Letter "In Defense of Creation"* (University Park: Pennsylvania State University Press, 1988), 7–9.

105. "BCS Criticizes Reagan for Budget Reductions, Wants Watt To Resign," *Newscope*, October 16, 1981, 1.

106. *Journal of the 1984 General Conference of the United Methodist Church* (Nashville: United Methodist Publishing House, 1984), 173–74.

107. *In Defense of Creation: The Nuclear Crisis and a Just Peace* (Nashville: Graded Press, 1986), 46.

108. Mark Tooley, *Methodism and Politics in the Twentieth Century: From William McKinley to 9-11* (Fort Valley, GA: Bristol House, 2011), 264.

109. "Speaking to Church and World Convictions about the Panama Invasion," *Christian Social Action*, February 1990, 2.

110. "Bishop Talbert, Other Religious Leaders Seek Peace in Gulf," *Newscope*, December 7, 1990, 3.

111. *The Book of Resolutions of The United Methodist Church 1992* (Nashville: United Methodist Publishing House, 1992), 605.

112. Ibid., 643.

113. "United Methodists Move to the Center," *UMAction Briefing*, Summer 2000, 1.

114. "United Methodist Bishops Neutral in War on Terror," *UMAction Briefing*, March 2002, 1.

115. "UM Bishops' Pastoral Letter Calls Violence 'Contrary to God's Purpose,'" *Newscope*, November 16, 2001, 1.

116. "The World Community," in *The Book of Discipline of the United Methodist Church 2016* (Nashville: United Methodist Publishing House, 2016), 143–44 (¶164.C, "War and Peace"), https://www.ctcumc.org/files/fileshare/2016-book-of-discipline.pdf.

117. "The Political Community," in *The Book of Discipline of the United Methodist Church 2016* (Nashville: United Methodist Publishing House, 2016), 141–42 (¶164.I, "Military Service"), https://www.ctcumc.org/files/fileshare/2016-book-of-discipline.pdf.

118. Ramsey, *Speak Up for Just War or Pacifism*, 36–37.

WORKS CITED

Bangs, Nathan. *A History of the Methodist Episcopal Church*. Vol. 2, *From the Year 1793 to the Year 1816*. New York: Carlton & Phillips, 1853.

"BCS Criticizes Reagan for Budget Reductions, Wants Watt to Resign." *Newscope*, October 16, 1981, 1.

"Bishops' Statement on Vietnam." *Concern*, December 1, 1967, 8.

"Bishop Talbert, Other Religious Leaders Seek Peace in Gulf." *Newscope*, December 7, 1990, 1.

The Book of Resolutions of the United Methodist Church 1968. Nashville: United Methodist Publishing House, 1968.

The Book of Resolutions of the United Methodist Church 1992. Nashville: United Methodist Publishing House, 1992.

The Book of Resolutions of the United Methodist Church 2016. Nashville: United Methodist Publishing House, 2016.

Bucke, Emory Stevens. *The History of American Methodism*. New York: Abingdon, 1964.

"Churches Must Endorse League or Be Traitors to the Lord." *Atlantic Constitution*, March 2, 1919, 4.

Crooks, George R. *The Life of Bishop Matthew Simpson of the Methodist Episcopal Church*. New York: Harper & Brothers, 1890.

Cummings, Joseph. "Address of the General Conference to President Lincoln." In *Journal of the General Conference of the Methodist Episcopal Church Held in Philadelphia, Pa., 1864*, edited by William L. Harris, 379–80. New York: Carlton & Porter, 1864.

General Conference Reports and Resolutions. Methodist Episcopal Church. New York: Methodist Book Concern, 1928.

General Conference Reports and Resolutions. Methodist Episcopal Church. New York: Methodist Book Concern, 1932.

General Conference Reports and Resolutions. Methodist Episcopal Church. New York: Methodist Book Concern, 1936.

"General Intelligence: Domestic." *Christian Advocate and Journal,* November 11, 1846.

Harmon, Nolan. *Ninety Years and Counting: Autobiography of Nolan B. Harmon.* Nashville: Upper Room, 1983.

In Defense of Creation: The Nuclear Crisis and a Just Peace. Nashville: Graded Press, 1986.

"John Wesley's Explanatory Notes – Matthew 26." Sermon Index Audio Sermons. www.sermonindex.net/modules/articles/index.php?view=article &aid=26197.

Journal of the Eighteenth General Conference. Nashville: Publishing House, Methodist Episcopal Church, South, 1918.

Journal of the First General Conference of the Methodist Church. Nashville: Methodist Publishing House, 1940.

Journal of the Fourteenth General Conference. Nashville: Methodist Publishing House, 1902.

Journal of the 1944 General Conference of the Methodist Church. Nashville: Methodist Publishing House, 1944.

Journal of the 1948 General Conference of the Methodist Church. Nashville: Methodist Publishing House, 1948.

Journal of the 1952 General Conference of the Methodist Church. Nashville: Methodist Publishing House, 1952.

Journal of the 1960 General Conference of the Methodist Church. Nashville: Methodist Publishing House, 1960.

Journal of the 1968 General Conference of the United Methodist Church. Nashville: United Methodist Publishing House, 1968.

Journal of the 1970 General Conference of the United Methodist Church. Nashville: United Methodist Publishing House, 1970.

Journal of the 1984 General Conference of the United Methodist Church. Nashville: United Methodist Publishing House, 1984.

Journal of the Nineteenth General Conference. Nashville: Methodist Publishing House, Methodist Episcopal Church, South, 1922.

Journal of the Thirtieth Delegated General Conference of the Methodist Episcopal Church. New York: Methodist Book Concern, 1928.

Journal of the Thirty-First Delegated General Conference of the Methodist Episcopal Church. New York: Methodist Book Concern, 1932.

Journal the Thirty-Second Delegated General Conference of the Methodist Episcopal Church. New York: Methodist Book Concern, 1936.

Journal of the Twentieth General Conference. Nashville: Methodist Publishing House, Methodist Episcopal Church, South, 1926.

Journal of the Twenty-Eighth Delegated General Conference of the Methodist Episcopal Church. New York: Methodist Book Concern, 1920.

Journal of the Twenty-First General Conference. Nashville: Publishing House, Methodist Episcopal Church, South, 1930.

Journal of the Twenty-Ninth Delegated General Conference of the Methodist Episcopal Church. New York: Methodist Book Concern, 1924.

Journal of the Twenty-Third General Conference. Nashville: Publishing House, Methodist Episcopal Church, South, 1938.

Journal of the Uniting Conference. New York: Methodist Publishing House, 1939.

Lincoln, Abraham. "President Lincoln's Reply to the Address." In *Journal of the General Conference of the Methodist Episcopal Church Held in Philadelphia, Pa., 1864,* edited by William L. Harris, 80. New York: Carlton & Porter, 1864.

"Methodist Officials Ask End of Viet Nam Conflict." *Concern,* March 1, 1965, 15.

"Methodists Favor 'Moral Embargo.'" *Baltimore Sun,* May 7, 1940, 15.

"Methodists Offer Aid to President." *New York Times,* May 28, 1916, 18.

"Methodists Vote Support of War, Reversing Position Taken in 1940." *New York Times,* May 5, 1944, 21.

"Methodists Wire Support to President." *Atlanta Constitution,* December 11, 1941, 12.

Minutes of the Methodist Conferences: From the First, Held in London by the Late Rev. John Wesley, A.M., in the Year 1744. Vol. 1. London: John Mason of the Wesleyan Methodist Church, 1862.

Miscellaneous Resolutions, Methodist Church General Conference (1944). Nashville: Methodist Publishing House, 1944.

"The Political Community." In *The Book of Discipline of the United Methodist Church 2016,* 138–42 (¶164). Nashville: United Methodist Publishing House, 2016. https://www.ctcumc.org/files/fileshare/2016-book-of -discipline.pdf.

Ramsey, Paul. *Speak Up for Just War or Pacifism: A Critique of the United Methodist Bishops' Pastoral Letter "In Defense of Creation."* University Park: Pennsylvania State University Press, 1988.

Rankin, Stephen W. "John Wesley and War: Guidance for Modern-Day Heirs?" *Methodist Review* 3 (2011): 101–39.

"Religion: Churchmen on War." *Time,* May 21, 1934. http://content.time.com /time/subscriber/article/0,33009,747448,00.html.

"Religion: In Springfield." *Time,* June 9, 1924. http://content.time.com/time /subscriber/article/0,33009,727967,00.html.

"Resolution on Vietnam." *Concern,* December 1, 1966, 9.

Resolutions. Methodist Church General Conference (1939). Nashville: Methodist Publishing House, 1939.

Rusling, James. "Interview with President William McKinley." *Christian Advocate*, January 22, 1903, 17. https://www.digitalhistory.uh.edu/disp_textbook .cfm?smtID=3&psid=1257.

Schleif, Luke. "That Her Religion May Be Uprooted: The Methodists and the Mexican-American War." *Methodist History* 52, no.1 (October 2013): 19–32.

"Some Remarks on the Twelfth Chapter of Revelation." *Quarterly Review of the Methodist Episcopal Church, South* 2 (July 1848): 474.

"Speaking to Church and World Convictions about the Panama Invasion." *Christian Social Action*, February 1990, 1.

"Statement of Vietnam." *Concern*, April 15, 1965, 5.

Telford, John, ed. *The Letters of the Rev. John Wesley.* 8 vols. London: Epworth Press, 1931.

Tooley, Mark. *Methodism and Politics in the Twentieth Century: From William McKinley to 9-11.* Fort Valley, GA: Bristol House, 2011.

Turley, Briane K. "John Wesley and War." *Methodist History* 29, no. 2 (January 1991): 96–111.

"UM Bishops' Pastoral Letter Calls Violence 'Contrary to God's Purpose.'" *Newscope*, November 16, 2001, 1.

"United Methodist Bishops Neutral in War on Terror." *UMAction Briefing*, March 2002, 1.

"United Methodists Move to the Center." *UMAction Briefing*, Summer 2000, 1.

"War Attitude of Methodists." *Miami Herald Record*, October 26, 1917, 7.

Weber, Theodore. *Politics in the Order of Salvation: Transforming Wesleyan Political Ethics.* Nashville: Abingdon, 2001.

Wesley, Charles. *The Journal of Charles Wesley.* Edited by S. T. Kimbrough Jr. and Kenneth G. C. Newport. Vol. 2. Nashville: Kingswood Books, 2007.

Wesley, John. *Compassionate Address to the Inhabitants of Ireland.* In *Works of John Wesley*, 11:149–53. Grand Rapids, MI: Zondervan, n.d. Reprint of edition published by the Wesleyan Conference Office (London, 1872).

———. *A Concise History of England: From the Earliest Times to the Death of George II.* 4 vols. London: R. Hawes, 1776.

———. *The Doctrine of Original Sin, according to Scripture, Reason, and Experience.* In *The Works of John Wesley*, vol. 9. Grand Rapids, MI: Zondervan, n.d. Reprint of edition published by the Wesleyan Conference Office (London, 1872).

———. *Free Thoughts on the Present State of Public Affairs.* In *The Works of John Wesley*, 11:14–33. Grand Rapids, MI: Zondervan, n.d. Reprint of edition published by the Wesleyan Conference Office (London, 1872).

———. "John Wesley's Explanatory Notes – Matthew 26." SermonIndex.net. www.sermonindex.net/modules/articles/index.php?view=article&aid=26197.

———. *National Sins and Miseries*. Sermon delivered on November 12, 1775. www.churchages.net/en/sermon/wesley/national-sins-and-miseries.

———. *Notes on the First Book of Moses Called Genesis*. Wesley Center Online. http://wesley.nnu.edu/john-wesley/john-wesleys-notes-on-the-bible/notes-on-the-first-book-of-moses-called-genesis/.

———. *A Seasonable Address to the More Serious Part of the Inhabitants of Great Britain, Respecting the Unhappy Contest between Us and Our American Brethren: With an Occasional Word Interspersed to Those of a Different Complexion; By a Lover of Peace*. In *Works of John Wesley*, 11:119–28. Grand Rapids, MI: Zondervan, n.d. Reprint of edition published by the Wesleyan Conference Office (London, 1872).

———. *Some Observations on Liberty*. In *The Works of John Wesley*, 11:90–118. Grand Rapids, MI: Zondervan, n.d. Reprint of edition published by the Wesleyan Conference Office (London, 1872).

———. *Thoughts on Slavery*. In *The Works of John Wesley*, vol. 11. Kansas City: Beacon Hill Press, 1979.

———. *Thoughts upon Liberty*. In *The Works of John Wesley*, 11:34–46. Grand Rapids, MI: Zondervan, n.d. Reprint of edition published by the Wesleyan Conference Office (London, 1872).

———. *Wesley's Notes on the Bible*. Christian Classics Ethereal Library. www.ccel.org/ccel/wesley/notes.

———. *A Word in Season: Or, Advice to an Englishman*. In *Works of John Wesley*, 11:182–86. Grand Rapids, MI: Zondervan, n.d. Reprint of edition published by the Wesleyan Conference Office (London, 1872).

———. *The Works of John Wesley*. Vol. 11. Grand Rapids, MI: Zondervan, n.d. Reprint of edition published by the Wesleyan Conference Office (London, 1872).

———. *The Works of John Wesley*. 14 vols. Kansas City: Beacon Hill Press, 1979.

Wesley, John, and Thomas Jackson. *The Journal of the Rev. John Wesley, from October 14th, 1735, to October 24th, 1790*. London: Wesleyan Conference Office, 1903.

Wesley, John, and John Taylor. *The Doctrine of Original Sin: According to Scripture, Reason, and Experience*. Bristol: F. Farley, 1757.

Will, Herman. *The Will for Peace*. Washington, DC: General Board of Church and Society, 1984.

Wilson, Robert L. *Biases and Blindspots: Methodism and Foreign Policy since World War II*. Wilmore, KY: Good News Books, 1988.

"The World Community." In *The Book of Discipline of the United Methodist Church 2016*, 142–44 (¶165). Nashville: United Methodist Publishing House, 2016. https://www.ctcumc.org/files/fileshare/2016-book-of-discipline.pdf.

EIGHT

Praying for Peace but Preparing for War

Baptists and the Just War Tradition

Timothy J. Demy

Baptists are no strangers to the trauma and tragedy of war. War has been part of the experience of Baptists throughout the centuries and has been characterized by several responses, among them adherence to the just war tradition. One of the most iconic images of the American Civil War is a photograph taken in the aftermath of September 17, 1862, America's bloodiest day, during the Battle of Antietam. Photographer Alexander Gardner took the photograph showing a whitewashed structure known as the Dunker Church in the background and Confederate victims in the foreground. The church was the focal point of a number of Union attacks against the Confederate left flank in the battle and served as a hospital and triage facility in the immediate aftermath of the fighting. The Dunkers were German Baptists with roots in Anabaptism and Pietism who traced their beginnings to Germany in 1708. Thus they had a very different history and lineage than English Baptists who began a century earlier, and this in itself illustrates the decentralized history of Baptist churches and Baptist ecclesiology.

Two hallmarks of Baptist ecclesiology make the subject of war and peace in Baptist thought difficult to address — self-governance and independence. These, coupled with a multiplicity of Baptist groups and a global history of Baptist faith, result in a rich but challenging study of any Baptist doctrine or practice. Therefore, after presentation of some early English Baptist history with respect to war and peace, this chapter will focus on Baptist just war thought in the United States.[1]

Ideas, like people, have genealogies. As with individuals, those genealogies are often complex. And so it is with how Baptists approach issues of war and peace. When considering Baptist perspectives on war, one immediately is confronted with answering not one question, but two questions: *Which* Baptists do we mean, and *Which* Christian perspective on war? No religious tradition is monolithic in its theology and practice. There is always a spectrum, or at least some variation. This is certainly true of Baptist responses to war. There is no uniform perspective on Baptists and war—many have been pacifists and many have been proponents of the idea of just war. Indeed, two prominent Baptist recipients of the Nobel Peace Prize, Martin Luther King Jr. and Jimmy Carter, rejected America's participation in two different wars (Vietnam and Operation Iraqi Freedom) as unjust.[2] In nineteenth-century England, Charles Spurgeon was staunchly antiwar (though not necessarily pacifist), and early twentieth-century American Baptist pacifists included Walter Rauschenbusch and Harry Emerson Fosdick.[3] More recently, Southern Baptist ethicist Glen Stassen (1936–2014) advocated a position he termed "just peacemaking"—one that he hoped would be an alternative to pacifism and the just war tradition. In any event, the purpose of this chapter is to explore Baptist belief and the just war tradition with a view to showing that the tradition has precedent in Baptist history and a strong presence in contemporary Baptist life.

No idea or movement arises in a vacuum. There is always a historical and intellectual context, and this is true of the emergence of the Baptist tradition. As Baptist historian Robert Johnson observes, "At its core, the Baptist movement began as a cause within the Anglo (English) culture. Its initial visionaries, though often well educated, addressed themes that became especially relevant to the Anglo understanding of post-Reformation English society. Those concerns were focused around matters of faith and theology but also reflected social issues associated with the struggles experienced by those classes in seventeenth-century Britain."[4] Throughout this chapter, we shall attempt to be sensitive to the historical and intellectual currents that have informed—and continue to inform—Baptist thought, particularly as they concern matters of war and peace.

BAPTISTS AND THE CHRISTIAN
SPECTRUM OF WAR

Christians throughout history have recognized that the formulation of a doctrine of war or approach to war is a theological and biblical deduction based upon the interpretation of numerous biblical passages (cf. Eccl. 3:1, 8; Matt. 5:44; 24:6–7; Acts 10:1–23; Rom. 13:1–7; 1 Tim. 2:2; and 1 Pet. 2:13–17). How one interprets those passages determines the position that one holds. There is no "red letter" biblical doctrine of war. Thus, the issue is not "What is the Bible's view of war?" but "What view best interprets and reflects the biblical passages regarding war?" It needs emphasizing that Baptists do not answer—and have not in the past answered—this question in unison. They agree, however, that the biblical worldview is one that values human life, animal life, the environment, and all that is in it as part of God's creation. Each of these parts of creation is affected by war. Created in the image of God, humans have infinite value and inherent dignity and worth. The loss of life or taking of life in any circumstance is among the most serious and severe things that occur in this world. No discussion of or comments about war should be lightly considered.

Baptist responses to war have represented a spectrum ranging from absolute rejection of war and participation in war to full participation with the proclamation of divine blessing and authority. For each of these views across the spectrum of response there are secular as well as religious counterparts—thus, for example, pacifism and Christian pacifism, just war and Christian just war. Each view also has strengths and weaknesses, with Baptists having debated, accepted, and rejected many variations throughout their complex history. For example, the largest Baptist group in the United States, the Southern Baptist Convention, was more supportive of the just war tradition and some aspects of national defense in the post–World War II era than was the American Baptist Churches USA. Although both groups sought peace rather than war, the latter denomination made various pronouncements on war (calling for its abolition), missile defense, and military policy throughout the 1970s, 1980s, and 1990s that strongly contrast with Southern Baptist views.[5] In the early 1970s, the American Baptist Churches USA also joined a group of denominations that called upon the US Congress to reevaluate missile defense spending.[6] Some Baptist denominations, by contrast, have not made pronouncements regarding war and peace beyond calling for working toward peace during times of conflict.

Baptist just war advocates contend with other proponents of the just war tradition that it is firmly and historically rooted in Christian moral-political thought and in the history of warfare in the West. It arose not in a vacuum but in the midst of the crucible of violence and upheaval that gave rise to values associated with Western civilization. Thinking about warfare within the just war tradition means wrestling with ideas and values that are upheld because they are considered greater than any individual, denomination, nation, or era.

In his seminal treatise *On War*, the Prussian military theorist Carl von Clausewitz insightfully understood that war and conflict are multidimensional, touching every facet of human and social experience. Entailed therein are dimensions of war that are psychological, intellectual, and spiritual in nature. Clausewitz observed that "theory becomes infinitely more difficult as soon as it touches the realm of moral values."[7] And, indeed, particular religious and ethical sentiments are part of the domain of what he terms "moral values." Although military forces of hundreds of thousands may clash in global conflict as experienced in twentieth century, it is ultimately individuals acting as moral agents who lead nations and forces in victory or defeat. Clausewitz continued, "Military activity is never directed at material force alone; it is always aimed simultaneously at the moral forces which give it life, and the two cannot be separated. But moral values can only be perceived by the inner eye, which differs in each person, and is often different in the same person at different times."[8] Whether one is a combatant, noncombatant, political leader, concerned citizen, or policy maker in any given war, religious and ethical values are part of the attitudes and actions in support of or dissent against the conflict. Values always have consequences. On this certainty, Baptists have never wavered.

BAPTIST BEGINNINGS AND THE PROBLEM OF WAR

It is important to understand the historical, political, and theological framework out of which the Baptist tradition arose, because it directly affected Baptist views on war, peace, freedom, and the state. The issue of Baptists and war is a derivative of a much broader, but foundational, aspect of Baptist history and the Baptist experience—namely, the relationship of Christians to the state, individually and corporately. Further, ideas regarding the Christian's relationship to the state are themselves reflective of historical experiences and theological convictions. The former derive largely from Christians in England who separated from the Church of England in the mid-to-late sixteenth and early seventeenth century. They did so because they believed that the process and theology of the Reformation were incomplete in Elizabethan England and the Church of England of Elizabeth's successor, James I.[9] In the words of one British historian, "Those who believed, by the early seventeenth century, that the national Reformation had failed were at the heart of the circles in which Baptist convictions first appeared."[10]

It was out of the experience of individual Christians in England in the early seventeenth century and what they believed about theology, worship, and polity that the beginnings of the multifaceted Baptist tradition are found. Several factors contributed the rise of the English Baptists: the English Separatist movement of the 1580s and 1590s; Parliament's enacting of the 1593 Act against Seditious Sectaries; religious life in England during the first decade of the seventeenth century; and the early years of the reign of James VI of Scotland, who inherited the crown of England in 1603 (and thus became James I). These led from some Christians being English Separatists in Amsterdam in 1609 to the beginnings of Baptist identity as it is known today.[11] It was, as Robert Johnson observes, "complex and variegated theological and cultural backgrounds out of which the numerous traditions that collectively constituted the early Baptist movement developed."[12]

When considering the relationship between the Baptist tradition and the just war tradition, as noted earlier, we find that there is no single Baptist perspective on war and peace. As with some theological doctrines and matters of Christian practice, there is a spectrum, and it began to develop rapidly, as early as the ecclesiastical separation of John Smyth and Thomas Helwys and their respective followers in the sixteenth century. Hence, any "attempts to define accurately Baptists under a single denominational rubric tend to generate confusion and frustration because this aggregation of churches lacks the centralizing authority often associated with an officially recognized denominational bishop, episcopacy, creed, or unifying structure."[13]

As Baptists grew in numerical strength, they also grew in varying ecclesiastical and doctrinal emphases. These resulted in numerous distinct groups that eventually spread around the globe. Johnson observes:

By the end of the eighteenth century, seven significant Baptist traditions could be identified: General Baptists, Particular-Regular Baptists, Separate Baptists, Free Will Baptists, Seventh Day Baptists, Amerindian Baptists, and black Baptists. . . . Separate Baptists had become the fastest-growing group of Baptists by the mid-eighteenth century because they strongly appealed to America's newly arriving frontier immigrants. Over time, Separates tended to merge with Regular Baptists to form a mainstream American Baptist body that included a mixture of qualities that had been drawn from the two groups.[14]

This multiplicity of groups and emphases created a vibrant theological tapestry with many strands, but it was one that makes tracing and surveying any single idea quite a challenge. As a result, one can speak of trends and examples of ideas that show the diversity of belief and practice under a common "Baptistic" umbrella.

It is possible to trace the Baptist lineage of just war support to one of the earliest advocates of the Baptist tradition, Thomas Helwys (1550–1616). After 1609–10, while living in Amsterdam, Helwys broke with John Smyth (1570–1612) when Smyth and supporters sought to join a Dutch Mennonite group known as the "Waterlanders." By 1612, Helwys and his supporters returned to England and created a congregation in Spitalfields, in north London. Smyth died in 1612, by which time his political leanings had been influenced strongly by Anabaptist political thought, causing Baptist historian Timothy George to note: "By the end of his life, then, Smyth had embraced an apolitical, radically pacifist view of the state. In good agreement with the Schleitheim Confession, Smyth believed that the sword was ordained by God outside the perfection of Christ."[15] Smyth's views were opposite those of Helwys. "In their attitude toward war, the distance that Helwys and the Baptists had placed between themselves and pacifistic Anabaptists is most clearly seen."[16]

In 1611, while still in Amsterdam, Helwys published two works repudiating several Waterlander doctrines that Smyth had embraced. Collectively, elements of these works present an early view of Baptist thought on government and the relationship of the Christian to it as well as the functions of government. One was titled *An Advertisement or Admonition to the Congregations, Which Men Call the New Fryelers, In the Lowe Countries, Written in Dutch and Published in English*. The second work was published under the title *A Declaration of Faith of English People Remaining at Amsterdam in Holland.* In these writings, Helwys addressed and rejected several teachings of the Waterlanders.

These writings show a belief in the validity of government as a divine institution, the necessity of Christian participation in government, government as an instrument of justice, and the rights of a government to go to war if necessary. With respect to individuals, Helwys's writings present one of the earliest calls for religious liberty and stress the importance of the individual conscience. By logical extension, Helwys argues for the Christian right to participate or not participate in matters of the state, including war, as one's conscience dictates.

On the matter of the doctrine of ecclesiology, Helwys argued against the Waterlanders' view of government and the magistracy. They held that if a person was involved with the government, the individual could not be a member of the true church. Helwys disagreed, arguing that the magistracy was a holy ordinance and did not debar a person from church membership. For instance, in his discussion of the magistracy in *A Declaration of Faith*, Helwys stated in part in article 24, the longest of the 27 articles:

> The Magistracy is a Holy ordinance of GOD, that every soul should be subject to it not for fear only, but for conscience sake. Magistrates are the ministers of GOD for our wealth, they do not bear the sword for nought [*sic*]. They are the ministers of GOD to take vengeance on them that do evil, Romans 13. It is fearful sin to speak evil of them that are in dignity, and to despise Government. 2 Peter 2.10. We should pay tribute, custom, and all other duties. We are to pray for them, for GOD would have them saved and come to the knowledge of his truth. 1 Timothy 2.1.4. And therefore they may be members of the Church of CHRIST, retaining their Magistracy, for no Holy Ordinance of GOD debars any from being a member of CHRIST'S Church. They bear the sword of GOD,—this sword in all Lawful administrations is to be defended and supported by the servants of GOD that are under their Government with their lives and all that they have according to the first Institution of that Holy Ordinance.[17]

For Helwys, government is divinely ordained, and participation in it by Christians is not prohibited.

In *An Advertisement or Admonition,* Helwys furthers his explanation of the magistracy by arguing that the use of the sword is permitted by magistracy:

> They are ministers of God and are applying themselves for the same thing. And let us with all grace and holiness to God and reverence to his holy ordinance consider what it is they are to apply themselves to. It is to punish evil doers with the sword and to reward or praise those that do well. . . . In applying themselves faithfully to the task they do the work that is proper to God. The divine property and work of God is to execute justice on the wicked and show mercy to those that do well. So far as the Lord has committed authority to magistrates to administer in these things, they do the proper work of God.[18]

Later in the treatise, he affirms apostolic teaching regarding bearing the sword and cites Romans 13:4. He then states: "Without any condition God has given magistrates power from himself and a sword to punish and take even vengeance on all evil doers. They may take vengeance of one, then of ten, and then of ten thousand, this God has appointed, ordained, and commanded. God is a gracious, merciful God, and full of pity and compassion. Yes, he is more compassionate than all men can be. Therefore do not let men pretend holiness in their compassionate and pitiful disposition that would not have magistrates administer with the sword."[19] With respect to Christians and the use of the sword, Helwys writes: "But the thing that misleads you all is that you can see no sword, but the sword of the spirit, and no armor but spiritual armor in the kingdom of Christ. Therefore the disciples of that kingdom (you say) must have no weapons nor put on any other armor. There then can be no putting to death, nor any war, neither should there be, but all is spiritual."[20] Helwys rejects this view as illogical and leading to foolish consequences. He reasons: "If then you will cast away all weapons and armor but such as the disciples of Christ use in the kingdom, you must also cast away all your bags and treasure, and all your buildings and houses, and you must wear no apparel but spiritual apparel, and eat not meat but spiritual meat."[21]

Collectively, the four statements above can be understood as permitting the magistracy and Christians to use the sword in causes deemed just. Helwys's use of "war" moves the discussion beyond the scope of civil governance narrowly.[22]

Although he acknowledges the tragedy of war, "where there is so much slaughter and bloodshed and which is accompanied with so many calamities and miseries," Helwys finds the work of the magistracy necessary and divinely approved based on Romans 13:4.[23] Were magistrates not to act, evil would prevail in the world. Chastising his opponents, he writes: "What a great sin of ingratitude and unthankfulness this is in all of you that so disapprove of magistrates and of their punishing of evil doers by the sword. If it were not for this ordinance all the godly on earth would be destroyed and the most godly first. Now we know that God is able to defend his own without the sword, but he has appointed this holy ordinance of the magistracy for the preservation and defense of all good men and for the subduing and keeping under and cutting off of evil doers."[24] For Helwys, government equally benefits Christians and non-Christians.

Helwys finds additional support for his views on war in the teachings of the Old Testament and the example of the Israelites, arguing that not only are Christians permitted to fight, but they may be preferred warriors because of their spiritual commitments: "Who are fitter to support and maintain the holy ordinance of God than those who profess to be children of God? Who are fitter to fight just and good battles than good and just men?"[25] Interestingly, he also speaks against use of mercenaries: "What simplicity is this to think that it is more lawful to hire men to fight a battle than to fight it themselves?"[26] And his argument against mercenaries, moreover, is grounded in Old Testament history: "The people of Israel, that were the people of God, never did so, but they fought the battles of the Lord themselves and the Lord went forth with their armies and gave them victory over their enemies and put their adversaries to flight. . . . It is as lawful now for servants of God to go to war as it was then."[27] Helwys will persist in his opposition to mercenaries and argue that personal safety and preservation are not reasons to use them.[28]

Helwys died in 1615 and was succeeded by John Murton (ca. 1582–1626). Nine years later, in 1624, several people separated (or were excommunicated) from Murton's congregation over doctrinal issues. However, one area on which they agreed with Murton was that of Christian participation in a just war. Regarding just war, Elias Tookey, the leader of this latter group, would write a letter, dated March 17, 1525, in which he stated:

And to these words (2 Cor. x. 4), *For the weapons of our warfare are not carnal*, we answer that, as we must use spiritual weapons in a spiritual war, it follows simply that it is allowed to Christians to use worldly weapons in a worldly warfare for a righteous matter; for formerly warriors have used both (for instance, Heb. Xi. 32. 33. 34). Indeed, we think that it is now not less allowed to Christians to use worldly weapons or arms in a just war, with which they must protect themselves, as it has been before, and even to perform all other exercises, on condition only that they govern their warfare by justice, faith, sufferance, fear, contentment, and all other virtues (virtues like some warriors formerly possessed). . . . We are also of the opinion that, if the enemies who carry on an unjust war are killed in that war, their blood will be on their heads, while the defenders are innocent.[29]

Writings such as those by Tookey and Helwys are among the earliest Baptist contributions on the subject of warfare. Of these writings, Baptist historian Anthony R. Cross writes: "If the interpretation put forward here of what Helwys was saying which was carried on by Tookey, is valid—that there are occasions when it is their patriotic duty for Baptists to employ violence in defense of their country—then it set a precedent for both General and Particular Baptists fighting in the civil wars of the 1640s, their serving as army chaplains."[30] The fledgling Baptist communities were not spared the social and political turmoil of the civil war era of 1638–60. Religious freedom during the 1640s facilitated growth of Baptist groups, permitting them to support and cooperate with the parliamentary regimes of the era as well as contribute to debates over a national confession, which would inform the Westminster Catechism and help create the New Model Army.[31]

BAPTISTS AND THE IDEAS OF POLITICAL LIBERTY AND CHRISTIAN LIBERTY

Significant for Baptist perspectives on war and peace is the foundational belief in—and practice of—liberty of conscience. This conviction is a historic and central component of Baptist thought and experience. It has been described variously as "soul freedom," "soul liberty," "soul competency," "religious liberty," and "religious freedom." Thereby it is understood that every person is free to follow his or her conscience in religious matters without any human coercion—especially ecclesiastical or political coercion. Part of the rationale behind this conviction is the Reformation principle of the spiritual equality of Christians ("priesthood of all believers"), while part of it stems from the historic environment of religious persecution in which the Baptist tradition arose.

In 1612, Helwys penned *A Short Declaration of the Mystery of Iniquity*, which contained a strong plea for religious liberty for all people. Two significant passages stand out with regard to religious liberty. In the first, he writes:

> We still pray our lord the king that we may be free from suspicion for having any thoughts of provoking evil against those of the Romish religion in regard of their profession, if they are true and faithful subjects to the king. For we do freely profess that our lord the king has no more power over their consciences than over ours, and that is none at all. For our lord the king is but an earthly king, and he has no authority as a king but in earthly causes. If the king's people are obedient and true subjects, obeying all human laws made by the king, our lord the king can require no more.[32]

In the second passage on religious liberty, Helwys writes: "For men's religion to God is between God and themselves. The king will not answer for it. Neither may the king be judge between God and man. Let them be heretics, Turks, Jews, or whatsoever, it does not appertain to the earthly power to punish them in the least measure. This is made evident to our lord the king by the scriptures."[33] Both of these passages are important for Helwys and later Baptists with respect to war and peace, because they argue for the primacy of the conscience and decision making. Whether or not a Christian participates in war is ultimately a matter of conscience once biblical grounds for participation have been established. Not only is the sword permitted; it is necessary. "If the sword of justice is taken away all government would be overthrown."[34]

Although the concept of "soul liberty" did not arise in the United States, it has been a strong part of the American idea of freedom of religion since the colonial era. Notable Baptists in the colonial and early national eras that championed and furthered this cause include Roger Williams (1603–83), John Clarke (1609–76), Isaac Backus (1724–1806), Samuel Stillman (1737–1807), James Manning (1738–91), and John Leland (1754–1841). Although a thorough study of their views of religious liberty and democracy is beyond the scope of this chapter, and their views on war are not just-war specific, each of them was very much aware of the tragedy and traumas of war. For example, Roger Williams attempted un-successfully to prevent the spread of King Philip's War in 1675–76. This failure resulted, in part, in the burning of Providence, Rhode Island (including Williams's own house) by Native Americans.[35]

Similarly, Isaac Backus was a leading pulpit orator of the American Revolution. In the aftermath of the revolution and context of the French Revolution, Samuel Stillman preached a 1794 sermon contrasting the two revolutions. In part, he proclaimed: "The events that have taken place in France are very different in their nature. Some of them are pleasing, others are painful—some we approve, others we condemn. We highly applaud the principles of the revolution, and the noble opposition of that nation to civil and ecclesiastical tyranny. But we are obliged to censure and lament their sanguinary measures, their numerous executions, their rejection of religion, and the fluctuating state of their politics."[36] Elsewhere in the sermon, Stillman calls for the congregation to be thankful for general peace and absence of war in America, though acknowledging the Indian war on the frontier that created difficulties for all on the frontier.[37]

Beyond matters of conscience, the idea of religious liberty and religious freedom, regardless of one's faith tradition, has always been a strong component of Baptist thought. Today, the largest evangelical denomination in the United States is the Southern Baptist Convention, and its Ethics & Religious Liberty Commission is the denominational entity promoting religious liberty.[38] For other Baptist groups in the United States such as the American Baptist Churches USA, Cooperative Baptist Fellowship, National Baptist Convention USA, Inc., National Baptist Convention of America, Seventh Day Baptist General Conference, Progressive National Baptist Convention, and others, the Baptist Joint Committee for Religious Liberty is the education and advocacy association that promotes religious liberty.[39]

BAPTISTS AND THE WARS OF AMERICA

Baptists in America have fought and died in every American war.[40] Re-latedly, the sacrifices of Baptist lives around the globe in national, regional, and international conflicts have been enormous. At the same time, many Baptists in the United States have also protested America's wars (just as other Baptists elsewhere have protested other wars). Yet when Baptists supported the decision to go to war, it was frequently more than patriotic fervor; it was from a belief that support was morally and biblically necessary. Baptists served in uniform as combatants and noncombatants (chaplains and otherwise) and as citizens on the home front. Yet, drawing on the Baptist emphasis of liberty of conscience, Baptists frequently addressed the treatment of conscientious objectors and supported those who made claims of conscientious objection, especially during World War II.[41]

During the American Revolution, there were about ninety-seven Baptist churches in the colonies, and the total Baptist population was less than ten thousand. Baptists overwhelmingly supported the colonists' fight for freedom. Because of religious persecution of Baptists in the colonies, they joined the revolutionary army fighting for religious and political freedom.[42] Nineteenth-century Baptist historian Thomas Armitage writes: "The colonies were not about to begin a revolution for religious liberty; that they had; but the Baptists demanded both, and this accounts for the desperation with which they threw themselves into the struggle, so that we have no record of so much as one thorough Baptist Tory."[43] Even when Armitage's declaration is somewhat exaggerated, its general sentiment is accurate.[44] Baptist leaders gave qualified support to the colonial cause but emphasized liberty of conscience as a guiding principle for participation. Historian Mark A. Noll observes, "Even though Baptists came to support independence in large numbers, they did not forget their fundamental religious commitments."[45] Although most Baptists supported the revolution, there were dissenters such as famed Baptist pastor and leader Morgan Edwards (1722–92).[46]

Due to the age and geography of the new American nation, regional interests, and the ecclesiology of Baptists, it is worth noting that it was extremely difficult to speak of Baptists as a "denomination" and major religious group in America for many decades after Americans gained independence. One can look at individual Baptists and individual Baptist churches and associations, but to do more and to attempt to make broader historical statements and conclusions is challenging. Thus, while some would argue that one cannot speak of "American Baptists" as a denomination during the nation's early decades, one can speak of "Baptist Americans" and argue that both words—"Baptist" and "American"—are definable and recognizable entities. During the War of 1812, Baptist Americans frequently viewed the young nation as the new Zion, imbuing it with theological significance that went far beyond patriotism.[47] Defending Zion was mandatory and, therefore, war was just.[48]

The tragedy of the American Civil War ripped apart the tapestry of the young nation less than one hundred years after its independence, and the scars of the war remained more than one hundred years after its conclusion. Baptists on both sides of the Mason-Dixon Line supported their respective armies and proclaimed their fighting justifiable.[49] For many, the war was a theological crisis as much as it was a political crisis, and it was during this war that ideas of sacrifice, death, duty, and valor became closely intertwined as military, political, and religious values.[50]

In the aftermath of the Spanish-American War, the United States rose to international prominence as an industrial and political power.[51] When America entered World War I, Baptists in the United States supported the effort as necessary, although prior to US entry there were pacifist and isolationist voices and sentiments among Baptists.[52] Baptists in America went to war but did so reluctantly.[53]

World War II came upon many Americans unexpectedly after the 1920s and 1930s, when pacifism was common in American churches, including many Baptist churches. With America's entry into the war, most Baptists recognized that at times war was necessary to combat evil. As a result, they broke away from the religious pacifism that was popular in most mainline American churches in the 1920s and 1930s. The war became a watershed and model for applying the just war tradition among many Baptist groups.[54]

Throughout the Cold War, including the conflicts in Korea and Vietnam, there were Baptist voices supporting the war efforts and those opposing them, especially in Vietnam, even when the majority of Baptists supported the nation's military efforts, as did most Baptist leaders.[55] Conflict engagement by the United States during the post–Cold War era typically was viewed by most Baptists in America as permitted under just war principles. This was especially true of the first Gulf War in 1991.

STATEMENTS OF FAITH

As noted by Timothy George, "Historically Baptists have been staunch advocates of religious liberty, the priesthood of all believers, and the inviolability of the individual conscience before God."[56] They have emphasized doctrine over formal creeds; yet they have affirmed their beliefs in various

types of statements of faith. In several of these documents, there are discussions of war and peace. In each one, where war and peace are men-
tioned, there is an emphasis, first, on the desirability and primacy of peace
and, second, on the necessity of war at times when peace is not to be had.
Liberty of conscience and the role of the civil magistrate (government) are
also a prominent feature.[57]

For the nation's largest Baptist group, the Southern Baptist Convention, the document "The Baptist Faith and Message" in its several editions
(1925, 1963, 2000) has been a guiding beacon for doctrinal beliefs and the
application of them. The article "Peace and War" (19 in the 1925 version,
16 in the 1963 and 2000 versions) remains the same in each edition with
the exception of one sentence that was included in 1925 but deleted in
1963 and then reinserted in part in 2000, in addition to the inclusion of
additional biblical references in 1963 and 2000. Deleted from the 1963
edition was the following: "We urge Christian people throughout the
world to pray for the reign of the Prince of Peace, and to oppose everything likely to provoke war." It was reinserted in the 2000 version but
omits the last phrase "and to oppose everything likely to provoke war."[58]
Regarding peace and war, the document states:

> It is the duty of Christians to seek peace with all men on principles of
> righteousness. In accordance with the spirit and teachings of Christ
> they should do all in their power to put an end to war.
>
> The true remedy for the war spirit is the gospel of our Lord. The
> supreme need of the world is the acceptance of His teachings in all
> the affairs of men and nations, and the practical application of His
> law of love. Christian people throughout the world should pray for
> the reign of the Prince of Peace.
>
> (Isaiah 2:4; Matthew 5:9, 38–48; 6:33; 26:52; Luke 22:36, 38;
> Romans 12:18–19; 13:1–7; 14:19; Hebrews 12:14; James 4:1–2)[59]

The article on religious liberty has not changed in the nearly one-hundred-
year history of the document. In part, it affirms, "God alone is Lord of the
conscience, and He has left it free from the doctrines and commandments
of men which are contrary to His Word or not contained in it."[60]

In addition to statements of faith, there have been numerous resolutions by Baptist groups regarding the topics of war and peace. For example,

there have been resolutions by the Southern Baptist Convention regarding peace and war (1936, 1940), conscientious objectors (1946), peace negotiations in Vietnam (1968), Operation Desert Storm (1991), terrorism (2002), and the liberation of Iraq (2003).

RECENT, CONTEMPORARY BAPTIST VOICES

One can find numerous just war proponents within the Baptist tradition. A brief glimpse at several of the more prominent ones from the latter half of the twentieth century to the present indicates that there is a strong tributary flowing from the historic Christian teaching regarding war and peace.

Billy Graham

One of a handful of Baptists with international name recognition, evangelist Billy Graham (1918–2018) was the most well-known evangelist of the twentieth century. His prominence in American Christianity afforded him opportunities of being heard by millions of people through his evangelistic crusades, through radio, and on television. He was the face and voice of American evangelicalism in post–World War II America.

The era of Graham's ministry paralleled the rise and duration of the Cold War and the conflicts in Korea and Vietnam.[61] He visited with and preached to troops during both wars. His Christmas 1953 visit to troops in South Korea was recorded in his diary of the trip, published as a small book *I Saw Your Sons at War.* He was also a guest, friend, and confidant of many political leaders, including US presidents — though not without controversy.[62] Under presidents Johnson and Nixon, Graham was a vocal supporter of the war in Vietnam, although as the war continued he became more ambivalent.[63] Graham and his ministry, Billy Graham Evangelistic Association (BGEA), supported American war efforts because of his concern regarding the atheistic nature of the global Communist threat.

Carl F. H. Henry

Carl F. H. Henry (1913–2003) was recognized widely as one of the preeminent evangelical leaders and theologians in the latter half of the twentieth century. He was an ordained Baptist minister and lifelong Baptist who earned a ThD from Northern Baptist Seminary and a PhD from Boston University and served as an instructor at Northern Baptist Seminary. In 1942, he participated in the founding of the National Association of Evangelicals, and in 1948 he became part of the original faculty of Fuller Theological Seminary. In 1956 he took a leave of absence and, at the invitation of Billy Graham and L. Nelson Bell, became the founding editor of *Christianity Today* as a journalistic alternative voice to the socially, politically, and theologically liberal magazine *Christian Century*.[64]

Henry is perhaps best known for his 1947 work *The Uneasy Conscience of Modern Fundamentalism*, which called for the development of a comprehensive worldview that addressed social and political issues as well as theology, as well as his subsequent six-volume magnum opus, *God, Revelation, and Authority* (1976–83). The latter defended the idea of divine propositional revelation as the philosophical and theological foundation of knowledge about God and the divine revelation of the Bible.

Giving voice to twentieth-century American evangelicalism, his writings echoed the beliefs of many Baptists and other evangelicals. Henry wrote on issues of war and peace in the broader context of evangelical social ethics. In *God, Revelation, and Authority* his comments regarding war come in rebuttal to the writings of Mennonite theologian John Howard Yoder (1927–97) and Yoder's staunch affirmation of pacifism as the clear teaching of Jesus and the New Testament.[65] Therein Henry upholds the Augustinian view that war is not the greatest evil and that war is at times, reluctantly, to be pursued in order to create a just peace and punish wrongdoing (as opposed to revenge).[66] He writes: "In regard to war, the church must stand unequivocally on the side of peace as its ultimate loyalty, even if war is not the worst of all possible evils and in fallen history justices sometimes requires it."[67] Significantly, in this statement Henry affirms two historic emphases—the Baptist desire for and emphasis on the primacy of peace in international relations and the Augustinian and just war tenet that in a fallen world justice may require war.

Henry's writings affirm the historic Baptist view of the state as divinely ordained, even with its many shortcomings and failures. It is a necessity in a fallen world. "Without the restraints of government to check men's evil lusts by the use of power in a sinful world, society would be reduced to anarchy."[68] Henry rejects Christian apathy toward government, politics, and social concern; but he also rejects Christian pacifism: "It is the Christian's duty to support government as an instrumentality for preserving justice and restraining disorder. To maintain Jesus' political relevance in the here and now does not require, as Yoder would have it, the repudiation of force as a moral principle in social ethics. One can transcend both an apolitical stance and the worldly political pattern without resorting to a pacifist ethic incompatible with the New Testament."[69] Specifically addressing Christian pacifism, he writes: "If Paul's intention was merely to teach 'a nonresistant attitude toward a tyrannical government [Yoder, *Politics of Jesus* p. 204],' then he surely had ample linguistic ability to state any such doctrine clearly. If the will of God in Christ concerning sociopolitical responsibility depends only upon inferences from the overall humiliation of Jesus, it becomes difficult to define the content of evangelical ethics at major levels. Nowhere in the New Testament does Jesus or Paul speak to the issue of war in terms of pacifism."[70] For Henry, there is no biblical mandate or template for pacifism. He believes that there are biblical guidelines for war and peace and that they must be understood as part of a larger biblical worldview.

Although Christians pray for peace, the just use of force is permitted and sometimes necessary in the contemporary world. Henry, in looking at history, the present, and the future, maintains a perspective that is Christocentric: "We stand in an interim period between Jesus' submission to the injustice of Pilate and his return as King of kings and Lord of lords when every knee and all the rulers will bow—an interim period in which the New Testament ethic evolves with its legitimate role for the state as an instrument for active promotion of justice and restraint of injustice by the use of force."[71] Wars will cease only with the return of the Prince of Peace.

The matters of personal conscience and liberty are dominant themes throughout Henry's writings. Henry recognizes that not all Christians agree with his views, and he supports the right of any to disagree. Noting the seriousness of Christian participation in the military, he observes:

> The matter of military participation or nonparticipation is, of course, critically important, for the tension in Christian ethics is nowhere more anguished than in regard to war. In either case, whether it takes up arms or refuses to do so, the church seems to cloud its mission.

This becomes all the more true since modern nuclear weaponry harbors the possibility of such monstrous destruction of civilian life and ecological values; what armed conflict achieves by way of restraining injustice often seems to be sacrificed in the disorder that follows. On the other hand, the victims of unresisted tyranny grieve for the loss of human freedom and dignity.[72]

Henry believes that individual conscience is important and is a corollary to religious liberty. Together, these two elements form a foundation freedom and human rights.[73]

Daniel R. Heimbach

In general terms, there has been a significant resurgence of just war thinking from the late 1980s to the present. This has come about nationally and internationally in academia as well as in political and policy-making realms. In the US context, the government's formulation of the just war idea in terms of policy, beginning in the late 1980s, can be traced in part to the work of Southern Baptist minister, ethicist, and professor Daniel R. Heimbach. Currently senior professor of Christian ethics at Southeastern Baptist Theological Seminary, Heimbach previously served in the US government as deputy assistant secretary of the navy for manpower. Prior to that, he served two years on the White House staff under President George H. W. Bush both as associate director for domestic policy and as deputy executive secretary to the Domestic Policy Council. It was through the efforts of Heimbach, a former naval officer who helped craft an internal White House staff memorandum written directly for the president, that assistance was given to President George H. W. Bush in providing conscious application and articulation of just war principles in his decision to use military force against Saddam Hussein in the 1991 Persian Gulf War.[74]

President Bush approved of Heimbach's memorandum and its content and "approved the recommendation and ordered the Office of Presidential Communications to use my [Heimbach's] outline of just war principles to compose an address in which he would explain to the nation and the world the moral framework for his leadership of forces opposing Iraqi aggression in the Persian Gulf."[75] Later, upon reviewing Heimbach's writing about this geopolitical development, Bush wrote to Heimbach and stated, "I read every word of 'The Bush Just War Doctrine' . . . ; and it accurately states my feelings. . . . Many thanks for setting the record straight."[76]

Beyond these efforts, Heimbach's writings, speeches, lectures, and influence on Baptist students have been significant in articulating just war principles among Southern Baptists. Several students educated under Heimbach currently have professorships in Southern Baptist seminaries and advocate the just war tradition—among them, Bruce A. Ashford, David W. Jones, and J. Alan Branch.[77]

Against those who argue that pacifism is the only viable position on war for a Christian, Heimbach contends that such is not the case, arguing: "Because evil is real in the world, sometimes we have to fight as a last resort against evil."[78] Heimbach's work has been instrumental in reinvigorating the just war tradition in US government and military venues and in influencing policy in support of the tradition in the last three decades.

Richard Land

Richard Land, currently president of Southern Evangelical Seminary, is the former president of the Southern Baptist Convention's Ethics & Religious Liberty Commission (ERLC). Operation Iraqi Freedom occurred during his tenure at ERLC, and he was a prominent and vocal supporter of the use of military force against Iraq. Three years after the conflict, when interviewed by *Religion & Ethics Newsweekly*, Land reaffirmed his belief that the conflict was justifiable on the basis of just war principles. He stated that even though no weapons of mass destruction were found, the conflict was still justifiable based on the just war tradition. His response contained the following:

> Q: Three years ago you told us the U.S. would be morally justified going into Iraq. Do you still believe that?
>
> A: Yes, I do. I think it's one of the nobler and finer things we've done as a nation, and I think that it's going to, in the end, produce a government in Iraq and a society in Iraq that is far more conscious of human rights and far more conscious of human freedom, and in the end it's going to remake the Middle East. . . .

Q: Has Iraq changed your thinking about the use of force?
A: It's certainly reminded me that war is a terrible thing. It's certainly reminded me that war should be a last resort, but not a last resort that's so defined down that you never get to it. Sometimes, you know, war is a terrible thing. But sometimes it's the least terrible thing.[79]

Three years earlier, at a February 2003 event on conflict in Iraq, Land, Heimbach, Mark Liederbach, and David Jones[80] all spoke at a public forum, with each affirming a commitment to the just war idea. Land and Heimbach, as it turned out, would disagree over whether regime change was justifiable within the framework. Land stated that "just cause can be a just cause of war if the regime is evil enough."[81] Heimbach, in response, disagreed that regime change alone was sufficient cause for a just war and invasion of Iraq. This disagreement is important in that it shows that even within acceptance of the just war tradition there can be difference of opinion and understanding. The tradition is one that offers moral principles and guidance, but it also has breadth, variation, and flexibility within it. Echoing aspects of the tradition, Land stated: "The resort to lethal force, authorized by a legitimate authority, is sometimes the price human beings have to pay for living in a moral universe."[82]

R. Albert Mohler Jr.

Albert Mohler Jr. serves as president of the Southern Baptist Theological Seminary in Louisville, Kentucky, and has frequently voiced advocacy of the just war tradition. Mohler's writings, daily podcasts, and Internet blog all offer analysis of current of events wherein he presents discussion and critique from the standpoint of an explicitly biblical worldview. He addresses difficult issues and does not avoid important social and cultural concerns.

Transcripts of his *The Briefing* podcasts not infrequently speak to topics related to war and peace—among these, "Is War Ever Justified? A Reality Check,"[83] "Just War Theory and North Korea,"[84] "Siege Warfare and the Syrian Civil War: Why the Christian Understanding of Just War Theory Matters," "Shouldn't We Just Ban the Bomb? Nuclear Weapons and the Problem of Sin and Knowledge," "Canadian Military Tackles the

Soul-Destroying Question of When to Shoot a Child Soldier,"[85] "Just War Theory,"[86] and "Hiroshima and the Burden of History."[87]

Throughout his podcasts and writings Mohler upholds the just war tradition. For example, he writes:

> The most thoughtful Christian tradition of moral reasoning on the question of lethal violence is customarily described as the Just War tradition. . . . The Christian conscience should struggle with the awful question of war. We know that every human life is sacred—and we know why. Christians must never grow to love war, nor to seek battle, yet those who righteously fight for life serve with honor. . . . War is a demonstration of the utter sinfulness of sin. In the name of the Prince of Peace, Christians must seek to establish and maintain our faltering and transient efforts at peacemaking until our Lord comes to establish the only peace that endures. In this fallen world, we must honestly acknowledge that peacemaking will sometimes lead to war. In the final analysis, war is the worst option imaginable, until it is the only option left.[88]

Mohler acknowledges that "the words of Jesus are unambiguous: 'Blessed are the peacemakers, for they shall be called sons of God.' [Matt. 5:9] These familiar words from the Sermon on the Mount form the basis of any Christian understanding of war and its morality. For the Christian, the standard is already set and the goal is absolutely clear—we are to seek the peace."[89]

Additional Proponents

The names presented above are illustrative of contemporary prominent Baptists who uphold the just war tradition. They are not the only voices, and their position is not the only position Baptists hold regarding matters of war and peace. However, their voices indicate the presence within the Baptist tradition of the just war tradition as a viable position. And as such, it is part of the historic mainstream Christian position regarding war and peace. Among other Baptists who are just war proponents one might cite D. A. Carson,[90] Russell Moore,[91] Jack Graham,[92] and Charles Stanley,[93] to name but a few.

A CONTINUING CONCERN OF INDIVIDUAL
LIBERTY AND CONSCIENCE

When, in the second century after the death of Jesus Christ, the early Christian theologian and apologist for the faith Tertullian asked the famous question "What has Athens to do with Jerusalem?,"[94] it was more than a simple rhetorical inquiry. Although the specific context of the question was a condemnation of philosophy, embedded in the question was an understanding that men and women simultaneously possess a physical dimension and a spiritual dimension as human beings and that both find individual and corporate manifestations in society.

But what is the proper relationship between these two dimensions, especially when experienced corporately and politically? What is the proper relationship between the secular and the sacred, the political and the religious, the state and the church? How are Christians to understand this relationship? How have they understood it in the past? And, most importantly, how does Scripture inform us in this regard?

Logically, there are only three answers to Tertullian's question — everything, nothing, or something. The answer may be simple, but it is not easy. Beneath a single-word answer, there are many complexities, nuances, and dimensions. Just as the roots are many and deep for a single tree, so too are there, for a one-word answer, many presuppositions, values, and ideas.

For two thousand years, Christians have wrestled with their answers, and in recent centuries Baptists around the globe have done so as well. Their responses have arisen in the midst of many changes socially, politically, and theologically. Those responses, it needs emphasizing, have by no means been monolithic; rather, they reflect emerging (and reemerging) ideas. Different times, systems, personalities, and events have shaped Christians' ideas about politics, law, government, and the state. That has surely been the case among Baptists.

Ultimately, for Baptists, it is not history, theory, culture, personalities, political parties, or movements that determine appropriate political values and actions, including matters of war and peace. It is, rather, a proper understanding of God and the role of individuals in upholding his plan in the created order. There is no "Baptist political blueprint" in the pages of Scripture, no schematic for a Christian political order; there are, however, principles to be discerned and applied. To the extent that they are capable of discernment and application, Baptists believe that Christians have a responsibility to act politically. As Carl F. H. Henry declared: "Christian duty requires courageous participation at the frontiers of public concern— education, mass media, politics, law, literature and the arts, labor and economics, and the whole realm of cultural pursuits."[95] And on occasion, with great sobriety and solemnity, Henry's "public concern" entails issues of war and peace.

In order to participate knowledgeably as Henry encourages, it is necessary to understand the realities of law, government, the state, and human rights in a biblical and historical framework. At that point, Baptists can join with others in pursuing a course of application of the principles to specific concerns and problems as they arise. It is in this application that the justified use of force based upon the principles of the just war tradition is to be considered as national and international events thus warrant.

Throughout American history the just war idea generally has been the tradition that most Baptist groups and declarations have affirmed. Although not all Baptists have been, are, or will be just war proponents, this tradition nevertheless remains a strong and viable framework by which Baptists can promote witness to a fallen world marred by sin. As they do so, Baptists prayerfully await the return of the Prince of Peace.

NOTES

1. The literature on Baptists and war is rich though somewhat fragmented for researchers, depending upon which country, war, and Baptist group one wishes to study. Two helpful volumes that are Baptist-specific in content and suitable for beginning such study are Gordon L. Heath and Michael A. G. Haykin, eds., *Baptists and War: Essays on Baptists and Military Conflict 1640s–1990s* (Eugene, OR: Pickwick, 2015), and Bruce T. Gourley, *Crucible of Faith and Freedom: Baptists and the Civil War* (Macon, GA: Nurturing Faith, 2015).

2. On Dr. King's views and statements, see Martin Luther King Jr., "Beyond Vietnam—a Time to Break Silence," speech delivered to participants of event "Clergy and Laymen Concerned about Vietnam" at Riverside Church, New York, April 4, 1967, available at American Rhetoric Online Speech Bank, https://www.americanrhetoric.com/speeches/mlkatimetobreaksilence.htm. On President Carter's opposition to Operation Iraqi Freedom, see his March 9, 2003, editorial "Just War—or a Just War?," in the *New York Times*, https://www.nytimes.com/2003/03/09/opinion/just-war-or-a-just-war.html.

3. See Jonathan Merritt, "Spurgeon: How the Politically Liberal Preacher Became a Conservative Christian Paragon," Religion News Service, June 17, 2008, https://religionnews.com/2013/08/12/surprised-by-spurgeon-how-a-politically -liberal-preacher-became-a-paragon-among-conservative-christians/.

4. Robert E. Johnson, *A Global Introduction to Baptist Churches* (Cambridge: Cambridge University Press, 2010), 1.

5. See, for example, the *American Baptist Resolution on National Missile Defense System*. American Baptist Churches USA, 2000. https://www.abc-usa .org/wp-content/uploads/2019/02/natmis.pdf.

6. See *Hearings before a Subcommittee of the Committee on Appropriations, United States Senate*, 92nd Cong. 1081 (1972).

7. Carl von Clausewitz, *On War*, ed. and trans. Michael Howard and Peter Paret (Princeton: Princeton University Press, 1976), 136.

8. Ibid., 137.

9. For a summary, see David W. Bebbington, *Baptists through the Centuries: A History of a Global People* (Waco, TX: Baylor University Press, 2010), 19–21.

10. Ibid., 21.

11. Early Baptist history is rich with contemporary relevance; notable histories thereof abound. Especially notable are Leon McBeth, *The Baptist Heritage: Four Centuries of Baptist Witness* (Nashville: Broadman, 1987); Bill J. Leonard, *Baptist Ways* (Valley Forge, PA: Judson Press, 2003); Tom Nettles, *The Baptists*, 3 vols. (Boston: Mentor, 2007–10); Johnson, *Global Introduction to Baptist Churches*; Bebbington, *Baptists through the Centuries*; Anthony L. Chute, Nathan A. Finn, and Michael A. G. Haykin, *The Baptist Story: From English Sect to Global Movement* (Nashville: Broadman & Holman, 2015).

12. Johnson, *Global Introduction to Baptist Churches*, 53.

13. Ibid.

14. Ibid., 94–95.

15. Timothy George, "Between Pacifism and Coercion: The English Baptist Doctrine of Religious Toleration," *Mennonite Quarterly Review* 58 (1984): 36.

16. Ibid., 37.

17. Thomas Helwys, *A Declaration of Faith*, in *The Life and Writings of Thomas Helwys*, ed. Joe Early Jr. (Macon, GA: Mercer University Press, 2009), 73.

18. Thomas Helwys, *An Advertisement or Admonition to the Congregations, Which Men Call the New Fryelers, In the Lowe Countries, Written in Dutch and Published in English*, in Early, *Life and Writings of Thomas Helwys*, 130.

19. Ibid., 140.

20. Ibid.

21. Ibid., 140–41.

22. Anthony R. Cross, "Baptists, Peace, and War: The Seventeenth-Century British Foundations," in Heath and Haykin, *Baptists and War*, 13.

23. Helwys, *Advertisement or Admonition*, 138, 140.

24. Ibid., 142–43.

25. Ibid., 143.

26. Ibid.

27. Ibid.

28. Ibid.

29. Elias Tookey, cited in Benjamin Evans, *The Early English Baptists* (London: J. Heaton & Son, 1864), 2:40. The letter is cited in full on pages 37–40.

30. Cross, "Baptists, Peace, and War," 16.

31. See Mark R. Bell, *Apocalypse How? Baptists Movements during the English Revolution* (Macon, GA: Mercer University Press, 2000).

32. Thomas Helwys, *A Short Declaration of the Mystery of Iniquity*, in Early, *Life and Writings of Thomas Helwys*, 209.

33. Ibid.

34. Helwys, *Advertisement or Admonition*, 144.

35. See James A. Warren, *God, War, and Providence: The Epic Struggle of Roger Williams and the Narragansett Indians against the Puritans of New England* (New York: Scribner, 2018), 205–44. On John Clarke and issues of liberty and democracy, see Theodore Dwight Bozeman, "John Clarke and the Complications of Liberty," *Church History* 75, no. 1 (March 2006): 69–93.

36. Samuel Stillman, *Being the Day of Annual Thanksgiving* (Boston: Manning and Loring, 1795), 12. This was a sermon delivered on November 20, 1794.

37. Ibid., 24–25.

38. See https://erlc.com.

39. See https://bjconline.org.

40. Baptist participation in—and attitudes toward—the wars of the United States is a topic that far exceeds the scope of this chapter. There are numerous sources available for each war, of which only a few will be cited in this section.

41. See "Resolution Concerning Conscientious Objectors," resolution passed at the Annual Meeting of the Southern Baptist Convention, Miami, Florida, May 1, 1946, available at https://www.sbc.net/resource-library/resolutions /resolution-concerning-conscientious-objectors/.

42. Not only had Baptists been restricted in colonies that had an established religion (e.g., Virginia's Episcopal Church), but there was a general fear in some quarters that the Church of England would enforce bishoprics on the colonies. This was one of the points made by the Continental Congress in its July 1775 "Declaration of the Rights and Grievances of the United Colonies."

43. Thomas Armitage, *A History of the Baptists* (New York: Bryan Taylor & Co., 1990), 690, https://archive.org/details/HistoryOfTheBaptists/page/n689.

44. Mark A. Noll, *Christians in the American Revolution* (Washington, DC: Christian College Consortium, 1977), 85. See especially his comments on Isaac

Backus (1724–1806) on pages 80–87. See also Backus's 1773 work, *An Appeal to the Public for Religious Liberty, against the Oppressions of the Present Day*, available at Classic Liberals, http://classicliberal.tripod.com/misc/appeal.html, and his 1778 work *Government and Liberty Described and Ecclesiastical Tyranny Exposed*, Evans Early American Imprint Collection, University of Michigan Library Digital Collections, https://quod.lib.umich.edu/cgi/t/text/text-idx?c=evans;cc=evans;rgn=main;view=text;idno=N12452.0001.001.

45. Noll, *Christians in the American Revolution*, 85.

46. Ibid., 118.

47. James Tyler Robertson, "A House Uniting: Americans, Baptists, and the War of 1812," in Heath and Haykin, *Baptists and War*, 64–66.

48. Ibid., 59–61. For the response of some Canadian Baptists to the war, see Gordon L. Heath, "Ontario Baptists and the War of 1812," *Ontario History* 103, no. 2 (November 2011): 169–91.

49. Gourley, *Crucible of Faith and Freedom*.

50. See Mark A. Noll, *The Civil War as a Theological Crisis* (Chapel Hill: University of North Carolina Press, 2006); Drew Gilpin Faust, *This Republic of Suffering: Death and the American Civil War* (New York: Knopf, 2008). Among the many works about religion and the war, see Robert J. Miller, *Both Prayed to the Same God: Religion and Faith in the American Civil War* (Lanham, MD: Lexington Books, 2007); Steven E. Woodworth, *While God Is Marching On: The Religious World of Civil War Soldiers* (Lawrence: University of Kansas Press, 2001).

51. Regarding the war and the just war tradition, see Timothy J. Demy, "Just War and the Spanish-American War," in *America and the Just War Tradition: A History of U.S. Conflicts*, ed. Mark David Hall and J. Daryl Charles (Notre Dame, IN: University of Notre Dame Press, 2019), 136–54; Eric D. Patterson, *Just American Wars: Ethical Dilemmas in U.S. Military History* (New York: Routledge, 2018), 124–39.

52. David Roach, "World War I Remembered as a 'Stand for Liberty' 100 Years Later," Baptist Press, August 7, 2014, http://www.bpnews.net/43111/world-war-i-remembered-as-stand-for-liberty-100-years-later.

53. Philip Jenkins, *The Great and Holy War: How World War I Became a Religious Crusade* (New York: HarperOne, 2014); Jonathan Ebel, *Faith in the Fight: Religion and the American Soldier in the Great War* (Princeton: Princeton University Press, 2010).

54. "War and Peace: Baptists' Opinions Have Shifted from Predecessors," Baptist News Global, August 5, 2007, https://baptistnews.com/article/war-and-peace-baptists-opinions-have-shifted-from-predecessors/#.XOgunda2Z08U. On Baptist pacifists and World War II, see Paul R. Dekar, "The 'Good War' and Baptists Who Refused to Fight It," *Peace & Change* 32, no. 2 (April 2007): 186–202.

55. On Vietnam, see Nathan A. Finn, "Baptists and the War in Vietnam: Responses to 'America's Longest War,'" in Heath and Haykin, *Baptists and War*, 202–29; David E. Settje, *Faith and War: How Christians Debated the Cold and Vietnam Wars* (New York: New York University Press, 2011), 34–37, 68–71, 133–38.

56. Timothy George, introduction to *Baptist Confessions, Covenants, and Catechisms*, ed. Timothy George and Denise George (Nashville: Broadman & Holman, 1996), 2.

57. See, for example, The Philadelphia Confession of Faith (1742), chaps. 21 and 25; The Orthodox Creed (1679), arts. 45 and 46; The New Hampshire Confession (1833), art. 14; and others in George and George, *Baptist Confessions, Covenants, and Catechisms*.

58. For comparison of the three versions, see "Comparison of the 1925, 1963 and 2000 Baptist Faith and Message," Southern Baptist Convention, https://bfm.sbc.net/comparison-chart/.

59. Ibid.

60. Ibid.

61. Settje, *Faith and War*, 131–34.

62. See Grant Wacker, *America's Pastor: Billy Graham and the Shaping of a Nation* (Cambridge, MA: Harvard University Press, 2014), 204–21; Nancy Gibbs and Michael Duffy, *The Preacher and the Presidents: Billy Graham in the White House* (New York: Center Street, 2007).

63. Wacker, *America's Pastor*, 17, 211. See also Richard V. Pierard, "Billy Graham and Vietnam: From Cold Warrior to Peacemaker," *Christian Scholar's Review* 10, no. 1 (1980): 37–51.

64. On Henry, *Christianity Today*, and the Cold War era, see Settje, *Faith and War*, 28–31, 41–43, 98–103, and 130–33.

65. Carl F. H. Henry, *God, Revelation and Authority*, vol. 4, *God Who Speaks and Shows: Fifteen Theses, Part Three* (Waco, TX: Word, 1979), 525–29, 531–37. It is in the latter pages just noted that Yoder's views on peace and war as mirrored in Yoder's *The Politics of Jesus* (1972) are found.

66. On Augustine and war, see J. Daryl Charles and Timothy J. Demy, *War, Peace, and Christianity: Questions and Answers from a Just-War Perspective* (Wheaton, IL: Crossway, 2010), 124–28.

67. Henry, *God, Revelation and Authority*, 4:551.

68. Henry, *A Plea for Evangelical Demonstration* (Grand Rapids, MI: Baker, 1971), 32.

69. Henry, *God, Revelation and Authority*, 4:535.

70. Ibid., 536.

71. Henry, *Carl Henry at His Best: A Lifetime of Quotable Thoughts* (Portland, OR: Multnomah, 1989), 89–90.

72. Henry, *God, Revelation and Authority*, 4:532–33.

73. Cf. Henry's address "Religious Freedom: Cornerstone of Human Rights," in *The Christian Mindset in a Secular Society* (Portland, OR: Multnomah, 1984), 63–80; "Religious Liberty as a Cause Celebre," in *Christian Citizens: The Rights and Responsibilities of Dual Citizenship*, ed. Richard D. Land and Louis A. Moore (Nashville: Broadman & Holman, 1994), 64–77.

74. Hereon see Daniel R. Heimbach, "The Bush Just War Doctrine: Genesis and Application of the President's Moral Leadership in the Persian Gulf War," in *From Cold War to New World Order: The Foreign Policy of George H. W. Bush*, ed. Meena Bose and Rosanna Perotti (Westport, CT: Greenwood, 2002), 443–44. The chapter devoted to Heimbach (441–64) offers a very interesting glimpse of policy and decision making at the highest levels of government.

75. Ibid., 445.

76. George Bush to Daniel Heimbach, May 27, 1997, cited in Heimbach, "Bush Just War Doctrine," 441.

77. Email of Daniel R. Heimbach to Eric D. Patterson, November 26, 2018; used with permission. See also Bruce Ashford and Chris Pappalardo, *One Nation under God: A Christian Hope for American Politics* (Nashville: B&H Academic, 2015), 125–33; Daniel R. Heimbach, "Distinguishing Just War from Crusade: Is Regime Change a Just Cause for Just War?," in *War in the Bible and Terrorism in the Twenty-First Century*, ed. Richard S. Hess and Elmer A. Martens, Bulletin for Biblical Research Supplement 2 (Winona Lake, IN: Eisenbrauns, 2008), 79–92.

78. Cited in Jason Hall, "Fighting a Just War in Iraq," *SBC Life*, April 1, 2003, available through Baptist Press, https://www.baptistpress.com/resource-library/sbc-life-articles/fighting-a-just-war-in-iraq/.

79. Richard Land, "Richard Land Extended Interview," interview by Kim Lawton, *Religion & Ethics Newsweekly*, March 24, 2006, https://www.pbs.org/wnet/religionandethics/2006/03/24/march–24–2006-richard-land-extended-interview/12482/.

80. Liederbach and Jones were assistant professors of ethics at Southeastern Baptist Theological Seminary.

81. Richard Land, cited in Hall, "Fighting a Just War In Iraq."

82. Richard Land, cited in ibid.

83. R. Albert Mohler Jr., *The Briefing* (podcast), April 19, 2004, https://albertmohler.com/2004/04/19/is-war-ever-justified-a-reality-check.

84. R. Albert Mohler Jr., *The Briefing* (podcast), August 11, 2017, https://albertmohler.com/2017/08/11/briefing-08-11-17.

85. R. Albert Mohler Jr., *The Briefing* (podcast), April 25, 2017, https://albertmohler.com/2017/04/25/briefing-04-25-17.

86. R. Albert Mohler Jr., *The Briefing* (podcast), February 8, 2013, https://albertmohler.com/2013/02/08/the-briefing-02-08-13.

87. R. Albert Mohler Jr., *The Briefing* (podcast), August 5, 2005, https://albertmohler.com/2005/08/05/hiroshima-and-the-burden-of-history.

88. R. Albert Mohler Jr., *The Briefing* (podcast), April 19, 2004, https://albertmohler.com/2004/04/19/is-war-ever-justified-a-reality-check.

89. Ibid.

90. D. A. Carson, "Just War," sermon at Capitol Hill Baptist Church, March 10, 2004, https://www.capitolhillbaptist.org/sermon/just-war/.

91. Russell Moore, "What Does the Gospel Teach Us about War?," Russell Moore.com, May 30, 2016, https://www.russellmoore.com/2016/05/30/what-does-the-gospel-teach-us-about-war/.

92. Stephanie Franks, "Religious Ethicists Ponder Justification of War," *Lariat*, April 29, 2003, https://www.baylor.edu/lariatarchives/news.php?action=story&story=18491.

93. Sam Hodges, "Looking Back at Conservative Evangelicals' Support for the Iraq War," *Dallas Morning News*, August 7, 2007, https://www.dallasnews.com/life/faith/2007/08/07/looking-back-at-conservative-e-1.

94. Tertullian, *De praescriptione haereticorum* 7.

95. Carl F. H. Henry, *Twilight of a Great Civilization* (Westchester, IL: Crossway Books, 1988), 44.

WORKS CITED

American Baptist Resolution on National Missile Defense System. American Baptist Churches USA, 2000. https://www.abc-usa.org/wp-content/uploads/2019/02/natmis.pdf.

Armitage, Thomas. *A History of the Baptists.* New York: Bryan Taylor & Co., 1990.

Ashford, Bruce, and Chris Pappalardo. *One Nation under God: A Christian Hope for American Politics.* Nashville: B&H Academic, 2015.

Backus, Isaac. *An Appeal to the Public for Religious Liberty, against the Oppressions of the Present Day.* 1773. Classic Liberals. http://classicliberal.tripod.com/misc/appeal.html.

———. *Government and Liberty Described and Ecclesiastical Tyranny Exposed.* 1778. Evans Early American Imprint Collection, University of Michigan Library Digital Collections. https://quod.lib.umich.edu/cgi/t/text/text-idx?c=evans;cc=evans;rgn=main;view=text;idno=N12452.0001.001.

Bebbington, David W. *Baptists through the Centuries: A History of a Global People.* Waco, TX: Baylor University Press, 2010.

Bell, Mark R. *Apocalypse How? Baptists Movements during the English Revolution.* Macon, GA: Mercer University Press, 2000.

Bozeman, Theodore Dwight. "John Clarke and the Complications of Liberty." *Church History* 75, no. 1 (March 2006): 69–93.

Carson, D. A. "Just War." Sermon at Capitol Hill Baptist Church, March 10, 2004. https://www.capitolhillbaptist.org/sermon/just-war/.

Carter, Jimmy. "Just War — or a Just War?" *New York Times*, March 9, 2003. https://www.nytimes.com/2003/03/09/opinion/just-war-or-a-just-war.html.

Charles, J. Daryl, and Timothy J. Demy. *War, Peace, and Christianity: Questions and Answers from a Just-War Perspective.* Wheaton, IL: Crossway, 2010.

Chute, Anthony L., Nathan A. Finn, and Michael A. G. Haykin. *The Baptist Story: From English Sect to Global Movement.* Nashville: Broadman & Holman, 2015.

Clausewitz, Carl von. *On War.* Edited and translated by Michael Howard and Peter Paret. Princeton: Princeton University Press, 1976.

"Comparison of the 1925, 1963 and 2000 Baptist Faith and Message." Southern Baptist Convention. https://bfm.sbc.net/comparison-chart/.

Cross, Anthony R. "Baptists, Peace, and War: The Seventeenth-Century British Foundations." In *Baptists and War: Essays on Baptists and Military Conflict, 1640s–1990s*, edited by Gordon L. Heath and Michael A. G. Haykin, 1–31. Eugene, OR: Pickwick, 2015.

Dekar, Paul R. "The 'Good War' and Baptists Who Refused to Fight It." *Peace & Change* 32, no. 2 (April 2007): 186–202.

Demy, Timothy J. "Just War and the Spanish-American War." In *America and the Just War Tradition: A History of U.S. Conflicts*, edited by Mark David Hall and J. Daryl Charles, 136–54. Notre Dame, IN: University of Notre Dame Press, 2019.

Early, Joe, Jr. *The Life and Writings of Thomas Helwys.* Macon, GA: Mercer University Press, 2009.

Ebel, Jonathan. *Faith in the Fight: Religion and the American Soldier in the Great War.* Princeton: Princeton University Press, 2010.

Evans, Benjamin. *The Early English Baptists.* Vol. 2. London: J. Heaton & Son, 1864.

Faust, Drew Gilpin. *This Republic of Suffering: Death and the American Civil War.* New York: Knopf, 2008.

Finn, Nathan A. "Baptists and the War in Vietnam: Responses to 'America's Longest War.'" In Heath and Haykin, *Baptists and War*, 202–9.

Franks, Stephanie. "Religious Ethicists Ponder Justification of War." *Lariat*, April 29, 2003.

George, Timothy. "Between Pacifism and Coercion: The English Baptist Doctrine of Religious Toleration." *Mennonite Quarterly Review* 58 (1984): 30–49.

———. Introduction to *Baptist Confessions, Covenants, and Catechisms*, edited by Timothy George and Denise George, 1–18. Nashville: Broadman & Holman, 1996.

George, Timothy, and Denise George, eds. *Baptist Confessions, Covenants, and Catechisms.* Nashville: Broadman & Holman, 1996.

Gibbs, Nancy, and Michael Duffy. *The Preacher and the Presidents: Billy Graham in the White House.* New York: Center Street, 2007.

Gourley, Bruce T. *Crucible of Faith & Freedom: Baptists and the Civil War.* Macon, GA: Nurturing Faith, 2015.

Hall, Jason. "Fighting a Just War in Iraq." *SBC Life*, April 1, 2003. Available through Baptist Press. https://www.baptistpress.com/resource-library/sbc -life-articles/fighting-a-just-war-in-iraq/.

Heath, Gordon L. "Ontario Baptists and the War of 1812." *Ontario History* 103, no. 2 (November 2011): 169–91.

Heath, Gordon L., and Michael A. G. Haykin, eds. *Baptists and War: Essays on Baptists and Military Conflict, 1640s–1990s.* Eugene, OR: Pickwick, 2015.

Heimbach, Daniel R. "The Bush Just War Doctrine: Genesis and Application of the President's Moral Leadership in the Persian Gulf War." In *From Cold War to New World Order: The Foreign Policy of George H. W. Bush*, edited by Meena Bose and Rosanna Perotti, 441–64. Westport, CT: Greenwood, 2002.

———. "Distinguishing Just War from Crusade: Is Regime Change a Just Cause for Just War?" In *War in the Bible and Terrorism in the Twenty-First Century*, edited by Richard S. Hess and Elmer A. Martens, 79–92. Bulletin for Biblical Research Supplement 2. Winona Lake, IN: Eisenbrauns, 2008.

Helwys, Thomas. *An Advertisement or Admonition to the Congregations, Which Men Call the New Fryelers, In the Lowe Countries, Written in Dutch and Published in English.* In Early, *Life and Writings of Thomas Helwys*, 93–154.

———. *A Declaration of Faith.* In Early, *Life and Writings of Thomas Helwys*, 64–73.

———. *A Short Declaration of the Mystery of Iniquity.* In Early, *Life and Writings of Thomas Helwys*, 155–310.

Henry, Carl F. H. *God, Revelation and Authority.* Vol. 4, *God Who Speaks and Shows: Fifteen Theses, Part Three.* Waco, TX: Word, 1979.

———. *A Plea for Evangelical Demonstration.* Grand Rapids, MI: Baker, 1971.

———. "Religious Freedom: Cornerstone of Human Rights." In *The Christian Mindset in a Secular Society*, 63–80. Portland, OR: Multnomah, 1984.

———. "Religious Liberty as a Cause Celebre." In *Christian Citizens: The Rights and Responsibilities of Dual Citizenship*, edited by Richard D. Land and Louis A. Moore, 64–77. Nashville: Broadman & Holman, 1994.

———. *Twilight of a Great Civilization.* Westchester, IL: Crossway Books, 1988.

Hodges, Sam. "Looking Back at Conservative Evangelicals' Support for the Iraq War." *Dallas Morning News*, August 7, 2007. https://www.dallasnews.com /life/faith/2007/08/07/looking-back-at-conservative-e-1.

Jenkins, Philip. *The Great and Holy War: How World War I Became a Religious Crusade*. New York: HarperOne, 2014.

Johnson, Robert E. *A Global Introduction to Baptist Churches*. Cambridge: Cambridge University Press, 2010.

King, Martin Luther, Jr. "Beyond Vietnam—a Time to Break Silence." Speech delivered to participants of event "Clergy and Laymen Concerned about Vietnam" at Riverside Church, New York, April 4, 1967. Available at American Rhetoric Online Speech Bank. https://www.americanrhetoric.com /speeches/mlkatimetobreaksilence.htm.

Leonard, Bill J. *Baptist Ways*. Valley Forge, PA: Judson Press, 2003.

McBeth, Leon. *The Baptist Heritage: Four Centuries of Baptist Witness*. Nashville: Broadman, 1987.

Merritt, Jonathan. "Spurgeon: How the Politically Liberal Preacher Became a Conservative Christian Paragon." Religion News Service, August 12, 2013. https://religionnews.com/2013/08/12/surprised-by-spurgeon-how-a -politically-liberal-preacher-became-a-paragon-among-conservative -christians/.

Miller, Robert J. *Both Prayed to the Same God: Religion and Faith in the American Civil War* Lanham, MD: Lexington Books, 2007.

Mohler, R. Albert, Jr. *The Briefing* (podcast), April 19, 2004. https://alber tmohler.com/2004/04/19/is-war-ever-justified-a-reality-check.

———. *The Briefing* (podcast), August 5, 2005. https://albertmohler.com/2005 /08/05/hiroshima-and-the-burden-of-history.

———. *The Briefing* (podcast), February 8, 2013. https://albertmohler.com/2013 /02/08/the-briefing-02-08-13.

———. *The Briefing* (podcast), April 25, 2017. https://albertmohler.com/2017 /04/25/briefing-04-25-17.

———. *The Briefing* (podcast), August 11, 2017. https://albertmohler.com/2017 /08/11/briefing-08-11-17.

Moore, Russell. "What Does the Gospel Teach Us about War?" RussellMoore .com, May 30, 2016. https://www.russellmoore.com/2016/05/30/what -does-the-gospel-teach-us-about-war/.

Nettles, Tom. *The Baptists*. 3 vols. Boston: Mentor, 2007–10.

Noll, Mark A. *Christians in the American Revolution*. Washington, DC: Christian College Consortium, 1977.

———. *The Civil War as a Theological Crisis*. Chapel Hill: University of North Carolina Press, 2006.

Patterson, Eric D. *Just American Wars: Ethical Dilemmas in U.S. Military History.* New York: Routledge, 2018.

Pierard, Richard V. "Billy Graham and Vietnam: From Cold Warrior to Peace-maker." *Christian Scholar's Review* 10, no. 1 (1980): 37–51.

"Resolution Concerning Conscientious Objectors." Resolution passed at the Annual Meeting of the Southern Baptist Convention, Miami, Florida, May 1, 1946. https://www.sbc.net/resource-library/resolutions/resolution-concerning-conscientious-objectors/.

Roach, David. "World War I Remembered as 'Stand for Liberty' 100 Years Later." Baptist Press, August 7, 2014. http://www.bpnews.net/43111/world-war-i-remembered-as-stand-for-liberty-100-years-later.

Robertson, James Tyler. "A House Uniting: Americans, Baptists, and the War of 1812." In Heath and Haykin, *Baptists and War*, 64–66.

Settje, David E. *Faith and War: How Christians Debated the Cold and Vietnam Wars.* New York: New York University Press, 2011.

Stillman, Samuel. *Being the Day of Annual Thanksgiving.* Boston: Manning and Loring, 1795.

Wacker, Grant. *America's Pastor: Billy Graham and the Shaping of a Nation.* Cambridge, MA: Harvard University Press, 2014.

"War and Peace: Baptists' Opinions Have Shifted from Predecessors." Baptist News Global, August 5, 2007. https://baptistnews.com/article/war-and-peace-baptists-opinions-have-shifted-from-predecessors/#.XOgunda2Z08U.

Warren, James A. *God, War, and Providence: The Epic Struggle of Roger Williams and the Narragansett Indians against the Puritans of New England.* New York: Scribner, 2018.

Woodworth, Steven E. *While God Is Marching On: The Religious World of Civil War Soldiers.* Lawrence: University of Kansas Press, 2001.

NINE

Anabaptists and the Sword

J. Daryl Charles

In considering the social-political currents that were swirling in Europe during the late fifteenth and early sixteenth centuries, even the casual reader comes to realize the remarkably diverse character of social upheaval that typified this period. Late-medieval society was markedly different from agrarian medieval society. Local as well as regional economies were changing, New World discoveries paralleled an expanding Ottoman Empire, populations were recovering from Black Death, and urban life was presenting civic authorities with new challenges, with the consequence, inter alia, that city governments and local polities were becoming more important. These developments were wholly aside from the exacerbation of the clergy-laity distinction within the Catholic Church, papal overreach, widespread (though not universal) ecclesiastical corruption, religious superstition, and the church's perceived failure to impart a Christian faith that was grace- rather than merit-centered.[1]

What gave force to the ideas of the "radical reformers" was a broader sense of moral, social, and economic dislocation that existed among significant parts of the population. What's more, many sensed that the behavior of both clergy and rulers contradicted the very values that they as common people professed.[2] Donald Durnbaugh well captures the existing cultural commotion, noting that scholars writing in retrospect often fail to capture the dynamics of early sixteenth-century Europe: "Stirred up by the preaching of evangelical freedom, excited by apocalyptic currents, frightened by the threat of Turkish invasion, caught between an ambitious, rising middle class and an increasingly desperate peasantry, Europeans found themselves in a veritable caldron."[3]

As a telling—and in many ways fascinating—sign of social-cultural foment during the period, one finds more and more common people submitting lists of grievances to city councils for action.[4] And with the recent invention of the printing press with movable type, the significance of these grievances would be felt with greater immediacy and impact. One of the trademarks of more recent late-medieval scholarship is to point to the sheer variety of movements associated with this period.[5] And as evidence thereof, it is not uncommon among historical overviews of this era to find book titles with the plural "reformations" rather than the singular "reformation."[6] Indeed, the language of *reformatio* seems to have saturated late-medieval culture—at least, late-medieval ecclesiastical culture. One religious historian frames it thus: "Movements once variously designated as the Christian Renaissance, the Protestant Reformation, the Protestant Revolt, the Catholic Reformation, and the Counter-Reformation are, from a historical point of view, perhaps now best understood as part of something that might be called the Age of Reformations—two centuries [ca. 1400–1600] of both notorious corruption and genuine renewal."[7]

This plurality or diversity applies, as well, to the phenomenon of Anabaptism, often referred to as the "radical reformation." While one particular strand of Anabaptist scholarship has tended to disassociate Anabaptism from its Protestant roots, preferring a self-designation that is "neither Catholic nor Protestant,"[8] it is accurate to say that Anabaptism, though it emerged in three different principal geographical regions—Switzerland, south and central-eastern Germany, and Holland—during this period, arose within the cradle of Zwinglian reform in and around Zürich. Hence, it was peculiarly Protestant, even when it was not normative Protestantism. Technically, there was no "Anabaptism" (literally, "baptism again") until the rebaptisms performed on January 21, 1525, by Conrad Grebel,[9] as a sign of the "true" church's restoration.[10] Thus, one can point to a substantial existing consensus among historians that the beginnings of Anabaptism are to be found in the Swiss Brethren; they are the first to articulate their baseline beliefs and practices and to bear witness to them with their lives.[11]

Broadly viewed, the main teachings of Anabaptism tended to cluster around the themes of Christianity as discipleship, restitution of the "true" church,[12] the church as a brotherhood, separation from "the world," and an ethic of nonviolence and nonresistance.[13] Late twentieth- and early twenty-first-century Anabaptist scholarship, while affirming the aforementioned foci, has tended to discredit accounts that attempt to link Anabaptism's genesis with Erasmian humanism as well as fanatical apocalyptic heresy associated with the "peasant revolts" (on which, see below).[14] And reasons for that detachment are not difficult to understand.

George H. Williams's typology of early sixteenth-century Anabaptism is generally accepted by both Anabaptist and non-Anabaptist historians. Williams identifies, as distinct from one another, three general categories of Anabaptist groups: "evangelical" (for example, the Swiss Brethren, Balthasar Hubmaier, Mennonites), "revolutionary" (for example, Hans Hut, Melchior Hoffmann, and the failed Münster experiment), and "contemplative" (for example, Hans Denck). Finding both radical and conservative theological tendencies among the Anabaptists, Williams rejects the notion that Anabaptists are "stepchildren" of the Reformation so-called; rather, they are to be properly viewed as a reflection of their time.[15] Williams's assessment would seem correct: Anabaptists were indeed a product of the Reformation (as conventionally understood).[16] For the sake of clarity, Michael Baylor, who has done us the great service of collecting key sixteenth-century texts, compares the vision of the magisterial reformers with that of the radical and Anabaptist reformers, against whom they would react, in the following way:

> Rejecting traditional ecclesiastical authority, they [magisterial reformers] clung more firmly to existing secular authority, which they held to be ordained by God. They also deeply distrusted the common man and feared that his participation in politics would lead to anarchy. They were willing to proceed only as far as authorization would allow. The ecclesiastical counterpart to this view of secular authority was the magisterial reformers' view that the power to proclaim the meaning of the gospel— and to advise secular authorities about the interpretation of Scripture— should remain in the hands of a university-trained, properly ordained clergy. Reformation radicalism was, in the first instance, "internal dissent'" within the Reformation—opposition to the paradigm for change set forth by such magisterial reformers as Luther and Zwingli.[17]

But a foremost practical interpretive issue emerges for those who wish to immerse themselves in early sixteenth-century European life. What of the causes of the aforementioned social and political ferment? And what role did the "radical reformation" play in these cultural developments? Late-medieval historian Hans-Jürgen Goertz disagrees with the dominant view among Anabaptist historians, arguing that Anabaptism indeed *was* closely connected to the revolutionary peasant struggles of the day, which then informs the social context of Anabaptism's birth in Switzerland.[18] Whether or not Goertz is accurate, a look at the evidence is highly instructive.

It is proper to insist that the "Reformation" (as conventionally understood) was *both* a religious *and* social protest movement; it both affirmed and protested the existing social-cultural-political as well as ecclesiastical order of the time. We find the decades prior to the "Lutheran affair" being marked by significant social upheaval, of which the "peasant revolts" of the mid–1520s were merely emblematic.[19] Issues at hand had decidedly religious, political, economic, and social repercussions. They ranged, for example, from a growing cleft between clergy and laity (which had religious as well as social repercussions) to a growing resistance toward paying a tithe to the landlord, from a growing demand of parishes to select their own preachers[20] to the socioeconomic developments attending the explosion of the mining industry in some regions,[21] to the deeply embedded distinctions (at least, in particular parts of Europe) between local authority and transnational authority.[22]

Contrary to what many proponents of the Anabaptist vision suggest, nonresistant pacifism was not universal among Anabaptists. Nor was it a "late" development, even when it grounded the vision of Menno Simons, who represents a second-generation manifestation of Anabaptism. Rather, it mirrored an absolute separation from society in a turbulent early sixteenth-century society. Such a response, we may reasonably conclude in retrospect, is natural insofar as violent civil responses *typically* met those who dissented.[23] And these responses came from both Catholic and "Protestant"— that is, "protesting"— sides.[24] After all, both Catholics and Protestants believed that political authority was obligated to "protect the faith"; both assumed that condemning heresy was central not only to protecting the church but to preventing civil unrest or civil war. It is surely no overstatement to observe that the sixteenth and seventeenth centuries were not conducive to religious tolerance.

CONRAD GREBEL AND THE SWISS BRETHREN

The Making of Conrad Grebel

If any normative assessment of Anabaptism must begin with the Swiss Brethren, then we must begin with Zwinglian reform—a reform that was independent of Luther and is anchored in the eloquent "people's priest" of Zürich,[25] Huldrych Zwingli (1484–1531). Two of the first "Anabaptist" (German: *Wiedertäufer*, literally, the "rebaptized")[26] leaders, Conrad Grebel and Felix Mantz, had been disciples of Zwingli in the early 1520s but subsequently broke with the reformer in their advocating a "believer's baptism." In January of 1525, Grebel baptized the first Anabaptist "convert," one Georg Blaurock. Shortly thereafter, in a letter dated November of 1526, Zwingli denounced Grebel as the Anabaptist "ringleader" (*coryphaeus*),[27] and Mantz would become the first Anabaptist martyr.[28] Without Grebel, according to the chief biographer of Grebel in the English-speaking world, Anabaptism in its historic form would probably not have come into existence.[29]

Any attempt to trace Grebel's history, theology, or impact encounters severe obstacles, given his very brief life; he died of the plague at age twenty-eight.[30] In bald contrast to other reformers—even other Anabaptist reformers—the only writing he prepared for publication, a brief pamphlet of under five thousand words, has been lost, though parts thereof have been somewhat reconstructed through Zwingli's counterattack that appeared in 1527.[31] At the same time, an important source of information comes through letters—some sixty-nine in number—that Grebel penned between September 1517 and July 1525, the year he baptized his first convert.[32]

It is generally thought that the phenomenon of Anabaptism arose from socially and economically oppressed lower classes.[33] But this was not the case with Grebel, whose family pedigree and education proved to be quite the opposite. Grebel was the "promising son of a Zürich patrician,"[34] the second of six children of Junker Jacob Grebel and Dorothea Fries. The Grebels had been a leading family in Zürich for generations in terms of political and economic affairs.[35] Thus it was that young Conrad was sent to the best universities—Basel,[36] Vienna,[37] and Paris[38]—to study. While a student in Paris in the years 1518–20 and without moorings,

Grebel was part of a group of students who were responsible for killing two Frenchmen as the result of nationalistic fervor. His conversion several years later was thoroughgoing, probably deepened by what had become an unhappy relationship to his father.[39]

The year 1522 would mark significant change for Grebel, whose education up to that point had not answered his questions regarding images, sacrifice in the mass, clerical benefits, and tithing, among other issues. At this time he was being increasingly drawn to the preaching of Zwingli and the idea of reform in Zürich; in short order the two would become close. This friendship would also be short-lived, lasting only until the second Zürich disputation of October 1523, due to a growing schism. By the fall of 1524 the break between the two was complete, leading to denunciation and counterdenunciation.[40]

As was particularly the case in the Swiss confederacy, public disputations were typically held to adjudicate over important issues bearing on the civic polity. As a rule, these usually lasted a day or two and were presided over by town or city councils. In the Swiss context, the public was generally allowed to attend.[41] In late 1523, Grebel and company began organizing, following the realization of a growing split with Zwingli. This breach would result in several disputations before the city council. Grebel's position was uncompromising: Zwingli, who had wished for a growing reformed consensus to emerge, with Zürich helping to lead the way, was too accommodating to the authorities, and this compromised the church in its essence and its witness to the world.

The October 1523 disputation, from the dissenters' vantage point, was intended to pressure the city council to institute reforms in the city's church life through abolishing the mass and removing images. At bottom, Zwingli was willing to be more patient with the council; Grebel was not. For Grebel, the issue reduced to this: should civil authorities dictate the faith and worship of the church, or should pastors and laity change things based on the requirements of the Word of God? That is, should the church be state controlled or voluntary? Grebel felt betrayed by Zwingli, while Zwingli viewed Grebel as a young radical. In the end, Zwingli was willing to accommodate the authorities, but Grebel was not. Meanwhile, Grebel would decide in the summer of 1524 to write to German theologian Andreas Karlstadt, who had broken with Luther along similar lines, and then Grebel would hear of another former Lutheran who had broken with the

Wittenberg reformer—a radical by the name of Thomas Müntzer. Since Müntzer had rejected Luther's sympathies toward the magistrate, Grebel wrote to him as well, assuming that he would find support.[42]

Following a public debate on January 17, 1525, strict mandates by the Zürich city council were put in place, whereby (a) a cessation of activity by Grebel and his fellow dissenters was ordered; (b) the group was forbidden from meeting; and (c) a baptizing of all unbaptized infants was mandated.[43] Both sides were hardened. On January 21, the dissenters met, with Grebel baptizing Blaurock, and with some eighty more baptisms occurring before the month's end.[44] The new mandates made it impossible for Grebel to remain in the city area; thus, he would begin to itinerate outside of Zürich, then return on two occasions. In October 1525 he was arrested and imprisoned, but escaped in March 1526 and continued to preach, until several months later, when his health would give out. Grebel was one of the few early Anabaptist leaders who were not executed.[45]

Grebel, Early-Anabaptist Theological Commitments, and Political Authority

In terms of the major Christian doctrines, Grebel was in basic agreement with Zwingli. Their chief differences, according to Zwingli himself, were baptism and the role of secular authority—and specifically, whether a Christian can serve as a magistrate.[46] Grebel's chief biographer in the English-speaking world, Harold Bender, has attempted to identify the theological underpinnings of Grebel's understanding of the Christian's relationship to the world; following are basic presuppositions that are thought to govern the true disciple:

- The Christian community must be separate from the world.
- Secular authorities cannot shape the church.
- The church must overcome the world by winning over individuals voluntarily.
- Since the church and the governing authorities are separate, the Christian can expect to suffer.
- The church is bound by the New Testament but not the Old.
- The Christian cannot participate with the state because of its use of coercive force and the sword.[47]

Anabaptist beliefs would be crystallized among the Swiss Brethren in the seven articles of the Schleitheim Confession (on which, see below) in 1527. The moniker "Swiss Brethren" was not foremost a geographical designation; rather, it referred more broadly to "Anabaptists" who were followers of Conrad Grebel. The fundamental differences between Swiss Anabaptists and Protestant reformed leaders in the 1520s and 1530s suggest that Anabaptists were first and foremost reacting against—and rejecting—an institutionalization of the Reformation cause. It is generally accurate to say that radical reformers—and the Anabaptists as the chief expression of the radical reformation—were equally distant from magisterial Protestantism and Roman Catholicism. And while fellow (magisterial) reformers worked toward reformation, the goal of Anabaptist reform was restitution—that is, a return to the apostolic church and the perceived New Testament model.[48]

A defining mark of these early Anabaptists was their deep-seated suspicion of the state and secular authority. Political authority, as embodied in the magistrate and represented by the sword, inevitably was used against them. Both ecclesiastical and political authority viewed radical reformers as heretical, seditious, treasonous, and a genuine threat to the common good, given their refusal to bear arms and take oaths (a common late-medieval expression of citizenship and loyalty to the city/political community),[49] their refusal to pay the tithe, and their rejection of the need for political authority or participation in military service.[50] As the Schleitheim Confession concisely states, the sword, taking oaths, and political coercion are necessary for unbelievers but not the community of Christ. Furthermore, radicals rejected the magisterial reformers' position due to the latter's "uncritical" and "undiscerning" attitude toward secular authority. Anabaptist reformers viewed themselves as "small islands of righteousness amidst an ocean of iniquity."[51] Thus, it is not surprising that Anabaptists were perceived as a threat, as social-political revolutionaries.

The matter of how to understand the relationship between the church and the state, between the Christian community and the secular authorities, was unquestionably one of the most controversial subjects that confronted leaders of Protestant reform—from Luther and Calvin to various kinds of Anabaptists—in the sixteenth century. In Luther's understanding, it will be remembered, the church was entrusted with the gospel, whereas the state existed to administer justice and maintain an ordered society. Insofar as Lutheran theology neither equated nor conflated the spheres—

or "estates"—of church and state, the sword properly belonged to only one domain, the magistrate, as distinct from medieval conceptions of authority that allowed for the "two swords" of papal theocracy and the political magistrate. Because, in Luther's theology, (a) Christians cannot dismiss their citizenship in either the earthly or heavenly kingdom and given that (b) human depravity is real, and thus (c) an ordered community needs maintaining, coercive force remains a necessary part of the state's function.

Despite the radical nature of early sixteenth-century Anabaptism—in which one can observe an oscillation between the polar antitheses of revolution and pacifism—most of these dissenters arrived at what historian James Stayer calls a "radical apoliticism"—that is, a denial that political involvement and coercive force might achieve ethical goals, given the explicit commitment to be separate from the world.[52] Unlike moderate apoliticism, radical apoliticism denies that force is necessary on occasion to preserve the common good.

From Grebel to the Swiss Brethren: The Schleitheim Confession of Faith and Practice

The earliest of Anabaptist documents was published under the title *Brüderliche Vereinigung etlicher Kinder Gottes/sieben Artickel betreffend . . ."* ("Brotherly Agreement of a Number of Children of God concerning Seven Articles"), otherwise known as the Schleitheim Confession of Faith, so named for the location of a synod that took place in Switzerland near the German border on February 24, 1527.[53] The Schleitheim Confession is significant not for its theological detail but rather because in time it would be considered normative among Anabaptists, enumerating those practices that were thought to distinguish true Christians, as embodied in their fellowship, from "the world."

The Brethren, under the leadership of Michael Sattler,[54] a former Benedictine monk, had been influenced by reform efforts in and around Zürich under the leadership of Grebel and Mantz. The particular aim of this synod was to discuss seven specific matters of the free-church movement that were thought to be of critical importance to their faith and practice. The seven matters, each being addressed in the form of an article of faith, were as follows: baptism, the ban (excommunication), the breaking of bread, separation from the world, pastoral duties, the sword, and the oath (vows). What these matters of faith and practice all have in common is a requisite *separation* of true believers from "the world." The confession was an attempt, if not to codify and consolidate creedal convictions, at least to formulate belief and practice in such a way as to (a) address those supposed "fringe" elements that deviated from Anabaptist belief and/or (b) emphasize what was shared by all Anabaptist groups and believers. The degree to which the confession is representative of Anabaptism continues to be debated today among scholars of its own tradition.[55] Nevertheless, for our own purposes we shall assume the significance of the confession as a charter document and the crystallization point of early Anabaptism.[56]

What is noteworthy about the confession is its oppositional tone and emphasis. Pronounced antagonism rather than differentiation undergirds the articles of faith. Correlatively, the chief argument being set forth appears to be that of separation from the world. In the introduction, the document reads, "We who have been and shall be separated from the world in everything . . . [are] completely at peace."[57] Alas, the clear thrust of the confession is that the Brethren are to be unified in their separation.

The sixth and longest of the seven articles of the confession concerns "the sword." Here one finds a dualism in the confession's formulation of what is required by Christian faith. On the one hand, the "sword" is "ordained by God," "guards and protects the good," and is "ordained to be used by the worldly magistrates." On the other hand, it is "outside the perfection of Christ" and for this reason is not to be employed by Christians. In anticipation of an objection, article 6 reasons: "Now it will be asked by many who do not recognize [this stance regarding the sword as] the will of Christ for us, whether a Christian may or should employ the sword against the wicked for the defense and protection of the good, or for the sake of love." The Brethren's reply to this question is "unanimous" and consists of a fourfold rationale:

- Christ's teaching and example point in the direction of mercy and forgiveness.
- Christ's example was not to pass judgment.
- Christ's example was not to rule as a king or prince, and in fact, Christ explicitly "forbids the [use of] the force of the sword saying 'The worldly princes lord it over them, etc. but not so shall it be with you'"[58]—an example that is supported by Paul's statement that God predestined his own to be conformed to the image of his

Son[59] and Peter's reminder that because Christ suffered, we are left with an example.[60]

- Christian citizenship is spiritual and heavenly; therefore, the work of ruling and magistracy, because it is "worldly," is out of line with the Christian's true nature.

The final point is the most substantial of the Brethren's answers to why a Christian may not employ the sword.

> Finally it will be observed that it is not appropriate for a Christian to serve as a magistrate because of these points: The government magistracy is according to the flesh, but the Christians' is according to the Spirit; their houses and dwellings remain in this world, but the Christians' are in heaven; their citizenship is in this world, but the Christians' citizenship is in heaven; the weapons of their conflict and war are carnal and against the flesh only, but the Christians' weapons are spiritual, against the fortification of the devil. The worldlings are armed with steel and iron, but the Christians are armed with the armor of God, with truth, righteousness, peace, faith, salvation and the Word of God.[61]

The absolutist approach to the confession's dualism inevitably and inexorably breeds withdrawal from the world. On the one hand, the Swiss Brethren, as reflective of most sixteenth-century Anabaptists, were true children of the Reformation, and they agreed to an extent with Luther on one temporal sword. At the same time, their separation was far more radical than that of Luther or any of the magisterial reformers, none of whom was apolitical. The Brethren, and the Anabaptists as a whole, derived their separation — and hence their radical apoliticism — from a particular view of Christian discipleship that issued out of their view of the world.

BALTHASAR HUBMAIER AND GERMAN ANABAPTISM

One of the few Anabaptist leaders who were university trained as theologians, Balthasar Hubmaier (1480–1528) receives surprisingly scant

264 J. Daryl Charles

attention in most historical overviews of the Reformation era.[62] Surely, part of the reason for this neglect is his premature death. Yet his influence, despite a very short life span, is illustrated by the fact that his name joins that of Luther, Calvin, and Zwingli at the Council of Trent in an official listing of "chief heretics" who are being denounced years after his martyrdom. "Rule II" of this official proclamation reads as follows: "Books of arch-heretics—those who after 1515 have invented or incited heresy or who have been or still are heads and leaders of heretics, such as Luther, Zwingli, Calvin, Hubmaier, Schwenckfeld, and the like—whatever their name, title or argumentation—are prohibited without exception."[63] One leader stood out among the early Anabaptists, and it was Balthasar Hubmaier. The reform brought about by this theologian and peer of Luther and Zwingli was one that "had the greatest potential for lasting success"— in the words of one observer[64]—given Hubmaier's willingness to support those in political authority rather than retreat into separatism. Unlike other Anabaptist leaders, he believed not only that secular authorities were ordained by God but that Christians should work with political authorities, even participating in the work of government.

On matters theological and ethical, Hubmaier seems to defy fixed categories, often taking positions that were between those of his Anabaptist brethren—sometimes agreeing and sometimes disagreeing. He found only "conditional sympathy" among fellow Anabaptists,[65] given his main points of disagreement—the chief one being his position on political authority and use of "the sword." In terms of temperament, most of the early Anabaptist leaders were spiritualistic and semimystical, which inclined them to stress understanding directly through the Holy Spirit's inspiration rather than through learning per se. This trend notwithstanding, Hubmaier was the real early Anabaptist theologian; as a writer he was prolific, writing on topics as diverse as baptism, the Lord's Supper, freedom of the will, the ban and Christian discipline, and "the sword."[66] Two of his writings that gave direction to the early Anabaptist movement were his *Von der brüderlichen Strafe* ("On Brotherly Discipline") and *Von dem christlichen Bann* ("On the Christian Ban"), both penned in 1527.[67] Thus, one may reasonably argue that Hubmaier inaugurated "Anabaptism" as we know it, for in addition to his teaching ministry it is he, not the Swiss Brethren, who was first to institute believer's baptism.[68] Remarkably, in the relatively few years of his work before being executed, Hubmaier would lead congregations totaling roughly twelve thousand people.[69]

The Making of Balthasar Hubmaier

Not much is known of Hubmaier's family, though this reformer was born in the Bavarian town of Friedburg. Hubmaier studied at the University of Freiburg, where he met and was inspired by Johannes Eck, who later would famously oppose Luther. From Freiburg, Hubmaier would follow Eck to the University of Ingolstadt and there earn a doctorate in theology in 1512. For the next three years he would serve as a professor and then take on administrative duties at the university, all the while serving as a parish priest.

Hubmaier's eloquence would open doors, so that in January 1516 Hubmaier resigned his university post at Ingolstadt to become *Domprediger* at the cathedral church in Regensburg. There he preached for five years, becoming one of the most popular Catholic preachers in south Germany.[70] Over time, the writings of both Erasmus and Luther would alter his thinking at a theological level,[71] moving him in a more evangelical direction and, eventually, bringing him into opposition with Eck, his former mentor, with baptism becoming a pivotal issue.[72]

In early 1521 Hubmaier moved to the town of Waldshut, where important travel and communications routes between Strasbourg, Freiburg, Zürich, and Basel crossed. In the spring of 1523, he would enter dialogue with Zwingli in Zürich over the scriptural basis for infant baptism, even when it is possible that he entertained doubts as early as 1520. Hubmaier would then participate in the Second Disputation of October 1523 in Zürich. Following these debates, he resumed his ministry in Waldshut, where he was rebaptized in April 1525 and where he himself, in turn, baptized around three hundred people shortly thereafter, including most of the members of the town council. Suddenly, in Waldshut "a parish church was transformed into an Anabaptist congregation."[73]

Von dem Schwert (1527)

Catholic reaction to Hubmaier's work in Waldshut would be swift and forceful, requiring Hubmaier to flee to Zürich. When Zwingli responded with a rebuttal to the Anabaptist phenomenon, Hubmaier ended up being imprisoned, then released, whereupon he went to the city of Nikolsburg in Moravia, known for its religious tolerance.[74] There he became pastor of a congregation with the support of Leonhard von Liechtenstein, the lord of the city. And it was there that he did most of his writing,[75] which frequently was dedicated to lords and knights—for example, Hans and Leonhard von Liechtenstein and Arkleb of Boskovice. Hubmaier's effectiveness in Nikolsburg can be measured by the fact that he was even successful in winning over an entire Lutheran congregation.[76]

Hubmaier departed from the traditional view of treating heretics. They should be admonished and rebuked, he argued, and not killed with the sword[77]—a position that made him clearly ahead of his time on the matter of religious toleration. In arguing for a distinction between church and state, Hubmaier insisted that execution should be reserved for criminals, not heretics. He believed that the government's right to use the sword was God-given, unlike other radical reformers who thought that government forfeited that right—Hans Hut, for example, whose revolutionary "holy violence" he would rebuff. Rejecting the revolutionary radicals' view of the sword as righteous retribution, Hubmaier also stood opposed to the contrary view, represented by the Swiss Brethren, in terms of their understanding of government's authority. For this, the Swiss Brethren would criticize Hubmaier, leading to his publication of *Von dem Schwert* (On the sword).

As influenced by the Brethren, divisions were arising among Nikolsburg Anabaptists as to whether Christians could rightfully participate in government and utilize the sword. In June 1527, then, Hubmaier would write a treatise to oppose the antigovernment sentiment among some Anabaptists and to counter their argument that Christians may not occupy positions of power or wield the sword. The document consists of Hubmaier's response to fifteen standard New Testament texts that were typically marshaled by his fellow pacifist opponents—for example, Jesus before Pilate (John 18:36), Jesus's rebuke of Peter (Matt. 26:52–54), Jesus's eye-for-an-eye comments on retaliation (5:38–42), Jesus's command to "love your enemy" (5:43–48), and his prohibition of vengeance (Rom. 12:14–21)—as well as an exposition of Romans 13:1–7. The treatise is dedicated to the "chancellor of the Margravate of Moravia," mirroring Hubmaier's commitment not to divorce Anabaptism from the wider polity.

Politics and Persecution: Hubmaier's Final Days

By 1527, the authorities' "military mop-up" and attempts at judicial retribution for various peasants' uprisings throughout Germany were giving way to more systematic efforts to track down and round up any supposed leaders. Anabaptism — that is, rebaptism, a crime punishable by death[78] — showed itself to be the most cohesive strand of radicalism emerging from the aforementioned uprisings, even when it sprang from diverse sources. Some within this movement affirmed the role of the secular authorities and the right to bear arms, while others — notably those who were dissatisfied by Zwinglian expectations of communal reform in or around Zürich — advocated not only nonresistance but separation from the existing polity, as reflected in Michael Sattler's formulation of the Schleitheim Confession articles.

Ferdinand I, the brother of Charles V whose imperial ascendency coincided with the outbreak of Protestant reform in the early 1520s, was determined to prevent Moravia from becoming an island of religious refuge. In August 1527 a general mandate against all non-Catholics was initiated, and in successive months a mandate against Anabaptists was issued by Ferdinand for every province (*Land*) under his rule.[79] Ferdinand was convinced that in the spring of 1528 the Anabaptists were planning uprisings comparable to those of 1525. This anxiety was fueled in part by published reports of "the end of the world" by some radicals. Although the feared spring-of-1528 riots did not materialize by Pentecost Sunday, Ferdinand continued his persecution. On July 24, he issued a mandate that "printers and booksellers of heretical books, as the chief seducers and 'poisoners' of all lands, be executed by drowning, without mercy and without delay."[80]

The Austrian authorities would repeatedly demand Hubmaier's extradition, and in the end, Hubmaier would be captured not by locals but by Austrians, who transferred him to Vienna, the capital, for trial and execution. In short order, the Nikolsburg congregation came to experience a schism over the matter of the sword. One group, led by a convert of Hubmaier, called themselves the *Schwertler* ("those of the sword") while another group, insisting on nonresistance and repudiating the sword, called themselves the *Stäbler* ("those of the staff"). The latter group would become the Moravian Anabaptists and, as a community, over time survive.

Hubmaier was tortured and burned at the stake on March 10, 1528, and his wife was drowned in the Danube three days later by the same Austrian authorities who considered her husband a threat. In the end, it would seem truly regrettable that Hubmaier's understanding of Christian faith — a faith that both accepted the reality of suffering in the world and assumed responsibility for the world — would find no acceptance in separatist

268   J. Daryl Charles

Anabaptism. His approach to faith and practice was active and no world-fleeing conception. For that reason alone he deserves a place alongside the fathers of sixteenth-century Reformation.

THE MÜNSTER TRAGEDY AND REVOLUTIONARY ANABAPTISM

Münster in the Making

In Germany, key events in the 1520s and the 1530s confirmed the fears of both secular rulers and magisterial reformers. Lodged at the center of these developments seemed to be the disruption of law and civil disorder. During these years the central-northern city of Münster (in Westphalia) acquired a reputation for religious tolerance, and hence became a haven for both German and Dutch "Anabaptists." The city had already become officially Lutheran in February of 1533, a development confirmed in a treaty between the prince-bishop and the city council and through the mediation of Landgrave Philip of Hesse. Aided by conflict between the Catholic bishop and the city council, what ensued shortly thereafter was a veritable "three-cornered struggle" over religion between Catholics, Lutherans, and Anabaptists.[81] Radical Anabaptists were strategically placed to build upon this fissure, and in short order they would attempt to usher in the "New Jerusalem."[82] Not even an eventual Lutheran-Catholic coalition could dislodge the radicals—until June 1535.

Among German cities, Münster assumed a somewhat unique position to the extent that it possessed a relatively high degree of self-rule. The city was governed by a city council and the prince-bishop, who ultimately had to answer to Charles V but was basically in charge of the city himself. The relationship between the city, which was overwhelmingly Lutheran, and the Catholic bishop had been strained for years. In July 1532 Charles V had demanded that evangelical ministers in the city be removed, which the city refused to do. When Franz von Waldeck was appointed prince-bishop in 1532, Lutherans had already started pushing the Catholics out of the city, with mobs inspired by an ex-Catholic priest and radical Lutheran pastor named Bernard Rothmann[83] who encouraged mob-led violence against Catholic churches in an attempt to destroy "idols." By 1533, Jan Matthias, a Dutch baker and professing Anabaptist, assumed leadership of the Anabaptist movement in the city and further encouraged violent rebellion. Urged on by these developments and inspired by Melchior Hoffmann, an eclectic, apocalyptic, though initially apolitical Anabaptist,[84] Anabaptists would continue to move to Münster in increasing numbers,[85] which in a short amount of time would affect the balance of power radically in terms of the constitution of the city council. Emergent leaders of the radical Anabaptist community in the city would take on "prophetic" authority and proclaim that Münster was to become "the city of the Lord" and a "New Jerusalem."

With rebaptisms now required by the city's leaders, Catholics and Lutherans fled the city, and their homes were taken over by the Anabaptists. By 1534, the prince-bishop initiated a blockade around the walled city in the hopes that a siege would bring the rebellion to a quick end. Inside Münster, under Matthias's leadership, the Anabaptists were radically restructuring their community. Community goods — food, clothing, and supplies — were held in common, stored in depots that were overseen by designated leaders. In the meantime, as well, a new leader named Jan van Leyden (otherwise known as John of Leiden or Jan Bockhold), a tailor's apprentice from Holland, decreed that polygamy was mandatory, whereby he took for himself fifteen wives. Anyone who opposed his rule would be imprisoned or killed. At the same time, the prince-bishop's siege was making things difficult for the city, and the Anabaptist leadership needed to find a way to keep their followers believing in the cause. On April 5, 1534, Easter Sunday, Matthias had a vision, after which he declared that God had told him to fight the prince-bishop's army single-handedly, whereupon he was killed immediately.[86] Van Leyden declared himself the city's sovereign and therewith disbanded the city council, setting up "twelve elders" to rule Münster as in ancient Zion, with himself as their head. On August 31, 1534, a second wave of siege was repelled, after which van Leyden was proclaimed "king of the New Zion." One of van Leyden's "ambassadors," a Jan van Geelen, traveled through the Netherlands in an attempt to recruit followers for the "New Jerusalem" movement at Münster and distributing Rothmann's latest book, *Van der Wrake* (Concerning revenge) in an attempt to create smaller "Zions" in the Netherlands.

All the while, the prince-bishop's army continued its encampment outside the city walls, having received military assistance from both Catholic and Lutheran rulers. Those inside held fast, with the city's double walls being guarded by Anabaptists loyal to the new "King's" vision. After roughly a year, starvation began to break the Anabaptist will. Thousands of people tried to escape the city, only to be killed by the prince-bishop's troops. Finally, on June 25, 1535, the prince-bishop's army gained entrance to the city as a result of betrayal from within. The three remaining leaders—van Leyden, Bernhard Knipperdolling,[87] and Bernhard Krechting[88]—were captured, tortured, and put on public display. They were put to death on January 23, 1536. The "spirit of Münster" would disappear; Anabaptists, however, would remain, though dispersed and purged greatly as a result of religious persecution.[89]

Münster upon Reflection

In retrospect, the apocalyptic crusade of Münster had only one parallel previously, and that consisted of the latter years of Thomas Müntzer's activity during the mid-1520s. The animating vision in Müntzer's program, reduced to its essence, was the destruction of the godless. Anabaptists in Münster had had the conviction that defense required a sword, and it is likely that Anabaptist leaders there had read Müntzer's *Sermon to the Princes*.[90] The sword of justice, in Münster, would become a sword for holy war,[91] leaving the "kingdom" of Münster to be variously described as a "revolution of the common man," an "antipatrician urban insurrection," a "sectarian revolution," a "reign of terror," a "millenarian psychodrama," and an "episode in collective religious fanaticism."[92]

As noted by one Anabaptist historian, Anabaptism "indeed experienced a setback in Münster and the surrounding territory, from which it never fully recuperated."[93] Not surprisingly, one of the important tasks in Anabaptist research has been to investigate troubling questions with a measure of objectivity. To what extent did Münster Anabaptism mirror original Anabaptist views? To what degree were the ideas and practices of the fanatical Anabaptists a reflection of local conditions in Münster or in the Netherlands? Some might be inclined to argue that it is one-sided merely to present the Münster episode purely as an attempt by the lower classes to improve their economic status. In fact, this stereotype collapses under a preponderance of evidence, for more recent scholarship has demonstrated that a large number of civic-minded citizens of relatively high standing in Münster in the end had sided with the Anabaptists, in order to preserve their own religious and political freedoms.[94] Others might argue, quite understandably, that the Münster tragedy was not really "Anabaptist" at heart but an aberration; thus, we should disassociate the episode from all Anabaptist ties. To this, however, one student of the sixteenth century responds: "The Münster Anabaptists were genuine Anabaptists, not a corrupt sect misusing the Anabaptist name."[95] One may, rather, legitimately conclude that the "kingdom" of Münster Anabaptism is improbable apart from the unusual alliance between forces working toward communal reform (communism) and the preaching of a distorted "Lutheran" message by radical apocalypticists such as Bernhard Rothmann and Melchior Hoffmann.[96]

MENNO SIMONS AND PACIFIST ANABAPTISM

In the aftermath of the peasant uprisings of 1524–26 and the failed "New Jerusalem" in Münster a decade later, what was unavoidable for radical reformers was how to make sense out of their cause. What were the lessons to be learned? And how were they to proceed in their mission? While "Anabaptism" arose in the cradle of Zwinglian reformation in Zürich, it would need to be refined through a full generation of testing and persecution before it would achieve its enduring form.

The tragic Münster episode, quite understandably, would reflect negatively on all Anabaptists, especially those in northern Germany and the Netherlands. Perhaps none felt the burden of this tragedy as much as Menno Simons (1496–1561). If, as one Anabaptist historian has argued, Menno's brother Peter, who happened to be one of the "twelve elders" of the radical Anabaptist community in Münster, was killed in the fighting that would lead to the community's downfall in 1535,[97] then Menno bore a heavy load as he sought to make sense of a purified Anabaptist community in the Netherlands.

In the years following Münster, Dutch Anabaptists would gather around the nonviolent vision of both Simons and Dirk Philips (1504–68). Simons's movement away from the Catholic Church and priesthood toward evangelical faith would be gradual; he did not leave the church at once. Over time, two features in particular would form the heart of Menno's strategy during the 1540s, when he would assume leadership among purified Anabaptist communities: combining (1) a nonviolent vision with the ban and shunning, which would have the effect of excluding those from the community who "fall into error" and therewith cannot accept nonviolence,[98] and (2) a community orientation or communalism that was distinct from mere spiritualism or mysticism.[99] While Menno Simons did not found the Anabaptist movement in the Netherlands, he had the heart of a founder, combining this vision with a pursuit of piety that would have lasting results. Menno's greatness, to be sure, was not eloquence, nor was it literary craftsmanship or being a theologian in the technical sense. Rather, it was lodged in the fact that he was a champion of "practical Christianity," stressing a faith-life of purity, charity, and good works.[100]

The Making of Menno

At age twenty-eight, Menno Simons was ordained in the priesthood and served in his native West Friesland in the Netherlands. In time, however, doubts would develop regarding both baptism and the Lord's Supper. Just as significant was the debacle at Münster and the need to move Anabaptism away from fanaticism and in the direction of inner renewal and holiness. Menno's emergence in the first decade after the uprisings in Münster, which left their effect as well in the Netherlands, mirrored a period of deep reflection. Was it necessary to break entirely with the existing order? What is the relationship between inward piety and outer social responsibilities? Radical reformers differed on these questions, and their differences were indeed profound. No clear, unifying answer was to be found.

As a Catholic priest, by 1531 Menno had come to reject infant baptism and the real presence in the Mass, based on personal study of the Bible. He served seven years in the priesthood before writing, "I examined the scriptures diligently and pondered them earnestly, but could find no report of infant baptism."[101] Being a parish priest made the break with the established church far from easy. During these years, he acknowledges Luther's influence and assistance, particularly in finding confidence in the testimony of Scripture[102] and disavowing the "erring sects." He acknowledges his two biggest obstacles to the faith: the matter of baptism and the debacle in Münster with its fanatical blasphemies. Issuing out of these dilemmas are several primary burdens that later surface in his writings— among these, brotherhood (i.e., community), nonviolence, separation from the world, and living under the cross.[103] Regarding Münster, he is deeply saddened that so many Dutch brethren were deceived—as sheep utterly without a shepherd.[104]

Following his baptism, Menno committed himself to public dissent in the form of separation and a disciplined community of believers, much in the tradition of the Swiss Brethren, whose Schleitheim Confession of 1527, with its seven articles of faith and practice, would be normative.[105] In his conversion reflections, not published until the year 1554 and appearing under the title *My Conversion, Call, and Testimony*,[106] Menno lists important steps in his search for truth. Among the most important,

- He sought out a "God-fearing, pious hero" named Sicke Snijder.[107]
- He consulted Martin Luther.
- He consulted Martin Bucer.
- He consulted Heinrich Bullinger.
- He concluded that the magisterial reformers had it wrong concerning baptism.
- He then began to preach publicly.
- He then renounced all things and submitted to Christ's cross.
- And he continued to anguish over Münster.

In January 1536, literally weeks after the authorities had quashed the radical Anabaptist attempt to institute the "New Jerusalem" in Münster, Menno would leave his parish priesthood to join the Anabaptist cause. From 1536 onward, he would itinerate in the Netherlands and in northern Germany, emphasizing, inter alia, the nature of true repentance and the "narrow way," separation from "the world," the efficacy of the scriptures, the Lord's Supper, and true baptism while denouncing sin, idolatry, and false worship. And, of course, he would disavow Münster as well as the use of the sword and coercive force.

As suggested thus far, it is impossible to appreciate the evolution of Menno's views without taking into account the role that the Münster tragedy played in his thinking. Following that calamity, an awareness in Menno of the need for godly shepherds who might guard the flock against false shepherds was clearly present. Upon serious reflection on the damage that Münster had caused, he decided to publish *A Reply to False Accusations*,[108] which was intended to repudiate violence and insist on personal holiness.

In addition to the "Münsterite" charge, Menno finds it necessary to answer one other major accusation — namely, that Anabaptists will not obey the magistrate. In similar terms, Menno rejects this charge, insisting that "our writings prove this accusation to be false": we "publicly and unequivocally confess," he insists, that the office of a magistrate is "ordained of God." "Taxes and tolls we pay," he notes, "as Christ taught and practiced." In addition, "we pray for all in authority." And yet "a public outcry of agitation" continues, he laments, which prompts "the bloody sword against us."[109]

This anguish and the need to disavow Münster deepen with Menno a commitment to ideological pacifism. A central error of Münsterites, he believes, was their preference for the Old Testament over the New, which had immense ethical repercussions. As Menno points out in *The Blasphemy of John of Leiden*,[110] "Now we should not imagine that the figure of the Old Testament [for example, a Moses or David] is so applied to the truth of the New Testament ... ; for the figure must reflect the reality ... and the letter, the Spirit."[111] Correlatively, Menno criticizes the apocalyptic view that God will shortly punish and destroy "Babylon" and "the wicked" and that Christians must be his agents. To believe such is to be deceived, Menno insists; "therefore we will oppose this view with Scriptures."[112] Not by Christians will the wicked be destroyed, he reminds his readers; rather, it is "the Lord Himself" who "will destroy at His coming and punish all His enemies."[113]

Therefore, a rereading of Scripture and particularly a certain reading of the "Sermon on the Mount" become central in Menno's thinking about Christian discipleship and Christian nonviolence. Moreover, Christ did not defend himself with Peter's sword; rather, he chose to suffer, "and in the same way all Christians must be minded [i.e., to suffer]."[114] For these reasons and more, then, it is not permitted that Christians fight with the sword.

"Foundation of Christian Doctrine": Post-Münster Anabaptist Reflections on the Magistrate and the Sword

The 1539 treatise *Foundation of Christian Doctrine*, which is the best known of Menno's writings,[115] was written with three primary aims: (1) to familiarize the world with the beliefs of Dutch Anabaptist Brethren, of which Menno became a bishop; (2) to ease persecution; and (3) to indoctrinate the brethren themselves. *Foundation* devotes an extended discussion to the magistrate and the sword. An important part of his reasoning would seem to stem from Menno's mission to correct erring brethren, many of whom were sympathetic to Münster. War, he was convinced, was the instrument of the Antichrist, whether Münsterite or Zwinglian or Papist.[116] Menno's views, however, according to one Anabaptist historian, were not the "radical apoliticism" of the Swiss Brethren,[117] insofar as Menno addresses princes in their tasks, admonishing them to be wise, just, and God-fearing. In so doing he counsels them to "rightly wield the Sword that God has given [them]."[118]

The language in one section of *Foundation*, "Request to the Magistracy," is one of pleading and supplication. Following are excerpts from this "Request" that mirror Menno's cry for tolerance and the beleaguered state of Anabaptists:

> We humbly intreat the Imperial Majesty, kings, lords, princes, magistrates, and officers, everyone in his calling, dignity, and rank. And all our dear and gracious rulers by the crimson blood and wounds of our blessed Lord Jesus Christ, that you would at long last lay aside all ill will and bad opinion concerning us. With proper pity be at least somewhat concerned about the inhuman and heavy oppression, misery, distress, cross, and torture of your sad and innocent subjects.
>
> Therefore condescend to read our writings diligently and ponder them, and that with a God-fearing and unbiased heart, so that you may know with certainty why you are unable to frighten us from our doctrine, faith, and practice by coercion, poverty, misery, persecution, and death.
>
> Therefore humble yourselves in the name of Jesus, that your poor souls may be excused. Examine, I say, our doctrine, and you will find through the grace of God that it is the pure and unadulterated doctrine of Christ. . . .
>
> O dear sirs, sheathe your sword. For as the Lord liveth you do not fight against flesh and blood, but against Him whose eyes are as a flame of fire; who judgeth and contends in righteousness; who is crowned with many crowns. . . . O illustrious lords and princes, it is against Him that you in this manner contend with your counsel and sword and weapon.[119]

In at least three other places, Menno entreats rulers and magistrates toward mercy and understanding, adjuring them to ease Anabaptist persecution and eschew unjust use of the sword. Elsewhere in *Foundation*, in a section titled "Appeals for Toleration," he affirms civil authority to the extent that it does not violate Scripture.[120]

In his 1552 treatise *A Pathetic Supplication to All Magistrates*, Menno continues his appeal to those in authority. Therein he distances the Anabaptists from heretical sects in the church's past and reaffirms Anabaptist commitment to the authority of Scripture, all the while exhorting leaders to rule in the fear of God and cease from the persecution of the godly.[121]

Anabaptist and Mennonite refusal to engage in violence or war follows directly from the Anabaptist view of the state and the disciple's separation from the world, not necessarily a refusal to serve as a soldier per se.[122] Moreover, European wars often were religious wars; hence, Anabaptist types viewed this as a denial of the Christian faith and the Prince of Peace. Menno Simons summarizes the Anabaptist and Mennonite view of war and coercive force: "All Christians are commanded to love their enemies; to do good unto those who abuse and persecute them; to give the mantle when the cloak is taken, the other cheek when one is struck. Tell me, how can a Christian defend scripturally retaliation, rebellion, war, striking, slaying, torturing, stealing, robbing and plundering and burning cities and conquering countries?"[123] Among Anabaptists, Menno Simons's view of coercive force—of *any* type—remains largely in place four and a half centuries after his death.

CONCLUDING REFLECTIONS ON ANABAPTIST ETHICS: THE PRIMACY OF SEPARATION AND "NONVIOLENCE"

In his *Epistle to Martin Micron* (1556), addressed to a Reformed theologian with whom he had exchanges, Menno mirrors something of a shift on the use of the sword. Up to this point he was ambiguous on its use in a "police function." This ambiguity, for example, can be seen in his 1552 tract *A Pathetic Supplication to All Magistrates*, noted earlier, wherein he writes, "Execute judgment and justice. Assist, against the violent, him that is robbed," while in the very same tract he admonishes, "Do violence to no man."[124] By 1558, in a later edition of *Foundation*, he writes that "Christ is our fortress; patience our weapon of defense; the word of God our sword . . . and iron and metal spears and swords we leave to those who, alas, regard human blood and swine's blood about alike."[125]

But already by 1530, right around the time of Menno's conversion, separatist and pacifist themes among Anabaptists had begun to congeal. Concurrent with this development was a growing theological controversy with non-Anabaptist Protestant reformers, who viewed the Anabaptists' radicalism as being rooted in a theologically deficient understanding of the relationship of the Old Testament to the New. Some Reformed leaders, such as Calvin and Bullinger, believed that this deficiency constituted the fulcrum of the debate. Not only a rejection of infant baptism but a cluster of important and related issues hinged on how to interpret the Old and New Testaments, including the Christian's view of the magistrate, the use of the sword, and the public sphere in general.[126]

The early sixteenth century constitutes something of a remarkable new chapter in reflection on war and coercive force. While magisterial Protestant thinkers maintain a dependence on the Augustinian theory that seeks to mediate the tension between two citizenships—the earthly and the heavenly—new developments begin to alter the landscape in dramatic ways. Rethinking the church's relationship to the sword gives rise to an emerging break with medieval life and tradition. In addition, the discovery of the Americas as well as an increasingly fragmented Europe called for attention.

The magisterial reformers held to the conviction that while retribution does not belong to the church, it is not only permitted but commanded of rulers. Thus, two differentiated spheres of authority were understood to coexist in tension.[127] How that tension was navigated differed considerably from Luther to Calvin and other magisterial reformers; at the same time, a tension was maintained nonetheless. From virtually the beginning, Anabaptists understood these two spheres to be staunchly oppositional; therefore, a Christian could not be a magistrate or punish with the sword. This position was generally affirmed by the second generation of Anabaptists, the "Mennonites." The Reformed-Anabaptist debate in this regard would come to a head in May and June 1571 at the Frankenthal Disputation.[128] The Reformed position seemed to expose a weak spot in the general Anabaptist/Mennonite argument: if a Christian could not be permitted to serve in any sort of ruling capacity, the implication is that the office *qua* office is not of God but of the devil and therefore intrinsically evil. A further inconsistency needed clarification, based on Article 6 of the Schleitheim Confession: three times in the opening paragraph of this article the confession states that the sword is "ordained." (1) It is "ordained of God" even when existing "outside the perfection of Christ"; (2) according to the law, the sword was "ordained" for the purpose of punishment; and (3) the same sword is presently "ordained" and "to be used by the worldly magistrates."[129]

By the end of the sixteenth century, Anabaptist types would maintain the stark polarity between Christ and "the world," resulting in an enduring form of separatism and pacifism that, at least in its practical expression, would necessitate a withdrawal from "the world" and be characterized by a narrow sectarianism. Both of these elements, to a measurable extent, remain five hundred years later.

NEO-ANABAPTISM, PACIFISM, AND THE STATE

Unlike other denominations and Christian traditions examined in this volume, Anabaptism has had no ongoing "dialogue" with the just war tradition. From its outset in the early sixteenth century, with the exception of the Münster tragedy, it was committed to a "nonviolent" expression of the faith, which has precluded any sort of dialogue that is meaningful either within or outside of the tradition.[130] The original ideological pacifist commitment remains lodged at the heart of contemporary Anabaptist faith. Thus, in the words of a professor of "peace theology" at a Mennonite university, "Modern-day Anabaptists should see themselves as . . . sharing the 16th-century Anabaptists' sense both (1) of separating themselves from many of the basic values of the wider society, especially those that undergird violence and domination and are underwritten by Christian rhetoric, and (2) of witnessing against that violence and domination, making known as widely as possible the peaceable message of Jesus."[131]

Hence, the commitment to ideological pacifism has not changed. What *has* changed, however, at least among Anabaptist academics and denominational leaders, is Anabaptist "political theology." Historically

viewed, this change in orientation is a relatively recent phenomenon, occurring since the Second World War. To a great extent, though with some
deviations, that shift is owing to the work of the most influential Anabaptist theologian of the twentieth century, John Howard Yoder. A prolific
writer and professor of Christian ethics at the University of Notre Dame
until his death in 1997, Yoder, in various ways, addressed, inter alia, Niebuhrian realism, the purported fallacy of just war thinking, and the church's
relationship to the state in his attempt to argue for an "absolute ethic of
Jesus."[132] For Yoder, individual Christians and the church as a community
must be pacifistic because killing is contrary to Christ's injunction to love
one's enemies and not to resist evil; such resistance, Yoder believed, is a
purely divine prerogative, reserved only for the eschaton.

A central component in Yoder's "peace" theology is the purported
"purity" of the early church. According to Yoder (and virtually all Anabaptist theologians as well as many non-Anabaptists who have uncritically
adopted this view), the great enemy of the church can be ascribed to
"Constantinianism," by which Yoder understands that in the fourth century the church "prostituted" herself before the political powers and became the maiden of the state. And until the "radical reformation" of the
early sixteenth century, this state of affairs—so it is argued—remained
uninterrupted. What is more, this state of affairs continues in the modern
era up to the present day and therefore requires "prophetic" denunciation,[133] which, as Yoder understands it, itself constitutes our "participation" in the culture. The early church was pacifistic, insists Yoder, and the
pacifist position alone is authentically Christian.

The best—and most serious—historical scholarship, it needs under-
scoring, has shown Yoder's position—namely, that the early church up
until the fourth century was uniformly pacifist—to be mythical. Rather,
what we find in the early centuries is a mixture of beliefs and practices.
Until the mid-second century we indeed find no evidence of Christians
serving in either a political or military capacity; this is as we would expect,
given the fact that the Christian community in its inception would have
been a small, marginalized social group through several generations.[134]
Moreover, serving in the Roman legions would have required Roman citizenship, which would have been well-nigh impossible for most Christian
believers in the early years. The historical record indicates that not "pacifism"
per se or the abhorrence of war and coercive force motivated early Christians, even when for some this was the case. Other factors—not least being

various idolatrous practices within the military[135]—would have been contributed to "nonparticipation" as well. James Turner Johnson has summarized the evidence coming to us from the second and third centuries: "Beginning with the second century, though, there is increasingly hard evidence [of military participation] . . . [and] this evidence presents a picture not of a single doctrine, but of plurality; not of universal rejection of war and military service, but of a mixture of acceptance and rejection of these phenomena in different sectors of the Christian world."[136]

In spite of pagan religious practices associated with the Roman legions, Christians were nevertheless already serving in the military by the mid- or late second century—a fact that is confirmed by both Christian and Roman sources.[137] Johnson once more summarizes Christian perspectives on military service in the early centuries:

> This alternative picture [to pacifism] is one that highlights the initial eschatological separatism of the earliest stages of the Christian movement, in which *not violence as such* but close involvement in the affairs of the world was to be shunned, followed by a gradual adjustment to such involvement in the wake of the realization that the new age was not immediately at hand—an adjustment that took place in different ways and at different rates among Christians in various parts of the empire, and one that did not compromise earlier moral purity but instead sought ways to direct it into life within the world at large.[138]

A more nuanced and composite reading of patristic texts during the first three-and-a-half centuries yields the conclusion that among Christians a diversity of views existed in the early centuries; we find evidence of the presence of both patriots and pacifists.[139] Thus, emerging attitudes among religious believers toward military life did not constitute a "falling away" from early Christian teaching or "apostolic purity," as the "Constantinianism" thesis advanced by Yoder and other Anabaptists has popularly assumed.[140] Rather, if indeed the early Christians avoided war and the military because of their eschatological expectations, it is only natural that with the change of those expectations theologically over time and their realization of the need to "occupy" in the world there would necessarily arise pluralistic interpretations of the role of Christians in society. This would be true of all vocations, not just military service.[141]

Article 6 of the Anabaptist Schleitheim Confession of 1527, noted earlier in this chapter, declares that the sword is "ordained" by God and "protects the good." It acknowledges that secular political authorities are *divinely established*, even when their establishment exists "outside the perfection of Christ." It needs emphasizing that the early Anabaptists, although they refused participation, nevertheless acknowledged the legitimacy of armed civil authority. Contemporary "neo-Anabaptists," by contrast, generally refuse to acknowledge this reality, rejecting all forms of coercive force and "violence," including state and military powers that are aimed at guarding the common good. This more recent version of Anabaptism, then, stands in contradiction of historic Anabaptist confession.

What compounds this lack of continuity with historic Anabaptism is yet another feature of neo-Anabaptist "political theology"—namely, the frequently strong calls for intervention by the state when it concerns matters of welfare, poverty, economic equality, or "social justice" issues. This occurs while Anabaptists simultaneously denounce those functions of the state which are described by St. Paul in Romans 13 as ordained for the common good. As it happens, contemporary Anabaptists—at least academic Anabaptists and Anabaptist leaders—tend to be aligned with a secular or religious political leftism.[142]

Relatedly, a common theme in contemporary Anabaptist political theology, regardless of its provenance, is the denouncing of "empire" and "violence." And in the words of the peace theologian cited above, "a mutually empowering encounter of the new awareness of the Bible's radical politics as seen on the evangelical left with the emergent interest in anarchism back in the 1970s" is something that "we can certainly use—more than ever now."[143] Moreover, this critique tends usually to be directed at the United States and not at totalitarian regimes around the globe where human rights are suppressed in the most basic of ways.

Positively, much current "political theology" by Anabaptists stresses the importance of cultural engagement by believers in the public realm. While not all Anabaptists will concede such, many more today seem willing to acknowledge the importance of participation in the institutions that make up our public life; hence, the historic commitment to separatism is being rethought, even when the "nonviolent" imperative remains absolute and nonnegotiable. Although Anabaptists refuse to run for public office, they are far more willing today to acknowledge that all of life is "political"; that is, that our common social life consists of interlocking spheres that are economic, social, civil, and political.

Historically, "public witness" for most Anabaptists—a "witness" that includes withdrawal—might be described as a "negative" public witness, which is to say, a refusal to participate or an institutional withdrawal from direct social involvement. Generally speaking, Anabaptist thinkers historically have devoted most of their efforts to justifying—historically, biblically, and ethically—their "peace theology" and an ideology of "nonviolence." This has not been accompanied, however, by a full-fledged, robust political theory that would underscore in a *positive* manner their public witness, in the recognition that wider culture is composed of myriads of social institutions that require our involvement—and not merely "discipleship," "purity," or separation.

The extent to which Anabaptism as a whole is capable in the twenty-first century of integrating itself in the public sphere remains to be seen.[144]

NOTES

1. Euan Cameron, *The European Reformation*, 2nd ed. (Oxford: Oxford University Press, 2012), 26, cautions us against appropriating the terms "corruption" or "decay" too readily in association with the church to describe this period; he prefers to speak of the church's "vulnerability." To employ the language of "vulnerability," however, fails to do justice to the *causes* of the church's vulnerability. Few have described the wider religious, social, and cultural climate of the late fifteenth, sixteenth, and early seventeenth centuries more lucidly than Carlos M. N. Eire, *Reformations: The Early Modern World, 1450–1650* (New Haven: Yale University Press, 2016).

2. Historian Michael G. Baylor summarizes both eloquently and concisely this sense of dislocation in the introduction to his important volume *The Radical Reformation*, ed. and trans. Michael G. Baylor, Cambridge Texts in the History of Political Thought (Cambridge: Cambridge University Press, 1991), xvii–xxi.

3. Donald F. Durnbaugh, *The Believers' Church: The History and Character of Radical Protestantism* (New York: Macmillan; London: Collier-Macmillan, 1968), 64–65.

4. Paul A. Russell, *Lay Theology in the Reformation* (Cambridge: Cambridge University Press, 1986), 31–33.

5. As the title of Peter G. Wallace's *The Long European Reformation: Religion, Political Conflict, and the Search for Conformity, 1350–1750*, 2nd ed. (New

York: Palgrave Macmillan, 2012), suggests, one might speak of a "late-medieval crisis" from the mid-fourteenth century until the early sixteenth century, with resistance, renewal, and reform intermittent and ongoing.

6. So, for example, Ulinka Rublack, ed., *The Oxford Handbook of the Protestant Reformations* (Oxford: Oxford University Press, 2017); Eire, *Reformations*; Heiko A. Oberman, *The Two Reformations: The Journey from the Last Days to the New World*, ed. Donald Weinstein (New Haven: Yale University Press, 2003); Carter Lindberg, ed., *The European Reformations Sourcebook* (Oxford: Blackwell, 2000); Katharine Jackson Lualdi and Anne T. Thayer, eds., *Penitence in the Age of Reformations* (Oxford: Ashgate, 2000); Carter Lindberg, *The European Reformations* (Oxford: Blackwell, 1996); Christopher Haigh, *English Reformations: Religion, Politics, and Society under the Tudors* (Oxford: Clarendon, 1993).

7. James Hitchcock, "The Age of Reformations," *Touchstone*, September/ October 2017, 36.

8. Walter Klaassen, *Anabaptism: Neither Catholic nor Protestant* (Waterloo, ON: Conrad Press, 1973). See, as well, Robert Friedmann, "Anabaptism and Protestantism," *Mennonite Quarterly Review* 24 (1950): 12–24. Even the author of "The Radical Reformation," appearing in volume 6 of *The Cambridge History of Christianity*, joins the chorus to argue that Anabaptism is not "Protestant" in character. See R. Emmett McLaughlin, "The Radical Reformation," in *The Cambridge History of Christianity*, vol. 6, *Reform and Expansion, 1500–1660*, ed. R. Po-Chia Hsia (Cambridge: Cambridge University Press, 2007), 37.

9. James M. Stayer, *Anabaptists and the Sword* (Lawrence, KS: Coronado Press, 1972), 95. Following the Swiss Brethren's break with Zwingli in 1524, Grebel took the lead in seeking allies outside of Zürich.

10. This demarcation is valid even though a group of like-minded individuals had existed since 1523, as tensions with Zwingli and the Zürich city council were growing. In fact, small meetings and Bible studies had been occurring since 1520.

11. So Durnbaugh, *Believers' Church*, 65: "It is therefore appropriate to choose the Swiss Brethren . . . as the foremost representatives of Believers' Churches in the sixteen century."

12. Restoration or restitution was a prominent sixteenth-century theme, particularly among the Anabaptists. Hereon see, for example, Frank J. Wray, "The Anabaptist Doctrine of the Restitution of the Church," *Mennonite Quarterly Review* 28 (1954): 186–96.

13. Hereon see Harold S. Bender, "The Anabaptist Vision," in *The Recovery of the Anabaptist Vision*, ed. Guy F. Hershberger (Scottdale, PA: Herald Press, 1957), 42. (Bender's chapter originally appeared as an essay in *Church History* 13 [March 1944]: 3–24, and was in turn republished with slight modifications in

284 J. Daryl Charles

the *Mennonite Quarterly Review* 18 [April 1944]: 67–88.) The same sort of thinking that has attempted to disassociate Anabaptism from Protestantism, noted above, has also led to the argument that Anabaptism has "no explicit theology" (so, for example, Robert Friedmann, *The Theology of Anabaptism: An Interpretation*, Studies in Anabaptist and Mennonite History 15 [Scottdale, PA: Herald Press, 1975], 27–35). In response, we may simply observe that "discipleship," "brotherhood," "nonresistance," and even martyrdom are underpinned by theological beliefs.

14. James M. Stayer discerningly notes: "Although Anabaptism is not important for understanding the Peasants' War, the Peasants' War is very important for understanding Anabaptism" (*The German Peasants' War and Anabaptist Community of Goods*, McGill-Queen's Studies in the History of Religion [Montreal: McGill-Queen's University Press, 1991], 4). Correlatively, Gunther Franz, *Der deutsche Bauernkrieg*, 12th ed. (Darmstadt: Wissenschaftliche Buchgesellschaft, 1984), has argued with considerable force that the "Peasants' War" was primarily a social, economic, and political phenomenon, and any relationship to Anabaptism was random. And Peter Blickle, *Revolution of 1525: The German Peasants' War from a New Perspective*, trans. T. A. Brady Jr. and H. C. Erik Midelfort (Baltimore: Johns Hopkins University Press, 1981), 185, considers Anabaptism to be an "after-effect" of the Peasants' War to the extent that uprisings often preceded Anabaptist communities.

15. George H. Williams, ed., *Spiritual and Anabaptist Writers: Documents Illustrative of the Radical Reformation*, Library of Christian Classics 25 (Philadelphia: Westminster, 1968), 20; Williams, *The Radical Reformation*, 3rd ed. (Kirksville, MO: Truman State University Press, 1995), xxiii–xxxi. With good reason, Hans J. Hillerbrand, editor of the seminal volume *The Reformation: A Narrative History Related by Contemporary Observers and Participants* (repr., Grand Rapids, MI: Baker, 1978), calls Williams's work "the best historiographical introduction" to the period (294).

16. The magisterial Protestant reformers agreed not only that there is one universal church but also that the "visible" church is coextensive with the local community in which its members live and worship (in relative peace, that is). Anabaptists initially shared this view—at least, in principle. But they were unable to actualize it to the degree that Luther, Calvin, Zwingli, and Bucer did. Failing to convince the entire community, early Anabaptist leaders separated themselves from the existing church, with its extended community, condemning it as "unbiblical" and hence voluntarily forming their own small communities— the "true believers."

17. Baylor, *Radical Reformation*, xiii.

18. Hans-Jürgen Goertz, *Die Täufer: Geschichte und Deutung* (Munich: C.H. Beck, 1980).

19. Manfred Hannemann, *The Diffusion of the Reformation in Southwestern Germany, 1518–1534* (Chicago: University of Chicago Press, 1975), 43, observes — correctly, in my assessment — that the expression "Peasants' War," which is frequently found in the relevant literature, is something of a misnomer insofar as revolts encompassed cities and towns in various regions — for example, massive revolts occurred in Swabia, Franconia, and Thuringia, to name only several regions — and took on a slightly different character depending on that particular region. One might argue, as well, that the term "peasant" is misleading since not all farmers (*Bauern*) were deprived or lowly; many were self-sufficient and esteemed in the community.

20. Evidence of this phenomenon was especially notable in Switzerland, given the back-and-forth movement of dissenters across the south German and Swiss border as well as the relative independence of some Swiss towns and cantons. "To be free like the Swiss" was a common adage at the time. On the character of this "freedom," see Gerald Strauss, "Three Kinds of 'Christian Freedom': Law, Liberty, and License in the German Reformation," in *Enacting the Reformation in Germany* (Aldershot: Variorum, 1993), 291–306.

21. In the late medieval period a mining explosion occurred, for example, in the German regions of Saxony and Thuringia as well as in the Black Forest, due to the presence and discovery of rare ores such as silver, copper, and lead.

22. By way of illustration, here we may distinguish between imperial cities, knightly territories, princely territories, and ecclesiastical territories.

23. Oberman, *Two Reformations*, xv, captures the early sixteenth-century moment quite vividly: "Among the thousands of letters I have read in the course of my Reformation researches, many contain a simple three-word postscript: 'Burn after reading.' The injunction conveys the need of sixteenth-century authors to conceal their identity and keep their ideas from falling into unfriendly hands. For similar reasons authors and printers commonly falsified or omitted names, places, and dates of publication in the thousands of pamphlets and tracts that circulated in Germany between 1500 and 1520. These were dangerous times: dissent was a well-understood risk and public opinion [was] a contested area, anxiously monitored by those who considered themselves to be the guardians of the public good."

24. At the same time, we should note that according to Augustine, Aquinas, the Protestant reformers, and early modern just war theorists, being a good citizen — that is, being "peaceful" — entails more than merely denying coercive force. Hence, both "Protestants" and those opposing them would be suspicious of — and likely oppose — the fundamental notion of being "separated from the world."

25. So Durnbaugh, *Believers' Church*, 67.

26. The early dissenters did not call themselves "Anabaptists" (*Wiedertäufer*); this was the name given to them by their opponents.

27. Emil Egli et al., eds. *Huldreich Zwinglis Sämtliche Werke* (Leipzig: Heinsius, 1914), 8:780. A second source refers to Grebel as the "arch-anabaptist" (*Erzwidertouffer*); see Johannes Kessler, *Johannes Kesslers Sabbata mit kleineren Schriften und Briefen*, edited by Emil Egli (St. Gall: Fehr, 1902), 142–43, 314.

28. Mantz was publicly executed by drowning in January of 1527.

29. Harold S. Bender, "Conrad Grebel," in *The Mennonite Encyclopedia: A Comprehensive Reference Work on the Anabaptist-Mennonite Movement*, ed. Harold S. Bender et al. (Scottdale, PA: Mennonite Publishing House, 1952), 2:566.

30. The only account of Grebel's origin is found in the chronicles of the Hutterian Brethren, under the title *Geschicht-Buch der Hutterischen Brüder* (Vienna: Carl Fromm, 1923). The Brethren, whose recorded history begins in 1524, settled in Austria but claim as their origin Zürich.

31. Huldrych Zwingli, *Catabaptistarum Strophas Elenchus* (Zürich: n.p., 1527), reprinted in *Huldreich Zwinglis Sämtliche Werke* (Zürich: Berichthaus, 1961), 6:1–196.

32. Two of these letters were written to Zwingli, one to Thomas Müntzer, one to a co-worker in Zürich (Andreas Castelberger), nine to an Oswald Myconius of Lucerne, and fifty-six to a close friend, Joachim von Watt, a fellow reformer in the Swiss city of St. Gall. Unfortunately, most of these letters were written when Grebel was a student in Paris and Vienna and not an "Anabaptist" leader.

33. So, for example, H. Richard Niebuhr, *The Social Sources of Denominationalism* (Cleveland: World Publishing Co., 1957), 38–39.

34. Heinold Fast, "Conrad Grebel: The Covenant on the Cross," in *Profiles of Radical Reformers: Biographical Sketches from Thomas Müntzer to Paracelsus*, ed. Hans-Jürgen Goertz and Walter Klaassen (Scottdale, PA: Herald Press, 1982), 118.

35. Harold S. Bender, an Anabaptist authority on Conrad Grebel, writes that for two generations prior to the Protestant Reformation, "no important political event took place in Zürich in which a Grebel did not have part" ("Conrad Grebel, the Founder of Swiss Anabaptism," *Church History* 7, no. 2 [June 1938]: 160).

36. Upon arriving at the university of Basel in October of 1514, where Erasmus had taken up a teaching position, Grebel would have been exposed to humanist scholarship.

37. Grebel's father transferred him to the university of Vienna, where he was to receive a four-year stipend from the emperor Maximillian (Bender, "Conrad Grebel, the Founder of Swiss Anabaptism," 162).

38. After three years at Vienna, Grebel would transfer to Paris for another two years of study; however, he would return to Zürich due to personal issues without finishing his education formally.

39. This is suggested by Fast, "Conrad Grebel," 129. Most sources are generally agreed that Conrad's marriage to a girl of lesser status alienated him from his family, resulting in a break in or about the year 1522.

40. Grebel's final break with Zwingli and the Zürich church would be over infant baptism. The issue, for Grebel, reduced to what constitutes the real church and true Christian discipleship.

41. Hereon see Claus-Peter Clasen, *Anabaptism: A Social History, 1525–1618; Switzerland, Austria, Moravia, South and Central Germany* (Cambridge: Cambridge University Press, 1972), 395–97.

42. It remains unknown whether Müntzer ever received the letter or responded.

43. At this time, Grebel happened to have a two-week-old daughter.

44. Lindberg, *European Reformations*, 214.

45. It was customary at the time that the "heretic" would be burned at the stake and his wife would be drowned.

46. Egli et al., *Huldreich Zwinglis Sämtliche Werke*, 3:872.

47. Bender, "Conrad Grebel," 571–73.

48. George H. Williams, "Radical Elements in the Reformation," in *The Reformation: Revival or Revolution?*, ed. W. Stanford Reid (New York: Rinehart and Winston, 1968), 33. Of course, one is justified in asking, *What does "restoration of the early church" mean?* After all, both magisterial and radical reformers desired such—*ad fontes*, "back to the sources."

49. Refusing to take oaths was important because citizens were sworn to maintain the common good, take up defense, avoid perjury, and uphold public service.

50. Citizen-soldiers guaranteed the public order, insofar as there was no standing army per se in sixteenth-century Switzerland.

51. Norman Cohn, *The Pursuit of the Millennium: A History of Popular Religious and Social Movements in Europe from the Eleventh to the Sixteenth Century* (London: Secker and Warburg, 1957), 254.

52. Stayer, *Anabaptists and the Sword*, 3–4.

53. For representative English translations, see John C. Wenger, "The Schleitheim Confession of Faith," *Mennonite Quarterly Review* 19 (1945): 243–53, and Michael Sattler, "The Schleitheim Articles," in Baylor, *Radical Reformation*, 172–80.

54. We know very little about Sattler; even the public records contain scant information about his life. For a profile of what we *do* know, see Martin Haas, "Michael Sattler: On the Way to Anabaptist Separation," in Goertz and Klaassen, *Profiles of Radical Reformers*, 132–43.

55. Some contemporary Anabaptist scholars bristle at the suggestion that their tradition, as mirrored in the Schleitheim Confession, is "separatist" and

that the document was influential, prototypical, or separatist in reality; rather, they would argue that documents such as the confession are a product of *cultural engagement* and *not* withdrawal. The nuances of this debate are helpfully illustrated in Gerald Biesecker-Mast's essay "Anabaptist Separation and Arguments against the Sword in the Schleitheim Brotherly Union," *Mennonite Quarterly Review* 74 (2000): 381–402. (Author note: I had a recent experience—in February 2019 at a Christian university in Florida—in which debate between two just war advocates—one being me, the author—and two ideological pacifists took place. When one of the pacifist representatives—who teaches at a Mennonite seminary—was pressed to account for her ideological pacifism, she refused to answer, given her intuited sense that *separatism*—for which Anabaptists are long known—suggests *detachment from the world*, which, in truth, it does. She had no real response, other than to express anger that her tradition, Anabaptism, might be perceived as being "separate" from the world or separatistic in character.)

56. This is the view of at least several contemporary Anabaptist writers—among these, for example, Beulah S. Hostetler, *American Mennonites and Protestant Movements* (Scottdale, PA: Herald Press, 1987), and Arnold Snyder, "The Influence of the Schleitheim Articles on the Anabaptist Movement: An Historical Evaluation," *Mennonite Quarterly Review* 63 (1989): 323–44.

57. And in the fourth article, we read: "We are agreed on separation: A separation shall be made from the evil and from the wickedness which the devil planted in the world; in this manner, simply that we shall not have fellowship with them [the wicked] and not run with them in the multitude of their abominations. . . . Since all who do not walk in the obedience of faith, and [who] have not united themselves with God so that they wish to do His will, are a great abomination before God, it is not possible for anything to grow or issue from them except abominable things. For truly all creatures are in but two classes, good and bad, believing and unbelieving, darkness and light, the world and those who have come out of the world, God's temple and idols, Christ and Belial; and none can have part with the other."

58. Gerald Biesecker-Mast, "Anabaptist Separation and Arguments against the Sword in the Schleitheim Brotherly Union," *Mennonite Quarterly Review* 74 (2000): 381–402. This statement, found in all three synoptic gospels, is taken out of context by the Brethren. The purpose of Jesus's teaching here is to emphasize the attitude of *being a servant of all* rather than wanting to be served and "lord it over" others.

59. Rom. 8:29.

60. 1 Pet. 2:21.

61. I am reliant on the Biesecker-Mast translation (see n. 55).

62. For example, Alister McGrath's seminal work *The Intellectual Origins of the European Reformation* (Oxford: Basil Blackwell, 1987) astonishingly contains not a single mention of Hubmaier. Neither does A. G. Dickens and John Tonkin's *The Reformation in Historical Thought* (Cambridge, MA: Harvard University Press, 1985). Nor does Heike A. Oberman's *The Reformation: Roots and Ramifications* (London: T&T Clark International, 2004). Nor, remarkably, any of the following: Lawrence P. Buck and Jonathan W. Zophy, eds., *The Social History of the Reformation* (Columbus: Ohio State University Press, 1972); Carlos M. N. Eire, *War against the Idols* (Cambridge and New York: Cambridge University Press, 1986); Andrew Pettegree, ed., *The Early Reformation in Europe* (Cambridge: Cambridge University Press, 1992); and G. R. Evan, *The Roots of the Reformation: Tradition, Emergence, and Rupture* (Downers Grove, IL: IVP Academic, 2012). As further evidence of undeserved neglect, Stephen Ozment's *The Age of Reform, 1250–1550: An Intellectual and Religious History of Late Medieval and Reformation Europe* (New Haven: Yale University Press, 1980) mentions Hubmaier merely once in passing, in a list; the same is true of B. A. Gerrish, ed., *Reformers in Profile* (Minneapolis: Fortress, 1967). Diarmaid MacCulloch's *Reformation: Europe's House Divided, 1490–1700* (New York: Penguin Books, 2003), considered by some to be *the* authoritative work on the Reformation, mentions Hubmaier four times in 864 pages; Hans J. Hillerbrand's *The Division of Christendom: Christianity in the Sixteenth Century* (Louisville: Westminster John Knox, 2007) also mentions Hubmaier's name only four times—this in 503 pages. And in part 5 ("Radical Theologians") of Carter Lindberg's *Reformation Theologians: An Introduction to Theology in the Early Modern Period* (Oxford: Blackwell, 2002), strangely, scant attention is devoted to Hubmaier.

63. The church's mandate has been reproduced in *Die Indices Librorum Prohibitorum des sechzehnten Jahrhunderts* (Tübingen: Mohr, 1886), 246–47, an English translation of which appears in Hillerbrand, *Reformation*, 474–75. The mandate continues: "Others will be permitted after Catholic theologians have examined and approved them by the orders of bishops and inquisitors. Likewise, Catholic books written by those who subsequently fell into heresy or by those who after their lapse returned into the bosom of the Church can be permitted after approval by a theological faculty or the inquisition."

64. Adrian John Roberts, "'Truth Is Unkillable': Non-Resistance, 'the Sword' and Magisterial Authority in the Theology of Balthasar Hubmaier, 1523–1528" (MPhil thesis, University of Birmingham, 2011), 2, https://etheses.bham.ac.uk//id/eprint/3624/1/Roberts12MPhil.pdf.

65. So Christof Windhorst, "Balthasar Hubmaier: Professor, Preacher, Politician," in Goertz and Klaassen, *Profiles of Radical Reformers*, 145.

66. For an English translation of Hubmaier's collected theological works, see H. Wayne Pipkin and John H. Yoder, eds. and trans., *Balthasar Hubmaier: Theologian of Anabaptism* (Scottdale, PA: Herald Press, 1989).

67. Significantly, the Schleitheim Confession, which is contemporary to these two documents (1527), devotes the second of seven articles to the ban.

68. This point is pressed by Kirk R. MacGregor, *A Central European Synthesis of Radical and Magisterial Reform: The Sacramental Theology of Balthasar Hubmaier* (Lanham, MD: University Press of America, 2006), 126.

69. Daniel Liechty, ed. and trans., *Early Anabaptist Spirituality: Select Writings*, Classics of Western Spirituality (New York: Paulist Press, 1994), 20.

70. During these years we read of unfortunate incidents of anti-Semitism involving Hubmaier and many other Christian leaders. Such would be perhaps the only real blemish on his work as a leader, even when such attitudes were the norm in "Christian Europe," characterizing even the Reformers themselves, as Luther's rather mixed testimony suggests.

71. We know this from his personal correspondence.

72. Sixteenth-century religious discourse had an unavoidable dimension of political reference, in the same way that political authority and the polity were articulated in religious language. Thus, to say that the radical reformers saw themselves as "religious" rather than "political" in the modern sense is simply inaccurate, and anachronistic, as Baylor, *Radical Reformation*, xvii, has well observed. Hence, baptism would have had enormous political significance, and rebaptizing would have been perceived as a threat to the very structure of authority in late-medieval society.

73. Thus, Jarold Knox Zeman, *The Anabaptists and the Czech Brethren in Moravia, 1526–1628*, Studies in European History 20 (The Hague: Mouton, 1969), 127.

74. Nikolsburg became for Hubmaier the "new Emmaus" (see Zeman, *Anabaptists and the Czech Brethren, 1526–1628*, 176), a very brief escape before severe persecution.

75. Hubmaier's writings are generally of two kinds: twenty-four printed booklets in the three-year period between May, 1524, and June, 1527, and various personal letters and appeals to the authorities.

76. Durnbaugh, *Believers' Church*, 84.

77. Thus his tract "On Heretics and Those Who Burn Them," published in 1524.

78. By 1529, a year after Hubmaier's execution, the Imperial Diet of Speyer proclaimed: "Every Anabaptist and rebaptized person of either sex should be put to death by fire, sword, or some other way" (as cited in Bender, "Anabaptist Vision," *Church History* 13 [March 1944]: 5–6).

79. See Grete Mecenseffy, ed., *Quellen zur Geschichte der Täufer*, vol. 11, *Österreich, I* (Gütersloh: Gerd Mohn, 1964), 26–60; see as well Zeman, *Anabaptists and the Czech Brethren in Moravia, 1526–1628*, 193–94.

80. Reproduced in Zeman, *Anabaptists and the Czech Brethren in Moravia, 1526–1628*, 199.

81. So Stayer, *Anabaptists and the Sword*, 254–55.

82. Based on a medallion found that dates to around 1535, five coats of arms signified five cities that were thought to have been chosen by God for the faithful; these were London, Amsterdam, Wesel, Deventer, and Münster. Hereon see Philipp Christiann Molhuysen, *Overijsselsche Almanak voor Oudheid en Letteren* (Oldenzaal: Deventer, 1839), 155.

83. Rothmann (1495–1535) was an independent and exceedingly eclectic theologian who had been in touch with reformers in Wittenberg and Strasbourg and who borrowed from various Swiss and south German Anabaptist sources. He served briefly in 1529 as preacher in the cathedral of St. Maurice in Münster. Rothmann's influence can be seen in the fact that he was successful in getting many of the city's leaders, including those presiding over the city's influential guilds, to endorse his radical theology. Williams, *Radical Reformation*, 574, writes: "Bernhard Rothmann was clearly the theological biblicist behind the Anabaptist theocracy of Münster. He was the city's university-trained ranking churchman." On Rothmann's background leading up to his role in Münster, see James M. Stayer, "The Münsterite Rationalization of Bernhard Rothmann," *Journal of the History of Ideas* 28 (1967): 179–92.

84. Stayer, *Anabaptists and the Sword*, 211–26. Northern German and Dutch Anabaptism seems to have been stamped peculiarly by Hofmann. The imminence of the end of the world was a defining feature of Hoffmann's theology. On his understanding of the governing authority and the sword, see James M. Stayer, "Melchior Hoffman and the Sword," *Mennonite Quarterly Review* 45 (1971): 270–77. Perhaps the best—and most thorough—critique of Hoffmann's theological framework and work is Klaus Deppermann, *Melchior Hoffman: Social Unrest and Apocalyptic Visions in the Age of Reformation*, trans. Malcolm Wren (Edinburgh: T&T Clark, 1987).

85. According to some estimates, between fourteen thousand and sixteen thousand people migrated to Münster during the mid-1530s. See, for example, Irvin B. Horst, *The Radical Brethren: Anabaptism and the English Reformation to 1558*, Bibliotheca Humanistica and Reformatorica 2 (Nieuwkoop: B. de Graaf, 1972), 66–67. Especially among Dutch Anabaptists, who were severely oppressed under Catholic authorities, news of what was going on in Münster was welcomed with considerable enthusiasm.

86. Although Matthias's iconoclastic rule lasted only six weeks, it orchestrated significant change.

87. Knipperdolling had been elected as mayor (*Bürgermeister*) in February 1534.

88. Krechting was the brother of the city's chancellor.

89. For a helpful overview of the development of the Münster project as well as its demise, see Cornelius Krahn, *Dutch Anabaptism: Origin, Spread, Life and Thought* (Scottdale, PA: Herald Press, 1981 [repr., Eugene, OR: Wipf & Stock, 2004]), 135–69. More recent research on Münster Anabaptism has tended to focus on the social, economic, and political preconditions for the Anabaptists' coming to power in the city, including the social composition of the fraction of the Münster citizenry that rallied to Anabaptism.

90. On July 13, 1524, Müntzer was invited before several Saxon princes to present his radicalized understanding of Protestant reform. In this presentation of his interpretation of Daniel 2, the radical Reformation reaches a "high-water mark" in terms of its "revolutionary spiritualism" and counter-Lutheran emphasis. The sermon is delivered in the presence of Duke John, brother of Frederick the Wise, protector of Luther, as well as multiple town officials. Herein Müntzer insists that divine revelation has not stopped; rather, it is a sign of the last days, he is a prophet, and the Spirit of God is speaking through him. Similar in character is Müntzer's first major writing, *The Prague Protest*, in 1521, a mixture of apocalyptic threats and vicious anticlericalism.

91. According to radical Anabaptist thinking in Münster, before the wicked could be punished, 144,000 saints needed to be found and gathered. Hence, there were attempts to draw sympathetic Anabaptist types from other parts of Germany and the Netherlands to Münster.

92. See the descriptive list compiled by R. Po-Chia Hsia, "Munster and the Anabaptists," in *The German People and the Reformation*, ed. R. Po-Chia Hsia (Ithaca, NY: Cornell University Press, 1988), 51–52.

93. Nanne van der Zijpp, "Münster Anabaptists," in Bender et al., *Mennonite Encyclopedia*, 3:779. See as well, in this vein, John Horsch, "Menno Simons' Attitude toward the Anabaptists of Münster," *Mennonite Quarterly Review* 10 (1936): 55–72.

94. See, for example, Karl-Heinz Kirchoff, *Die Täufer in Münster, 1534/35* (Münster: Aschendorff, 1973).

95. Stayer, *Anabaptists and the Sword*, 123.

96. For a helpful survey of the historiographical debate over Münster Anabaptism, see James M. Stayer, "Was Dr. Kuehler's Conception of Early Dutch Anabaptism Historically Sound? The Historical Discussion of Anabaptist Münster 450 Years Later," *Mennonite Quarterly Review* 60 (1986): 261–88.

97. Stayer, *Anabaptists and the Sword*, 273.

98. Significantly, the ban constituted the second of the seven articles of the 1527 Schleitheim Confession. The ban was a literalistic interpretation and application of Matt. 18:15–18.

99. McLaughlin, "Radical Reformation."

100. Harold S. Bender, "A Brief Biography of Menno Simons," in *The Complete Writings of Menno Simons*, ed. John C. Wenger, trans. Leonard Verduin (Scottdale, PA: Mennonite Publishing House, 1956), 3–29. Cornelius Krahn writes: "Menno Simons was a Biblicist in the truest and best meaning of the word; he turned away from tradition and became Bible-centered in all his beliefs and practices." "Menno Simons," in Bender et al., *Mennonite Encyclopedia*, 3:582.

101. Menno Simons, *Reply to Gellius Faber . . . Conversion, Call, and Testimony*, in *Complete Writings*, 668.

102. Ibid.

103. Irvin B. Horst, "Menno Simons: The New Man in Community," in Goertz and Klaassen, *Profiles of Radical Reformers*, 209–10.

104. Menno Simons, *Reply to Gellius Faber*, 670–71.

105. On the Schleitheim Confession, see above.

106. Menno Simons, *Reply to Gellius Faber*, 668–74.

107. Snijder was martyred in 1531, following his rebaptism.

108. Menno Simons, *A Reply to False Accusations*, in *Complete Writings*, 543–77.

109. Ibid., 549.

110. Menno Simons, *The Blasphemy of John of Leiden*, in *Complete Writings*, 33–50.

111. Ibid., 42.

112. Ibid., 46.

113. Ibid., 46.

114. Ibid., 44.

115. *Foundation* was begun in 1539 and finished in 1540; it was thoroughly revised in 1554. However, it would not be translated into German until 1575.

116. Menno Simons, *Foundation of Christian Doctrine* (1539), in *Complete Writings*, 190, although the wider argument is laid out on pp. 190–206.

117. Stayer, *Anabaptists and the Sword*, 309–38.

118. Simons, *Foundation of Christian Doctrine*, 200.

119. Ibid., 117–18.

120. Part of this section reads: "But as to the flesh, we teach and exhort to obedience to the emperor, king, lords, magistrates, yea, to all in authority in all temporary affairs, and civil regulations in so far as they are not contrary to the Word of God. Rom. 13:1–3 . . . *We teach and acknowledge no other sword, nor*

tumult in the kingdom or church of Christ than the sharp sword of the Spirit, God's Word, as has been made quite plain in this and our other writings: a sword which is sharp and more penetrating than any sword, two-edged, and proceeding from the mouth of the Lord.... But the civil sword we leave to those to whom it is committed. Let everyone be careful lest he transgress in the matter of the sword, lest he perish with the sword. Matt. 26:52." Ibid., 200 (emphasis added).

121. Menno Simons, *A Pathetic Supplication to All Magistrates* (1552), in *Complete Writings*, 525–31.

122. However, the latter follows from the former. Here we need to remember that there was no conscription; European armies were a mixture of volunteers and mercenaries.

123. Menno Simons, *Reply to False Accusations*, in *Complete Writings*, 555.

124. Simons, *Pathetic Supplication to All Magistrates*, 526.

125. Menno Simons, *Foundation of Christian Doctrine*, 198.

126. John D. Roth, "Harmonizing the Scriptures: Swiss Brethren Understandings of the Relationship between the Old and New Testament during the Last Half of the Sixteenth Century," in *Radical Reformation Studies: Essays Presented to James M. Stayer*, ed. Werner O. Packull and Geoffrey L. Dipple (Aldershot: Ashgate, 1999), 36, has perceptively written: "At stake in the minds of the Reformers was not an abstract scholarly quibble over allegorical or tropological readings of Old Testament passages, but rather basic understandings of the sovereignty of God, the meaning of the Incarnation, the foundation of Christian ethics and the principles of order and authority essential to a stable society. Indeed, as subsequent debates would show, virtually every distinctive Anabaptist argument—on baptism, the sword, the oath, the Christian magistracy, and so on—hinged on their insistence that the New Testament was more authoritative than the Old in matters of Christian ethics."

127. When Anabaptist scholars refer to a "two kingdom" theological framework, this is not to be confused with the Lutheran model.

128. Hereon see Jess Yoder, "The Frankenthal Debate with the Anabaptists in 1571: Purpose, Procedure, Participants," *Mennonite Quarterly Review* 36 (1962): 14–35; Yoder, "The Frankenthal Disputation, Part II: Outcome Issues, Debating Methods," *Mennonite Quarterly Review* 36 (1962): 116–42.

129. This inconsistency, which fails to see the God-ordained necessity of political order due to human nature, largely remains to the present day, as evidenced by one representative Anabaptist historian: "Men will not come to the truth by violence and killing. Only patience and love and gentleness can accomplish that. Violence and killing are rejected in obedience to Christ because they are not the means to be used to achieve Christian ends." Klaassen, *Anabaptism*, 57.

130. The notable exception to Anabaptism's pacifist beginnings, as discussed earlier in this essay, was Balthasar Hubmaier, whose views on political authority and coercive force were more Lutheran than "Anabaptist."

131. Ted Grimsrud, "Anabaptism for the 21st Century," Peace Theology, https://peacetheology.net/anabaptist-convictions/anabaptism-for-the-21st -century/.

132. Representative of Yoder's work are *The Original Revolution: Essays on Christian Pacifism* (Scottdale, PA: Herald Press, 1971); *What Would You Do?* (Scottdale, PA: Herald, 1983); *Nevertheless: The Varieties and Shortcomings of Religious Pacifism*, 2nd ed. (Scottdale, PA: Herald Press, 1992); *The Politics of Jesus*, 2nd ed. (Grand Rapids, MI: Eerdmans, 1994); *When War Is Unjust: Being Honest in Just-War Thinking*, 2nd ed. (Maryknoll, NY: Orbis Books, 1996). Also representative of the Anabaptist position is Myron Augsburger, "Christian Pacifism," in *War: Four Christian Views*, ed. Robert G. Klouse, rev. ed. (Downers Grove, IL: InterVarsity, 1991), 79–97.

133. Through his writings, the Methodist Stanley Hauerwas, a "disciple" of Yoder, has continued this line of thinking, as have most Anabaptist academics.

134. But even this assumption and pattern are challenged by the New Testament—for example, by Cornelius the centurion (and Acts 10 and 11), a gentile convert, and by the soldiers whom John the Baptist encounters (Luke 3:14).

135. These practices would have included, inter alia, taking an oath to the emperor, who was appointed as *Pontifex Maximus*, and participating in a military system that included oaths to the standards of the legion. The discovery of *Feriale duranum*, a calendar of Roman army religious celebrations for the year AD 226, indicates festivals for the imperial cult and the army that included sacrifices and other activities that Christians would have viewed as idolatrous.

136. James Turner Johnson, *The Quest for Peace: Three Moral Traditions in Western Cultural History* (Princeton: Princeton University Press, 1987), 17.

137. We find this in Tertullian's *Apology* 5 and in Eusebius's *Ecclesiastical History* 5.5, as well as in Dio Cassius, *Dio's Roman History*, trans. Earnest Cary, vol. 9, Loeb Classical Library (Cambridge, MA: Harvard University Press, 1969), 72.8–10 (pp. 27–31).

138. Johnson, *Quest for Peace*, 61 (emphasis added).

139. In this regard see Stephen Gero, "Miles Gloriosus: The Christian and Military Service according to Tertullian," *Church History* 39, no. 3 (1970): 285–98; John Helgeland, "Christians and the Roman Army, A.D.173–337," *Church History* 43, no. 2 (1974): 149–63, 200, an expanded version of which appears as "Christians and the Roman Army from Marcus Aurelius to Constantine," in *Aufstieg und Niedergang der römischen Welt: Geschichte und Kultur Roms im Spiegel der neueren Forschung*, ed. Hildegard Temporini and Wolfgang Haase

(Berlin: de Gruyter, 1997), 2.23.1:724–834; Louis J. Swift, *The Early Fathers on War and Military Service,* Message of the Fathers of the Church 19 (Wilmington, DE: Michael Glazier, 1983); John Helgeland, Robert J. Daly, and J. Patout Burns, *Christians and the Military: The Early Experience* (Philadelphia: Fortress, 1985); Johnson, *Quest for Peace,* 4–66; Frances Young, "The Early Church: Military Service, War and Peace," *Theology* 92 (1989): 491–503; David G. Hunter, "A Decade of Research on Early Christians and Military Service," *Religious Studies Review* 18, no. 2 (1992): 87–94; J. Daryl Charles, "Patriots, Pacifists, or Both? Second Thoughts on Pre-Constantinian Early-Christian Attitudes toward Soldiering and War," *Logos: A Journal of Catholic Thought and Culture* 13, no. 2 (2010): 17–55; and J. Daryl Charles and Timothy J. Demy, *War, Peace, and Christianity: Questions and Answers from a Just-War Perspective* (Wheaton, IL: Crossway, 2010), 108–28.

140. More recently a vigorous attempt to rebut Yoder and the "Constantinian" thesis has been offered by Peter J. Leithart in *Defending Constantine: The Twilight of an Empire and the Dawn of Christendom* (Downers Grove, IL: IVP Academic, 2010), given the extent to which Yoder's polemic has influenced countless theologians, even outside of the Anabaptist context. An important part of Leithart's argument is historical, for Yoder "gets the fourth century wrong" in many particulars, which then "distorts his entire reading of church history" (11). Among those "particulars," as Leithart is well aware, is Yoder's unwillingness to acknowledge what the most serious historical scholarship on the early centuries has demonstrated—namely, "there is practically no evidence from the Fathers which would support the argument that the early church denied enlistment [into the Roman Legions] on the ground that killing and war were opposed to the Christian ethics" (so Helgeland, "Christians and the Roman Army from Marcus Aurelius to Constantine," 764). Alas, Yoder works with a prior, *closed* narrative of the church's "fall"—one that Leithart properly perceives as being "inherited from sixteenth-century Anabaptists" (319). Moreover, this presumed narrative shapes the manner in which Yoder treats not only the fourth century but "the whole of church history" (317). Leithart rightly concludes: "The church did not 'fall' in the fourth century. It was more resilient than that" (331). And in her constitution, the church of the early centuries was far more diverse than Yoder and most pacifists are willing to acknowledge.

141. According to the Anabaptist model (to the present day), Christians may not—indeed, must not—serve as magistrates or military personnel. But the list of illicit vocations is not confined merely to rulers and soldiers. It includes policy makers and government service, politicians (whether local, state, or national), public clerks, civil servants, virtually all sales agents, bankers, legal theorists and lawyers, economists and accountants, property managers and real estate agents, not to mention police, law-enforcement agents, and those in security (e.g., from Brinks truck drivers to watchmen and security guards).

142. Among Anabaptist academics (when not the average Anabaptist lay person), there is a fascination with — and appeal toward — "radicalism," and much of the rationale for this appeal is to be found in Yoder's emphasis on the "radicalism" and "countercultural" mode of Jesus. Not only the politically left-leaning tendency but the remarkable disjuncture between historic Anabaptism and non-Anabaptism as well as the seeming double standard noted above (of appealing to political powers when convenient) is well illustrated by John Roth, a professor of history at Goshen College, a Mennonite college in Indiana. Roth writes: "Christian pacifists may be resolutely opposed [to military service] and still actively support the Military Code of Conduct, which forbids such things as torture and extrajudicial killing; and they can publicly denounce the nation's decision to go to war, while also expecting it to abide by the Just War principles it has agreed to follow. *Christians who believe in the sanctity of life may have strong views against abortion, while still advocating for legislative measures that make contraception widely available or provide economic support to young teens struggling with life choices.*" "The Anabaptist Vision of Politics," *Plough Quarterly*, no. 24 (March 25, 2020), https://www.plough.com/en/topics/justice/politics/religious-liberty/the-anabaptist-vision-of-politics (emphasis added).

143. Ted Grimsrud, "The Anarchistic Appeal of the Bible: A Needed Story of Human Wellbeing," Thinking Pacifism, https://thinkingpacifism.net/2021/02/16/the-anarchistic-appeal-of-the-bible-a-needed-story-for-human-wellbeing-theological-memoir-11/. Also illustrating neo-Anabaptists' break with historic Anabaptist confession on social issues, see, for example, by the same author, *Mennonites and "Homosexuality": The Struggle to Become a Welcoming Church* (Harrisonburg, VA: Peace Theology Books, 2016), as well as *Gay and Mennonite* (blog), https://gaymenno.blogspot.com/p/home.html, and Rachel Waltner Goossen, "The Rise of LGBTQ Mennonite Leaders," *Anabaptist Historians* (blog), February 2, 2021, https://anabaptisthistorians.org/2021/02/02/the-rise-of-lgbtq-mennonite-leaders/. Not insignificantly, on September 21, 2015, two Anabaptist institutions, Goshen College and Eastern Mennonite University, jointly released a statement declaring that they were withdrawing as member institutions from the Coalition of Christian College and Universities (CCCU) because of the issue of sexuality, in order "to update their non-discrimination policies and allow the hiring of married gay and lesbian faculty." EMU's president added: "Eastern Mennonite University remains fully committed to our Christian mission and will do so as an institution rooted in the Anabaptist-Mennonite tradition which attempts to reflect Jesus' call to peacemaking and justice."

144. Parts of this chapter have been reproduced, with permission, from chapters 11, 12, and 13 of Timothy J. Demy, Mark J. Larson, and J. Daryl Charles, *The Reformers on War, Peace, and Justice* (Eugene, OR: Pickwick, 2019).

WORKS CITED

Augsburger, Myron. "Christian Pacifism." In *War: Four Christian Views*, edited by Robert G. Klouse, 79–97. Downers Grove, IL: InterVarsity, 1991.

Baylor, Michael G., ed. and trans. *The Radical Reformation.* Cambridge Texts in the History of Political Thought. Cambridge: Cambridge University Press, 1991.

Bender, Harold S. "The Anabaptist Vision." In *The Recovery of the Anabaptist Vision*, edited by Guy F. Hershberger, 29–56. Scottdale, PA: Herald Press, 1957. First published in *Church History* 13 [March 1944]: 3–24. Repr., *Mennonite Quarterly Review* 18 (April 1944): 67–88.

———. "A Brief Biography of Menno Simons." In *The Complete Writings of Menno Simons, c. 1496–1561*, edited by John C. Wenger, translated by Leonard Verduin, 3–29. Scottdale, PA: Mennonite Publishing House, 1956.

———. "Conrad Grebel." In *The Mennonite Encyclopedia: A Comprehensive Reference Work on the Anabaptist-Mennonite Movement*, edited by Harold S. Bender et al., 2:566–75. Scottdale, PA: Mennonite Publishing House, 1952.

———. "Conrad Grebel, the Founder of Swiss Anabaptism." *Church History* 7, no. 2 (June 1938): 157–78.

Biesecker-Mast, Gerald. "Anabaptist Separation and Arguments against the Sword in the Schleitheim Brotherly Union." *Mennonite Quarterly Review* 74 (2000): 381–402.

Blickle, Peter. *Revolution of 1525: The German Peasants' War from a New Perspective.* Translated by T. A. Brady Jr. and H. C. Erik Midelfort. Baltimore: Johns Hopkins University Press, 1981.

Buck, Lawrence P., and Jonathan W. Zophy, eds. *The Social History of the Reformation.* Columbus: Ohio State University Press, 1972.

Cameron, Euan. *The European Reformation.* 2nd ed. Oxford: Oxford University Press, 2012.

Charles, J. Daryl. "Patriots, Pacifists, or Both? Second Thoughts on Pre-Constantinian Early-Christian Attitudes toward Soldiering and War." *Logos: A Journal of Catholic Thought and Culture* 13, no. 2 (2010): 17–55.

Charles, J. Daryl, and Timothy J. Demy. *War, Peace, and Christianity: Questions and Answers from a Just-War Perspective.* Wheaton, IL: Crossway, 2010.

Clasen, Claus-Peter. *Anabaptism: A Social History, 1525–1618; Switzerland, Austria, Moravia, South and Central Germany.* Cambridge: Cambridge University Press, 1972.

Cohn, Norman. *The Pursuit of the Millennium: A History of Popular Religious and Social Movements in Europe from the Eleventh to the Sixteenth Century.* London: Secker & Warburg, 1957.

Demy, Timothy J., Mark J. Larson, and J. Daryl Charles. *The Reformers on War, Peace, and Justice*. Eugene, OR: Pickwick, 2019.

Deppermann, Klaus. *Melchior Hoffman: Social Unrest and Apocalyptic Visions in the Age of Reformation*. Translated by Malcolm Wren. Edinburgh: T&T Clark, 1987.

Dickens, A. G., and John Tonkin. *The Reformation in Historical Thought*. Cambridge, MA: Harvard University Press, 1985.

Dio Cassius. *Dio's Roman History*. Translated by Earnest Cary. Vol. 9. Loeb Classical Library. Cambridge, MA: Harvard University Press, 1969.

Durnbaugh, Donald F. *The Believers' Church: The History and Character of Radical Protestantism*. New York: Macmillan; London: Collier-Macmillan, 1968.

Egli, Emil, et al., eds. *Huldreich Zwinglis Sämtliche Werke*. Vol. 8. Leipzig: Heinsius, 1914.

Eire, Carlos M. N. *Reformations: The Early Modern World, 1450–1650*. New Haven: Yale University Press, 2016.

———. *War against the Idols*. Cambridge: Cambridge University Press, 1986.

Evan, G. R. *The Roots of the Reformation: Tradition, Emergence, and Rupture*. Downers Grove, IL: IVP Academic, 2012.

Fast, Heinold. "Conrad Grebel: The Covenant on the Cross." In Goertz and Klaassen, *Profiles of Radical Reformers*, 118–31.

Franz, Gunther. *Der deutsche Bauernkrieg*. 12th ed. Darmstadt: Wissenschaftliche Buchgesellschaft, 1984.

Friedmann, Robert. "Anabaptism and Protestantism." *Mennonite Quarterly Review* 24 (1950): 12–24.

———. *The Theology of Anabaptism: An Interpretation*. Studies in Anabaptist and Mennonite History 15. Scottdale, PA: Herald Press, 1975.

Gay and Mennonite (blog). https://gaymenno.blogspot.com/p/home.html.

Gero, Stephen. "Miles Gloriosus: The Christian and Military Service according to Tertullian." *Church History* 39, no. 3 (1970): 285–98.

Gerrish, B. A., ed. *Reformers in Profile*. Minneapolis: Fortress, 1967.

Geschicht-Buch der Hutterischen Brüder. Vienna: Carl Fromm, 1923.

Goertz, Hans-Jürgen. *Die Täufer: Geschichte und Deutung*. Munich: C.H. Beck, 1980.

Goertz, Hans-Jürgen, and Walter Klaassen, eds. *Profiles of Radical Reformers: Biographical Sketches from Thomas Müntzer to Paracelsus*. Scottdale, PA: Herald Press, 1982.

Goossen, Rachel Waltner. "The Rise of LGBTQ Mennonite Leaders." *Anabaptist Historians* (blog), February 2, 2021. https://anabaptisthistorians.org/2021/02/02/the-rise-of-lgbtq-mennonite-leaders/.

Grimsrud, Ted. "Anabaptism for the 21st Century." Peace Theology. https://peacetheology.net/anabaptist-convictions/anabaptism-for-the-21st-century/.

———. "The Anarchistic Appeal of the Bible: A Needed Story for Human Wellbeing." Thinking Pacifism. https://thinkingpacifism.net/2021/02/16/the-anarchistic-appeal-of-the-bible-a-needed-story-for-human-wellbeing-theological-memoir-11/.

———. *Mennonites and "Homosexuality": The Struggle to Become a Welcoming Church.* Harrisonburg, VA: Peace Theology Books, 2016.

Haas, Martin. "Michael Sattler: On the Way to Anabaptist Separation." In Goertz and Klaassen, *Profiles of Radical Reformers*, 132–43.

Haigh, Christopher. *English Reformations: Religion, Politics, and Society under the Tudors.* Oxford: Clarendon, 1993.

Hannemann, Manfred. *The Diffusion of the Reformation in South-Western Germany, 1518–1534.* Chicago: University of Chicago Press, 1975.

Helgeland, John. "Christians and the Roman Army, A.D. 173–337." *Church History* 43, no. 2 (1974): 149–63, 200.

———. "Christians and the Roman Army from Marcus Aurelius to Constantine." In *Aufstieg und Niedergang der römischen Welt: Geschichte und Kultur Roms im Spiegel der neueren Forschung*, edited by Hildegard Temporini and Wolfgang Haase, 2.23.1:724–834. Berlin: de Gruyter, 1979.

Helgeland, John, Robert J. Daly, and J. Patout Burns. *Christians and the Military: The Early Experience.* Philadelphia: Fortress, 1985.

Hillerbrand, Hans J. *The Division of Christendom: Christianity in the Sixteenth Century.* Louisville: Westminster John Knox, 2007.

———, ed. *The Reformation: A Narrative History Related by Contemporary Observers and Participants.* Repr., Grand Rapids, MI: Baker, 1978.

Hitchcock, James. "The Age of Reformations." *Touchstone*, September/October 2017, 36–40.

Horsch, John. "Menno Simons' Attitude toward the Anabaptists of Münster." *Mennonite Quarterly Review* 10 (1936): 55–72.

Horst, Irvin B. "Menno Simons: The New Man in Community." In Goertz and Klaassen, *Profiles of Radical Reformers*, 203–13.

———. *The Radical Brethren: Anabaptism and the English Reformation to 1558.* Bibliotheca Humanistica and Reformatorica 2. Nieuwkoop: B. de Graaf, 1972.

Hostetler, Beulah S. *American Mennonites and Protestant Movements.* Scottdale, PA: Herald Press, 1987.

Hsia, R. Po-Chia. "Munster and the Anabaptists." In *The German People and the Reformation*, edited by R. Po-Chia Hsia, 51–69. Ithaca, NY: Cornell University Press, 1988.

Hunter, David G. "A Decade of Research on Early Christians and Military Service." *Religious Studies Review* 18, no. 2 (1992): 87–94.

Die Indices Librorum Prohibitorum des sechzehnten Jahrhunderts. Tübingen: Mohr, 1886.

Johnson, James Turner. *The Quest for Peace: Three Moral Traditions in Western Cultural History.* Princeton: Princeton University Press, 1987.

Kessler, Johannes. *Johannes Kesslers Sabbata mit kleineren Schriften und Briefen.* Edited by Emil Egli. St. Gall: Fehr, 1902.

Kirchoff, Karl-Heinz. *Die Täufer in Münster, 1534/35.* Münster: Aschendorff, 1973.

Klaassen, Walter. *Anabaptism: Neither Catholic nor Protestant.* Waterloo, ON: Conrad Press, 1973.

Krahn, Cornelius. *Dutch Anabaptism: Origin, Spread, Life and Thought.* Scottdale, PA: Herald Press, 1981. Reprint, Eugene, OR: Wipf & Stock, 2004.

———. "Menno Simons." In *The Mennonite Encyclopedia: A Comprehensive Reference Work on the Anabaptist-Mennonite Movement,* vol. 3, edited by Harold S. Bender et al., 577–84. Scottdale, PA: Mennonite Publishing House, 1957.

Leithart, Peter J. *Defending Constantine: The Twilight of an Empire and the Dawn of Christendom.* Downers Grove, IL: IVP Academic, 2010.

Liechty, Daniel, ed. *Early Anabaptist Spirituality: Select Writings.* Classics of Western Spirituality. New York: Paulist Press, 1994.

Lindberg, Carter. *The European Reformations.* Oxford: Blackwell, 1996.

———, ed. *The European Reformations Sourcebook.* Oxford: Blackwell, 2000.

———. "Part V: 'Radical' Theologians." In *The Reformation Theologians: An Introduction to Theology in the Early Modern Period,* edited by Carter Lindberg, 325–77. Oxford: Blackwell, 2002.

Lualdi, Katharine Jackson, and Anne T. Thayer, eds. *Penitence in the Age of Reformations.* Aldershot: Ashgate, 2000.

MacCulloch, Diarmaid. *Reformation: Europe's House Divided, 1490–1700.* New York: Penguin Books, 2003.

MacGregor, Kirk R. *A Central European Synthesis of Radical and Magisterial Reform: The Sacramental Theology of Balthasar Hubmaier.* Lanham, MD: University Press of America, 2006.

McGrath, Alister. *The Intellectual Origins of the European Reformation.* Oxford: Basil Blackwell, 1987.

McLaughlin, R. Emmett. "The Radical Reformation." In *The Cambridge History of Christianity,* vol. 6, *Reform and Expansion, 1500–1660,* edited by R. Po-Chia Hsia, 37–55. Cambridge: Cambridge University Press, 2007.

Mecenseffy, Grete, ed. *Quellen zur Geschichte der Täufer,* vol. 11, Österreich, I. Gütersloh: Gerd Mohn, 1964.

Molhuysen, Philipp Christiann. *Overijsselsche Almanak voor Oudheid en Letteren.* Oldenzaal: Deventer, 1839.

Niebuhr, H. Richard. *The Social Sources of Denominationalism*. Cleveland: World Publishing Co., 1957.

Oberman, Heiko A. *The Reformation: Roots and Ramifications*. London: T&T Clark International, 2004.

———. *The Two Reformations: The Journey from the Last Days to the New World*. Edited by Donald Weinstein. New Haven: Yale University Press, 2003.

Ozment, Stephen. *The Age of Reform, 1250–1550: An Intellectual and Religious History of Late Medieval and Reformation Europe*. New Haven: Yale University Press, 1980.

Pettegree, Andrew, ed. *The Early Reformation in Europe*. Cambridge: Cambridge University Press, 1992.

Pipkin, H. Wayne, and John H. Yoder, eds. and trans. *Balthasar Hubmaier: Theologian of Anabaptism*. Scottdale, PA: Herald Press, 1989.

Roberts, Adrian John. "'Truth Is Unkillable': Non-Resistance, 'the Sword' and Magisterial Authority in the Theology of Balthasar Hubmaier, 1523–1528." MPhil thesis, University of Birmingham, 2011. https://etheses.bham.ac.uk//id/eprint/3624/1/Roberts12MPhil.pdf.

Roth, John D. "The Anabaptist Vision of Politics." *Plough Quarterly*, no. 24 (March 25, 2020), https://www.plough.com/en/topics/justice/politics/religious-liberty/the-anabaptist-vision-of-politics.

———. "Harmonizing the Scriptures: Swiss Brethren Understandings of the Relationship between the Old and New Testament during the Last Half of the Sixteenth Century." In *Radical Reformation Studies: Essays Presented to James M. Stayer*, edited by Werner O. Packull and Geoffrey L. Dipple, 35–52. Aldershot: Ashgate, 1999.

Rublack, Ulinka, ed. *The Oxford Handbook of the Protestant Reformations*. Oxford: Oxford University Press, 2017.

Russell, Paul A. *Lay Theology in the Reformation*. Cambridge: Cambridge University Press, 1986.

Sattler, Michael. "The Schleitheim Articles." In *The Radical Reformation*, edited by Michael G. Baylor, 172–80. Cambridge Texts in the History of Political Thought. Cambridge: Cambridge University Press, 1991.

Simons, Menno. *The Blasphemy of John of Leiden*. In *Complete Writings*, 33–50.

———. *The Complete Writings of Menno Simons, c. 1496–1561*. Edited by John C. Wenger. Translated by Leonard Verduin. Scottdale, PA: Mennonite Publishing House, 1956.

———. *Foundation of Christian Doctrine*. In *Complete Writings*, 105–226.

———. *A Pathetic Supplication to All Magistrates*. In *Complete Writings*, 525–31.

———. *A Reply to False Accusations*. In *Complete Writings*, 543–77.

———. *Reply to Gellius Faber . . . Conversion, Call, and Testimony*. In *Complete Writings*, 668–76.

Snyder, Arnold. "The Influence of the Schleitheim Articles on the Anabaptist Movement: An Historical Evaluation." *Mennonite Quarterly Review* 63 (1989): 323–44.

Stayer, James M. *Anabaptists and the Sword*. Lawrence, KS: Coronado Press, 1972.

———. *The German Peasants' War and Anabaptist Community of Goods*. McGill-Queen's Studies in the History of Religion. Montreal: McGill-Queen's University Press, 1991.

———. "Melchior Hoffman and the Sword." *Mennonite Quarterly Review* 45 (1971): 270–77.

———. "The Münsterite Rationalization of Bernhard Rothmann." *Journal of the History of Ideas* 28 (1967): 179–92.

———. "Was Dr. Kuehler's Conception of Early Dutch Anabaptism Historically Sound? The Historical Discussion of Anabaptist Münster 450 Years Later." *Mennonite Quarterly Review* 60 (1986): 261–88.

Strauss, Gerald. "Three Kinds of 'Christian Freedom': Law, Liberty, and License in the German Reformation." In *Enacting the Reformation in Germany*, 291–306. Aldershot: Variorum, 1993.

Swift, Louis J. *The Early Fathers on War and Military Service*. Message of the Fathers of the Church 19. Wilmington, DE: Michael Glazier, 1983.

Wallace, Peter G. *The Long European Reformation: Religion, Political Conflict, and the Search for Conformity, 1350–1750*. 2nd ed. New York: Palgrave Macmillan, 2012.

Wenger, John C. "The Schleitheim Confession of Faith." *Mennonite Quarterly Review* 19 (1945): 243–53.

Williams, George H. "Radical Elements in the Reformation." In *The Reformation: Revival or Revolution?*, edited by W. Stanford Reid, 30–36. New York: Rinehart and Winston, 1968.

———. *The Radical Reformation*. 3rd ed. Kirksville, MO: Truman State University Press, 1995.

———, ed. *Spiritual and Anabaptist Writers: Documents Illustrative of the Radical Reformation*. Library of Christian Classics 25. Philadelphia: Westminster, 1968.

Windhorst, Christof. "Balthasar Hubmaier: Professor, Preacher, Politician." In Goertz and Klaassen, *Profiles of Radical Reformers*, 44–57.

Wray, Frank J. "The Anabaptist Doctrine of the Restitution of the Church." *Mennonite Quarterly Review* 28 (1954): 186–96.

Yoder, Jess. "The Frankenthal Debate with the Anabaptists in 1571: Purpose, Procedure, Participants." *Mennonite Quarterly Review* 36 (1962): 14–35.

———. "The Frankenthal Disputation, Part II: Outcome Issues, Debating Methods." *Mennonite Quarterly Review* 36 (1962): 116–42.

Yoder, John Howard. *Nevertheless: The Varieties and Shortcomings of Religious Pacifism.* 2nd ed. Scottdale, PA: Herald Press, 1992.

———. *The Original Revolution: Essays on Christian Pacifism.* Scottdale, PA: Herald Press, 1971.

———. *The Politics of Jesus.* 2nd ed. Grand Rapids, MI: Eerdmans, 1994.

———. *What Would You Do?* Scottdale, PA: Herald Press, 1983.

———. *When War Is Unjust: Being Honest in Just-War Thinking.* 2nd ed. Maryknoll, NY: Orbis Books, 1996.

Young, Frances. "The Early Church: Military Service, War and Peace." *Theology* 92 (1989): 491–503.

Zeman, Jarold Knox. *The Anabaptists and the Czech Brethren in Moravia, 1526–1628.* Studies in European History 20. The Hague: Mouton, 1969.

Zijpp, Nanne van der. "Münster Anabaptists." In *The Mennonite Encyclopedia: A Comprehensive Reference Work on the Anabaptist-Mennonite Movement,* vol. 3, edited by Harold S. Bender et al., 779–85. Scottdale, PA: Mennonite Publishing House, 1969.

Zwingli, Ulrich. *Catabaptistarum Strophas Elenchus.* Zürich: Christoph Fropschauer, 1545. Reprinted in *Huldreich Zwinglis Sämtliche Werke* (Zürich: Berichthaus, 1961), 6:1–196.

CONTRIBUTORS

JOHN ASHCROFT served as the seventy-ninth attorney general of the United States of America. He received his degree with honors from Yale in 1964, and he earned his JD from the University of Chicago Law School in 1967 and then went on to practice law in Missouri until entering politics in 1972, when he became the state auditor for Missouri. He then became the assistant attorney general, serving from 1975 to 1977. In 1977, he became the attorney general of Missouri, serving in that capacity until 1984. From 1985 to 1992, Mr. Ashcroft was the governor of Missouri. In 1995, he was elected a US senator from Missouri. Mr. Ashcroft has the distinction of having dealt with issues of security and peace in a variety of roles, having served in both the executive and legislative branches and at the state and federal level, most notably as Missouri's governor (and thus commander in chief of the state militia and chief law enforcement official). President George W. Bush announced Mr. Ashcroft as his pick for attorney general on December 22, 2000, and he served for four years (through February 2005). Upon reentering private life, he serves in numerous capacities, including as Distinguished Professor of Law and Government at Regent University in Virginia Beach, Virginia.

H. DAVID BAER, PHD, is a professor in the Department of Theology, Philosophy, and Classical Languages at Texas Lutheran University. His areas of specialization include religious freedom, communism, Lutherans in Hungary, history, and ethics and politics. He took his BA from Oberlin College, his MTS from Candler School of Theology at Emory University, and his PhD from the University of Notre Dame. The author of *The Struggle of Hungarian Lutherans under Communism* (Texas A&M

University Press, 2006), Baer received the 2013 Ambassador for Peace Award from the European Leadership Conference of Universal Peace. The award is given to those individuals whose lives exemplify the ideal of living for the sake of others and who dedicate themselves to practices that promote universal moral values, strong family life, interreligious cooperation, international harmony, renewal of the United Nations, a responsible public media, and the establishment of a culture of peace.

NIGEL BIGGAR, PHD, is a member of the Faculty of Theology and Religion at the University of Oxford, serves as the Regius Professor of Moral and Pastoral Theology, and is director of the McDonald Centre for Theology, Ethics, and Public Life, a research institute at the University of Oxford. Biggar's research interests include the ethics of nationalism and empire, the ethics of individual rights and of jurisprudence, just war reasoning, the principle of double effect and the ethics of killing, the concept of proportionality, the moral vocation of universities, and the relationship between Christian religious concepts and moral life. He is the author of *Between Kin and Cosmopolis: An Ethic of the Nation* (James Clarke, 2014), *In Defence of War* (Oxford University Press, 2013, 2014), and *Behaving in Public: How to Do Christian Ethics* (Eerdmans, 2011); editor of *Burying the Past: Making Peace and Doing Justice after Civil Conflict* (Georgetown University Press, 2003); and coeditor of *Religious Voices in Public Places* (Oxford University Press, 2009).

JOSEPH E. CAPIZZI, PHD, is the Ordinary Professor of Moral Theology/Ethics and associate dean for graduate studies in the School of Theology and Religious Studies at the Catholic University of America. Capizzi is also the executive director of the Institute for Human Ecology at CUA. The author of *Politics, Justice, and War: Christian Governance and the Ethics of Warfare* (Oxford University Press, 2015) and coauthor of *A Catechism for Business: Tough Ethical Questions and Insights from Catholic Teaching* (CUA Press, 2014), he teaches in the areas of social and political theology, with special interests in issues of peace and war, citizenship, political authority, and Augustinian theology. He has written, lectured, and published widely on just war doctrine, bioethics, the history of moral theology, and political liberalism. He received his BA from the University of Virginia, his MTS from Emory University, and his MA and PhD in theology from the University of Notre Dame.

J. DARYL CHARLES, PhD, is an affiliate scholar of the John Jay Institute and has served as the Acton Institute Affiliated Scholar in Theology & Ethics. Charles also serves as a contributing editor of *Providence: A Journal of Christianity and American Foreign Policy* and is author, co-author, or coeditor of twenty-one books, including *Virtue amidst Vice* (Sheffield Academic Press, 1997), *Between Pacifism and Jihad: Just War and Christian Tradition* (InterVarsity Press, 2005), *Retrieving the Natural Law* (Eerdmans, 2008), *War, Peace, and Christianity: Questions and Answers from a Just-War Perspective* (Crossway, 2010), *The Just War Tradition: An Introduction* (ISI Books, 2012), *Natural Law and Religious Freedom* (Routledge, 2018), and most recently, *America and the Just War Tradition: A History of U.S. Conflicts* (University of Notre Dame Press, 2019), and *The Reformers on War, Peace, and Justice* (Pickwick, 2019). His work has appeared in both academic and more popular journals including *Journal of Church and State*, *Philosophia Christi*, *Journal of Religious Ethics*, *First Things*, *Logos: A Journal of Catholic Thought and Culture*, *Journal of Lutheran Ethics*, *Ethics & Medicine*, *Christian Scholar's Review*, *Modern Age*, *National Catholic Bioethics Quarterly*, *Pro Ecclesia*, *Christianity Today*, *Public Discourse*, and *Touchstone*. Charles has been invited to address the US Army's Command and General Staff College in Ft. Leavenworth, Kansas, in 2012, 2016, and 2018 on the topic of just war as part of the CGSC's ethics training. He has taught at Taylor University and Union University, was a 2013–14 visiting professor in the honors program at Berry College, was a 2003–4 visiting fellow at the Institute for Faith & Learning at Baylor University, was a 2007–8 William E. Simon visiting fellow in religion and public life at the James Madison Program, Princeton University, and is a fellow of the James Madison Society. Charles's research interests include faith and public life, the ethics of war and peace, the natural law, and criminal justice ethics. Before entering the university classroom full-time he did public-policy work in criminal justice in Washington, DC.

DARRELL COLE, PHD, is assistant professor of religion at Drew University and has been part of the Drew faculty since 2002. Cole teaches courses in religious ethics and theology. His primary areas of specialization are religious engagement with politics, business, and medicine. Author of *When God Says War Is Right: A Christian Perspective on When and How to Fight* (Waterbrook, 2002) and coauthor of *The Virtue of War: Reclaiming the Classic Christian Traditions East and West* (Regina Orthodox

Press, 2004), he has a BA from Lynchburg College, an MA Phil From Ohio University, an MAR from Yale Divinity School, a ThM from Duke Divinity School, and a PhD from the University of Virginia. Cole's work has appeared in scholarly and popular journals such as *The Journal of Religious Ethics, Pro Ecclesia, Notre Dame Journal of Law, Ethics and Public Policy,* and *First Things.*

TIMOTHY J. DEMY, PHD, THD, is a retired commander in the US Navy and teaches military ethics, international relations, and leadership at the US Naval War College. Demy served twenty-seven years as a chaplain in the US Navy, the United States Marine Corps, and the United States Coast Guard. From 2010 to the present he has served as academic fellow of the Potomac Institute for Policy Studies (Center for Neurotechnology Studies, and Program in History, Social and Strategic Studies) and is a US Adviser for International Network for the Study of War and Religion in the Modern World. He is coauthor of *War, Peace, and Christianity: Questions and Answers from a Just-War Perspective* (Crossway, 2011), editor of *The U.S. Naval Institute on Leadership Ethics* (Naval Institute Press, 2017), and coeditor of *War and Religion: An Encyclopedia of Faith and Conflict* (3 vols.; ABC-CLIO, 2017) and *Military Ethics and Emerging Technologies* (Routledge, 2014).

ERIC PATTERSON, PHD, is a professor at and the former dean of the Robertson School of Government at Regent University. His research and teaching focus on religion and politics, ethics and international affairs, and just war thinking in the context of contemporary conflict. Prior to his arrival at Regent, Patterson served as associate director of the Berkley Center for Religion, Peace & World Affairs and visiting assistant professor in the Department of Government at Georgetown University. As part of the Berkley Center's government outreach program he has spoken to and led seminars at the US Military Academy (West Point), the US Naval Academy (Annapolis), the Armed Forces Chaplains Center, National Defense University, the Pentagon, the Naval Postgraduate School, the Foreign Service Institute, and other government venues. As part of his considerable US government experience, Patterson served as a White House Fellow and special assistant to the director of the US Office of Personnel Management and spent two stints in the State Department's Bureau of Political and Military Affairs. He continues to serve as an officer and commander in the Air National Guard. Patterson is the author or editor of fourteen books, including *Just American Wars: Ethical Dilemmas in U.S. Military History* (Routledge, 2018), *Ending Wars Well: Just War Thinking and Post-Conflict* (Yale University Press, 2012), and *Ethics beyond War's End* (Georgetown University Press, 2012). He has also edited two volumes on Christian realism and has been published in numerous journals including *Survival, International Studies Perspectives, Journal for the Scientific Study of Religion, International Politics, Journal of Diplomacy and International Affairs,* and *Journal of Political Science,* among others.

KEITH J. PAVLISCHEK, PhD, is a contributing editor of *Providence: A Journal of Christianity and American Foreign Policy* and a military affairs expert with a focus on just war doctrine and the ethics of war. He retired as a colonel in the US Marine Corps in 2007 after thirty years of active and reserve service, having served in Desert Storm, Bosnia, and Iraq and with the US Central Command and the Office of the Director of National Intelligence. He is the author of *John Courtney Murray and the Dilemma of Religious Toleration* (Truman State University Press, 1994) and numerous articles, including a chapter on the ethics of asymmetric warfare in the Ashgate Research Companion to Military Ethics (2015).

DANIEL STRAND, PhD, is a professor at the US Air Force's Air War College at Maxwell Air Force Base, Alabama. He previously was a postdoctoral fellow in the Center for Political Thought and Leadership at the Arizona State University and a contributing editor of *Providence: A Journal of Christianity and American Foreign Policy*. His scholarly interests are in history of political thought, religion and politics, and the thought of St. Augustine of Hippo.

MARK TOOLEY is president of the Washington, DC–based Institute on Religion and Democracy and editor of IRD's foreign policy journal *Providence: A Journal of Christianity and American Foreign Policy*. Prior to joining the IRD in 1994, Tooley worked for the Central Intelligence Agency. A graduate of Georgetown University and lifelong United Methodist, he has been active in United Methodist renewal since 1988. He is the author of *The Peace That Almost Was: The Forgotten Story of the 1861 Washington Peace Conference and the Final Attempt to Avert the Civil War* (Thomas Nelson, 2015), *Methodism and Politics in the 20th Century* (Bristol House, 2012), and *Taking Back the United Methodist Church* (Bristol House, 2008).

accountability (political), 1, 18, 70. *See also* legitimate authority

Adams, John: on Jonathan Mayhew's sermon "A Discourse concerning the Unlimited Submission and Non-Resistance to the High Powers," (1750), ixn.1, 152n.79

Afghanistan, 171–72; Church of England's response to war in, 172, 177n.50; Methodist Bishops' response to war in, 205

Alexander of Hales: and Catholic doctrine of punishment by legitimate authority, 37

Ambrose of Milan, St.: belief that just wars are always either defensive in nature or waged for the punishment of wrongdoing, 70; letter to Emperor Theodosius on massacre and ecclesiastical discipline due to emperor's disproportionate act of punishment in Thessalonica, 70; similar views as St. John Chrysostom on need for charity (*caritas*) to rule in matters of war and peace, 69. *See also* Orthodox churches

American Baptist Churches USA. *See* Baptists

American ethics in war: John Ashcroft on, vii

American Civil War. *See* Civil War (U.S.)

American War for Independence: John Wesley and early Methodism's responses to, 186–87; and Reformed view of war, 145

Ames, William, 162; considered "wrong intention" in wars, 163; straightforward presentation of *jus ad bellum* and *jus in bello* Just War criteria as from Aquinas, 162–63, 177; use of method of casuistry used by Thomas Aquinas in moral reasoning, 158–59

Anabaptism/Anabaptists: arguments against war and use of force, 253–303; birth of, in Switzerland with Swiss Brethren, 256; creation of "The New Jerusalem" and lethal resistance to magistrates in Münster, 274; development of two early branches of "evangelicals" and "pacifists," and "apocalyptic" and "revolutionary" in, 255; and "failed Münster experiment," 255; and Melchior Hoffman,

311

Anabaptism/Anabaptists (*cont.*)
Hans Hut, and Bernhard
Rothman as "apocalyptic"
visionaries "in early sixteenth
century revolutionary" movement
and takeover of Münster by force,
251, 255, 266, 269, 271,
291nn.83–84; as part of the
"radical Reformation," according
to Zwingli, 159; as reaction to
violence in society (religious and
state), 256; and *Schleitheim
Confession of Faith* as charter
document of, 261–62;. *See also*
Grebel, Conrad; Mantz, Felix;
Sattler, Michael; Simons, Menno
Anglicanism/Anglicans. *See* Church
of England
Aquinas, St. Thomas (on Just War),
3, 7–9, 12, 23n.7, 35–36, 51, 111,
115n.53, 134–35, 145, 148n.27,
149n.37, 153nn81–82, 158–59,
161–62, 175n.6, 285n.24; moral
reasoning, 158–59; on principles
of *jus ad bellum* in *Summa
Theologica*, 159
armed humanitarian intervention.
See humanitarian intervention
armed resistance, 124–26; Calvin and
John Knox's views on political
authority, 142–45; Lutheran
doctrine of resistance, 99–100,
107–11
Asbury, Francis, 187; avoidance of
comment on his support of
American War for Independence,
186–87, 192
assassination, of U.S. President
McKinley in 1901, 195
Augustine, St., vii, xn.4, 1–2, 5*f*, 9, 12,
23n.1, 24n.10, 24n.15, 25n.16,

38–39, 50–51, 52n.9, 55n53,
55n.55, 73, 75, 81n.57, 89, 111,
132–34, 149n.44, 159, 161, 184,
246n.66, 285n.24; on concept of
caritas, 1, 9, 159; Cranmer on,
161; and criteria for Just War, ix;
discussed in *Augustine on War &
Military Service* (Wynn), 31;
on end of war as "better state
of peace," ix; Luther on, 161
authority. *See* legitimate authority

Backus, Isaac: *An Appeal to the Public
for Religious Liberty, against the
Oppressions of the Present Day*
(1773), 244n.44; leading pulpit
orator of the American Revolu-
tion who helped champion the
cause of religious ("soul") liberty
in the colonies, 230, 244n.44
Bainton, Roland, 23n.9, 135–36,
149n.42
Balkans Conflict: response by Church
of England Bishop Richard
Harries in *Inside-Out: The
Balkans Conflict*, 171, 177n.46;
and use of NATO in, 171
Baptists: American Baptist Churches
USA, Cooperative Baptist
Fellowship, National Baptist
Convention USA, National
Baptist Convention of America,
Seventh Day Baptist General
Conference, Progressive National
Baptist Convention, and other
Baptist churches in the United
States' participation in the
Baptist Joint Committee for
Religious Liberty, 231; on the
American Civil War, 232,
242n.1, 245n.50, 250–52;

on championing religious (soul) liberty, 230; churches and theology falling under the "Baptistic umbrella," 224; on the Cold War, 232; early Baptist Americans' views on America as "the new Zion" and defense of War of 1812, 231; German Baptists 'Dunkers' in U.S. Civil War, 219; on Just War Tradition, 219–52; notable Baptist authors on issues of war, 229; religious freedom and, 228–30; responses to America's involvement in various wars, 242; "soul freedom" and "soul liberty" concern of Baptists in America, 228–29; Southern Baptist Convention resolutions on peace and war (1936, 1940), conscientious objectors (1946), peace negotiations in Vietnam (1968), Operation Desert Storm (1991), terrorism (2002), and the liberation of Iraq (2003), 234; Southern Baptist Convention's Ethics & Religious Liberty Commission (ERLC), 238; Southern Baptists Ethics & Religious Liberty Commission as the denominational entity promoting religious liberty, 231; and wars involving America, 230–32; on World War I, 232; on World War II, 232. *See also* George, Timothy; Graham, Billy; Helwys, Thomas; King, Martin Luther, Jr.; Land, Richard; Leland, John; Mohler, R. Albert, Jr.; Smyth, John; Stillman, Stanley; Tookey, Elia

Barth, Karl: on just wars, 149n.39; opposition to casuistry as method of moral reasoning, 162

Basil the Great, St.: on evil in war-fighting, 73; on need for moderation in soldiering, 69–70; recognition and discussion of moral hazards of waging war, 67–68. *See also* Orthodox churches

Baylor, Michael: comparing vision of the magisterial reformers with that of the radical and Anabaptist reformers in *The Radical Reformation*, 255, 282n.2, 284n.17, 287n.53, 290n.72, 298

Bell, George (G. K. A.): on war with Germany and the Nazi State, 162, 176n.19

Bell, Nelson L., 236

Bellarmine, Robert, 33, 37–46, 51, 53n.22, 53n.30, 53n.33, 55n.55

Bender, Harold: writing on theological underpinnings of Conrad Grebel's understanding of Christians' relationship to the world and political authority, 259, 283n.13, 286n.29, 286n.35, 286n.37, 287n.47, 290n.78, 292n.93, 293n.100, 298, 301, 304

Beza, Theodore, 107; teaching on lesser magistrates and legitimate authority, 144–45, 146n.3, 152nn.76–77

Biggar, Niger: on Balkans Conflict response, 171, 177n.43; on importance on "national life" versus "cosmopolitanism," 166; on Just War tradition in *In Defense of War*, 169

Bosnian War, xiii, 309

Bouwsma, William J., 154; on Calvin's demythologizing of war, 133; on Calvin's opposition to a "heroic" view of war as an end in itself, 133; on Calvin's support for a Republican form of government (in last chapter of his *Institutes*), 125, 147n.9; quoting Calvin's commentary on Genesis 14 (on *Imago Dei*), 148n.32

Bullinger, Heinrich, 124, 139–44, 146n.4, 147n.16, 148n.27, 151n.58, 151n.67, 152n.78, 273, 277; as "key source for the revival of the holy war idea among some Puritans during the English Civil War," 140

Calvin, John, 2, 4, 12, 20, 112n.6, 116n.99; on Cicero and just war doctrine, 139, 150n55; on "distinct roles for ecclesiastical and civil authorities," 127; and Heinrich Bullinger more cautious than John Knox on "armed resistance," 152n.78; on "just war," 123–54; on "law of charity" for armed men who cast down their arms after being conquered, 139; refusal to support rebellion by "private persons," 144; teaching on legitimate political authority, 107; and treatment of noncombatants in war, 138; wary of democracy, especially rebellion or revolt, degenerating into anarchy, 126

Canada/Canadians, 182, 239; Canadian Baptists response to War of 1812, 245n.48

caritas (biblical and Christian concept of "charity," "love of neighbor,"

"neighbor-love" concepts in just war thinking), ix, 1, 6, 16, 159; Ambrose of Milan and John Chrysostom on need for, in war to achieve peace, 69–70; "Golden Rule" as, 3; meaning of, as "protecting one's neighbor," 9; Pope Benedict XVI on, in *Caritas in veritate* (2009), 46, 54n.44, 54n.48, 55; St. Ambrose and other early Church Fathers on, as making justice more likely by working against the motives of self-interest in and after war, 70; St. Augustine's writing on his conception of, 1, 9, 159; Thomas Aquinas on, 175n.6

Carter, Jimmy: on Vietnam War and Operation Iraqi Freedom as unjust wars, 220. *See also* Baptists; Evangelicalism/Evangelicals

Catholicism/Catholics: Catechism sections on "just war," 29; and just war thinking, 29–55; Pope Pius XII's 1944 Christmas address seeming to recognize the contemporary irrelevance of war, 44; and pre-Constantinian view of Church against use of force by Christians and shift after Constantine became a Christian and began ruling over Rome, 32; statements and teaching on the "use of force as an instrument of peace," 32–37; statements by the National Council of Catholic Bishops (U.S. Catholic Bishops) in pastoral letters on war and the threat of war, including nuclear war, 16, 26n.24, 27, 32, 52n.10, 52n.13, 55, 56, 167, 176n.30, 178;

views on use of force by the state
to protect the common good, 37.
See also Aquinas, St. Thomas;
Augustine, St.; Bellarmine,
Robert; *Challenge of Peace, The*;
Gentili, Alberico; *Harvest of
Justice Is Sown in Peace, The*;
Jerome, St.; Súarez, Francisco;
Vitoria, Francisco de
Challenge of Peace, The (U.S. Catholic
Bishops' pastoral letter, 1983), 16,
26n.24, 27, 52n.10, 52n.13, 55,
167, 176n.30, 178
charter. *See* UN Charter
child soldiers: R. Albert Mohler, Jr.
podcast on, 240, 247n.85
China: and consideration of humanitarian intervention as member of
UN Security Council, 174
Chrysostom, St. John, 68–69
Church of England: appreciation
and application of "casuistry"
style of moral reasoning, 162;
Board for Social Responsibility
of the General Synod on nuclear
deterrence, 167–68; connection
with scholastic traditions and
natural law scholarship of the pre-
Reformation era in modern era,
158–59; maintaining of Luther's
soteriology while sympathizing
with desire for unity of Church
and maintaining scholarship from
classic Catholic scholars such as
Aquinas and some yearning for
reunification of Christendom in
1630s and 1640s as well as in the
Anglo-Catholic movement from
1830ff, 158; position on nuclear
weapons in *The Church and the
Bomb*, 167–68; on rediscovery of

just war tradition, 167; response
to Afghanistan War, 172;
response to Iraq War, 171;
response to Kosovo War, 171;
Richard Harries on nuclear
deterrence in *Christianity and
War in the Nuclear Age*, 169; on
use of force, 158–59; use of
"multidisciplinary working
parties" to discuss issues and
determine positions and
responses to government on wars,
nuclear weapons, and other
issues, 162. *See also* Ames,
William; Bell, George (G. K. A.);
Biggar, Nigel; Fisher, David;
Maurice, Frederick Dennison
Cicero, Marcus Tullius: Calvin on,
139, 150n.55; influence on
classical just war thinking
and tradition, 6, 150n.55, 154;
On Duties, 150n.55, 154;
outside influence on Just War
Tradition referred to by Calvin
and others, 6
civilians. *See* discrimination
Civil War (U.S.): Baptists' response in,
232; Methodist's support in, 194
civil wars: Catholic mediation in
Mozambique civil war, 22;
ending, through use of Track 2
diplomacy of faith-based
institutions, 22; English Civil
War and Puritan revival of
Holy War idea, 24; from Old
Testament Israelite encounters,
24, 141; prevention of civil
war and protection of churches
by political authorities, 256;
Syrian civil war, 174, 239
Clausewitz, Carl von, 16, 222, 243n.7

Clement of Alexandria, 78n.9; on moral limitations of the use of force as being built into the very theological justification of force, which is a peace-seeking justice, 62–63. *See also* Orthodox churches

combatants: distinguishing from noncombatants, 2; and laws of armed conflict (LOAC), 2. *See also* noncombatants, Numbers 31 on; nonstate actors; terrorism/ terrorists

conciliation: defined, 5*f*; discussed in *Ending Wars Well* (Patterson); third element of *jus post bellum*, 5*f*, ultimate, 5*f*. See also *jus post bellum*; just war thinking; reconciliation

Constantine the Great: as Christian warrior and view of Eusebius, 64; and pre-Constantinian view against use of force by Christians and shift after Constantine became a Christian and began ruling over Rome, 32

conventions (international treaties). *See* international law; UN Charter; *specific conventions and international treatiesby name*

Cooperative Baptist Fellowship. *See* Baptists

counterterrorism. *See* terrorism/ terrorists

crusades/crusaders, 10–11, 135, 245n.53, 247n.77, 270; Calvin on the "Holy War idea," 135; Crusades (Christian), 13; 85; crusading idea as understood by England's Puritans, 135; evangelistic crusaders, 234;

Luther's rejection of, 95–99, 110–11; of Münster (Germany), 270–71; *Reconquista* (reconquered) and meaning of, in terms of taking back territory conquered by advancing Muslim armies from Western Europe to Persia, 13; *See also* Holy War

Declaration of Independence, U.S. (1776), vii, 107

"Declaration of the United Colonies on the Causes and Necessities of Taking Up Arms" (1775), 242n.42

democracy: Calvin on, 125–26, 142; Methodism political involvement in and support of wars by U.S. and, 193–94, 201; and resistance to tyranny, 152n77; Roger Williams on tragedy of war and, 235, 244n.35

deterrence (nuclear): and David Fisher's moral defense of UK policy on, in *Morality and the Bomb*, 169; and denouncing of, by Methodist Bishops in 1984, 204; Oliver O'Donovan's moral argument against, in *Peace and Certainty*, 168, 176n.34; United Methodist Bishops' statement against, in *In Defense of Creation*, 204. *See also* nuclear war; nuclear weapons

diplomacy: formal during prewar phase, 21; and the need for "holistic approach to Christian thinking" on war and peacemaking, 21; outside of traditional government-to-government channels, 21–22; *See also* Track 2 diplomacy

disarmament: bilateral, 168;
multilateral, to avoid instability,
167; Methodist Bishops calling
for "total" (of all weapons, both
nuclear and conventional) in
1984 General Conference, 204;
Methodist Bishops in 1960
calling for "mutual" and
"complete," 202; northern
Methodist Bishops for
"complete," in 1928, 198;
southern Methodist Bishops in
1922 on, 197; unilateral, and
dangers of, 168. *See also* nuclear
war; nuclear weapons
discrimination (*jus in bello* principle
of civilian/noncombatant
immunity), 5*f*, Aquinas on, 35;
and asymmetrical warfare and
air strike technology, 46; contemporary Orthodox teaching on, 70;
St. Basil (the Great) on, 68
distinction (*jus in bello* principle in
determining combatants and
noncombatants), 5*f*, 6, 164
Durnbaugh, Donald, on "radical
Reformation," cultural upheaval
during era of Reformation,
253–54; 283n.3, 283n.11,
285n.25, 290n.76, 299

Eastern Orthodox Churches.
*See Eastern Orthodox churches
by autocephalous church names*
Elshtain, Jean Bethke: presentation
on "Just War and Humanitarian
Intervention" (2001), 27; writing
on Just War Doctrine in *Just War
Theory* (1992), 25, 27
Estates (Luther's Three Estates).
See Three Estates, or "Orders"

Eusebius of Caesarea: on military
service by Christians as allowable,
64–65; view of Constantine, a
political leader of the Byzantine
Empire and a warrior, as the
consummate Christian soldier
and model for the lower level
of Christianity, 64. *See also*
Orthodox Churches
Evangelicalism/Evangelicals: avoiding
national security issues in some
cases, 2; Billy Graham as leader,
234, 252; Carl F. H. Henry as
voice, 234–37, 247n.72, 248n.95;
former U.S. president Jimmy
Carter on Vietnam War and
Operation Iraqi Freedom as
unjust wars, 220; on Iraq War,
248n.93; movement among
Protestant mainline and
nondenominational churches,
colleges, and universities, 2;
Protestant evangelicals typically
unaware of the historic teachings
on just war thinking, 2–3; R.
Albert Mohler, Jr., addressing
difficult issues and not avoiding
important social and cultural
concerns, 239–40. *See also*
Anabaptism/Anabaptists;
Baptists; Carter, Jimmy; Graham,
Billy; Henry, Carl F. H.; King,
Martin Luther, Jr.; Methodism/
Methodists

faith-based NGOs, use in Track 2
diplomacy to end civil wars, 22.
See also *jus post bellum*
Fisher, David: defense of nuclear
deterrence programs in *Morality
and the Bomb*, 169; on Just War

Fisher, David (*cont.*)
Tradition's application to Gulf
War (2003), invasion of Iraq,
terrorism, and genocide in
Morality and War, 169, 176n.41
force (use of): Church of England
thought on, 158–59; C. S. Lewis
on distinction in Jesus's directive
to avoid use of force in personal
interactions, 17; defined, 16;
distinguished from violence, 7,16;
as an instrument of peace in
Catholic statements and teaching,
32–37; and "levels-of-analysis
error," 17; in Orthodox Church
thinking about war and international relations and never using
immoral means,175; presumption
against use of force, 16–17;
Reinhold Niebuhr on use of force
as "lesser evil," 15; restrained use
of force, 22; Thomas Aquinas on,
7–8, 159; as viewed by classic
and Anglican scholars, 158–59;
See also *jus in bello*
forgiveness. *See* conciliation;
reconciliation; *jus post bellum*

Geneva Conventions (and additional
protocols). *See* international law
genocide: application of Just War
Tradition with regard to, in
Morality and War (Fisher), 169,
176n.41; Methodists' 2000
General Conference on response
to, 204; moral failure to intervene
in Rwanda, 173
Gentili, Alberico: definition of just
war, 163; distinction between
"preventative" and "preemptive"
war, 163; influence on Hugo

Grotius, 164; on just cause in
jus ad bellum, 163
George, Timothy: on Baptists as
"staunch advocates of religious
liberty, the priesthood of all
believers, and the inviolability of
the individual conscience before
God," 232–33, 243n.15, 246n.56,
250; on Puritan views of war,
141, 152n.68, 224
Global War on Terrorism (GWOT).
See terrorism/terrorists
Goertz, Hans-Jürgen: argument that
Anabaptism indeed *was* closely
connected to the revolutionary
peasant struggles of the day,
which then informs the social
context of Anabaptism's birth in
Switzerland, 256, 284n.18,
286n.34, 287n.54, 289n,65,
293n.103, 299–300, 303
Gouge, William, 151n.66, 154;
adoption of Old Testament views
on war as valid, 140; among more
radical Puritan revolutionaries,
139; and Heinrich Bullinger's
thought as compared to Calvin
on the Christian understanding
of restraint in war and distinction
of non-combatants, 142;
understanding of Puritan and
Protestant communities as
analogous to Israel in biblical
interpretation of defense and war,
141; views on "Holy War," 136
Graham, Billy: and evangelistic
crusades, 234; as "face and voice
of American evangelicalism in
post–World War II America,"
234; visits to South Korea and
Vietnam, 234, 246n.63, 252

Grebel, Conrad, 254, 257–63, 283n.9, 286n.27, 286n.30, 286n.32, 286nn.35–38, 287nn.39–40; 287n.43; 287n.47, 298; baptizing of adult believer for first time in 1525, 259; break with Zwingli over "believer's baptism," security authority over church affairs, and whether a Christian could serve as a magistrate, 257–58; questioning of state control of church affairs in October 1523 disputation, 258

Grotius, Hugo, 3, 152n.80, 153n.83, 156, 163–64, 178; *De jure belli et pacis* (1625), 164; as just war theorist, 184; among writers who developed Just War Tradition as the Western moral tradition on war during the modern period, 141, 153, 164

guerrillas (Marxist): *Should a Christian Support Guerrillas?* (Harries), 169; United Methodists' Board of Global Ministries granting to groups in support of, in El Salvador, 204

Gulf War (Persian Gulf), 24n.14, 28, 169, 237, 247n.74, 250; Anglican response to in 1991, 69; Baptists' response to in 1991, 232

Harakas, Stanley, as contributor to debates on war as a "lesser evil" or "lesser good," 76

Harries, Richard: on nuclear deterrence programs in UK in *Christianity and War in the Nuclear Age*, 169; *Should a Christian Support Guerrillas?*, 169

Harvest of Justice Is Sown in Peace, The, 26n.24, 27, 52n.13, 56

Helwys, Thomas, 223–24; belief that government is divinely ordained, and participation in it by Christians is not prohibited, 225–26; break with John Smyth's apolitical, pacificist Anabaptist group and return to England, 224; on Christians permitted to serve in the military, 227; and just causes for war, 226–27; against use of mercenaries in war, 227; writing on religious liberty for all, 229

Henry, Carl F. H., 234–37; *God, Revelation, and Authority*, 247n.72; *Twilight of a Great Civilization*, 248n.95. *See also* Baptists; Evangelicalism/ Evangelicals

Henson, Hensley, distinguishing patriotism from nationalism, 166

Hitler, Adolf, 110; Reinhold Niebuhr on response to, 10, 15

Holy War: Bullinger and William Gouge compared to Calvin's thinking of, in Just War Tradition, 142; concept as defined by the Puritans (in England during Puritan Revolution), 135; as "crusading idea," 135; redefined by James Turner Johnson, 136; Roland Bainton's description of, as warfare "prosecuted unsparingly," 136

Hubmaier, Balthasar: attending the Council of Trent with Calvin, Luther, and Zwingli, 263–64; not only believing that secular authorities were ordained by God but that Christians should work with political authorities instead of separating themselves from

Hubmaier, Balthasar (*cont.*)
    public life/government, 264;
    as one of the few Anabaptists
    trained as a theologian, 265;
    premature death as martyr,
    263–64
humanitarian intervention, 48; and
    Anglicans on, 174; and just
    war, 23n.4, 27; Methodist
    academic Paul Ramsey on, 180;
    morality of, by other countries
    and international bodies, 174;
    in unjust wars, 6; and UN
    Security Council great-power
    competition preventing, 174
Hussein, Saddam, 207; Daniel R.
    Heimbach on, 237

impressment (into military service):
    defied by Methodist preacher
    John Nelson, 186
international community: duty of
    states in, 43–44; "failed to put
    into place the political conditions
    sufficient to pursue peace without
    lapsing into war," 50; and League
    of Nations 155; not addressing
    issues of humanitarian atrocities
    in states or between states, 174;
    shared duty of for human rights
    171; status to be considered a
    member of, 43; threatened by
    terrorism, 181
International Criminal Court (ICC),
    54n.37, 180
international law, vii; Alberico
    Gentili's argument that the
    limitation of warfare by, involves
    moral constraints, 164; Biggar on
    the nature and authority of, 167;
    Biggar's argument that moral law

transcends national legal systems
    and positive international law,
    172; codified in international
    humanitarian law (IHL) and in
    the articles of the United
    Nations, has narrowed the
    justification to which individual
    states can appeal when
    considering forceful defense
    against armed attack, 44; on
    Immanuel Kant's understanding
    that the "path to peace lies in a
    cooperative international order
    with mutual rights and duties
    regulated by," 109; implicit and
    explicit, 43; and the International
    Criminal Court (ICC) and
    Rome Statute, 180; invisible in
    matters of war between nations
    reserved solely to states' legitimate
    authorities, 39; and *justa causa* in
    war, 39; in limiting *just cause* to
    defense, as did Luther, 96; Oliver
    O'Donovan's biblical case for
    international order of plural
    nations unified by, as opposed to
    universal, imperial government,
    166; Paul Ramsey on the
    responsibility to intervene and,
    170; presumption of war evident
    in, 39; on the prospect that the
    concept of just war is obsolete,
    even if the moral principles that
    inspired the just war criteria still
    have use and validity, 110; and
    state sovereignty, 43
international security: in Just War, 5*f*
Iraq War, 171; Church of England's
    response to, 172; Methodism's
    response to, 205
Israel, 185. *See also* Holy War

Jerome, St., 38

jihadists, 10–11. *See also* terrorism/ terrorists

John of Leiden (Jan van Leyden or Jan Bockhold): decree that polygamy was mandatory, 269; Menno Simons on *The Blasphemy of John of Leiden*, 274, 293n.110, 302. *See also* Anabaptism/ Anabaptists

John Paul II (Pope): Catechism of the Catholic Church on Just War, 29

Johnson, James Turner, 95–96, 114n.49, 115n.53, 119, 127, 138, 150n.46, 301; articles on Holy War, 8, 148n.17, 149n.43, 151n.58, 151n.64, 155; articles and responses on pacifism, 8; on Christian views of military service, 280, 295n.139, 295nn.140–41; on difference between *duellum* (private quarrels between individuals) and *bellum* (wars between groups/states) in Medieval understanding of Just War, 96; on Luther's concept of sovereignty as differing from earlier authors on Just War Tradition, 95; on re-envisaging of Just War Tradition and just war thinking by James F. Childress and others, 16, 23n.9, 26n.22, 26n.24, 27; response to Roland Bainton on "Holy War" concept, 136; view on sovereignty, 96

Johnson, Lyndon Baines, 34

Judeo-Christian worldview: debates over American War for Independence grounded in, viii; evident in career of Abraham Lincoln, viii; national law

principles embedded in, 3; roots and denominational frameworks undergirding the moral structure for statesmanship and policy referred to as just war thinking, ix; values in American responses at end of war in World Wars I and II, ix

jus ad bellum, as criteria of just cause, right authority, right intention, likelihood of success, proportionality of ends, and last resort derived from St. Augustine (Bishop of Hippo) and recorded by Thomas Aquinas in *Summa Theologica* II-II.40, 5f. *See also* just cause; last resort; likelihood of success; proportionality; right intention

jus in bello. See discrimination; distinction

jus post bellum: Eric Patterson discussing cases and aspects of, in *Ending Wars Well* and *Ethics beyond War's End*, 5f; evident in American generosity at war's end in World Wars I and II, ix; involvement of faith-based NGOs in, 22; "love of neighbor" as motivation in, ix; *See also* conciliation; justice; order

just cause (principle in *jus ad bellum*), 2, 5f, 226–27; defining of just cause, 94–97; Francisco de Vitoria on, 41; Gentili on, in *jus ad bellum*,163; limitation for, related to the Two Kingdom Doctrine and Luther's Three Estates, 96; restriction by Luther to self-defense, 111 justice (as second principle of *jus post bellum*), 5f; Ambrose and Early Church fathers on, being tempered by *caritas* in matters of war and at end of war, 69–70; charity and justice connected, 70; in international relations should always be based upon the principles of love of neighbor and understanding the needs of others, and never by immoral means according to understanding by contemporary Orthodox bishops, 75

Just War Theory: Jean Bethke Elshtain and *Just War Theory*, 25, 27; as misnomer for Just War Tradition, 3

just war thinking (as based upon Christian concepts): alternatives to, 8–14; Anglican application of, 161–74; Baptist theologians meet and speak on involvement in Iraq War, 239; Catholicism on, 29–55; commentaries on New Testament passages, 3, 18, 74, 159; criteria for, 5f, 6–7; debates about, 14–21; Francisco de Vitoria's use of, 12; and goal of peace in, 7–8; guidelines for, and general principles in, 6–7; in Old Testament, 39; Orthodox liturgies and devotional texts support of, 71; *See also* Anabaptism/Anabaptists; Aquinas, St. Thomas; Augustine, St.; Baptists; Chrysostom, St. John; Grotius, Hugo; Jerome, St.; *jus ad bellum*; *jus in bello*; *jus post bellum*; Methodism/Methodists; Orthodox churches; Vitoria, Francisco de

Just War Tradition: application in Gulf War (2003), invasion of Iraq, terrorism, and genocide in *Morality and War* (Fisher), 169, 176n.41; Baptist theologians meeting and speaking on, in Iraq, 239; in Christian traditions as "chief moral grammar by which moral judgments concerning [use of] force [in war] have been shaped," 6; commentaries on, from New Testament, 3, 18; concept of sovereignty as differing from earlier authors on Just War Tradition, 95; debates within, 14–21; developed within Christian-based scholarship mainly, 6; influence on, development by Cicero outside Christianity, 6; Luther's writings as contribution to, 85–119; Methodist Bishops criticism of, 204; misnomer as "just war theory," 3. *See also* New Testament; Old Testament

King, Martin Luther, Jr.: on Vietnam War, 242n.2, 251; on Vietnam War and Operation Iraqi Freedom as unjust wars, 220. See also Baptists

Knox, John, 137n.13, 152n.78; refusal to support rebellion by "private persons," 144, 155; on Scottish resistance to English kings as justified, ix, ixn.1, 144; views as more radical than that of Calvin's on resistance to tyrants, 126

Korean War: as Methodism's last official support for any major US military action, 202

Kosovo War, 171–72; Church of England response to, 172; 1999 armed humanitarian intervention in, 170

Land, Richard, 238–39; on use of force in Iraq War, 239

Larson, Mark, 118, 127, 299, 140–41; *Calvin's Doctrine of the State*, 146n.3, 147nn.15–16, 148n.19, 148n.27, 149n.35, 150n.47, 150n.50, 150n.55, 152n.77, 155; on Heinrich Bullinger's understanding of *jus in bello*, 140

last resort (principle in Just War Tradition): Baptists on, 238–39; Church of England (Anglican) authors on, 171–72; criteria for in *jus ad bellum*, 5f; Orthodox Church on defensive war, 71, 75–76, 109; See also *jus ad bellum*

legitimate authority (political; concept in *jus ad bellum*), ix, 2; Aquinas on, 35, 153n.83; Baptist scholars on, 239; Bible and Christian teaching on, 16; Calvin on, 134, 144; Catholic teaching on, 36–37, 40; Francisco de Vitoria on (following Aquinas and Augustine), 12; Church of England on, for going to war, 165; Heinrich Bullinger on, 140; Luther on, in *Temporal Authority*, 90, 94; Orthodox Church on, 75; presumptions in teaching on, 17; systematic teaching on, by John Calvin and Theodore Beza, 144; threat of Ottoman conquest and, 98; tyrant as illegitimate authority according to Aquinas, 153;

Wesley on, 185–87; *See also* lesser magistrates; tyranny/tyrants

Leland, John, championing "soul liberty" and religious liberty in America, 229

lesser magistrates, 107; doctrine developed by Reformers calling on intermediate authority between the tyrant and the citizenry, 4; Huguenot tract *Vindiciae contra tyrannos* (1579) justifying armed rebellion if those suffering persecution are led by a lesser magistrate, 144; John Calvin and Theodore Beza on doctrine of, 145, 146n.3; in John Calvin's teaching, 144; Lutheran teaching on, 96; Theodore Beza's argument that "those who possess the authority to elect a king also have the authority to depose him," 144. *See also* legitimate authority; tyranny/tyrants

likelihood of success (principle in *jus ad bellum*): description of, in just war criteria, 5f, 7

Lincoln, Abraham, viii, 195; inaugural speeches and Gettysburg Address on war and peace, viii; introduction of "Spot Resolutions" to determine the *casus belli* of the Mexican-American War, viii, xn.2; response to 1864 Methodist Episcopal General Conference statement on support for the Union in the U.S. Civil War, 194, 210n.55, 213, 215

Luther, Martin: concept of sovereignty as differing from earlier authors on Just War

Luther, Martin (*cont.*)
   Tradition, 95; contribution to
   Christian political thought, 107;
   and defining of just cause, 94–97;
   and Diet of Augsburg in 1530 as
   pivotal in developing his thought
   on resistance, 100; influenced by
   Aristotelean tradition, 92; on
   limitation of war to defense, 97;
   opposition to casuistry as method
   of moral reasoning, 162; political
   thought contribution to Just War
   Tradition, 85–19; on record as
   opposing not only rebellion but
   any sort of resistance against a
   superior authority, 100–102;
   reputation as an authoritarian,
   100; on *telos* of peace, 102;
   Three Estates of, 110; use of Two
   Kingdoms Doctrine, 110; *See also*
   Three Estates, or "Orders";
   Two Kingdoms Doctrine
Lutheranism/Lutherans, 20–21, 30;
   drafting of Augsburg Confession
   in response to Ottoman
   aggression, 102–3; 1555 Peace of
   Augsburg leading to legal status
   in the empire,106; following
   Augustinian Just War Tradition,
   2–3; involvement in debates on
   just war and peace, 85–88;
   Magdeburg Confession of 1550,
   106–7; "right of resistance"
   doctrine developed by Luther's
   Wittenberg circle and
   transmission to Geneva,
   Scotland, England, and America,
   103, 107; theological foundation
   of political thought, 88–89; on
   theological foundation of secular
   government, 89; three estates

concepts of, 90–93; tradition
   of Christian political thought
   within, 107–11; "two kingdoms
   doctrine" in, 88–90. *See also*
   Bullinger, Heinrich; Three
   Estates, or "Orders"; Two
   Kingdoms Doctrine

Manning, James: Baptist who
   championed the cause of
   "soul liberty," "soul freedom,"
   and religious freedom, 229
Mantz, Felix, 257; martyrdom of,
   286n.28
Maurice, Frederick Dennison: on
   sanctity of "national life" versus
   "cosmopolitanism," 162–63
McKinley, William: as devout
   Methodist President, 195; and
   Spanish-American War, 195
McNeill, John T.: *John Calvin: On
   God and Political Duty*, 146n.5,
   147n.6, 155; on John Calvin and
   forms of government, 123–26
Melanchthon, Philipp: co-author of
   Lutheran treatise on war and
   just cause with Justus Menius,
   Von der Notwehr (*On Defense*),
   106, 116n.95, 120; Luther and
   Melanchthon distinguishing
   between the two kingdoms but
   relegating matters of discipline
   and ecclesiastical order to the
   civil realm, 146n.4; on the
   Peasants' War, 102; on Smalcald
   War with Catholic princes, 106
Mennonites, 255. *See also*
   Anabaptism/Anabaptists
Methodism/Methodists: 1864
   Methodist Episcopal General
   Conference statement on support

for the Union in the U.S. Civil
War, 210n.54, 213, 215; historical
view of "America as God's
instrument in peace and war," 195;
"idealism" and "pacifism" defended
with respect to war, 198–99;
response on war in Iraq, 205;
response on War of 1812, 186–87;
responses on American War for
Independence and avoidance of
public comment by first
Methodist-Episcopal Bishop
Francis Asbury, 186–87; response
to war in Afghanistan, 205;
support of U.S. involvement in
Mexican-American War, 193;
support of U.S. involvement in
World Wars I and II, 193–94, 201;
United Methodist Bishops'
statement in *In Defense of Creation*,
204; United Methodists' General
Board of Church and Society
stance on nuclear disarmament,
203–4; United Methodists' official
policy of pacifism from 1972 until
2000, 203–4; United Methodists'
statements on war and military
service from 2016, 205–6. *See also*
Asbury, Francis; Wesley, John
Mexican-American War (1846–1848):
Abraham Lincoln on, vii;
Methodist support of U.S.
involvement in, 193, 209n.49, 216
military force. *See* force (use of)
military humanitarian intervention.
See humanitarian intervention
military necessity (principle of *jus in
bello*), 5f
Mohler, R. Albert, Jr.: addressing
difficult issues and not avoiding
important social and cultural

concerns, 239–40; on just war
thinking, 239–40; podcasts
(*The Briefing*) on crucial issues
related to war and peace, 239–40;
proponent of Just War Tradition
along with other Baptist
theologians, 240. *See also* Baptists

National Baptist Convention USA.
See Baptists
National Baptist Convention of
America. See Baptists
NATO (North Atlantic Treaty
Organization): as able and willing
to use defensive force unlike the
United Nations, 174; dependence
on nuclear weapons, 168; 1999
Kosovo intervention by, 170–72.
See also Balkans Conflict; Biggar,
Nigel; Kosovo War
New Testament (passages related to
Christian just war thinking):
Acts 10, 3, 233; Hebrews 12:14,
233; James 4:1–2, 233; Luke
3:14, 3; Luke 22:36, 38, 233;
Matthew 5:9, 38–48, 233;
Matthew 6:33, 233; Matthew
26:52, 233; 1 Peter 2:13–17, 3;
Romans 12 and 13, 18, 233;
Romans 13:1–7 and exposition
of John Chrysostom on Paul's
teaching in, 74, 159
Niebuhr, H. Richard, 286n.33, 302
Niebuhr, Reinhold, 25n.17, 25n.20, 28,
51n.4, 149n.39, 155; arguments
against Christian pacifism, 30, 56;
critique of pacifism, 9–10; debate
within Just War Tradition, 14–15;
denouncing of "political pacifists,"
10; force as a "lesser evil," 15;
John Howard Yoder denouncing

Niebuhr, Reinhold (*cont.*)
of "Niebuhrian realism," 279;
as pacifist until the rise of Hitler
and fascism in Europe, 10
9/11: Church of England's response
to, 172; just war thinking since,
2; United Methodists' response
to, 204–5
Nixon, Richard M., 34
noncombatant immunity. *See*
discrimination
noncombatants, Numbers 31 on, 140
nonstate actors, 164
North Korea, 239; Baptist theologian
R. Albert Mohler, Jr. podcast on,
239
nuclear war: Anglicans on, 167–69;
United Methodist Bishops on,
204; U.S. Catholic Bishops on,
16, 26n.24, 27, 52n.10, 52n.13,
55, 167, 176n.30, 178; *See also*
deterrence
nuclear weapons: David Fisher's
defense of the policy of nuclear
deterrence in *Morality and the
Bomb*, 169; Oliver O'Donovan's
position against deterrence
strategy in *Peace and Certainty*,
168, 176n.34; position of the
Church of England on, in *The
Church and the Bomb*, 167–68;
position of U.S. Catholic Bishops
in 1983 letter, *The Challenge of
Peace*, 16, 26n.24, 27, 52n.10,
52n.13, 55, 167, 176n.30, 178;
position of U.S. Catholic Bishops
in 1993 letter, *The Harvest of
Justice Is Sown in Peace*, 26n.24,
27, 52n.13, 56; United Methodist
Bishops' statement against
nuclear deterrence programs in
In Defense of Creation, 204

O'Donovan, Oliver, 166–68; position
against nuclear deterrence
strategy in *Peace and Certainty:
A Theological Essay on Deterrence*,
168, 176n.34
Old Testament (commentaries on
Just War): Augustine commentary on Psalm 37, 39; Bullinger
commentary on Numbers 31
(war between Midianites and the
Israelites), 22; John Wesley's
commentary on Genesis 14 and
principle of charity in waging
war to rescue Lot, 185; John
Wesley's view of "war in the Old
Testament as a soteriological
tool," 185; Robert Bellarmine's
commentary on war as punishment in, 37–38; St. Jerome
commentary on Jeremiah 22, 38;
William Gouge's interpretation
of Deuteronomy 25:17–19
regarding Holy War, 141
order (in *jus post bellum* criteria), 60,
294n.126; defined, 121; divine,
101; as first basic principle of
jus post bellum that needs to be
established after a war's end, 5f, 8,
22; international, ix, 43–45, 109,
166, 184; and justice, 127, 183;
law and, 89; 101, 144, 159; and
legitimate authority responsibility
for, 17–18; local, 194; peace and,
62–64, 68–69, 71, 74–75, 77;
political, 1–2, 65–68, 160, 182,
196, 241; public, 93, 287n.50,
294n.129; in society, 62, 101, 260;
sovereign national, 43; Wesley
on, 15; world, 172, 201
Origen: his pacifism was not of a strict
nature because he did not believe
that the use of force is inherently

evil but is sometimes necessary,
64; teaching that the state serves a
necessary function for an ordered
and peaceful life, 63–64
Orthodox churches: following the
early church fathers, Orthodox
Bishops declare that moral law
from God is the basis of relative
(i.e., less than perfect) peace,
order, and justice that earthly
political authorities are supposed
to seek, 75. *See also various
Orthodox churches by particular
autocephalous church name*

pacifism/pacifists, 17, 30; defined as
commitment against violence
and an allegianceto peace,
defined as "nonviolence," 9;
as official policy of United
Methodists from 1972 until
2000, 203–4; as policy of
Anabaptists such as Mennonites,
Church of the Brethren, and
Brethren in Christ, Quakers, as
well as some other Protestant
groups, and since 1980s among
Catholics, 10
Persian Gulf War. *See* Gulf War
preventative war: Alberico Gentili
distinguished from preemptive
war, 163; the Church of England
on, 172
preemptive war: Alberico Gentili
distinguished from preventative
war, 163; the Church of England
on, 172–73; United Methodists
on, 205
Progressive National Baptist
Convention. *See* Baptists
proportionality (as *jus in bello*
principle), 26n.27; Ambrose of

Milan's letter to Emperor
Theodosius on massacre and
ecclesiastical discipline due to
emperor's *disproportionate* act of
punishment in Thessalonica, 70;
Aquinas on, 35; in Catholic
teaching, 44–46; Luther on, 109;
Nigel Biggar on, 170, 306.
See also force (use of)
punishment: Ambrose of Milan's
belief that just wars are always
either defensive in nature or
waged for punishing of
wrongdoing, 70; Ambrose of
Milan's letter to Emperor
Theodosius on massacre and
ecclesiastical discipline due to
emperor's disproportionate act
of punishment in Thessalonica,
70; Anabaptists on use of the
sword for, by authorities, 128;
Augustine on punishment of
lawbreakers as way of loving
one's neighbors and as aspect of
the "law of love," 9; as built upon
the principles associated with
judgment extend outward when
the civil community faces
aggressors against it, 37; Calvin
on magistrates carrying out,
by decree of God, 131–32; in
jus post bellum principle of justice,
a matter of "just deserts,"
including consideration of
individual punishment for those
who violated the law of armed
conflict and restitution policies
for victims when appropriate, 5*f*;
as just political action, 49;
legitimate public authority's right
to administer, proportionate to
gravity of the offense, 37; logic of,

punishment (*cont.*)
  in Catholic doctrine going back
    as far as Alexander of Hales and
    drawing on concepts nascent in
    St. Augustine, 36–37; Martin
    Luther on use of sword for
    punishing the wicked, 92, 98;
    Orthodox understanding in war
    for wrongdoing, 71; Robert
    Bellarmine's commentary on
    Catholic understanding of war as,
    40–46; "sovereign equality" as
    shredding concept of, in war, 47;
    St. John Chrysostom on, 68;
    uncritical confidence in United
    Nations and International
    Criminal Court in respect to,
    54n.37; war as form of, in
    Catholic thinking, 54n.46, 56
Puritans (in America and England):
    and Bullinger's influence on
    Holy War concepts of, 185;
    movement from just war to
    Holy War in Puritan thought,
    141; Puritan Revolution in
    England, 135

Ramsey, (Robert) Paul; as contem-
    porary Methodist ethicist
    championing just war thinking,
    166–67, 182; initiating
    "resurgence of just war
    scholarship in the 1960s" that
    influenced moral reasoning of
    Anglicans, 166–67; voting
    down attempt to change
    wording of Methodist Bishops'
    denouncement of all war as
    "immoral" and a "crime against
    humanity" in 1972, 203; writing
    on nuclear deterrence, 167

Reagan, Ronald: aggressive stance on
    Soviet Union and threat of
    nuclear war, 167–68
reconciliation; after genocide in
    Rwanda, 126. *See also* conciliation
Reformed Churches: turn by some
    after Reformation to "Radical
    Reformed" sectarian Christian
    denominations, which explicitly
    forbade Christians to serve as
    soldiers, and to varying degrees,
    that prohibition applied to
    political office, 128. *See also*
    Protestant churches in the
    Reformed tradition by name
    of reformer or churches
regime change: debate on justifiability,
    239, 247n.77, 250
reparations. See *jus post bellum*
responsibility (political). *See* legitimate
    authority
restitution. See *jus post bellum*
restoration. See *jus post bellum*
restraint. *See* just war thinking; Just
    War Tradition
right authority. *See* legitimate authority
right intention (principle of *jus ad*
    bellum): Anglican thinking on,
    162; in Catholic teaching, 35,
    41; in Reformed thinking, 133,
    137, 144
rogue regimes: and corruption in, 74;
    fighting in, ix
Roman Catholicism. *See* Catholicism/
    Catholics
Rome Statute. *See* International
    Criminal Court
Roosevelt, Franklin D.: and
    Methodist Bishop's affirmation
    of decision to join after Pearl
    Harbor attack, 199

Russia: and humanitarian intervention considered as member of UN Security Council, 174; Putin's confessor views on understanding of just war concepts of the need to go to war, 74; and war with Ukraine, 72

Russian Orthodox Church: contemporary voices in, on just and unjust wars, 75–77; in debates over whether war is a "lesser evil" or a "lesser good," 76; after fall of the Soviet Union reaffirmation of commitment to the just war tradition, 74; John Chrysostom's exposition of Paul in Romans 13 with respect to duties of authorities and Christians, 74; on just war and corrupt regimes, 74; moral tension within, on war-making, 74–78; on peacemaking as the primary task of the church, 74; proclamation on relationship between church and state authority in *The Basis of the Social Concept*, 74–75; regarding Basil's warning to avoid injustice in war, 74; Russian novelists, philosophers, clerics, and theologians' contributions to the Orthodox approach to moral questions surrounding war in the twentieth century, 73–75; and thinking on war as the "lesser evil," 73–74; and use of force in Russia's War in Ukraine, 72; Vladimir Putin's confessor in, and understanding of just war concepts, 74; Western post-Augustinian bewilderment of views, 75

Rwandan genocide: moral failure to intervene in, 173. *See also* genocide

Sattler, Michael, 300, 302; influenced by Conrad Grebel and Felix Mantz, 261; *Schleitheim Confession of Faith*, 128, 261, 287nn.53–54

Seventh Day Baptist General Conference. *See* Baptists

Simons, Menno: complete writings of, 302; helping form a doctrine of pacificism in Anabaptism, 271–74; on Münsterites' preference for the Old Testament over the New Testament, 274; response to charges of "not obeying the Magistrate" in Münster, the city to which Anabaptists were moving in greater numbers, 274

Smyth, John: embrace of apolitical, radically pacifist view of the state, 224; separation from Thomas Helwys's Baptist group to join Dutch Mennonite group "Waterlanders," 223–24

Southern Baptists. *See* Baptists

South Korea: Billy Graham's 1953 visit to U.S. troops in, 234

South Sudan: warring factions brought to Vatican by pope and archbishop of Canterbury for "retreat" to discuss terms of conflict resolution, 22. *See also* Sudan

sovereignty, 12, Catholic claim resting state sovereignty in the existence of a good beyond the state, 43, 46–47; of God, 294; questions on, 47

Soviet Union, and prospect of nuclear war, 167–68

Spanish-American War, Baptists' response to, 232

Spurgeon, Charles, 220, 243n.3, 251. *See also* Baptists

Stayer, James: *Anabaptists and the Sword*, 287n.52, 291n.81, 292n.95, 292n.97, 293n.117; on Bernhard Rothmann's background leading up to his role in Münster, on "radical apoliticism" of Anabaptists, 261, 283n.9, 284nn.14–15, 291nn.83–84, 292n.96, 294n.126, 302–3

Stillman, Samuel: preaching famous 1794 sermon contrasting the American and French revolutions, 230, 244n.36, 252. *See also* Baptists

Súarez, Francisco: in Just War tradition, 3, 159

Sudan (Darfur): moral failure to intervene in, 173

surrender, 139; Grotius and Whewell on combatants who surrender no longer being treated as active belligerents, 164

Swiss Brethren, the (in Anabaptist movement), 257; and birth of, 257; and break with Reformers over "believer's baptism," 257; reaction to religious and state violence against peasants, 257. *See also* Grebel, Conrad; Mantz, Felix

Taliban: Church of England's General Synod position paper on war on terror asking if war against, is a Just War, 172

Temple, William: and deriving of moral wisdom from nonscriptural sources, 162; on importance of the "nation-state"' versus "cosmopolitanism," 166

temporal authority: Calvin on, 127; Luther and, 88, 92, 96, 97; treatise by Luther on, 90–93; and *jus ad bellum*, 96, 100, 113n.10, 113n.12, 115n.66, 115n.68, 119; *See also* Three Estates, or "Orders"; Two Kingdoms Doctrine

terrorism/terrorists: by al-Qaeda, 11, 172; application of Just War Tradition to in *Morality and War: Can War Be Just in the Twenty-First Century?* (Fisher), 169, 176n.41; fighting against, ix; Methodist Bishops on fighting against, 204; war in Afghanistan to stop Taliban and al-Qaeda, 172, 177, 177n.50. *See also* jihadists

Tertullian: Baptists' attempts to answer his question on order in society and culture, 241

Three Estates, or "Orders" (of Martin Luther), 113n.31, 120; as bulwark against the devil, 104; in Calvin's writing, 143; including "*ecclesia* (the church), *oeconomica* (household), and *politia* (government)," 91; Luther on assault on, by papacy, and Turks destruction of, 98–99; Luther's doctrine of resistance built upon, 106–7; as "orders" of creation, 91; relation of papacy to, 104; Second Estate *oeconomica* influenced by Aristotelian tradition, 92. *See also* Two Kingdoms Doctrine

Tookey, Elias, 227–28, 244n.29

torture: Wesley on, for prisoners of war, 189

Track 2 diplomacy: documented by Eric Patterson, 22; using non-State, private communication channels of faith-based NGOs, 21–22

Turley, Briane, on Wesley, 184, 191

Two Kingdoms Doctrine (in Just War Tradition), 112n.8; arising because of conflict between God and the devil, 91–92; distinction between church and state as well as sacred versus secular, 20–21, 266; distinction between kingdom of God and kingdom of earth, 89; eschatological dimension of, as compared to the "Three Estates" of Luther, which do not have an eschatological dimension, 91–92; and foundation of Luther's political thought and later Lutheran thought on war, 88–91, 100, 110, 112n.8; in Luther's polemic against the medieval church, 90; reminiscent of Augustine's two cities, 89
See also Three Estates, or "Orders"

tyranny/tyrants: Calvin on tyranny and monarchy, 126, 152n.77; in Calvin's and Beza's conception of ability of Parliaments or "lesser magistrates" to resist through force, 145; Calvin teaching in the Institutes that republicanism and democratic system are required to prevent tyranny, 126; Calvin's teaching that "magistrates of the people" (populares magistratus) have duty to serve as resistance

against tyranny, 124; Church of England on tyranny of the Nazi State, 165; "early" Luther on resistance to mad leaders and tyrants, 95, 100; Eusebius on soldiers not being allowed to fight on behalf of corrupt leaders with selfish ambitions in Canon 12 of the Council of Nicaea, 65; Huguenot tract Vindiciae contra tyrannos (1579) justifying armed rebellion if those suffering persecution are led by a lesser magistrate, 144; "later" Luther's on government overstepping legitimate authority and Protestants' ability to resist Catholic princes, 100; Lutherans on resistance to tyrants as different from Calvin's and Beza's (Reformers') view, 144–45; Luther developing teaching on when magistrates turn against what is true and right itself and persecute God in an attempt to destroy all good works, they are like an antichrist, 107, 117n.96, 120; Luther on magistrates' duty to serve as a check on tyranny, and by armed resistance if necessary, 144; Methodists' 2000 General Conference on response to unchecked aggression and, 204; Reformed emphasis on the right and duty of armed resistance of populares magistratus, 145; Reformed theologians who advocated resistance to tyrants, xn.1; Reformers' logical outcome supporting the Puritan cause in

tyranny/tyrants (*cont.*)
the English Civil War and in
self-defense-against-tyranny
argument in the American War
for Independence, 145; response
to French Revolution by pastors
in American Revolution, 230,
244n.44, 248; victims of
unresisted, 237

Ukrainian Orthodox Church
(autocephalous Eastern
Orthodox Church), 81n.53; and
just use of force by states, 72
UN Charter, 54n.38, 56, 96, 171
United Methodists. *See* Methodism/
Methodists
United Nations Security Council:
Anglican scholar Nigel Biggar
on lack of moral authority to
determine *jus ad bellum* as
opposed to principles of just war,
172–74; and humanitarian
intervention considered by
permanent members of UN
Security Council, 174; paralyzed
on how to address humanitarian
injustice when involving one
of the great-powers on the
Council, 174; on stalemates
due to great-power competition
between China, Russia, and
the United States, 174
U.S. Civil War. *See* Civil War (U.S.)

Vietnam War, 252; and Baptists'
official responses and resolutions
on the, 220, 232, 234, 246n.55,
249; Baptist Evangelist Billy
Graham visiting troops and
supporting war efforts due to

atheistic, Communist threat
during, 234, 246n.63, 252; and
Catholic pacifism, 10; Dr. Martin
Luther King, Jr., on, 242n.2, 251;
Methodists' Board's response to,
in 1965, 1966, 1967, 1968, 1970,
and 1972, 202–3, 213, 215–16;
United Methodists growing
political leftism that embraced
liberation theology since
Vietnam Era, 182
Vitoria, Francisco de, 12, 25n.18, 28,
33, 37, 41, 43, 51, 53n.31, 54n.36,
57; and civilian immunity, 25;
On the Law of War, 53n.31, 57;
as Thomistic voice on Just War
since the beginning of the
modern era, 33, 53n.31, 159

War of 1812: American Baptists'
theological reasons to support,
231; Canadian Baptists' response
to, 245n.48; Methodism's
response to, 186–87
weapons of mass destruction
(WMDs): in Iraq, 238
Weber, Theodore R., 32
Webster, Alexander: debate with
Stanley Harakas on just war, 76
Wesley, John: on Christians' duty to
advance a just and lasting peace,
192; failure to outline theoretical
just war teaching and avoidance
of articulating, 192; on Jacobite
Rebellion, 187; view on
American Revolution against
Britain, 186
Whewell, William: addressing "the
rights of war" in *Elements of
Morality, Including Polity* (1855),
164, 175n.14, 179; stance that,

following Grotius, combatants who surrender must no longer be treated as active belligerents, 164

Williams, George H., 255, 284n.15, 303

Williams, Roger: attempted unsuccessfully to prevent the spread of King Philip's War in 1675–1676, 230, 235n.35, 252; Baptist champion on "soul liberty," "soul freedom," and religious freedom, 229

Wilson, Woodrow: envisaging of the concepts of self-determination, collective security, and freedom of the seas, ix

WMDs. *See* weapons of mass destruction

Yoder, John Howard, 30, 302, 304; emphasis on "radicalism" and "countercultural" mode of Jesus, 297n.142; "peace" theology based upon "purity" in the early church, 278–79; Peter J. Leithart's rebuttal of, 296n.140; as prolific writer and professor of Christian

ethics at the University of Notre Dame until his death in 1997 addressed, inter alia, Niebuhrian realism, the purported fallacy of just war thinking, and the church's relationship to the state as an "absolute ethic of Jesus," 279, 295n.132; staunch pacifist based upon his view of Jesus's teachings, 235–36, 146n.65, 279. *See also* Anabaptism/Anabaptists; pacifism/pacifists

Zwingli, Huldrych, 254–55, 264; adopted "caesaropapist position" (along with Heinrich Bullinger), subjecting church and discipline to the control of the civil magistrate, 146n.4, 147n.16; denounced Anabaptist Conrad Grebel, 257; friendship and break with Anabaptist Conrad Grebel, 258; participation in Second Disputation in October 1523 with Balthazar Hubmaier, 265; Zwinglian reform, 257, 257

ERIC PATTERSON

is executive vice president at the Religious Freedom Institute
and scholar at large at Regent University.
He is author or editor of eighteen books, including
Just American Wars: Ethical Dilemmas in U.S. Military History.

J. DARYL CHARLES

is affiliate scholar of the John Jay Institute and a contributing editor
of *Providence: A Journal of Christianity and American Foreign Policy.*
He is the author or editor of twenty-one books, including
America and the Just War Tradition: A History of U.S. Conflicts
(University of Notre Dame Press, 2019).

JOHN ASHCROFT

served as the seventy-ninth attorney general of the United States of America.
He serves in numerous capacities, including as Distinguished Professor
of Law and Government at Regent University.

CPSIA information can be obtained
at www.ICGtesting.com
Printed in the USA
LVHW081553051222
734621LV00003B/577